KT-228-773

THEORIES OF INTERNATIONAL RELATIONS

Scott Burchill and Andrew Linklater

with Richard Devetak, Matthew Paterson and Jacqui True

First published 1996 by
MACMILLAN PRESS LTD
Houndmills, Basingstoke, Hampshire RG21 6XS
and London
Companies and representatives
throughout the world

ISBN 0-333-66088-9 hardcover
ISBN 0-333-66089-7 paperback

A catalogue record for this book is available from the British Library.

10   9   8   7   6   5   4   3   2
05   04   03   02   01   00   99   98   97

Copy-edited and typeset by Povey-Edmondson
Okehampton and Rochdale, England

Printed in Great Britain by
Antony Rowe Ltd, Chippenham, Wiltshire

Published in the United States of America 1996 by
ST.MARTIN'S PRESS, INC.,
Scholarly and Reference Division
175 Fifth Avenue, New York, N.Y. 10010

ISBN 0-312-16244-8 (cloth)
ISBN 0-312-16245-6 (paperback)

THEORIES OF INTERNATIONAL RELATIONS

Contents

For W. J. (Bill) Adams

Preface

The origins of this book lie in the decision of the School of Australian and International Studies at Deakin University to introduce a Master of Arts (International Relations) programme in 1995 for students learning via distance education. The provision of high-quality course materials for every off-campus student enabling them to study for their degree anywhere in Australia or overseas was considered essential to the success of the programme.

As preparation of the programme proceeded it was decided that each student should receive a solid grounding in international theory before choosing a range of specialist options. However, it was felt that no one existing text adequately covered all the approaches the course designers believed should be included: the books were either too narrow in their theoretical focus or did not take sufficient account of contemporary developments in the field. It was therefore decided to write an entirely new book which would meet the requirements of both staff and students. Early drafts of Chapters 1 to 7 were piloted in the initial year of the programme, after which they were redrafted for publication. At this point Chapters 8 and 9 were added to broaden the coverage of more recent theoretical influences in International Relations.

I am very grateful to Andrew Linklater of Keele University for his excellent contributions to this volume, his invaluable comments on the other chapters, and for suggesting the other contributors. I am similarly grateful to Richard Devetak, Matthew Paterson and Jacqui True, whose work has been a pleasure to edit. I would also like to acknowledge the encouragement and support given by Gary Smith of Deakin University. The comments of an anonymous reviewer and our publisher, Steven Kennedy, have also significantly improved the quality of the manuscript.

SCOTT BURCHILL

CHAPTER 1

Introduction

Scott Burchill

Although in the modern era we have grown accustomed to the idea of theories within the 'natural sciences', the suggestion that the political and social worlds also lend themselves to theoretical enquiry remains problematic for many. As one sceptic has noted, in the analysis of international relations for example, 'historical conditions are too varied and complex for anything that might plausibly be called "a theory" to apply uniformly'.[1] If by theory our sceptic is referring to the levels of certainty and exactness, standards of proof and 'scientific rigour' normally associated with the 'physical' sciences, then he has a point when he claims that 'if there is a body of theory, well tested and verified, that applies to the conduct of foreign affairs or the resolution of domestic or international conflict, its existence has been kept a well guarded secret'.[2] There is a world of difference between the 'physical' and the 'social' sciences, and it is difficult to argue that the methodology of the former, with its emphasis on testable propositions and the production of falsifiable hypotheses, can be automatically applied to theoretical endeavours in the latter without serious problems arising. Is it therefore misleading to speak of 'theories of international relations'?

One of the purposes of this book will be to argue that the term 'theory' is not limited to its 'scientific' or positivist formulation and that explanatory theories, of the kind which flow from the adoption of a positivist methodology, are only one type of international theory. There is now an increasingly large group of theorists who recognize a second category of theory which reflects upon the very process of theorizing. These theorists are concerned with the social and political purposes of knowledge, the cognitive interests and assumptions of the observer and the way in which the principal actors construct their images of the political world. They believe we should be just as concerned with how we approach the study of world politics as we are with explaining events, issues and the behaviour of actors in the global system. One commentator has argued that these two categories of theory represent a fundamental division within the discipline 'between theories which seek to offer *explanatory* accounts of international relations, and those that see theory as *constitutive* of that reality'.[3] Recognizing and understanding these two 'types' of theory will be the entry point for this introduction to international theory. The contributors to this book believe that both types of theory represent important paths of intellectual enquiry and that no contemporary survey of international theory could legitimately ignore either category.

It would be a mistake to regard constitutive theories as merely a prevailing or transitory intellectual fashion, after which the discipline will return to its normal explanatory concerns. As early as 1972 Hedley Bull argued that

> the reason we must be concerned with the theory as well as the history of the subject is that all discussions of international politics. . .proceed upon theoretical assumptions which we should acknowledge and investigate rather than ignore or leave unchallenged. The enterprise of theoretical investigation is at its minimum one directed towards criticism: towards identifying, formulating, refining, and questioning the general assumptions on which the everyday discussion of international politics proceeds. At its maximum, the enterprise is concerned with theoretical construction: with establishing that certain assumptions are true while others are false, certain arguments valid while others are invalid, and so proceeding to erect a firm structure of knowledge.[4]

In other words, Bull believes that not only is there room for explanatory and constitutive theory, but that theoretical enterprise itself would be incomplete without both processes. Although he wrote this in the early 1970s, it was not until later in the decade that constitutive theory began to leave its mark on the discipline, thanks largely to the influence of the cognate fields of political and social theory. Since then, the growth of interest in international theory and the recent production of texts which address theoretical concerns in International Relations, indicates a widening acceptance that constitutive theory has a important place in the study of global politics.

At the outset our sceptic betrayed his positivist bias by implying that 'theory' should be defined as the opposite of 'reality'. The authors of this book reject the suggestion that 'theory' and 'reality' are antonyms or 'binary opposites' on the grounds that, as theoreticians, they are active agents in research which is conditioned by their own historical experiences. These experiences cannot be artificially separated from their work because they are embedded in the theoretical worlds they construct. As Cox explains, theorists cannot stand outside of the political and social worlds that they are examining because

> theory follows reality. It also precedes and shapes reality. That is to say, there is a real historical world in which things happen; and theory is made through reflection upon what has happened. The separation of theory from historical happenings is. . .only a way of thinking, because theory feeds back into the

making of history by virtue of the way those who make history. . .think about what they are doing. Their understanding of what the historical context allows them to do, prohibits them from doing, or requires them to do, and the way they formulate their purposes in acting, is the product of theory.[5]

As we shall discover, although it is extremely difficult to reach an agreed single definition of theory within the study of international relations, the contributors to this volume share a sense of the importance of theory because they regard the *theory versus reality* divide as a false dichotomy. Whether they like it or not, even those in the field of international relations who reject the value and purpose of international theory cannot avoid the fact that their work is theoretically informed and has theoretical and political implications.

International Relations can be cast as a discipline of theoretical disagreements. Though it is a comparatively new subject in the Western academy, almost every aspect of its nature is contested. What should be studied in the discipline? How should it be studied? Is the discipline politically biased, or conceived in such a way as to limit the possibilities for discussion and analysis? In other words, the discipline of International Relations (IR) is internally divided on the notions of the *subject matter* to be analysed, the appropriate *methodology* to be used when studying international politics, and the *epistemological structure* of the theories. These internal divisions have sometimes taken the form of 'great debates' which have served as watersheds in the short history of the discipline. More recently, they have been reconsidered as a consequence of the application of contemporary developments in social theory to the study of global politics. International Relations has belatedly joined the ranks of the introspective academic disciplines.[6]

In this introductory chapter we shall examine these and other issues under the following headings:

1. the foundation of the discipline of International Relations
2. theories and disciplines
3. explanatory and constitutive theory
4. what do theories of international relations differ about?
5. what criteria exist for evaluating, comparing and contrasting theories?

Initially we shall discuss the notion of 'theory' in the context of studying international relations and briefly examine how the term is variously understood. This has become a more complex task since questions of methodology, epistemology and ontology joined the discipline's theoretical agenda, first in the 1960s with the 'behaviourist revolution' and again in the 1980s with the application of critical, feminist and postmodern theory to IR. We shall then examine the relationship between theories and academic disciplines, before distinguishing between two broad categories of international theory – explanatory and constitutive. It will also be necessary to examine a range of criteria for differentiating between the theories selected for explication in the book. This should help to explain the proliferation of theories over the last two decades and why a number of theoreticians appear to 'talk past' each other rather than engage in intellectual exchanges. We shall also identify ways in which meaningful comparisons between the various perspectives of international relations can be made. It will be important to bear these points in mind as we sweep through a selection of some of the most influential theoretical traditions in the field. Before then, however, a brief introduction to the foundation of the discipline will help to set the scene for the more specific analysis to follow.

The Foundation of International Relations

Though scholars and thinkers have long devoted their thoughts to international politics, the formal recognition of international relations as a separate discipline within the Western academy dates from the end of the First World War with the establishment of a Chair of International Relations at the University of Wales at Aberystwyth in 1919. Until this time, the province of international politics was shared by a number of older disciplines, including law, philosophy, economics, politics and diplomatic history.

It is difficult to separate the foundation of the discipline of International Relations from the intellectual reaction to the horrors of the First World War. As far as the historians were concerned there was relatively little interest in the war itself. The great subject which eclipsed all others and monopolised their interest was how and why the war began. Historians established their reputations as authorities on the origins of the First World War – Gooch in England, Fay and Schmitt in the United States, Renouvin and Camille Bloch in France, Thimme, Brandenburg, and von Wegerer in Germany, Pribram in Austria, Pokovsky in Russia, to name just a few.[7] Their task was one guided by a genuinely moral purpose: to discover the causes of the war so the world might avoid a similar catastrophe in the future.

At least initially, the experiences of 1914–18 brought into intellectual and diplomatic prominence those who considered the old assumptions and prescriptions of power politics to be totally discredited (for example, Zimmern, Noel-Baker, Wilson). Peace, they believed, could only be preserved by a system of collective security; this involved transferring the concepts and practices of domestic society to the international sphere. Together with a nineteenth-century belief in the inevitable progress of mankind, these 'idealists' or 'utopians' as they came to be pejoratively called, invested their hopes for a new, peaceful world order in the idea of a 'Concert', and specifically in international organisations such as the League of Nations. At the basis of their proposals was a critique of the doctrine of the balance of power as the main guarantor of state sovereignty, and an emphasis on the need to extend the concept of citizenship to include membership of the global community of nation-states.

However, it was widely felt amongst students of the causes of the First World War that, to a certain extent, the war had highlighted the inadequacy of history as a guide to the future. In its aftermath, therefore, a discipline devoted specifically to the comprehensive and systematic study of international conflict emerged within universities in the victorious nations, specifically the United Kingdom and the United States. The discipline of International Relations was founded in reaction to the unprecedented horrors of the conflict. The war had shaken the confidence of those who thought diplomacy operated effectively and was properly understood. As an instrument of statecraft war had proven to be immoral, costly and dysfunctional. Early scholars in the field, almost exclusively from the 'satisfied' or 'status quo' nations, therefore agreed that three questions would dominate their studies:

1. What had war achieved, other than death and misery for millions?
2. Were there lessons from the war that could be learnt to prevent a recurrence of conflict on this scale?
3. Was the war caused by mistake, misunderstanding or evil intent?

In response to these questions, the first 'school' or 'theory' of international relations emerged to dominate the discipline's early history. The idealists (also known as liberals and utopians) argued that war was not a product of human nature, but the result of misunderstandings by politicians who had lost control of events leading up to hostilities in 1914. If 'secret diplomacy' could be replaced by collective security, and autocratic rule by democracy, war would be seen as a senseless and destructive tool of international statecraft. In other words, a more peaceful and just world order could be established if the lessons of the First World War were understood and acted upon.[8] According to Bull,

> the distinctive characteristic of these writers was their belief in progress: the belief, in particular, that the system of international relations that had given rise to the First World War was capable of being transformed into a fundamentally more peaceful and just world order; that under the impact of the awakening of democracy, the growth of the 'international mind', the development of the League of Nations, the good works of men of peace or the enlightenment spread by their own teachings, it was in fact being transformed; and that their respon-

sibility as students of international relations was to assist this march of progress
to overcome the ignorance, the prejudices, the ill-will, and the sinister interests
that stood in its way.[9]

The important point to note here is the normative character of the early
discipline. Founded in a climate of reaction against the barbarity of the First
World War, the discipline was established with the conviction that war
must never happen again: the Great War, as it was initially called, was to be
the 'war to end all wars'. Only the rigorous study of the phenomenon of
war could reveal its underlying causes so that its recurrence could be
prevented. The initial preoccupation of the discipline with this subject
coloured the questions that practitioners in the field asked about the world,
the methods they employed to conduct their studies and the conclusions
they eventually reached. With each generation of scholars, these questions
were re-asked and re-answered. What is significant is not so much the
answers the first generation of thinkers emerged with, but the direction
they initially gave to the discipline's trajectory. The reaction of scholars to
the liberal-utopians dominates the discipline's early life. The realist critique
of the liberal-utopian school launched by E. H. Carr immediately before the
Second World War, sometimes referred to as the discipline's first 'great
debate', gave the discipline of International Relations its early definition:
the dualism between idealism and realism. As we shall see in subsequent
chapters, as each theoretical approach rises to dominance in the discipline it
exercises its hegemony over the field of study, in part, by restructuring the
focus and content of the entire discipline.

It should be obvious from this that in the discipline's formative stages
there was an explicit connection between theory and practice and between
means and ends. The very purpose of intellectual endeavour was to change
the world for the better by eradicating the scourge of war. This was really
the only function international theory had. It was not a remote and disconnected vocation. Idealism was 'a way of thinking in which some higher
or better state is projected as a way of judging conduct or of indicating
action'.[10] Liberals were intellectuals who believed 'the world to be profoundly other than it should be, and who have faith in the power of human
reason and human action so to change it that the inner potential of all
human beings can be more fully realised'.[11]

As the discipline grew this foundational normative concern of International Relations became supplemented by other theoretical issues. Though
the preoccupation with conflict and war remained, the discipline became
more generally concerned with a wider range of other international actors
and phenomena as well as a series of introspective philosophical questions.
By the 1990s, the discipline had undergone a 'rapid transition from an
essentially problem-solving approach to strategic interaction between existing bounded communities to a normatively engaged analysis of the

history of bounded communities and the possibility of improved forms of political community'.[12] This represents nothing short of a revolutionary transformation of the discipline's principal focus. The early consensus about the nature of the discipline has collapsed and been replaced by a spectrum of contending theoretical approaches. The traditional intellectual boundaries of International Relations have been widened to the point where it would be barely recognizable to its early practitioners. Interdisciplinary research and influences from cognate fields have so deeply affected the subject it is now possible to ask whether International Relations still has a clearly bounded intellectual domain or even a distinctive subject matter.[13] One of the tasks of this book will be to map many of these changes and offer a range of answers to this question.

Theories and Disciplines

Although earlier it was claimed that 'idealism' or 'liberal internationalism' constituted the first school or theory of International Relations, this is in many ways a retrospective judgement. As late as 1966 Martin Wight posed the question, 'why is there no international theory?', by which he meant an equivalent body of knowledge to that which comprised political theory. Wight argued that there was no body of international theory ('speculation about the society of states, or the family of nations, or the international community') to match the achievements of political theory ('speculation about the state') because the character of international politics was 'incompatible with progressivist theory'. Political theory was philosophically rich because it was concerned with the 'theory of the good life', whereas 'international theory is the theory of survival' in a world where 'international politics is the realm of recurrence and repetition'. Because theorizing 'has to be done in the language of political theory and law', a language 'appropriate to man's control of his social life', Wight believed it was inappropriate for thinking about the international domain where state survival was the principal concern.[14]

Three decades later the poverty of international theory which Wight identified has been substantially alleviated. We hope to demonstrate in this book that there is now a rich and diverse field of international theory which is not constrained by a preoccupation with state survival or the absence of an appropriate vocabulary with which to theorize about global politics. We hope to refute the claim that the character of international politics is either consensually recognized or determined, and challenge the view that the discipline needed to create an autonomous theory of international relations. By arguing that international theory is not analytically distinct from the cognate fields of social and political theory, it is possible to open up new areas of theoretical endeavour which Wight could not have anticipated in the 1960s.

Thanks to an explosion of theoretical activity in the field since the 1970s, it is now possible to regard International Relations as a discipline comprising a range of alternative, overlapping and competing theories of world politics. As we proceed through this book we shall be examining a number of the most influential theories, including liberal internationalism, neo-realism, and rationalism, as well as less influential approaches such as Marxism and new perspectives such as feminism and green political theory. We are unable to trace the intellectual history of the entire discipline, but it is possible to examine a broad range of theories, both explanatory and constitutive, which currently influence the discipline's agenda.

We will call these approaches theories, but in the literature we will also see them referred to as perspectives, paradigms, discourses, schools of thought, images and philosophical traditions: there is no agreement within the discipline about what these divisions of knowledge should be called. For convenience we will call them theories or theoretical traditions, but what are they? What do they seek to do? And how do they differ from each other? The following definitions of theory show how varied the notion of theory can be for scholars in the field:

- theories explain laws which identify invariant or probable associations (Waltz)
- to abstract, generalise and to connect (Hollis and Smith)
- a tradition of speculation about relations between states (Wight)
- using observation to test hypotheses about the world (empirical theory)
- a representation of the way the world ought to be (normative theory)
- ideological critique of the present which opens up alternative future paths to change, freedom and human autonomy (critical theory)
- reflections upon the process of theorizing, including questions of epistemology and ontology (constitutive theory).

Putting aside for a moment the difficulty of formulating coherent ideas about an area of such complexity and diversity as world politics, it is clear from the above list that practitioners in the field do not agree about what they are actually doing when they theorize about international relations. This makes comparisons between their work all the more difficult, for we might in effect be comparing and contrasting unlike things. Postmodernists, for example, would deny the worthiness of 'grand theories' and reject the suggestion that their own contribution to the study of world politics constitutes a 'school' or even a unified theoretical approach. If further evidence of diversity is needed, the plurality of names used to describe essentially the same theoretical approach is another indication of this confusion (for example, utopianism, idealism, liberal internationalism and interdependency theory are alternative descriptions of essentially the same theoretical tradition). We may have to live with the fact that there are categories of theory, such as the division made earlier between explanatory and constitutive theory, which are incommensurable and perhaps incompatible.

Even the term 'international relations' is misleading. It implies that all we are concerned with is relations between the nations of the world, which in effect means relationships between nation-states. And yet in the contemporary world, this is only one of the discipline's principal concerns. It is now a broader and more eclectic field of study, which in part accounts for the diversity of definitions of theory, and explains why some argue that 'global politics' is a more appropriate description of the subject. Though by no means an exhaustive list, below are some of the discipline's recent preoccupations:

- *relationships* – economic interdependence, Third World debt and dependence, international trade, inequality, new forms of political identity and citizenship, regimes, international society of states, the nature of anarchy, regional economic associations, balances of power, democratization, post-Cold War security;
- *actors* – nation-states, transnational corporations, finance markets, non-government organisations, supra and sub-national political communities, UN peacekeepers, new social movements, G7, IMF-World Bank;
- *empirical issues* – globalisation and fragmentation, human rights, intervention and sovereignty, aid, refugees, ethnicity, women's issues, environmental conservation, aids, drugs, organised crime;
- *philosophical issues* – questions of epistemology, ontology and methodology, gender perspectives, inter-paradigm debates, ethics and foreign policy.

According to Halliday, who argues that International Relations retains its distinctive subject matter, it is possible to identify three 'constituent elements' which have produced an enormous variety of specialist sub-fields, interdisciplinary studies and theoretical approaches. They are: (1) the inter-state; (2) the transnational; and (3) the systemic.[15] Halliday is suggesting that international relations occur on more than one level, and possibly three. When it was founded over seventy-five years ago, the subject was primarily, though not exclusively concerned with (1) the inter-state. However, within the framework of a contemporary International Relations syllabus you might find scholars working on US–Russia diplomatic relations side by side with a finance market or Third World debt analyst who could be sitting across the table from a neo-Marxist theoretician. The field is now more open and, despite Halliday's assertion, it is almost as difficult to see where the discipline's distinctive subject matter ends as it is to pinpoint where it actually begins.

In contrast to Halliday, critical theorists and postmodern approaches refuse to treat the discipline of International Relations as a separate or discrete discourse with its own distinctive concepts, language and subject matter. For postmodernists this would involve an intolerable process of exclusion – an arbitrary and unjustifiable choice of what goes in and what is left out of academic consideration. Instead, they regard disciplinary bound-aries, such as the division between sociology and history, for example, as artificially imposed demarcation lines which distort our capacity to under-stand the world. For them, knowledge has no boundaries – the borders between neatly packaged fields of study merely reflect the conservative nature of the academy, a process which, in turn, obstructs our intellectual endeavours. Marxists would want to make a similar point by rejecting 'the epistemological and methodological foundations of "bourgeois" social science with its fragmentation into arbitrarily delimited disciplines'.[16] Clearly, then, the domain of International Relations is a matter of some dispute.

Another question which affects our study of the discipline's theoretical terrain, is the changing fortunes of each theory in policy-making circles. In his study of US foreign policy at the beginning of the Cold War, Daniel Yergin traces the alternating influence which realism (the 'Yalta axioms') and totalitarian theory (the 'Riga axioms') had over the Roosevelt and Truman administrations in the 1940s.[17] His purpose was to demonstrate how intellectuals and arguments compete for influence over government policy, and why any one particular perspective can move from being in the ascendancy (hegemonic) to the margins (dissenting) in influencing govern-ment policy, depending on the turn of world events and changing political personalities. What needs to be stressed here is that there are two domains in which theories compete for hegemony, and they can often be unrelated to each other: there is (1) the (foreign policy) behaviour of the state and (2) debate and discussion within the academy (the universities and the general intellectual domain). Realism's clear dominance over US foreign policy during the Nixon and Kissinger years occurred at a time when its influence within the academy was under one of its first important challenges. In the 1980s, when neo-liberalism dominated the economic agendas of many Western governments, it was under substantial attack from neo-mercanti-lists and economic nationalists within the discipline of political economy. Dominance in one domain does not necessarily mean control in the other: the reasons can be quite different.[18]

In response to this uncertainty, a number of scholars have sought to explain the relationship between *theories* and *disciplines*. In an attempt to understand how academic disciplines in the natural sciences evolved, Kuhn suggested that the growth of knowledge proceeds via a series of distinct stages, each dominated by a particular frame of assumptions (paradigms) which render knowledge in one particular period of time incommensurate with knowledge in another. These successive periods of knowledge are separated by confrontations between opposing sets of ideas which in turn change the actual shape of the discipline. As human knowledge expands, paradigms become intellectually exhausted and impoverished, and are continually superseded as scholars find within them anomalies which cannot be explained.

Instead of viewing research as a procession of random and momentary fads without apparent logic or justification, Kuhn's model claims that what passes for knowledge at any given time in the history of a discipline is not objective but 'paradigm dependent'. A dominant paradigm is primarily a frame of assumptions dialectically conceived and consensually recognized as the cumulative wisdom of the discipline at any specific time in its evolution. These dominant paradigms give direction to the field of study within the discipline, shape the fundamental assumptions that can be made about the world, and determine the kind of questions that can be meaningfully posed and answered.[19]

There is much debate over the relevance and applicability of Kuhn's epistemological model to the social sciences, with suggestions that realism, for example, has been the dominant paradigm within the discipline of International Relations. It then becomes possible for scholars to cast theoretical disagreements and rivalries within the discipline as representing 'inter-paradigm debates', the implication being that a dominant theory becomes hegemonic within a discipline because of its intellectual merit.[20] This explanation may err in discounting the role played by politics, and specifically ideology, in the structure of the western academy. Kuhn's approach may also militate against theoretical diversity by arguing that the emergence of *one* dominant paradigm within a discipline is both normal and desirable.[21]

Bull poses an interesting challenge for Kuhn's approach by arguing that intellectual progress in International Relations is quite different from intellectual progress in the natural or 'hard' sciences. Research in the 'hard' sciences proceeds on the assumption that logical argument and empirical verification will render certain hypotheses proven beyond reasonable doubt. Once a consensus of view within the scientific community is formed, theoretical enquiry can be built upon the acceptance of certain views as established fact: progress occurs as old ideas are superseded by superior accounts. According to Bull, this type of intellectual progress is not possible within the study of international relations because the matter under investigation cannot be subject to proof or strict confirmation. New ideas will certainly add to knowledge about an issue or event but their superiority to previous accounts can never be conclusively demonstrated. In International Relations, there is rarely a consensus about when theoretical progress is made and the central questions of the discipline are never finally settled: they will always be open to new interpretations and further refinement.

Applying Kuhn's model to a subject such as International Relations, therefore, may in fact impede theoretical progress. 'The rhetoric of scientific
progress itself, misapplied to a field in which progress of a strictly scientific
sort does not take place, has the effect of constricting and obscuring the sort
of advance that is possible'.[22]

However appropriate Kuhn's model may be, without further elaboration
it is clear that the factors which determine whether a theory within a
discipline is the dominant paradigm at any point may be quite different
from the reasons why a government appears to be following a particular
policy path. The world of international diplomacy is affected by a range of
factors which may have nothing to do with the intellectual merits of the
protagonists in a theoretical dispute, including most importantly, economic
and political interests. It is therefore important to keep the domains separate in our minds as we survey the field of international theory.

It is necessary to stress the politicized nature of the discipline because
the politics of International Relations can determine how broad the spectrum of 'legitimate theoretical opinion' can actually be. A brief review of
the early history of the discipline can serve to illustrate the point more
clearly. A number of Marxist scholars have highlighted the limits of
expressible dissent in the discipline's attempt to uncover the cause of the
First World War. They point to the conceptual and ideological parameters
beyond which the investigators into war causes could not, or would not
proceed. For opinion to be considered legitimate it had to fall between the
poles of 'idealism' at one end of the spectrum and 'realism' at the other.
According to these Marxists, certain facts were axiomatically excluded as
not belonging to the enquiry at all. Tensions within society, such as class
struggles, and economic competition between colonial powers – during
this period a popular Marxist explanation of the origins of war – were not
considered seriously within the discipline at this time. One commentator
has suggested that the theory of imperialism was deliberately excluded
because, since it located the causes of war within the nature of the capitalist
system, it posed a direct threat to the social order of capitalist states:
'. . .this false doctrine had to be refuted in the interest of stabilising
bourgeois society. . .the [historians] acted and reflected within the social
context the bourgeois university, which structurally obstructed such revolutionary insights'.[23] Feminists have made a similar claim about the exclusion of their identity and perspectives from the concerns of International
Relations, arguing that the organization of the academy is designed in a
way which prevents enquiry into masculine power. We need to be aware
that because of its very subject matter, International Relations is a politicized discipline and this can affect the way we read texts and theorize
about the world. We cannot take it for granted that any question can be
posed or that the discipline values each theoretical approach equally, or on
the same terms.

Explanatory and Constitutive Theory

Rather than proclaiming an 'official' definition of international relations theory, it might be better to state the purpose to which these theories are being put. This will enable us to distinguish between *explanatory* and *constitutive* international theory.

One aim of studying a wide variety of IR theories is to make international politics more intelligible and better understood. In other words, to make better sense of the institutions, events and processes which exist in the contemporary world. At times the theories will involve testing hypotheses, proposing causal explanations, describing events and explaining general trends and phenomena, with the aim of constructing a plausible image of the world. We will call these *explanatory* theories of international relations. To the extent that these theories broaden and deepen our understanding of contemporary world politics, they will be performing an important function.

But why study international relations in this way, that is via explanatory theories? Do we need theories at all? Surely facts are sufficient? Halliday's three answers to this question are instructive.

> First, there needs to be some preconception of which facts are significant and which are not. The facts are myriad and do not speak for themselves. For anyone, academic or not, there need to be criteria of significance. Secondly, any one set of facts, even if accepted as true and as significant, can yield different interpretations: the debate on the 'lessons of the 1930s' is not about what happened in the 1930s, but about how these events are to be interpreted. The same applies to the end of the Cold War in the 1980s. Thirdly, no human agent, again whether academic or not, can rest content with facts alone: all social activity involves moral questions, of right and wrong, and these can, by definition, not be decided by facts. In the international domain such ethical issues are pervasive: the question of legitimacy and loyalty – should one obey the nation, a broader community (even the world, the cosmopolis), or some smaller sub-national group; the issues of intervention – whether sovereignty is a supreme value or whether states or agents can intervene in the internal affairs of states; the question of human rights and their definition and universality.[24]

Theories provide intellectual order to the subject matter of international relations. They enable us to conceptualize and contextualize both past and contemporary events. They also provide us with a range of ways of interpreting complex issues. Theories help us to orientate and discipline our minds in response to the bewildering phenomena around us. They help us to think critically, logically and coherently. A solid grounding in explanatory theories of International Relations will make empirical studies of world politics that much more intelligible. As Banks argues, theory consists of both analysis and synthesis. To analyse is to unravel, to separate the strands, or to take to pieces. To synthesise is to reassemble, to piece together the parts in such a way as to compose a whole that makes sense. General theory in IR, then, consists of dividing the human race into sections, noting the significant properties of each, examining the relationships between them, and describing the patterns formed by the relationships. Interesting problems arise at every stage. Some of these are methodological. How should we set about observing things, defining them, measuring them and comparing them? Others are theoretical, because theory consists of forming ideas or concepts to describe aspects of the world, classifying them, and considering the various ways in which they interact. . . In short, what are the appropriate units of analysis, what are the significant links between them, and what are the right levels on which to conduct the analysis? And there are further theoretical questions even beyond these, because all theories of society are, at root, ideological. Theories simultaneously express the political values of the theorist, and also help to shape the world which is being analysed.[25]

To the scholar of the 'international', theories are unavoidable. After all, the interpretation of 'reality' is always contingent on theoretical assumptions of one kind or another. To reiterate the point, the events and issues which comprise international relations can only be interpreted and understood by reference to a conceptual framework. The theory of International Relations provides us with a choice of conceptual frameworks.

The functions we perform when theorizing are also in dispute and, as Bull insisted, they require critical and reflective examination. Gellner asks whether is it possible or meaningful to distinguish 'between a world of fact "out there" and a cognitive realm of theory that *retrospectively* orders and gives meaning to factual data'?[26] In separating 'theory and practice', 'object and subject' in this way, might we place ourselves in debt to positivist-based empirical science when this methodology may be ideologically biased or inappropriate to our task? In other words, are we fooling our-selves in pretending to be detached from the task of theorizing – the process by which we give meaning to an allegedly objectified world 'out there' – if, as some postmodernists tell us, there is no Archimedean point of ultimate reference from which we can make judgements about the world?

These questions lead us to a second category of theory, *constitutive* international theory. Everyone comes to the study of international relations with preconceptions, experiences and beliefs which affect the way they understand the subject. Language, culture, religion, ethnicity, class and ideology are just a few of the factors which shape our world view. Indeed it is only possible to understand and interpret the world within particular cultural and linguistic frameworks: these are the *lenses* through which we see the world. One of the primary purposes for studying theory is to enable us to examine our own lenses to discover just how controlled or distorted our world view is. Why do we focus on some images (for example, states) and why are we unable to see others (such as class)? Why do we gaze in one direction (for example, the international system) and seemingly turn a blind eye to others (such as the domestic environment)? And in which interpretation of *social reality* are our intellectual endeavours grounded?

We need to examine our own background assumptions to reveal and explain our selections, priorities and prejudices because 'all forms of social analysis. . .raise important questions about the moral and cultural constitution of the observer'.[27] In the theory of international relations we are as concerned with how we *approach* the study of world politics as we are with the events, issues and actors in the global system. We need to understand how individuals think about their world by promoting a wider self-awareness of our belief systems. As Linklater argues, 'all social analysts [should] reflect upon the cognitive interests and normative assumptions which underpin their research'.[28] It should be remembered that the 'international' is refracted through the mind of the observer. Constitutive international theory is directly concerned with the importance of human reflection on the nature and character of world politics.

Often our views may not be particularly coherent, rigorous or well-founded in knowledge. This is accepted as inevitable, given that no one's mind is completely blank on questions concerning the study of international relations, however poorly informed they may be. All that can be asked is that as human beings we need to be acutely aware of our own assumptions, prejudices and biases. We should not attempt anything as futile or unrealistic as dispensing with our intellectual and emotional baggage, but we are duty bound to subject these assumptions to critical analysis and review. We cannot hope to understand the complex field of international politics until we understand ourselves, in particular the inherent assumptions we bring to the task. International relations theory is fundamentally concerned with asking questions about these prior assumptions.

What do Theories of International Relations Differ About?

We should not assume that even within the same theoretical tradition, scholars share a consensus of views. Although they may share many basic assumptions, there can be as much diversity within one school of thought as there is between the various theoretical perspectives. Marxism and feminism are examples of very broad 'churches' with almost as many variations, strains and factions as there are scholars in each field. They could not be described as monolithic or homogenous theoretical traditions. This should not come as a surprise to students in the field of international relations. It is perfectly normal for there to be scope for differences of views within the same theoretical school. Indeed some of the most interesting debates within IR theory are between intellectuals from the same theoretical tradition. Heterogeneity can be a strength. There are few benefits to be gained from theoretical purity.

Comparing unlike things would be a fruitless activity. However, theories of international relations have enough in common to make contrasts and comparisons an insightful activity. Perhaps an odd starting point for this task is the identification of things about which the theories *disagree*. According to Linklater there are four fundamental points on which the various theories of international relations differ.[29] These will be used as the basis for our discussion.

The first is the *object of analysis and the scope of the enquiry*. This is sometimes called the level of analysis debate. Here the differences centre on the very nature of the subject matter under analysis. Which actors or phenomena should be studied in International Relations – nation-states, war, international organisations, class, transnational corporations, bureaucracies, the environment or the makers of foreign policy? What characteristics of global political processes should theorists be concerned with – the pursuit of power, the successful management of the international system, the exclusion of women, the evolution of a diplomatic culture or the exploitation of classes and the dependent relationships between states? And what kinds of outcomes are favoured – preservation of the existing state-system, greater levels of interdependency between individuals across the world or the revolutionary transformation of the international order?[30]

In his survey of approaches to the causes of wars, Kenneth Waltz argued that there were three levels of analysis: (1) the nature of individuals; (2) the nature of states and societies; and (3) the nature of the international system. According to which level of analysis is chosen, certain actors will be emphasized and de-emphasized in any study of the causes of war. So for a neo-realist like Waltz, the object of analysis in the study of international relations is the struggle for power and security by nation-states in an anarchical international system (level 3). For a Marxist, however, who wishes to understand the prospects for global political and economic change, it is the internal class nature of capitalist societies which is significant (level 2). A psychologist, who explains war by looking at the innate aggressiveness of humankind, will focus on the individual in her explanation of its causes (level 1). Again, depending on the level at which the question is addressed, certain actors or agents will be privileged over others.

The scope of the enquiry can often extend to questions of ontology and epistemology which underpin the very nature of theorizing. Here we are indebted to the work of critical theorists and postmodernists who correctly point out that debates over the nature of knowledge, meaning, interpretation, language and reality have been largely ignored, or at best margin-alized within the discipline of International Relations. And yet questions which focus on what is the 'knowable reality' of global politics, for example, are central to our task. For many theorists, the scope of their inquiries extends to subjecting the reality 'out there', and assumptions that this reality is palpable, perceptible, universally accepted and understood, to ideological critique. Postmodernists, for example, believe the interpretation of social reality which underwrites neo-realism is narrowly conceived and highly contestable: it is not widely agreed as Waltz and others assume. For them 'reality' is a discursive phenomenon and is 'never a complete, entirely coherent "thing", accessible to universalized, essentialist or totalized understandings of it. . .[it] is always characterised by ambiguity, disunity, discrepancy, contradiction and difference'.[31] Feminists would similarly argue that women are too often excluded from the neo-realist 'reality' of international politics. Women should no longer be an invisible feature of the theoretical landscape, as the hegemonic perspectives would have them drawn.

For the theorist of international relations, questions of ontology are unavoidable. As Cox argues, 'ontology lies at the beginning of any enquiry. We cannot define a problem in global politics without presupposing a certain basic structure consisting of the significant kinds of entities involved and the form of significant relationships among them'. All theories have ontological foundations of some kind because ontology is the study of 'how political actors construct the political world and imagine its purposes'.[32] Even the shape of the discipline itself and the content of its curriculum are an expression of ontological preference. Again Cox reminds us that 'onto-logical presuppositions [are] inherent in. . .terms such as "international relations", which seems to equate nation with state and to define the field as limited to the interactions among states'. Perhaps the term 'global politics' is less restrictive and more appropriate?[33] At the very least these ontological questions cast doubt on whether a politically neutral or objec-tive interpretation of an external 'reality' is possible, or even makes sense.[34]

Over the last decade discussion of exactly what constitutes the 'knowable reality' of international relations (that is, ontological questions) has been matched by debates over how knowledge is generated in theories of inter-national relations (epistemological questions). The focus of an increasing number of theoreticians has been on the social and political purposes of knowledge, specifically the relationship between knowledge and power. The intellectual inquiries of critical theorists have centred on the construc-tion of an epistemological taxonomy, the most frequently cited being Habermas's three categories of knowledge-constitutive interests (technical, practical and emancipatory), and their application across the theoretical breadth of the discipline. The purpose of this approach has been to evaluate the respective perspectives on international relations by revealing the theory of knowledge which underpins each of them. Linklater, for example, has suggested that in this way neo-realism can be seen to be based on positivist methodology, rationalism on hermeneutics and critical theory on an emancipatory cognitive interest. The epistemological basis of each theory is said to be an important factor in determining what it privileges and assumes in its account of world politics.

Cox has distinguished between theories such as neo-realism which produce knowledge 'which made it possible for a political order that favoured dominant interests to function more smoothly', and critical approaches which generate knowledge with an emancipatory interest and a transformative intent.[35] Similarly, feminists can demonstrate how knowledge about structures and beliefs functions to exclude, subordinate or marginalize a specific social group, while ecological theorists can show how positivism is biased towards producing knowledge which privileges anthropocentricism, industrialism and economic growth, thus giving legitimacy to humankind's mastery over nature.

Evaluating the theories of International Relations from an epistemological perspective can be difficult because it involves a high order of abstraction. Nevertheless, it can tell us much about the assumptions each theorist makes and the conclusions each perspective on world politics reaches. The only danger in pursuing the philosophy of social science as an avenue of research (constitutive theory) is that scholars may, in the process, neglect or be distracted from the important fields of empirical research which deserve to be explored.[36]

The second point of difference between theories is the *purpose of social and political enquiry*. In other words, what is the underlying reason behind the theoretical undertaking? For neo-realists like Waltz, it is to ensure, by understanding the international system better, that relations between states are managed as smoothly as possible in an effort to minimize the potential for conflict and war: in other words, its purpose is problem-solving. For neo-liberals the purpose of social and political enquiry is to produce optimal economic outcomes for the citizens of each country based on efficiencies produced by market applications. Specifically, this means exposing and removing the corrupting influence of the state from the lives of individual citizens. Critical theorists and feminists are normatively committed to promoting human understanding and emancipation by explaining and exposing the constraints upon human autonomy in the contemporary world. For them, the purpose of social enquiry is to be actively libertarian by opening the paths to changing the international system. They are seeking new arrangements which will improve the circumstances of subordinate and marginal groups.[37]

Different purposes for social and political enquiry is the basis of the distinction between *problem solving theory* and *critical theory* made by Robert Cox in his assessment of the impact of recent developments in social theory for the study of International Relations. Drawing on the influence of the Frankfurt School, in particular Horkheimer's distinction between 'traditional' and 'critical' theory, and Habermas's division of knowledge-constitutive interests (technical, practical and emancipatory cognitive interests), Cox distinguishes between theoretical approaches on the basis of the *purpose* of theory: 'theory is always *for* someone and *for* some purpose. . . . The world is seen from a standpoint definable in terms of nation or social class. . . . There is . . . no such thing as theory in itself, divorced from a standpoint in time and space. When any theory so represents itself, it is the more important to examine it as ideology, and to lay bare its concealed perspective'.[38] Theory never exists in a void. It can 'either be a guide [to] solving problems within the terms of a particular perspective [problem-solving theory], or it can reflect on the process of theorizing itself, which raises the possibility of choosing a different perspective [critical theory]'.[39]

Cox claims that problem-solving theory 'takes the world as it finds it, with the prevailing social and political relations and institutions into which they are organised, as the given framework for action.[40] The general aim of problem-solving theory is to make these relationships and institutions work smoothly by dealing effectively with particular sources of trouble'. Problem-solving theory does not question the pattern of relationships and institutions in question and can 'fix limits or parameters to a problem area' which in turn limits 'the number of variables which are amenable to relatively close and precise examination'.[41] Problem-solving theory has the effect of legitimizing the status quo.

Critical theory, on the other hand, 'stands apart from the prevailing order of the world and asks how that order came about. Critical theory, unlike problem-solving theory, does not take institutions and social and power relations for granted but calls them into question by concerning itself with their origins and how and whether they might be in the process of changing. It is directed towards an appraisal of the very framework of action. . .- which problem-solving theory accepts as its parameters'. Whereas problem-solving theory is 'a guide to tactical actions which, intended or unintended, sustain the existing order', critical theory provides a 'a guide to strategic action for bringing about an alternative order'.[42]

This is just one scholar's method of distinguishing between theoretical approaches to the study of international relations. In this case Cox wants to expose the ideology of neo-realism by demonstrating that it is a 'problem-solving' theory in contrast to 'critical theory' which is informed by the emancipatory commitment of the Marxist tradition. There are many different approaches to theoretical distinction and classification in International Relations. And there are obviously a variety of purposes which animate the work of international theorists. Some want to bring greater intellectual cohesion to the field while others want to abandon the search for a resolution of the discipline's major theoretical disputes. More recent practitioners want to subvert governing orthodoxies and break-down disciplinary boundaries. Others want to admit previously marginal and dissident concerns into the mainstream of the discipline.[43] The proliferation of purposes and motives reflects the discipline's recent receptiveness to new theoretical possibilities. International Relations is now more inclusive than at any time in its short history.

The third point of difference centres on the *appropriate methodology for the study of international relations*. Should it be an empirical vocation, one based on the rigorous application of the scientific method, or should there be a clear preference for either a systemic or reductionist approach? In the discipline's 'great debate' over methodology in the 1960s, 'traditionalists' emphasised the relative utility of history, law, philosophy and other classical methods of academic enquiry, whereas the 'behaviourists' argued in favour of scientific conceptualisation, including the quantification of variables, formal hypothesis testing and model building, to reveal the 'realities' of the international system.

This debate formed part of a much larger discussion about the extent to which like the natural world, the 'laws' of the social world could also be uncovered by applying the scientific method. At the end of the eighteenth century, when science had contributed so much to our understanding of the natural world and our own physical nature, it began to be asked whether science might also further our understanding of the social world. Could the method by which science studied the natural world be applied to the study of human affairs? The creation of 'social science' therefore sprung from the application of a specific set of methodological principles (scientific empiricism) which had proved so successful in other disciplines. Methodological debates in the 'social sciences' generally, and International Relations specifically, have therefore centred on the relevance and applicability of this approach. Does emulating the natural sciences make sense when the subject matter is human and social?

In the 1980s more critically-orientated theorists reopened the debate by attacking the positivist methodology of neo-realism, believing that this explained both the dominance and conservative nature of the perspective. According to critical theorists influenced by the Frankfurt School and the work of Habermas, methodology should be grounded in an emancipatory interest in freeing human beings from unnecessary social constraints and not a technical interest in social control.[44] Debates over methodology are relatively common in the 'social sciences', with certain approaches being more widely favoured over others in one country (the impact of behaviourism on the US IR community was much greater than its impact elsewhere). In International Relations these arguments are a long way from being resolved. Perhaps they should not or can not be resolved, only debated? After all, different modes of social enquiry will inevitably produce different outcomes.

By the 1980s the idea of a politically neutral, value-free methodology came under challenge as the study of International Relations became influenced by intellectual developments in other fields, most notably European political and social theory. Borrowing ideas from critical theory, writers such as Cox and Ashley began to expose the links between theoretical methodology and the legitimation of political orders which favoured the interests of ruling elites. Having subverted the somewhat naïve belief that positivism could provide the student of International Relations with an impartial or politically objective world view, these influences ensured that questions of methodology, and subsequently ontology and epistemology, would be brought in from the margins of the discipline to occupy a central place on its research agenda.

The fourth point of departure centres on *whether each theory sees International Relations as being distinct from, or related to, other areas of intellectual endeavour*. In other words, is the study of international relations distinct from political science, sociology, diplomatic history, political philosophy, and so on, or are these demarcation lines contrived and artificial? Is it important to have a separate, specialised field dealing with the international context? These are epistemological questions as well as questions concerned with the history and structure of the Western academy. What do these disciplinary boundaries represent anyway? Do they facilitate or limit enquiry? What do they tell us about the way the university system packages knowledge? Can the disciplinary boundaries be explained by the careerist motives of academics?

Each theoretical approach has different answers to these questions and places greater or lesser emphasis on the importance of disciplinary boundaries. Though they might borrow their methodological approach from other disciplines, neo-realists see the international system as a 'domain apart' (Waltz) which deserves separate treatment in the academy. For them, the discipline is unique. Critical theorists, on the other hand, dispute the discrete nature of the discipline and are concerned with the relevance of recent developments in social theory and historical sociology for the study of international politics. Many postmodernists are highly suspicious of what they call the 'metanarratives' of liberation and progress. Unlike anarchists, who believe the libertarian promise of the Enlightenment is still to be consummated, and critical theorists, who wish to recast the Enlightenment project, many postmodernists want to abandon it altogether, believing it to be a dehumanizing and ultimately oppressive tradition. They regard disciplinary boundaries as exclusionary and part of a structure of intellectual repression.

Feminists and ecologists have recently joined the debates within International Relations because of the increasingly porous state of the discipline's boundaries. Their perspectives could no longer be ignored or marginalized, and their influence is a direct product of interdisciplinary research. Questions of identity, patriarchy and exclusion are central to the concerns of feminists, although most discussion of these topics has taken place outside the IR pantheon. Similarly, it is research into ecological sustainability and environmental degradation conducted in other disciplines, such as environmental studies, which is finally impacting on international theory.

Just as the shape of contemporary political boundaries was being altered by the forces of globalization and fragmentation, so too the intellectual boundaries of International Relations were being eroded by the influences of cognate disciplines such as jurisprudence and international law, sociology and political economy. In a sense, the fate of the nation-state became a metaphor for the discipline which has claimed exclusive jurisdiction over the study of its external behaviour. The power of finance markets, transnational corporations and regional trade associations, together with developments in information technology and the end of the Cold War, have undermined the immutability of political boundaries and the sovereign integrity of the modern nation-state. Similarly, the ideas of theorists such as Habermas, Foucault, Derrida, and the political force of social and intellectual movements centred on feminism and environmentalism, have undermined the safe and traditional certainties of international thought: as a result, the intellectual boundaries of International Relations have been contested and are being redrawn. Given the collapse of the consensus about its actual nature, whether International Relations should continue to stand alone as a separate discipline within the academy is now a central question for those who work in the field.

It is possible to find other points of difference between the theories of International Relations. In fact in the 1980s debates about this issue often filled the discipline's journals and preoccupied the intellectual lives of teachers and students. The four points of difference just outlined can be seen as a template for conceptualizing the seemingly endless and complex disputes within the field.

Evaluating Theories for Contrasts and Comparisons

We should not ask too much of these theories. For scholars who locate themselves in the postmodern tradition, grand theories are by definition problematic and should be either treated with suspicion or dispensed with. A single theory cannot, by itself, completely identify and explain all the key structures and dynamics in the international system. Some will be more convincing in explaining certain specific features of international politics.

Others will be more persuasive in their understanding of the process of theorizing. Most are deficient in some way. This may be initially frustrating for students seeking a single comprehensive meta-theory of international relations. It will soon be apparent, however, that each approach has something important and insightful to say, though this may depend on each theory's relevance for a specific topic or period of history. The end of the Cold War and the process of globalization has forced scholars to reconsider the relevance of their theoretical outlooks in the 1990s. The failure of IR theory to adequately detect and predict patterns of behaviour at the global level has been particularly noticeable in recent years. Neither the collapse of the Soviet Union, the Gulf War nor the ethnic conflicts in the Balkans were anticipated or adequately explained by any of the major traditions of speculation about international politics.

As has been suggested earlier, the selection of theories for this book has been based on what the authors regard as the most influential and informative in contemporary theoretical discussion. Our approach has therefore been pluralist and, at times, interdisciplinary – or to put it in religious terms, we have tried to be ecumenical and non-denominational. We do not claim that this is a definitive survey covering all theoretical traditions. Nor do we deny that other theories of IR cannot lay claim for representation here. We have selected eight theoretical traditions with at least one eye on where we believe theoretical research in the discipline is currently heading. By definition the process of selection demands a degree of arbitrary decision-making.

The biases of the authors should be apparent because there has been no conscious attempt to conceal them. And it is quite normal for scholars to identify, or be identified, with one perspective in preference to others, however misleading or inaccurate the label may be. This is often no more than a form of intellectual shorthand which purports to make the process of classifying intellectuals easier. Readers, however, are encouraged to reach their own conclusions about the strengths and weaknesses of each perspective, regardless of the preferences of the authors. The important point to remember is one made by Wight, that no one theory can ever be proven correct, but it is the debate between them that is important: truth is not an attribute of any one tradition, but of the dialogue between them.[45]

Establishing criteria for evaluating theories of international relations is not an easy task. Kegley argues that 'a theory of international relations needs to perform four principal tasks. It should describe, explain, predict and prescribe'.[46] As criteria for evaluating the performance of explanatory theories, this list may be sufficient. However, it would exclude from consideration constitutive theory which, by definition, could not meet these criteria. It is only possible, then, to suggest that theories of international relations can be evaluated against one or more of the following criteria:

1. a theory's *understanding* of an issue or process;
2. the *explanatory power* of the theory;
3. the theory's success in *predicting* events;
4. the theory's intellectual *consistency* and *coherence*;
5. the *scope* of the theory; and
6. the theory's capacity for *critical self-reflection* and intellectual *engagement* with contending theories.

This list of six points is not a definitive one but it should help the reader to conceptualise the complex field of alternative conceptions of international relations. The processes of appraisal and discrimination are higher order cognitive skills which make considerable demands upon the student of international theory. In this book we hope to make these tasks both stimulating and rewarding.

In Chapters 2 and 3 Scott Burchill discusses the traditions of liberal internationalism and realism. These theories represent the oldest and arguably the most influential perspectives in the field, dominating speculation for at least the first fifty years of the discipline's life. Although no longer unchallenged for theoretical dominance, they remain highly influential within the field. As far as economic relationships are concerned, global politics in the 1990s resonates with many of the ideas originally promoted by nineteenth-century liberals. Conversely, the writings of early realists such as Carr and Morgenthau still influence discussion within the discipline half a century after they were published. Neo-realism emerged in the 1970s to occupy a position of intellectual hegemony in the discipline, particularly in the United States, though its influence would appear to be currently in decline. A measure of neo-realism's dominance, however, has been the extent to which dissenting approaches have felt obliged to address many of the central concerns of theorists such as Waltz, most notably the nature and importance of anarchy in the international system.

In Chapters 4 and 5 Andrew Linklater analyses rationalism and Marxism, two perspectives which have had less historical influence on the discipline than the first two, but have nevertheless had a significant impact upon contemporary thought. Rationalism came to prominence in the 1970s in Australia and the United Kingdom as a substantial theoretical qualification to the pessimism of realism and the idealism of liberal internationalism. The work of Wight, Vincent and Bull remains central to any discussion of an 'international society of states' and the prospects for universal human rights. Marxism, which was widely thought to have neglected the central foci of International Relations, re-emerged in the 1980s to stake its claim as a progressivist account of international politics based on its emancipatory credentials. Although it is still widely seen as a theory of domestic society, Marxism nevertheless mounts an important critique of neo-realism's exogenous approach to world politics.

Marxism also provides the intellectual inheritance for critical theory, which is discussed by Richard Devetak in Chapter 6. The relevance of critical theory for the study of international relations reflects the influence of European social theory across disciplinary boundaries. The importance of the work of Habermas, Ashley, Cox and Linklater can be measured by both their reclamation of the emancipatory spirit of Marxism, and their exploration of the epistemological bases of the most influential traditions of thought within International Relations. In Chapter 7, on postmodernism, Richard Devetak evaluates the theoretical contribution of Derrida, Foucault and Lyotard, and the likely effects of their writings on the trajectory of the discipline. Challenging the premises of the Enlightenment 'project', including the assumption that modernity is linear and progressive, is at the core of much postmodernist theory. Together with a focus on issues such as *exclusion, difference* and *ontology*, these central themes pose a fundamental challenge to the way scholars have thought about international politics. Depending on the reader's own position, the influence of postmodernism on International Relations can be viewed as either an exciting development which opens up new avenues of research or a disturbing trend which threatens to tear the discipline apart.

In Chapter 8 Jacqui True sheds light on a subject which, until recently, has been largely neglected: feminist perspectives on international relations. Ostensibly invisible to a male-dominated discipline, the contributions of feminist scholarship are some of the most innovative and original challenges to orthodoxy within the field and should no longer be seen as marginal. Feminist approaches to international relations have developed their own distinctive foci and agendas, in particular highlighting the extent to which masculinity has distorted conceptions of power and epistemology within the discipline. As arguments for theory which is sensitive to the concerns of gender, they have significantly enriched the study of world politics.

Developments within ecological theory, discussed by Matthew Paterson in Chapter 9, also have important implications for the study of global politics. Environmental degradation and threats to the continuing diversity of species caused by assumptions of infinite economic growth and unbridled capitalism pose problems which can only be seriously addressed at the global level. Ecological theory and green politics are responses which will continue to reorientate the discipline of International Relations towards ways of thinking which consider humanity's common fate and the shared destiny of life on earth as the moral starting point for intellectual research.

The authors of this book believe that theoretical developments within the discipline of International Relations have reached a new and exciting stage marked by rapid intellectual challenges, most notably the influences of cognate fields of research, and need to grasp the extraordinary changes currently taking place in global politics. They do not share the pessimism of our early sceptic, believing that a knowledge of a range of theories of international relations, both explanatory and constitutive, is not only possible but is actually an essential prerequisite to understanding the modern world. This volume is their contribution to an ongoing dialogue.

Notes

1. N. Chomsky, *World Orders, Old and New* (London, 1994), p. 120.
2. N. Chomsky, *American Power and the New Mandarins* (Harmondsworth, 1969), p. 271.
3. S. Smith, 'The Self-Image of a Discipline: A Genealogy of International Relations Theory', in K. Booth, and S. Smith (eds), *International Relations Theory Today* (Cambridge, 1995), pp. 26–7.
4. H. Bull, 'The Theory of International Politics, 1919–1969' (1972), reproduced in J. Der Derian (ed.), *International Theory: Critical Investigations* (Basingstoke, 1995), pp. 183–4.
5. R. W. Cox, 'Towards a post-hegemonic conceptualization of world order: reflections on the relevancy of Ibn Khaldun', in J.N. Rosenau and E-O. Czempiel (eds), *Governance Without Government: Order and Change in World Politics* (Cambridge, 1992), p. 133.
6. Economics remains an obvious exception.
7. A.J.P. Taylor, *The Origins of the Second World War* (Harmondsworth, 1961), p. 30.
8. For a fuller discussion see Chapter 2 on Liberal Internationalism.
9. Bull quoted in M. Hollis and S. Smith, *Explaining and Understanding International Relations* (Oxford, 1990), p. 20.
10. R. Williams, *Keywords* (London, 1983), p. 152.
11. M. Howard, *War and the Liberal Conscience* (Oxford, 1978), p. 11.
12. J. MacMillan and A. Linklater (eds), *Boundaries in Question: New Directions in International Relations* (London, 1995), p. 15.
13. Ibid., p. 4.
14. M. Wight, 'Why is there No International Theory?' (1966), reprinted in J. Der Derian (ed), *International Theory: Critical Investigations* (Basingstoke, 1995), pp. 15, 25–6 and 32.
15. F. Halliday, 'The Pertinence of International Relations', *Political Studies*, vol. 38 (1990) p. 503.
16. V. Kubalkova, and A. Cruickshank, 'The 'new cold war' in critical international relations studies, *Review of International Studies*, vol. 12 (1986) p. 164.
17. D. Yergin, *Shattered Peace* (rev. ed., London, 1990).
18. Think of the influence of prevailing intellectual fashions and careerism on the academy.
19. T. Kuhn, *The Structure of Scientific Revolutions* (Chicago, 1970).

20. See M. Banks, 'The inter-paradigm debate', in M. Light and A. J. R. Groom (eds), *International Relations: A Handbook of Current Theory* (London, 1985) and M. Hoffman, 'Critical theory and the inter-paradigm debate', *Millennium*, vol. 16, no. 2 (1987).

21. For a celebration of theoretical diversity from an anarchist perspective, see P. Feyerabend, *Against Method* (London, 1975).

22. Bull (1972) in Der Derian, p. 204. See also pp. 202–6.

23. E. Krippendorff, *International Relations as a Social Science* (Brighton, 1982), p. 27.

24. F. Halliday, *Rethinking International Relations* (London, 1994), p. 25.

25. Banks, 1985, pp. 8–9.

26. E. Gellner, *Legitimation of Belief* (Cambridge, 1974), p. 175.

27. MacMillan and Linklater (1995), p. 9.

28. A. Linklater, 'The question of the next stage in international relations theory: a critical-theoretical point of view', *Millennium*, vol. 21, no. 1 (1992).

29. See Linklater (1992).

30. See R. Little and M. Smith (eds), *Perspectives on World Politics* (London, 1991), pp. 4–12.

31. J. George, *Discourses of Global Politics: A Critical (Re)Introduction* (Boulder, 1994), p. 11.

32. MacMillan and Linklater (1995), p. 10.

33. Cox (1992) p. 132.

34. MacMillan and Linklater (1995), p. 8.

35. Ibid.

36. R. Keohane, 'International Institutions: Two Approaches', *International Studies Quarterly*, 32(4), pp. 379–91.

37. MacMillan and Linklater (1995), p. 9.

38. R. W. Cox, 'Social forces, states and world orders: beyond international relations theory', *Millennium*, vol. 10 (1981), p. 128.

39. Hoffman (1987), p. 237.

40. For a discussion of both Horkheimer's and Habermas' theoretical constructions, see R. Bernstein, *The Restructuring of Social and Political Theory* (London, 1976), pp. 191–200; and Hoffman (1987), pp. 231–8.

41. Cox (1981), pp. 128–9.

42. Ibid., pp. 128–30.

43. Linklater (1992).

44. Linklater (1992).

45. S. Smith, 'The Self-Image of a Discipline: A Genealogy of International Relations Theory', in K. Booth and S. Smith (eds), *International Relations Theory Today* (Cambridge, 1995), p. 13.

46. C. W. Kegley, Jr. (ed.), *Controversies in International Relations Theory: Realism and the Neo-Liberal Challenge* (New York, 1995), p. 8.

CHAPTER 2

Liberal Internationalism

Scott Burchill

The end of the Cold War generally, but specifically the demise of Soviet Communism, has revived the fortunes of liberal internationalism within the academy, a theoretical approach long thought to have been discredited by perspectives which emphasize the recurrent features of international relations. In a confident reassertion of the teleology of liberalism, Fukuyama has recently claimed that the collapse of the Soviet Union proves that liberal democracy has no serious ideological competitor: it is 'the end point of mankind's ideological evolution' and the 'final form of human government'. Furthermore, the end of the Cold War represents the triumph of the 'ideal state' and a particular form of political economy, 'liberal capitalism', which 'cannot be improved upon': there can be 'no further progress in the development of underlying principles and institutions'. For Fukuyama, the end of the East–West conflict confirms that liberal capitalism is now unchallenged as a model of, and endpoint for, humankind's political and economic development. Like most liberals he sees history as progressive, linear and 'directional', and is convinced that 'there is a fundamental process at work that dictates a common evolutionary pattern for *all* human societies – in short, something like a Universal History of mankind in the direction of liberal democracy'.[1]

Fukuyama's belief that Western forms of government, political economy and political community are the ultimate destination which the entire human race will eventually reach poses at least three challenges for orthodoxy within International Relations. First, his claim that political and economic development always terminates at liberal-capitalist democracy assumes that the non-Western world is striving to imitate the Western route to modernization: to put in another way, that the Western path to modernity will eventually command universal consent. Secondly, Fukuyama's approach assumes that the West is the keeper of moral truths which 'progress' will oblige all societies to observe, regardless of national and cultural distinction.

Thirdly, Fukuyama believes that progress in human history can be measured by the elimination of global conflict and the international adoption of principles of legitimacy which have evolved over time in certain domestic political orders. This constitutes an 'inside-out' approach to international relations, where the exogenous behaviour of states can be explained by examining their endogenous political and economic dispositions. It also leads to Doyle's claim that 'liberal democracies are uniquely willing to eschew the use of force in their relations with one another', a view which refutes the realist contention that the anarchical nature of the international system means states are trapped in a struggle for power and security.[2] In this chapter we shall be primarily concerned with the third challenge to international theory posed by Fukuyama's liberalism.

Liberal Internationalism: Inside Looking Out

Fukuyama revives a long-held view among liberal internationalists that the spread of legitimate political orders will eventually bring an end to international conflict. This neo-Kantian position assumes that particular states, with liberal-democratic credentials, constitute an ideal or model which the rest of the world will emulate. Fukuyama is struck by the extent to which liberal democracies have transcended their violent instincts and institutionalized norms which pacify relations between each other. He is particularly impressed with the emergence of shared principles of legitimacy amongst the great powers, a trend which can be expected to continue now that the ideological contest of the Cold War is over. The progressive translation of liberal-democratic principles to the international realm is said to provide the best prospect for a peaceful world order because 'a world made up of liberal democracies. . .should have much less incentive for war, since all nations would reciprocally recognise one another's legitimacy'.[3]

This approach is rejected by neo-realists such as Waltz, who claim that the moral aspirations of states are thwarted by the absence of an overarching authority which regulates their behaviour towards each other. The anarchical nature of the international system homogenises foreign policy behaviour by socializing states into the system of power politics. The requirements of strategic power and security are paramount in an insecure world, and they soon override the ethical pursuits of states, regardless of their domestic political complexions. Waltz highlights the similarity of foreign policy behaviour among states with diverse political orders, and argues that if any state was to become a model for the rest of the world, one would have to conclude that 'most of the impetus behind foreign policy is internally generated'. The similarity of United States and Soviet foreign policy during the Cold War would suggest that this is unlikely, and that their common location in the international system is a superior explanation.[4]

By stressing the importance of legitimate domestic orders in explaining foreign policy behaviour, Waltz believes that liberals such as Fukuyama and Doyle are guilty of 'reductionism' when they should be highlighting the 'systemic' features of international relations. This conflict between 'inside-out' and 'outside-in' approaches to international relations has become an important line of demarcation in international theory. The extent to which the neo-realist critique of liberal internationalism can be sustained in the post-Cold War era will be a major feature of this analysis.[5]

Fukuyama's argument is not simply a celebration of the fact that liberal-democratic capitalism has survived the threat posed by Marxism. It also implies that neo-realism has overlooked the 'the foremost macropolitical trend in contemporary world politics: the expansion of the liberal zone of peace'.[6] Challenging the view that the nature of anarchy conditions international behaviour is Doyle's argument that there is a growing core of pacific states which have learnt to resolve their differences without resorting to violence. The likely expansion of this pacific realm is said to be the most significant feature of the post-Communist landscape. If this claim can be upheld it will constitute a remarkable resuscitation for an international theory widely thought to have been refuted by Carr in his critique of liberal utopianism over fifty years ago. It will also pose a serious challenge to a discipline which until recently has been dominated by assumptions that war is a recurrent and endemic feature of international life.

Does liberal democracy have universal validity? What is it about liberal-democratic states which predisposes them towards peace with one another? What are the prospects for an expansion of the zone of peace? And can liberal states overcome their feelings of insecurity engendered by the anarchical international system? These questions, and the answers offered by liberal theorists, will be revisited throughout this chapter. To understand their importance and how they gave contemporary form to liberal internationalism, we shall need to trace through some of the history of this theoretical tradition. Part I of this chapter examines the liberal diagnosis of the causes of wars and a range of suggestions for its remediation. Part II considers two critiques of liberal economic theory and the manner in which it has been applied as policy. Part III assesses the relevance of liberal internationalism for the era of globalisation. The conclusion to this chapter offers an overview of the location of liberal internationalism within contemporary international theory.

I   War: Causes and Cures

The foundations of contemporary liberal internationalism were laid in the eighteenth and nineteenth centuries by liberals proposing preconditions for a peaceful world order. In broad summary they concluded that the prospects for the elimination of war lay with a preference for democracy over aristocracy, free trade over autarky, and collective security over the balance of power system. In this section we shall examine each of these arguments in turn and the extent to which these views have informed contemporary liberal thought.

Prospects for peace

For liberals, peace is the normal state of affairs: in Kant's words, peace can be perpetual. The laws of nature dictated harmony and co-operation between peoples. War is therefore both unnatural and irrational: it is an artificial contrivance and not a product of imperfect social relations or some peculiarity of human nature. Liberals have a belief in progress and the perfectibility of the human condition. Through their faith in the power of human reason and the capacity of human beings to realise their inner potential, they remain confident that the stain of war can be removed from human experience.[7]

A common thread running through liberal thought, from Rousseau, Kant and Cobden, to Schumpeter and Doyle, is that wars were created by militaristic and undemocratic governments for their own vested interests. Wars were engineered by a 'warrior class' bent on extending their power and wealth through territorial conquest. According to Paine in *The Rights of Man*, the ' "war system" was contrived to preserve the power and the employment of princes, statesmen, soldiers, diplomats and armaments manufacturers, and to bind their tyranny ever more firmly upon the necks of the people'.[8] Wars provided governments with excuses to raise taxes, expand their bureaucratic apparatus and thus increase their control over their citizens. 'The people', on the other hand, were peace-loving by nature, and only plunged into conflict by the whims of their unrepresentative rulers.

War was a cancer on the body politic. But it was an ailment that human beings themselves had the capacity to cure. The treatment which liberals began prescribing in the eighteenth century has never changed: the 'disease' of war could be successfully treated with the twin medicines of *democracy* and *free trade*. Democratic processes and institutions would break the power of the ruling elites and curb their propensity for violence. Free trade and commerce would overcome the artificial barriers between individuals and unite them everywhere into one community.

For liberals like Schumpeter, war was the product of the aggressive instincts of authoritarian and unrepresentative elites. The warlike disposition of these rulers drove the reluctant masses into violent conflicts which, while profitable for the arms industries and the military aristocrats, were disastrous for those who did the fighting. For Kant, the establishment of republican forms of government in which rulers were accountable and individual rights were respected would lead to peaceful international relations because the ultimate consent for war would rest with the citizens of the state.[9] For both Kant and Schumpeter, war was the outcome of minority rule. Liberal states, founded on individual rights such as equality before the law, free speech and civil liberty, respect for private property and representative government, would not have the same appetite for conflict and war. Peace was fundamentally a question of establishing legitimate domestic orders throughout the world. 'When the citizens who bear the burdens of war elect their governments, wars become impossible'.[10]

The dual themes of domestic legitimacy and the extent to which liberal-democratic states exercise restraint and peaceful intentions in their foreign policy have been taken up again more recently by Doyle. In a restatement of Kant's argument that a 'pacific federation' (*foedus pacificum*) can be built by expanding the number of states with democratic constitutions, Doyle claims that liberal democracies are unique in their ability and willingness to establish peaceful relations between themselves. This pacification of foreign relations among liberal states is said to be a direct product of their shared legitimate political orders based on democratic principles and institutions. The reciprocal recognition of these common principles – a commitment to the rule of law, individual rights and equality before the law, representative government based on popular consent – means that liberal democracies evince little interest in conflict with each other and have no grounds on which to contest each other's legitimacy: they have constructed a 'separate peace'.[11] This does not mean that they are less inclined to make war with non-democratic states, and Doyle is correct to point out that democracies maintain a healthy appetite for conflicts with authoritarian states. But it does suggest that the best prospect for bringing an end to war between states lies with the spread of liberal-democratic governments across the globe. The expansion of the zone of peace from the core to the periphery is the basis of Fukuyama's optimism about the post-Communist era.[12]

A related argument by Mueller claims that we are already witnessing the obsolescence of war between the major powers. Reviving the liberal faith in the capacity of people to improve the moral and material conditions of their lives, Mueller attempts to demonstrate that, just as duelling and slavery were eventually seen as morally unacceptable, war is increasingly viewed in the developed world as repulsive, immoral and uncivilised. That violence is more widely seen as an anachronistic form of social intercourse is not due to any change in human nature or the structure of the international system. According to Mueller, the obsolescence of major war in the late twentieth century is the product of moral learning, a shift in ethical consciousness away from coercive forms of social behaviour. Because war brings more costs than gains and is no longer seen as a romantic or noble pursuit, it has become 'rationally unthinkable'.[13]

The long peace between states of the industrialized world is a cause for profound optimism for liberals such as Mueller and Fukuyama, who are confident that we have already entered a period in which war as an instrument of international diplomacy is becoming obsolete. But if war has been an important factor in nation-building, as Giddens, Mann and Tilly have argued, the fact that states are learning to curb their propensity for violence will also have important consequences for forms of political community which are likely to emerge in the industrial centres of the world. The end of war between the great powers may have the ironic effect of weakening the rigidity of their political boundaries and inspiring a wave of sub-national revolts. If war has been a binding as well as destructive force in international relations, the problem of maintaining cohesive communities will be a major challenge for metropolitan centres.

Far from sharing the optimism of the liberals, neo-realists such as Waltz and Mearsheimer are profoundly disturbed by the collapse of Soviet strategic power. If mutual nuclear deterrence between the United States and the Soviet Union accounted for the high level of international stability in the post-war period, the end of bipolarity casts an ominous shadow over the future world order. Because there is no obvious replacement for the Soviet Union which can restore the balance of strategic power, the world is entering a new and dangerous phase of uncertainty and instability. As Waltz concedes, 'in international politics, unbalanced power constitutes a danger even when it is American power that is out of balance'.[14]

Waltz and Mearsheimer continue to stress the importance of strategic interaction in shaping the contours of international relations. For them, the distribution and character of military power remain the root causes of war and peace.[15] Instead of highlighting the spread of liberal democracy and a concomitant zone of peace, they regard the rapid demise of bipolarity as the single most dramatic change in contemporary world politics. The pacification of the core, while desirable and perhaps even encouraging, is merely a transient stage which needs to be superseded by a restoration of the strategic balance among the great powers. Echoing Carr's critique of liberal-utopianism on the eve of the Second World War, Waltz believes that the 'peace and justice' which liberals claim is spreading beyond the central core 'will be defined to the liking of the powerful'.[16]

According to Waltz and Mearsheimer, the recurrent features of international relations, most notably the struggle for power and security, will eventually reassert themselves: 'in international politics, overwhelming power repels and leads others to try to balance against it'.[17] However, the immediate absence of a likely countervailing power to the United States means there are few clues about the period we are now entering. According to Mearsheimer, the long peace of the Cold War was a result of three factors: the bipolar distribution of military power in continental Europe, the rough equality of military power between the United States and the Soviet Union, and the pacifying effect of the presence of nuclear weapons.[18] The collapse of the Soviet Union removes the central pillar upon which the bipolar stability was built. Multipolar systems, on the other hand, are notoriously less stable than bipolar systems because the number of potential bilateral conflicts is greater, deterrence is more difficult to achieve, and the potential for misunderstandings and miscalculations of power and motive is increased.[19] Based on the experience of previous multipolar systems, in particular the periods before both world wars, the new era is therefore more a cause for concern than celebration: according to Mearsheimer, the stability of the last forty-five years is unlikely to be repeated.

Neo-realists have regarded nuclear weapons, and the rough parity between East and West, as a source of stability and pacification during the Cold War. They provided security to both blocs, generated caution amongst decision-makers, imposed a rough equality, and created a clarity of relative power between both camps.[20] The absence of a first strike capability and the destructive potential of a direct conflict forced the United States and the Soviet Union to learn to manage their differences without recourse to violence. In addition, the binding force of having a common enemy – a form of bonding by exclusion – imposed a discipline upon and within each bloc. According to Mearsheimer, if this level of stability is to be reached in the new multipolar environment, the carefully managed proliferation of nuclear weapons in Europe may be required to preserve the peace, or at least keep a check on the strategic primacy of the United States.[21]

Maintaining strategic stability in Europe in a multipolar environment is just one of a number of major challenges for liberal internationalists. On the question of how liberal states should conduct themselves with non-liberal states, Fukuyama and Doyle are equally and surprisingly silent. As the number of East Asian societies which reject the normative superiority of liberal democracy grows, considerable doubt is cast on the belief that the non-European world is seeking to imitate the Western route to political modernisation. Perhaps the answer here, as Linklater suggests, is not so much the spread of liberal democracy *per se*, 'but the idea of limited power which is present within, but not entirely synonymous with, liberal democracy'.[22] The notion of limited power and respect for the rule of law contained within the idea of 'constitutionalism' may be one means of solving the exclusionary character of the liberal zone of peace. It is a less ambitious project and potentially more sensitive to the cultural and political differences among states in the current international system. It may avoid the danger of the system bifurcating into a privileged inner circle and a disadvantaged and disregarded outer circle.[23] The greatest barrier to the expansion of the zone of peace from the core is the perception within the periphery that this constitutes little more than the domination of one culture by another. These suspicions are well-founded given that peripheral states have traditionally been the victims of Western intervention. A commitment to constitutionalism rather than liberal democracy may therefore be a more acceptable and inclusive precondition for spreading the zone of peace.

The spirit of commerce

In the eighteenth and nineteenth centuries liberals felt that the spirits of war and commerce were mutually incompatible. Most wars were fought by states to achieve their mercantilist goals. Free trade, however, was a more effective and peaceful means of achieving national wealth because, according to the theory of comparative advantage, each economy would be materially better off than if it had been pursuing nationalism and self-sufficiency (autarky). Free trade would also break down the divisions between states and unite individuals everywhere in one community. Artificial barriers to commerce distort perceptions and relations between individuals, thereby causing international conflict. Free trade would expand the range of contacts and levels of communication between the peoples of the world and encourage international friendship and understanding. According to Kant, unhindered commerce between the peoples of the world would unite them in a common, peaceful enterprise. 'Trade. . .would increase the wealth and power of the peace-loving, productive sections of the population at the expense of the war-orientated aristocracy, and. . .would bring men of different nations into constant contact with one another; contact which would make clear to all of them their fundamental community of interests'.[24] Similarly Ricardo believed that free trade 'binds together, by one common tie of interest and intercourse, the universal society of nations throughout the civilized world'.[25]

Conflicts were caused by states erecting barriers which distorted and concealed the natural harmony of interests commonly shared by individuals across the world. The solution to the problem, argued Adam Smith and Tom Paine, was the free movement of commodities, capital and labour. 'If commerce were permitted to act to the universal extent it is capable, it would extirpate the system of war and produce a revolution in the uncivilized state of governments'.[26] Writing in 1848, John Stuart Mill also claimed free trade was the means to bring about the end of war: 'it is commerce which is rapidly rendering war obsolete, by strengthening and multiplying the personal interests which act in natural opposition to it'.[27] The spread of markets would place societies on an entirely new foundation. Instead of conflicts over limited resources such as land, the industrial revolution raised the prospect of unlimited and unprecedented prosperity for all: material production, so long as it was freely exchanged, would bring human progress. Trade would create relations of mutual dependence which would foster understanding between peoples and reduce conflict. Economic self-interest would then be a powerful disincentive for war.

Free trade, according to Cobden, was 'eternal in its truth and universal in its application'. It was the key to global harmony and peace: 'the triumph of free trade was a triumph of pacific principles between all nations of the earth'.[28] As it was understood by Bright, free trade was the means for 'undermining the nationalist ambitions of nation-states by encouraging cosmopolitanism (meaning free from national limitations), and making nations so interdependent that wars and military budgets became unthinkable. Imperialism and autarky were regarded by liberals as the work of illiberal and reactionary forces and as a direct cause of wars'.[29]

It was felt that free trade would encourage links across frontiers and shift loyalties away from the nation-state. Leaders would eventually come to recognize that the benefits of free trade outweighed the costs of territorial conquest and colonial expansion. The attraction of going to war to promote mercantilist interests would be weakened as societies learn that war can only disrupt trade and therefore the prospects for economic prosperity.[30]

It was believed that free trade would also reduce misunderstandings between states, because the often contentious issues of industrial production and distribution would be taken from the jurisdiction of the state and handed over to the market. States would then be removed from direct responsibility for commercial behaviour which might upset, or threaten a rival state. State officials and commercial interests would be free to establish 'crosscutting transnational ties that serve as lobbies for mutual accommodation'.[31] Interdependence would replace national competition and diffuse unilateral acts of aggression and reciprocal retaliation.

Free trade and the removal of barriers to commerce is at the heart of modern interdependency theory. The rise of regional economic integration in Europe, for example, was inspired by the liberal belief that the likelihood of conflict between states would be reduced by creating a common interest in trade and economic collaboration among members of the same geographical region. This would encourage states such as France and Germany, which traditionally resolved their differences militarily, to co-operate within a commonly agreed economic and political framework. States would then have a joint stake in each other's peace and prosperity. The European Union is the best example of economic integration engendering closer economic and political co-operation in a region historically bedevilled by national conflicts. As Mitrany argued, initially co-operation between states would be achieved in technical areas where it was mutually convenient, but once successful it could 'spill over' into other functional areas where states found that mutual advantages could be gained.[32] In a development of this argument, Keohane and Nye have explained how, via membership of international institutions, states can significantly broaden their conceptions of self-interest in order to widen the scope for co-operation. Compliance with the rules of these organizations not only discourages the narrow pursuit of 'national interests', it also weakens the meaning and appeal of state sovereignty.[33] This suggests that the international system is more normatively regulated than realists would have us believe, a position further developed by rationalists such as Wight and Bull.

According to Rosencrance, the growth of economic interdependency has been matched by a corresponding decline in the value and importance of territorial conquest for states. In the contemporary world the benefits of trade and co-operation among states greatly exceeds that of military competition and territorial control. Nation-states have traditionally regarded the acquisition of territory as the principal means of increasing national wealth. In recent years, however, it has become apparent that additional territory does not necessarily help states to compete in an international system where the 'trading state' rather than the 'military state' is becoming dominant. In the 1970s state elites began to realise that wealth is determined by their share of the world market in value-added goods and services. This understanding has had two significant effects. First, the age of the independent, self-sufficient state is over. Complex layers of economic interdependency ensure that states cannot act aggressively without risking economic penalties exacted by other members of the international community. It also makes little sense for a state to threaten its commercial partners, whose markets are essential for economic growth. Secondly, territorial conquest in the nuclear age is both dangerous and costly for rogue states. The alternative, economic development through trade and foreign investment, is a much more attractive and potentially beneficial strategy. In an environment of free and open trade, the conquest of territory would not only be burdensome, it would also undermine the system upon which economic success in the global economy rests.[34]

Neo-realists have two responses to the liberal claim that economic interdependency is pacifying international relations. First, they argue that in any struggle between competing disciplines, the anarchic environment and the insecurity it engenders will always override the quest for economic prosperity. Economic interdependency will never take precedence over strategic security because states must always be primarily concerned with their survival. Their capacity to explore avenues of economic co-operation will therefore be limited by how secure they feel, and the extent to which they are required to engage in military competition with others. Secondly, the idea of economic interdependence implies a misleading degree of equality and shared vulnerability to economic forces in the global economy. Interdependence does not eliminate hegemony and dependency in interstate relations because power is very unevenly distributed throughout the world's trade and financial markets. Dominant players such as the United States have always framed the rules under which interdependency has flourished. Conflict and co-operation is therefore unlikely to disappear, though it may be channelled into more peaceful forms.

The advocacy of democracy and free trade foreshadows another issue which liberal internationalism has introduced to international theory. Liberals have always believed that the legitimacy of domestic political orders was largely contingent upon upholding the rule of law and the state's respect for the human rights of its citizens. Human beings are said to be endowed – purely by reason of their humanity – with certain fundamental and inalienable rights, benefits and protections. The extension of these rights to all peoples has a particularly important place in liberal thinking about foreign policy and international relations because states which treated their own citizens ethically and allowed them meaningful participation in the political process were thought to be less likely to behave aggressively internationally. The task for liberals was to develop ethical and moral standards which would be universally observed. This has proved to be a difficult task. How could liberals avoid the charge that their conceptions of democracy and human rights were culturally specific, ethnocentric and therefore irrelevant to societies which were not Western in cultural orientation? To recipient societies the claim to universality may merely conceal the means by which one dominant society imposes its culture upon another. The promotion of human rights from the core to the periphery assumes that the West not only possesses moral truths which others are bound to observe, but that the West can sit in judgement on other societies. And even if universal rules could be agreed upon, how could compliance with these standards be enforced? Liberals have always been divided over this issue, between non-interventionists who defend state sovereignty, and those who feel that the promotion of ethical principles justifies intervention in the internal affairs of other states.

The liberal solution to the problem of war contains within it a fortuitous coincidence of ethical and utilitarian arguments: for liberals, peace and profit are coterminous. There is, however, a third aspect to their prescription for peace which centres on the structure of the international system and the conduct of international diplomacy.

Secret diplomacy, the balance of power and collective security

As much as any other factor, liberals argue for democracy because they are profoundly suspicious of concentrated forms of power, especially state power. When they looked at the international system, liberals of the nineteenth and early twentieth centuries saw power being exercised in the interests of governing elites and against the wishes of the masses. 'Secret diplomacy' was the name they gave to the way unrepresentative elites practised international relations in the pre-democratic era. They disputed the view that foreign policy was a specialized art which was best made by professional diplomats behind closed doors and away from the influences of national politics. If the democratization of domestic politics could produce important economic and social reforms there would be a commensurate improvement in the conduct of foreign policy as a result of popular participation.[35] And if the 'free consent' of the populace was to be fully realized in the liberal state, there would need to be an adequate machinery for ensuring the democratic control of foreign policy. This would change forever the nature of international relations, presaging a new era of peaceful co-operation.

From the time of Bright and Cobden, liberals have regarded the balance of power as the most pernicious aspect of 'secret diplomacy'. It was, in Bright's words, 'a foul thing' which gave no credence to the common interests of humankind and the just claims of small nations seeking self-determination. The balance of power was the product of elite collusion which resulted in international relations being 'arranged' to suit the interests of those who ruled Great Powers. 'This excessive love for the *balance of power*', claimed Bright, 'is neither more or less than a gigantic system of outdoor relief for the aristocracy of Great Britain'.[36] For Cobden the 'balance of power' was the veil behind which the armaments industries enriched themselves through state expenditure on weapons of war. It was also a smokescreen which concealed British imperial interests, with the word 'balance' designed 'to please the public ear; it implied something of equity; whilst England, holding the balance of Europe in her hand, sounded like filling the office of Justice herself to one-half of the globe'.[37]

Liberal internationalists in the nineteenth century were fundamentally anti-statist in their approach to international relations. Governments, especially undemocratic ones, were seen as the major cause of international conflict and insecurity. Consistent with their preference for the minimalist state was their belief that governments get in the way of peaceful relations between individuals, hence Cobden's call for 'as little intercourse as possible between Governments, as much connection as possible between nations of the world'. To realise their world view, liberals wanted to replace autocratic regimes with regimes based on democratic accountability and values. However, a major obstacle to the transformation of international relations was the balance of power system, which helped to sustain tyrannical regimes by denying nationalities the opportunity to overthrow the structures of state power. Empires and authoritarian governments were propped up by those with vested interests in maintaining the integrity of the European states system, regardless of the political aspirations of the peoples of Europe. Until this system was radically revised, by bringing the balance of power mechanism to an end, the liberal world order would have to wait.[38]

The balance of power is technically defined as the absence of a preponderant military power in the international system. As it operated in Europe, the balance of power system described the process whereby smaller powers would form temporary alliances of convenience which would act as a countervailing power to the dominant military state in the region. Membership of these alliances would change over time as new potential hegemons emerged, and from time to time war would be necessary to cut down the dominant state and distribute strategic power in the region more evenly. To defenders of the balance of power, conflict was a regrettable though necessary and sometimes desirable feature of the international system.

Liberal critics of the balance of power claim the concept is vague and unintelligible. Criticism 'focuses upon the alleged obscurity or meaninglessness of the concept, the untested or untestable nature of the historical generalisations upon which it rests, and the reliance of the theory upon the notion that all international behaviour consists of the pursuit of power'.[39] In addition, they assert that attempts to preserve a balance of power in the international system are often a source of war. Liberals have claimed that the balance of power is the method by which great powers pursue their commercial and strategic interests at the expense of small powers, often in violation of international law. Defenders of the concept, on the other hand, argue that liberals have missed the point of the system. The principle function of the balance of power is not to preserve peace, but to preserve the system of states. On certain occasions war may in fact be necessary to recalibrate the differentials of power in the international system. Smaller powers may be absorbed or partitioned in the process, and international law may be sporadically breached, but this is the necessary cost of keeping order in the system.[40]

Until 1914 most scholars and statesmen assumed that the 'balance of power' was a self-regulating system, the political equivalent of the law of economics. The First World War discredited the laws of both economics and politics. The self-operating laws had failed to prevent the most destructive conflict in human history. The experiences of 1914–18 brought to the fore liberal thinkers and politicians who 'considered the old assumptions and prescriptions of power politics to be totally discredited and who helped to substitute for its erratic procedures a firm system of international law and organisation preserving peace by a system of collective security'.[41] The balance of power had failed to prevent the war because, instead of allowing for the flexibility of realigning each other against the aggressor, the great powers had locked themselves into two antagonistic blocs. The commitment to collective security was designed to prevent this situation recurring by ensuring that in the future, the aggressor would be confronted by all other states. In other words, a balance of power would be institutionalized. According to supporters of the theory, this would have two beneficial results. First, it would make the balance of power more effective because there would be less chance of a preponderant power emerging. Secondly, it would ensure that violence, if necessary, would always be used in a legitimate manner. Since power would be vested in the international community, it would not be abused in the way it was by individual nation states.[42] Henceforth, all members of the international community would take collective responsibility for keeping the peace. This responsibility would be formally enshrined in the institutional form of the League of Nations.

Consistent with their view that peace depended on the spread of democracy, collective security was an attempt by liberal internationalists to reproduce the concepts and processes of domestic law at the international level. Liberals believed that the destructive forces of international anarchy could only be brought to an end if the international system was regulated in the same way as domestic society. President Wilson's 14 points were therefore an attempt to incorporate US constitutional prescriptions globally.[43] The League of Nations was designed as an overarching authority which would regulate the behaviour of states towards each other. Members would be required to submit their disputes to arbitration and, if necessary, use sanctions to compel aggressor states to conform to a peaceful method of conflict resolution. Under the organization's rules, an act of war against one member of the League would be considered an act of aggression against the entire international community (Article 16 of the Covenant of the League of Nations). The League would, in theory, be run by an alliance of major powers permanently committed to opposing aggression on the grounds of principle. According to President Wilson, 'there must be, not a balance of power but a community of power; not organized rivalries but an organised common peace'.[44] There would no longer be any need for covert alliances between governments because secret diplomacy would be replaced by open discussion in the Assembly of the League. The commitment of member states to the principle of collective security would override any other alliance or strategic obligations. States would formally renounce the use of force as a means of settling international disputes.

Regrettably, it was all a forlorn hope. The idea of collective security failed in the 1930s because it depended on the general acceptance by states of a particular configuration of international power: a distribution of influence, territory and military potential that clearly favoured the victors of the First World War at the expense of the defeated powers. Why should Germany, for example, accept forever the inequity, and what many saw as the injustice, of a discriminatory peace settlement imposed on it in 1918? To those states which lost the First World War, and who wished to revise the frontiers and conditions imposed by the Versailles settlement, the League of Nations seemed dedicated to the preservation of the status quo rather than the preservation of peace.

And what could be done about states which did not accept these new diplomatic norms, such as the rule of law, controls on the use of force in international disputes, and the authority of the collective security organization? When Japan moved into Manchuria in 1931 and Italy invaded Abyssinia in 1935–6, the League of Nations lacked both the collective will and the enforcement power to reverse these acts of aggression. Collective security was seen as inherently contradictory, if not hypocritical. If its principal motivation was outlawing the recourse to war, should the enforcement of its provisions in the final instance be dependent on the threat of the use of force?

Ironically, although the League of Nations was properly seen as one of the principal instruments of collective security, its creation had the effect of consolidating conceptions of national sovereignty as the 'natural' political condition of humankind. Far from representing a stage beyond the nation-state as a representation of political community, the League operated on the principle that 'statehood' was universally applicable: it should be extended to all ethnic and national groups. As a critique of the balance of power as the principal guarantor of sovereignty, the League of Nations was an alternative means of legitimating national sovereignty, not an alternative to national sovereignty. The restructured territorial divisions which arose as a result of the new entitlement to statehood merely ensured that, after 1918, hostilities between ethnic or national minorities would become conflicts between states.[45]

It was the weakness of the concept of collective security itself which finally discredited the organization. Although it was in theory a superior form of strategic organization, the principle of collective security was prone to failure because it assumed an overriding, if not universal, normative commitment to peace by states. Opposition to war on the grounds of principle not only relied on the goodwill and determination of all participants in the arrangement, it also assumed that states would be prepared to forgo their national interests for the sake of a peaceful international order. As Carr and other realists were soon to point out, the insecurity states feel in the international system does not afford them the luxury of forswearing the use of violence to uphold a principle. States are extremely reluctant to surrender their sovereign powers in an anarchical international environment.

Liberal internationalists had been wrong to assume that there was a self-evident value system, committed to international harmony and co-operation, which had universal validity. As Carr commented, 'these supposedly absolute and universal principles were not principles at all, but the unconscious reflections of national policy based on a particular interpretation of national interest at a particular time'.[46] Collective security, as it was practised in the early phase of the inter-war years, was little more than the preservation of the status quo by the victorious powers, in their own interests. The great powers had never really stopped playing 'balance of power' politics: the process was simply mediated through the League. Rather than removing considerations of power from the domain of international politics, the League of Nations represented the exploitation of the changing equilibrium of power, initially by the status quo powers and later by the revisionist states. Ironically its eventual collapse was provoked by a collapse in the European balance, another triumph of power over principle.[47]

At the very least, a collective security system requires 'a degree of mutual confidence, a homogeneity of values and a coincidence of perceived interests'.[48] This level of cultural homogeneity is never easy to find in the international system. Later in the century collective security would prove to be more successful when attempted at the regional level, especially in limited strategic alliances against a common enemy. But in 1939 it appeared that European society was permanently organized into a system of states in which war was an inescapable part of the process of settling differences in the absence of a higher jurisdiction. As much as it distressed liberals, 'for better or worse war was an institution which could not be eliminated from the international system. All that could be done about it was, so far as possible, to codify its rationale and to civilise its means'.[49]

II   Liberal Internationalism: The Economic Dimension

Fukuyama's post-Cold War optimism is on firmer ground if we consider the extent to which economic liberalism has become the dominant perspective and ideology of the contemporary period. The move towards a global political economy organized along neo-liberal lines is a trend as significant as the likely expansion of the zone of peace. As the end of the century approaches, the world economy more closely resembles the prescriptions of Smith and Ricardo than at any previous time.

In this section we shall assess the significance of this trend for both the internal nature of modern capitalist societies and the relationships between nation-states in the modern period. We shall begin by examining a previous attempt to construct a 'market society', in nineteenth-century Britain, followed by an exploration of the ideology of free trade.

Society and the 'free market' (Polanyi's critique)

In his seminal account of the abandonment of *laissez-faire* capitalism, Karl Polanyi argues that by the 1830s, economic liberalism in Britain had 'burst forth as a crusading passion, and *laissez-faire* had become a militant creed'. But contrary to economic orthodoxy, the arrival of *laissez-faire* was neither inevitable nor the result of an evolutionary process. According to Polanyi, it was the product of deliberate state policy and 'nothing less than a self-regulating market on a world scale' could ensure its proper functioning. The crucial step towards the laissez-faire economy was the commodification of land and labour in the eighteenth century, while the expansion of the market system in the nineteenth century was dependent on the spread of international free trade, the creation of a competitive (national) labour market, and the linking of the currency to the gold standard.[50] *Laissez-faire* capitalism was the creation of conscious political intervention by the state. 'The road to the free market was paved with continuous political manipulation, whether the state was involved in removing old restrictive regulations. . . . or building new political administrative bodies to bolster the factors of production of the new market economy'.[51]

According to Polanyi, the market economy created a new type of society. An 'economic sphere' came into existence which was sharply delimited from other domains in society. Henceforth, society's institutions were 'determined' by this economic sphere while the market mechanism created the 'delusion' of economic determinism as a general law for all human society.[52] From these developments, three 'misleading generalisations' about the nature of humankind, forms of possible economic organization, and approaches to the study of society and economy, emerged from the specific case of *laissez-faire* capitalism. According to Polanyi, the institutionalization of these generalizations has distorted our understanding of ourselves and our society, and successfully blocked alternative paths to human emancipation.

The first of these generalizations suggests that the pursuit of material self-gain is the natural condition of humankind. This has been an article of faith for economic liberals who, since the time of Adam Smith, have argued that society is comprised of individuals with an innate propensity to 'truck, barter and trade' – for the rational pursuit of self-interest. Polanyi, on the other hand, argues that the pursuit of material self-gain was an institutionally enforced incentive which, without the intervention and protection of the state, threatened to tear apart the fabric of community life in nineteenth-century England. 'Only in the nineteenth-century self-regulating market did economic self-interest become the dominant principle of social life, and both liberalism and Marxism made the ahistorical error of assuming that what was dominant in that society had been dominant throughout human history'.[53] Yet, despite being historically specific to the rise of industrial capitalism, 'the pursuit of material gain compelled by laissez-faire market rules is still not seen as behaviour forced on people as the only way to earn a living in a market system, but as an expression of their inner being; individualism is regarded as the norm, and society remains invisible as a cluster of individual persons who happen to live together without responsibility for anyone other than kin'.[54] According to George and Sabelli, man has been 'ontologically reconstructed and redeemed as homo economicus'. His dwelling place is the market and his desire to accumulate, pursue his self-interests and maximize profit in all things are his natural expressions.[55]

Secondly, despite the experience of modern economic development, *laissez-faire* capitalism has been reified in Western economic and political culture. 'When contrasted with earlier and later economies, laissez-faire capitalism can be seen to be a unique and transitory event'. It was born in England between 1750 and 1850, and died in Europe and America during the 1930s and 1940s.[56] Polanyi recognized that the great achievement of economic liberals, therefore, has been to represent a transitory, historical state of economic and social relations as if it were permanent, neutral and eternal. 'The market mechanism. . ..created the delusion of economic determinism as a general law for all human society'.[57] Most contemporary discussion of industrial capitalism in the 'problem-solving' positivist disciplines (economics, policy studies, and so on) remains ahistorical to the extent that it fails to acknowledge the collapse of *laissez-faire* capitalism in the 1930s and 1940s.

This leads to the third of Polanyi's generalizations, which highlights the epistemological peculiarities of the discipline of economics. Polanyi stresses that neo-classical economics, still the discipline's governing orthodoxy, was a product *of* the Industrial Revolution *for* the Industrial Revolution. Its claims for universal relevance beyond the period of *laissez-faire* capitalism are therefore unjustified – an 'economistic fallacy'.

In Polanyi's terms, the institutional structure of laissez-faire industrial capitalism separated out economy from society and polity by turning labour, land and other natural resources into commodities. . . . One consequence of this great institutional transformation was that classical and then neo-classical economics could be created: the analysis of this separate and autonomous sphere of uncontrolled resource and product markets. With Adam Smith, political economy ended: with David Ricardo, economics began.[58]

Economics was invented on the assumption of the artificial separation of the polity and the economy: this remains its ideological foundation. As Block points out, 'the neo-classical insistence that the economy is analytically distinct from the rest of society makes it logical to see government regulation of business or government provision of welfare as an external interference with a market economy. While economists may disagree as to whether particular types of interference are benign or malignant, they share the view that they are *external*'.[59]

The artificial separation of economic and politics created an imaginary vision of how the world could theoretically be structured, if only society could be returned to its natural state: 'the illusion of the international character of the world system rested on the conviction that it was not an artificial creation of man but part of an order of nature'.[60] This utopian image, with its normative assumptions, then became the starting point for prescriptions about what constitutes a desirable economic and social order. According to Carr,

> the [liberal] protest against these restrictions [on trade] took the form of a wishful vision of free trade; and out of this vision. . .Adam Smith created a science of political economy. The new science was primarily based on a negation of existing reality and on certain artificial and universal generalizations about the behaviour of hypothetical economic man. . . But economic theory long retained its utopian character; and even today some 'classical economists' insist on regarding universal free trade – an imaginary condition which has never existed – as the normal postulate of economic science and all reality as a deviation from this utopian prototype.

The science of economics could not be profitably studied in isolation from politics: after all, it presupposes a given political order. The separation of economics from politics was an imaginary and unsustainable theoretical divorce, 'an illusion'. For Carr, the *laissez-faire* period was therefore an 'abnormal interlude' when utopian dreams broke free from the realities of social and economic life.[61]

Importantly, argues Polanyi, the expansion of the market system after the Industrial Revolution could only be maintained by state intervention. 'The road to the free market was opened and kept open by an enormous increase in continuous, centrally organized and controlled intervention'. Despite the claims of liberals that laissez-faire was a natural, organic development, 'there was nothing natural about *laissez-faire*; free markets could never have come into being merely by allowing things to take their course'. *Laissez-faire* capitalism was enforced by the state, which resulted in an enormous increase in its administrative and bureaucratic functions.[62] The liberal doctrine of non-intervention disguised the extent to which governments were expected to maintain conditions for markets to function.

According to Polanyi, the commodification of land, labour and money was purely fictitious. To subject the fate of these fictitious commodities – human beings, their natural environment and their means of financial exchange – to the vagaries of a self-regulating market, was to invite a social disaster. Accordingly, by the 1870s an anti-*laissez-faire* movement had emerged in Britain to ameliorate the social effects of the self-regulating market. It took the familiar forms of social and national protection, and foreshadowed a steady period of economic decline in Britain. According to the liberals, this movement was an organized, anti-liberal 'collectivist' conspiracy, determined to deny the promise of the Enlightenment. The liberal dream of peace and prosperity was 'frustrated by the passions of nationalism and class war, vested interests and monopolists, and above all, by the blindness of the working people to the ultimate beneficence of unrestricted economic freedom to all human interests, including their own'. Economic liberalism could have produced a prosperous society. Only the incomplete application of its principles caused its failure. The fault lay not with the competitive system and the self-regulating market itself, but with those who interfered with and intervened in the system.

Polanyi refutes the liberal diagnosis and claims that the anti-*laissez-faire* movement was in fact a spontaneous social reaction to the pernicious effects of the self-regulating market. The abandonment of market principles and the protective intervention of the state arose out the need to safeguard the public from the more odious conditions of modern industrial life: 'the market economy was a threat to the human and natural components of the social fabric':

> To allow the market mechanism to be the sole director of the fate of human beings and their natural environment, indeed, even of the amount and use of purchasing power, would result in the demolition of society. . .Undoubtedly, labour, land and money markets are essential to a market economy. But no society could stand the effects of such a system of crude fictions even for the shortest stretch of time unless its human and natural substance as well as its business organization was protected against the ravages of this satanic mill.[63]

Far from being 'strangled by shortsighted trade unionists, Marxist intellectuals, greedy manufacturers and reactionary landlords', the abandonment of *laissez-faire* principles was demanded by a public which required protection from the perils inherent within the market system.[64] Social legislation covering working hours, public health, factory conditions and trades unions were acts of community self-defence. They were a response of both the organized working class and the middle class protecting their own respective interests. Farmers wanted insulation from fluctuating prices, workers protested against unemployment, and capitalists wanted a national banking system to protect their investments against the vagaries of the world market: 'paradoxically enough, not human beings and natural resources only but also the organization of capitalistic production itself had to be sheltered from the devastating effects of a self-regulating market'.[65] According to Polanyi, 'the anti-liberal conspiracy is pure invention. The great variety of forms in which the "collectivist" counter movement appeared was not due to any preference for socialism or nationalism on the part of concerted interests, but exclusively to the broader range of vital social interests affected by the expanding market mechanism'.[66]

Paradoxically, liberal attempts to re-establish the self-regulating market system have always required state intervention: 'for as long as that system is not established, economic liberals must and will unhesitatingly call for the intervention of the state in order to establish it, and once established, in order to maintain it'.[67] Markets in this sense are often the products of states, not their alternatives or rivals.

> Economic history reveals that the emergence of national markets was in no way the result of the gradual and spontaneous emancipation of the economic sphere from governmental control. On the contrary, the market has been the outcome of a conscious and often violent intervention on the part of government which imposed the market organization on a society for non-economic needs.[68]

Gramsci endorses this view, claiming that 'it must be made clear that *laissez-faire* too is a form of State "regulation", introduced and maintained by legislative and coercive means. It is a deliberate policy, conscious of its own ends, and not the spontaneous, automatic expression of economic facts'.[69] The history of US hegemonic intervention in the Third World during the Cold War is often cited by critics of liberal internationalism as an example of the state creating 'market conditions', as is the transition of the world economy from national to global markets, which began in the 1970s.

According to critics of liberalism, the lessons of last century have important implications for our own. Nineteenth-century civilization, they believe, was destroyed 'by the measures which society adopted in order *not* to be, in its turn, annihilated by the action of the self-regulating market. . .the conflict between the market and the elementary requirements of an organized social life provided the century with its dynamics and produced the typical strains which ultimately destroyed that society'.[70] From Polanyi's analysis of the abandonment of *laissez-faire* in the nineteenth century, three 'lessons' have contemporary relevance for the prospects for liberal internationalism in the post-Cold War period.

First, *laissez-faire* capitalism in the nineteenth century did not fail because of 'covert action' planned by vested interests determined to thwart the liberal dream. It was the effects of unfettered capitalism and the free operation of the self-regulating market which prompted calls for state protection. The movement away from the liberal doctrine sprang from a genuine social need: without state intervention, society would be annihilated by the market.[71] Uncontrolled market exchange had led to social division: the fabric of community life had been torn by the Industrial Revolution and could only be repaired with the subordination of economic forces to social control.

Secondly, *laissez-faire* capitalism had depended for its systemic existence upon the very forms of state intervention it claimed obstructed the free workings of the market. Only the state could provide and maintain the legal and commercial infrastructure upon which the operation of the market depended. Ironically, some of the loudest calls for state intervention came from liberal capitalists who demanded that the system be enforced by the state, both for defensive and aggressive motives. Nothing of significance has changed in the present century. As one commentator has observed, 'state power has regularly been invoked by the capitalist class to protect it from the destructive effects of an unregulated market, to secure resources, markets, and opportunities for investment, and in general to safeguard and protect their profits and power'.[72] Another observer agrees, adding that 'in the last analysis, markets come out of the barrel of a gun, and to establish an integrated world economy on capitalist lines requires the international mobilization of political power'.[73]

Thirdly, as Chomsky has noted, economic historians such as Friedrich Pollock, Karl Polanyi and Alexander Gerschenkron have long been arguing that a sharp departure from neo-liberal doctrines was a prerequisite for economic development in our own century. In fact in the post-war period, the experience of Japan and the other dynamic economies of East Asia has demonstrated that 'late development' would appear to be critically dependent on state intervention.[74] There are few, if any examples of *laissez-faire* transitions to economic development. This has not deterred some liberal intellectuals who seem 'genuinely incapable of entertaining the possibility that deliberately devised and sustained Japanese policies of government intervention and protection, in conscious rejection of Western textbook precepts, have played an essential role in Japan's rise to industrial ascendancy'.[75] They continue to regard the state as an 'artificial' impediment to the 'free' and 'natural' operation of the market, and deny that it is capable of playing a positive role in resource allocation or economic development.

The implications of Polanyi's critique are crucial to any claim that liberal capitalism is the ultimate form of political economy for all societies. *Laissez-faire* capitalism was abandoned in the nineteenth century for ethical and social reasons. The state intervened to mitigate many of the hardships and cruelties of the self-regulating market. Legislative controls were introduced to regulate the impact of unfettered capitalism on the work force and the environment. Trade unions legitimized themselves and, for a period, exercised countervailing power to the entrepreneurial capitalists. Social cohesion and the legitimacy of the system could only be sustained if the state

assumed the role of smoothing out the business cycle, thus limiting associated hardship and despair. Furthermore, there is a close correlation in
advanced Western societies between state co-ordinated economic development and global financial and trading success. If, as Susan Strange says,
'world market shares are the name of the game' for national governments,
the most successful contemporary players are those which recognize that
the state has a necessary role to play.[76]

While it may be possible for liberals to defend the market on the grounds
of economic efficiency, it is much more difficult to support the idea of the
market society on moral grounds. Many of the evils of unrestricted economic competition were only overcome in the industrialized North by
protecting society from market forces. In the post-Cold War period, however, 'protection' is now widely demonized: in the discourse of the ruling
elites in many industrialized societies it is a pejorative term, associated with
intrusive and inefficient government. In the developing world, in particular
the economically dynamic states of East Asia, the moral battle against
unregulated markets has only just begun. In these regions the full impact
of economic liberalism on the fabric of community life in both communist
and authoritarian states is only beginning to be felt. Attempts to create a
'market society' on a global scale may not be as desirable as some liberals
would have us believe. Fukuyama's excitement may be somewhat premature, for as Derrida remarks 'never in history has the horizon of the whole
thing whose survival is being celebrated (namely, all the old models of the
capitalist and liberal worlds) been seen as dark, threatening and threatened'.[77]

From Polanyi's critique of liberal economic principles, and their effects
on industrial society, we can now turn to the second category of concerns
about liberal internationalism: the ideology of 'free trade'.

Free trade imperialism

Two of the difficulties we face with the term 'free trade' is its benign
symbolism and the gap which often exists between the rhetoric of its
progenitors and the reality of their behaviour. As we shall see later, in
contemporary world politics free trade agreements, for example, are rarely
'free' nor are they specifically about 'trade'. Moreover, the most prominent
advocates of free trade often behave as if the idea was non-reciprocal: it is a
policy honoured more in the breach than in the observance. These distinctions will become more obvious in the next section when we examine the
nature of contemporary world trade.

To those societies which have had the 'beneficence' of free trade thrust
upon them by metropolitan powers, the policy appears anything but be-

nign. After all, free trade and market forces tend to overwhelm and even dissolve traditional social relations and institutions: they are a powerful source of social and political change. The introduction of free trade and market relations produces a competition for efficiency which drives out the inefficient and forces all members of society to adapt to new ways. Free trade also affects the distribution of wealth and power within and between societies, establishing new hierarchies, dependencies and power relationships. Within states, community life is transformed into market life, in accordance with the requirements of efficient production, export earnings and the international division of labour. Outside, in the international system, not all states are able to take advantage of the opportunities presented by free trade or capable of influencing market forces to their own advantage. Only wealthy societies seem capable of harnessing the power of the market.

'Recipients' therefore frequently view free trade as a rationale for the exploitation of subordinate sectors by rich and powerful states determined to secure domestic economic advantages for themselves. 'Free trade undermines national autonomy and state control by exposing the economy to the vicissitudes and instabilities of the world market and exploitation by other, more powerful economies'.[78] This argument was first articulated during the middle of the nineteenth century, the so called 'golden age' of liberalism when British colonialism and industrial expansion was at its peak.[79]

The case of those who felt the malign effects of 'free trade' has been argued by political economists such as Friedrich List who regarded free trade in the mid-nineteenth century as merely the 'veil behind which the British state ruthlessly pursued its own national interests and exploited its particular advantages – the great productivity of its industries and their consequent dominance of world trade'.[80] It was not until 1846 that British manufacturers were sufficiently powerful to allow the Corn Laws to be repealed, confident in the knowledge that free trade policies would now serve their particular interests. According to List, the British had used the power of the state to protect their own infant industries against foreign competition while weakening their opponents by military force, and they only became champions of free trade after having achieved technological and industrial supremacy over their rivals. They had pursued protectionist policies until British industry was strong enough to out-compete every other economy. Having reached this point, they then sought to advance their own 'national' economic interests by gaining unimpeded access to foreign markets through free trade.[81] 'In contemporary terms, once they had established the 'level playing field' to their incontestable advantage, nothing seemed more high-minded than an 'open world' with no irrational and arbitrary interference with the honest entrepreneur, seeking the welfare of all'.[82] Free trade, as List argued, was the correct policy for an industrially dominant nation like Great Britain in the nineteenth century, but only policies of protection could enable weaker powers to challenge the hegemon's supremacy.

From the very beginning free trade was a middle-class movement. Though it was only to last until 1931, when free trade was introduced in Britain in 1846 it was rightly seen by Cobden as a victory for the interests of manufacturers over aristocratic and landed interests. Having discovered that free trade policies promoted their own prosperity, British manufacturers were convinced that free trade also promoted British prosperity as a whole: their interests were said to be indivisible and 'in harmony' with the interests of the state. According to Marx, 'the assertion that free competition is the final form of development of productive forces, and thus of human freedom, means only that the domination of the middle class is the end of world history'.[83] Thus when workers struck for higher pay and better working conditions they damaged the manufacturers and merchants, and therefore by definition, they hurt Britain. Logically, industrial action became unpatriotic, if not treacherous behaviour. 'Once industrial capitalism and the class system had become the recognized structure of society, the doctrine of the harmony of interests acquired a new significance, and became. . .the ideology of a dominant group concerned to maintain its predominance by asserting the identity of its interests with those of the community as a whole'.[84] It was not a huge leap for British statesmen of the time, having discovered that free trade promoted 'British' prosperity, to believe that it also promoted the prosperity of the entire world.

The class-based nature of free trade advocacy continues to be reflected in the second half of the twentieth century.[85] Few economic historians would contest the view that the rise of Britain to industrial and commercial superiority at this time had little to do with methods guided by free trade principles: hence the suffix 'imperialism' was attached by critics of 'free trade' to the original description of international market relations. As one American commentator declared in 1866, 'free trade was a system devised by England to enable her to plunder the world'.[86]

Little needs to be added to the truism that all the modern advanced societies in this century also industrialized behind protective walls (the USA in 1816 and most advanced states by the 1880s): 'it seems altogether rash to suppose that economic nationalism is necessarily detrimental to states which practice it'.[87] On this subject, economic history remains almost uniform. However, what is not generally acknowledged in the scholarly literature is the dual standards of economic development which hegemonic states apply on the one hand to themselves, and on the other to those economically subordinate societies. Nowhere is this more graphically illustrated than in the post-war period where the means by which the burgeoning USA had climbed to economic maturity were to be denied to later entrants in the race. As Chomsky argues, 'it should be stressed that the economic doctrines preached by the powerful are intended for others, so they can be more efficiently robbed and exploited. No wealthy developed society accepts these conditions for itself, unless they happen to confer temporary advantage; and their history reveals that sharp departure from these doctrines was a prerequisite for development'.[88]

The creation of a liberal free trading regime by the United States in the post-war period was a conscious act of state policy. The United States emerged from the Second World War with 'preponderant power' and in an unprecedented position to reconstruct the world economy so American business could trade, operate and profit without restrictions everywhere.[89] This meant creating an open world economy conducive to the free movement of goods, capital and technology. US planners wanted to break down England's sterling bloc, create convertible currencies, and establish conditions for free trade. Crucially, raw materials had to be made available to all nations, though particularly to the advanced industrialized states, without discrimination. It was clear from official statements that the USA was ready to assume Britain's former role as the world's financial hegemon, and realized this could only be achieved by exercising considerable state power.[90]

The regions of the world would have to be 'opened' – to investment, the repatriation of profits, access to resources, and so on – and dominated by the United States.[91] It flows from this analysis that the Soviet Union was considered by US planners to be the major threat to the liberal international order because of its very existence as a great power controlling an imperial system that could not be incorporated within the US sphere.[92] Any country or bloc which succeeded in either extricating or exempting itself from the US-dominated system could expect hostility from the United States because this would constitute a reduction in the potential resource base and market opportunities available to the hegemonic economy. 'We believe passionately', Acheson stated, 'that the dissemination of free enterprise abroad was essential to its preservation at home'.[93] If necessary the doors barring access to US capital could be opened by force.

The historical record suggests two fundamental exceptions to the free trade model of economic development. The doors which barred free and non-discriminatory access to raw materials, and which blocked the path to currency convertibility, could only be pushed open by the state, in the post-war period by the United States. Left alone they would have remained shut. As Calleo and Rowland have argued, 'it is, in fact, difficult to sustain any free trade system without a concomitant political hegemony'.[94] Beyond that, the markets so necessary to absorb America's vast industrial production at the end of the war had to be artificially created by the state. Foreign trade had to be state financed. The reconstruction of the economies of Western Europe was therefore only partially altruistic. It was also the only way US capitalism could expand at the necessary rate. Needless to say, in the Third World the doors of independent economic nationalism have been more regularly, and more forcefully opened during this period.[95]

Secondly, the distinction between the state and the private economy as separate and discrete agents is more blurred than the liberals would argue. Not only does the state periodically intervene on behalf of private companies, the transnationals frequently return the compliment. As Leffler argues, 'in a world free of barriers to the movement of goods and capital. . .the private sector could serve as an instrument, albeit not a docile one, of state power'. Thus US-based multinational oil companies could help ensure American control over the world's most important raw material.[96]

The critique of 'free trade imperialism' exposed both the hypocrisy of states which espoused free trade (its selective and non-reciprocal aspects) and the extent to which the economic world order advocated by the liberals paradoxically required state intervention for its realization. For these and other reasons, free trade has never been embraced as enthusiastically in developing societies as it has by the elites in wealthy industrial states. They tended to see free trade as an imperial weapon used by dominant players to open up their societies to resource exploitation, foreign investment and the repatriation of profits. Invariably this meant that free trade led to a serious diminution in their economic sovereignty, at the same time blocking their paths to alternative forms of economic development.

In the modern period – the era of globalization – the case for free trade has been revived again by state elites in advanced sectors, and business elites which operate in global rather than national markets. This resuscitation of economic liberalism, which we will call neo-liberalism, has had a profound effect upon the lives of people around the world. It is the most significant legacy of eighteenth-century liberal internationalism.

III   Neo-liberalism in the Era of Globalization

To a significant extent, the globalization of the world economy coincided with a renaissance of neo-liberal thinking in the Western world. The political triumph of the 'New Right' in Britain and the United States in particular during the late 1970s and 1980s was achieved at the expense of Keynesianism, the first coherent philosophy of state intervention in economic life. According to the Keynesian formula, the state intervened in the economy to smooth out the business cycle, provide a degree of social equity and security, and maintain full employment. Neo-liberals, who had always favoured the free play of 'market forces' and a minimal role for the state in economic life, wanted to 'roll back' the welfare state, in the process challenging the social-democratic consensus established in most Western states during the post-war period.

Just as the ideological predilection of Western governments became more concerned with efficiency and productivity and less concerned with welfare and social justice, the power of the state to regulate the market was eroded by the forces of globalization, in particular the deregulation of finance and currency markets. The means by which domestic societies could be managed to reduce inequalities produced by inherited social structures and accentuated by the natural workings of the market, declined significantly. In addition, the disappearance of many traditional industries in Western economies, the effects of technological change, increased competition for investment and production, and the mobility of capital, undermined the bargaining power of labour. The sovereignty of capital began to reign over both the interventionary behaviour of the state and the collective power of organized working people.

In this section we shall examine both the contemporary relevance of liberal-internationalism in explaining the present form of the world economy and the extent to which liberal ideas have shaped the world order of the 1990s. Specifically we will focus on the contemporary nature of world trade and the question of sovereignty and foreign investment.

The nature of 'free trade'

For neo-liberals, the principles of free trade first enunciated by Smith and Ricardo, continue to have contemporary relevance. Commercial traders should be allowed to exchange money and goods without concern for national barriers. There should be few legal constraints on international commerce, and no artificial protection or subsidies constraining the freedom to exchange. An open global market, where goods and services can pass freely across national boundaries, should be the objective of policy-makers in all nation-states. Only free trade will generate the competition that will promote the most efficient use of resources, people and capital.

Conversely, 'protectionism' is seen as a pernicious influence on the body politic. Policies which protect uncompetitive industries from market principles corrupt international trade, distort market demand, artificially lower prices and encourage inefficiency, while penalising fair traders. Protection is the cry of 'special' or 'vested' interests in society and should be resisted by government in 'the national interest'.

The cornerstone of the free trade argument is the theory of 'comparative advantage', which discourages national self-sufficiency and autarky by advising states to specialise in goods and services they can produce most cheaply – their 'factor endowments'. They can then exchange their goods for what is produced more cheaply elsewhere. As everything is then produced most efficiently, according to the price mechanism, the production of wealth is maximized and everyone is better off. For Smith, the 'invisible hand' of market forces directs every member of society in every state to the most advantageous position in the global economy. The self-interest of one becomes the general interest of all.

The relevance of the theory of comparative advantage in the era of globalization has recently come under question.[97] The first difficulty that it faces is that it was devised at a time when there were national controls on capital movements. Ricardo and Smith assumed capital was immobile and only available for national investment. They also assumed that the capitalist was first and foremost a member of a national political community, which was the context in which he established his commercial identity: Smith's 'invisible hand' presupposed the internal relations and bondings of community, so that the capitalist feels a 'natural disinclination' to invest abroad. Smith and Ricardo could not have foreseen 'a world of cosmopolitan money managers and transnational corporations which, in addition to having limited liability and immorality conferred on them by national governments, have now transcended those very governments and no longer see the national community as their context'. The emergence of capitalists who had freed themselves from community obligations and loyalties, and who had no 'natural disinclination' to invest abroad, would have appeared absurd.[98] Highly mobile and volatile capital markets are a major challenge for the theory of comparative advantage.

The second problem arises from the fact that the forms of international trade have dramatically changed over recent decades. The idea of national, sovereign states trading with each other as discrete economic units is becoming an anachronism. Intra-industry or intra-firm trade dominates the manufacturing sector of the world economy. Over 40 per cent of all trade is now comprised of intra-firm transactions, which are centrally managed interchanges within transnational corporations (that cross international borders) guided by a highly 'visible hand', to quote Alfred Chandler: these are what Robert Reich has called a 'global web' of linkages and exchanges. Intra-firm trade runs counter to the theory of comparative advantage which advises nations to specialize in products where factor endowments provide a comparative cost advantage. The mobility of capital and technology, and the extent to which firms trade with each other, means that 'governments in virtually all industrial societies now take an active interest in trying to facilitate links between their own domestic firms – including offshoots of multinationals – and the global networks' in the strategic industries. They can no longer remain at arms length from business as neo-liberal economic theory demands.[99]

Similarly, the globalization of the world economy has seen the spread of manufacturing industries to many developing countries and the relocation of transnational manufacturing centres to what are often low wage, high repression areas – regions with low health and safety standards where

organized labour is frequently suppressed or illegal. Transnational corporations are becoming increasingly adept at finding ways of circumventing
national borders in their search for cheap labour and access to raw materials, and few states can refuse to play host to them. The creation of centres of
production occurs wherever profit opportunities can be maximized because
investment decisions are governed by absolute profitability and no longer
by comparative advantage.

Trading conditions in the 1990s have therefore diverged significantly
from the assumptions which underpin the neo-liberal analysis of how
markets and trade actually work. The internationalization of production,
the mobility of capital and the dominance of transnational corporations are
just three developments which render theories of comparative advantage
anachronistic. The idea of national sovereign states trading with each other
as discrete economic units is steadily becoming the exception rather than
the rule. Neo-mercantilist theory, which stresses the maximization of national wealth, also fails to explain contemporary trade realities. A more
accurate description is 'corporate mercantilism', with 'managed commercial
interactions within and among huge corporate groupings, and regular state
intervention in the three major Northern blocs to subsidise and protect
domestically-based international corporations and financial institutions'.[100]
If there is such a thing as a nation's comparative advantage it is clearly a
human achievement and certainly not a gift of nature.

The third challenge to the relevance of the theory of comparative advantage is the steady erosion of the rules which have underpinned multilateral
trade in the post-war era. Protectionism and neo-mercantilism are actually
on the rise, particularly in Europe and North America, where declining
international competitiveness has forced governments to move even further
away from free market principles.[101] While there has been a reduction in
barriers to trade *within* blocs such as the EU and NAFTA, they have been
raised *between* blocs. Tariffs have come down but they have been replaced
by a wide assortment of non-tariff barriers, including import quotas and
voluntary restraint agreements. This is a concern to small, 'fair' traders
which are incapable of matching the subsidies provided by the Europeans
and North Americans. States which unilaterally adopt free market doctrines
while leading industrial societies head in the opposite direction, place
themselves in a very vulnerable position in the world economy. But regardless of whether tariff and non-tariff barriers were dismantled, the world
market would not be 'free' in any meaningful sense, because of the power of
transnational corporations to control and distort markets through transfer
pricing and other devices.

The recent proliferation of free trade agreements and associations such as
NAFTA, APEC and GATT (now the WTO) and the growing importance of
international organizations such as the G7, IMF and World Bank is indica-
tive of the influence of liberal internationalism in post-Cold War period.

These are powerful transnational bodies which embody free trade liberalism as their governing ideology. To their critics, however, they impose free market strictures on developing societies. They are primarily organizations which formalize and institutionalize market relationships between states. By locking peripheral states into agreements which force them to lower their protective barriers, NAFTA and GATT for example, prevent Third World nations from developing trade profiles which diverge from the model dictated by their supposed 'comparative advantage'. The IMF and the World Bank, on the other hand, make the provision of finance (or more accurately 'debt') to developing societies conditional on their unilateral acceptance of free market rules for their economies – the 'conditionality' of so called 'structural adjustment programs'. Needless to say these conditions are rarely, if ever applied to the industrialized world.

The new institutions of governance, such as the World Bank and NAFTA, are dominated by the wealthy industrialized societies of the North. They enshrine the liberal principle that unfettered competition between privately owned enterprises is the only efficient form of economic organization. And they believe that economic growth is the one and only road to development for all societies. Critics, on the other hand, highlight the devastating effects of free trade policies which are imposed on subordinate societies, including environmental degradation, growing disparities of wealth and income, and the creation of economic dependencies. They are also concerned by the lack of democratic accountability of these institutions.

Most importantly, they criticise these free trade institutions for legitimizing only one kind of global order, based on unequal market relations. Specifically, the institutions are attacked for imposing identical prescriptions for economic development on all countries, regardless of what conditions prevail locally. Developing societies are expected to adopt the free market blueprint – opening their economies up to foreign investment, financial deregulation, reductions in government expenditure and budgetary deficits, the privitization of government-owned enterprises, the abolition of protection and subsidies, developing export-orientated economies – or risk the withholding of much-needed aid and finance. And because they are required to remove national controls on capital movements – which make it possible for states to reach their own conclusions about investment and spending priorities – the direction of their economic development is increasingly set by amorphous financial markets which act on profit opportunities rather than out of any consideration of national or community interest. To put it another way, the price of financial assistance to and investment in these states is the loss of their economic sovereignty. This fulfils the traditional requirements of liberal internationalism: the power of the state to interfere in commercial relations between individuals is removed. The sovereignty of the state is replaced by the sovereignty of capital.

Although arguments for free trade can still be made on the grounds of economic efficiency, for leading players free trade is often non-reciprocal and an ideological weapon used to regulate the economic development of subordinate societies. Their rhetoric supporting the sanctity of market principles is rarely matched by their own economic behaviour. This tendency, together with fundamental changes to the structure of the world economy and the forms of international trade, casts considerable doubt on the extent to which liberal internationalism can justify the globalization of the world economy on its own terms.

Sovereignty and foreign investment

The enormous volumes of unregulated investment capital liberated by the collapse of the Bretton Woods system in the early 1970s has transformed the relationships between states and markets. The resulting increase in the power of transnational capital and the diminution of national economic sovereignty is perhaps the most dramatic example of the realization of liberal economic ideas.

The relationship between a nation's economic prosperity and the world's money markets is decisive. Because most states are incapable of generating sufficient endogenous wealth to finance their economic development, governments need to provide domestic economic conditions which will attract foreign investment into their countries. In a world where capital markets are globally linked and money can be electronically transferred around the world in microseconds, states are judges in terms of their comparative 'hospitality' to foreign capital: that is, they must offer the most attractive investment climates to relatively scarce supplies of money. This gives the foreign investment community enormous influence over the course of the nation's economic development, and constitutes a significant diminution in the country's economic sovereignty.

The power of transnational finance capital in the modern period can scarcely be overestimated. The volume of foreign exchange trading in the major financial centres of the world, estimated at $US 640 bn per day, has come to dwarf international trade by at least 32 times.[102] Recent UN statistics suggest that the world's 100 largest transnational corporations, with assets of over $A4.6 trillion, account for a third of the total foreign direct investment of their home states, giving them enormous leverage over the economies of host countries.[103]

The brokers on Wall Street and in Tokyo, the clients of the 'screen jockeys' in the foreign exchange rooms, and the auditors from credit ratings agencies such as Moody's and Standard & Poors, can now pass daily judgements on the management of individual economies, and signal to the world's financial community the comparative profit opportunities to be found through investment in a particular country. Inappropriate interventionary policies by government can be quickly deterred or penalized with a (threatened) reduction in the nation's credit rating, a 'run' (sell off) on its currency or an investment 'strike'. The requirements of the international markets can only be ignored at a nation's economic peril. Not only have nation-states lost control over the value of their currencies and the movements of capital around the world, they can no longer determine the institutional settings in which capital markets operate. Many neo-liberal financial commentators regard this development as a positive change, believing that markets rather than the governments know what is in the nation's best interests.

Finance markets, dominated by large banks and financial institutions, insurance companies, brokers and speculators, exist only to maximise their own wealth. There is no reason for them to act in the interests of the poor, the homeless, the infirm or those who are deprived of basic human rights by their own governments. These are irrelevant considerations, unless they impinge in some way on the 'stability' of the host economy. States which cede economic sovereignty to these global players in the name of free trade and commerce therefore run the risk of elevating private commercial gain to the primary foreign policy objective of the state. As Marx wrote in 1848,

> What is free trade under the present conditions of society? It is freedom of capital. When you have overthrown the few national barriers which still restrict the progress of capital, you will merely have given it complete freedom of action. . . . All the destructive phenomena which unlimited competition gives rise to within one country, are reproduced in more gigantic proportions on the world market. It breaks up old nationalities and pushes the antagonism of the proletariat and the bourgeoisie to the extreme point.[104]

When the foreign investment community is freed from state barriers and controls, and able to choose the most profitable location for its capital, it has the effect of homogenising the economic development of nation-states across the globe. In what is effectively a bidding war for much-needed infusions of capital, states are driven by the lowest common denominator effect to reduce their regulations, standards, wages and conditions, in order to appear attractive to the investor community: in contemporary parlance, this is what is meant by 'international competitiveness'. Priority is given to the drive for efficiency and profits. The threat of disinvestment becomes the stick for markets to wield over the heads of government. Ironically, in many instances the key to attracting overseas investment is for the host government to provide the transnational investor with subsidies and protection from market forces. In some cases this is the only way states can win and maintain the confidence of global markets.

The demand for the liberalization of finance and services by the investment community allows transnational banks to displace domestic rivals so that it is difficult for developing economies to carry out the kind of national economic planning that enabled the rich countries to develop – usually behind high protectionist walls with extensive state intervention to protect domestic elites from the destructive effects of the market. This is another illustration of the changing differentials of power between states and markets in the last two decades. In effect, the world economy has come to resemble the global strategic environment. It has become anarchic in character and, as a consequence, the competition for economic security is as intense as the search for strategic security.

In the nineteenth century citizens were able to look to the state to protect them from market forces which, according to Polanyi, if left unregulated would demolish industrial society. The transition from *laissez-faire* capitalism to state capitalism acknowledged the need for interventionary behaviour by the state. Earlier this century Keynes provided the intellectual justification for abandoning free market principles. In the 1990s, however, globalization has again liberated the power of markets from the clutches of the overarching state. The state is in decline and no longer capable of providing its citizens with protection from the power and vicissitudes of global markets. In many ways international relations in the 1990s fulfils the dream of eighteenth and nineteenth-century liberals. The state is in decline, democracy is spreading and international commerce is unfettered. Only the recurrence of war outside the central core defies the liberal prescription for a better world order.

Conclusion

At the beginning of this chapter it was argued that liberal internationalism was an 'inside-out' approach to international relations, because liberals favour a world in which the endogenous determines the exogenous. The challenge is to extend the legitimacy of domestic political arrangements found within democratic states to the relationships between all nation-states. To put it another way, liberals believe democratic society, in which civil liberties are protected and market relations prevail, can have an international analogue in the form of a peaceful global order. The domestic free market has its counterpart in the open, globalized world economy. Parliamentary debate and accountability is reproduced in international fora such as the United Nations. And the legal protection of civil rights within liberal democracies is extended to the promotion of human rights across the world. With the collapse of Communism as an alternative political and economic order, the potential for continuity between the domestic and the international is greater than in any previous period.

Fukuyama has reason to be optimistic. The spread of liberal democracies and the zone of peace is an encouraging development, as is the realization by states that trade and commerce is more closely correlated with economic success than territorial conquest. The number of governments enjoying civilian rather than military rule is increasing, and there are signs that ethical considerations have a permanent place in the diplomatic domain. The collapse of Communism as a legitimate political order removes a substantial barrier to the spread of liberal democracies, and there can be little doubt that the great powers are now much less inclined to use force to resolve their political differences.

The globalization of the world economy means there are few obstacles to international trade. Liberals have long sought to remove the influence of the state in commercial relations between businesses and individuals, and the collapse of national economic sovereignty is an indication that the corrupting influence of the state is rapidly diminishing. Transnational corporations and capital markets wield unprecedented influence over the shape of the world economy, in the process homogenizing the political economies of every member state of the international community. The objective of creating a market society on a global scale is within sight.

On the other hand, there is a growing number of states which reject the argument that Western modernity is universally valid or that political development always terminates at liberal-capitalist democracy. They claim that the West's political and human rights agenda is a form of cultural imperialism and have demonstrated impressive economic success without the procedural freedoms championed by liberal internationalists. Liberal states have yet to learn how to conduct themselves peacefully with these societies, nor have they explained how the zone of peace can include those who have traditionally been the victims of Western intervention. Liberal internationalists have not shown how even liberal states can overcome their feelings of insecurity engendered by the anarchic international system, a condition further aggravated by the collapse of the balance of power and mutual nuclear deterrence with the end of the Cold War. The uncertainties of a multipolar world and the inherent weaknesses of collective security arrangements are a cause of considerable disquiet among neo-realists.

Furthermore, the triumph of free trade appears somewhat misleading given that the leading economic powers have achieved economic success by explicitly violating the market principles they are seeking to impose on the developing world. Left unregulated, free trade policies exacerbate disparities of wealth internally and between the rich and poor worlds. They overwhelm and often destroy community life in traditional societies by prescribing only one path to economic development. Meanwhile the globalization of the world economy leaves the power of transnational corporations and financial markets unchallenged and unaccountable.

The end of the Cold War has resuscitated liberal internationalism in the academy. No matter how flawed, its claims about the future of the international order deserve serious investigation and intellectual engagement with contending approaches. To continue to believe that it was fatally discredited in the 1930s would be to grossly underestimate its intellectual resilience and the extent to which the contours of contemporary international relations have come to resemble its teleology.

Notes

1. F. Fukuyama, *The End of History and the Last Man* (London, 1992), pp. xi–xii and 48.
2. A. Linklater, 'Liberal Democracy, Constitutionalism and the New World Order', in R. Leaver and J. Richardson (eds), *The Post-Cold War Order: Diagnoses and Prognoses* (St Leonards, 1993), p. 29.
3. Fukuyama (1992), p. xx.
4. K. Waltz, 'America as a Model for the World?', *PS: Political Science and Politics*, vol. 24, no. 4 (1991), p. 667. See also Linklater (1993), pp. 29–31.
5. See M. Doyle, 'Liberalism and World politics', *American Political Science Review*, vol. 80, no. 4 (1986), pp. 1151–69.
6. Linklater (1993), p. 29.
7. For a survey of liberal internationalism, see M.W. Zacher and R.A. Matthew, 'Liberal International Theory: Common Threads, Divergent Strands', in C.W. Kegley Jr (ed.), *Controversies in International Relations Theory* (New York, 1995), pp. 107–50. See also, R.N. Gardner, 'The Comeback of Liberal Internationalism', *The Washington Quarterly*, 13, 3 (Summer 1990), pp. 23–39.
8. M. Howard, *War and the Liberal Conscience* (Oxford, 1978), p. 31.
9. I. Kant, *Kant's Political Writings*, ed. H. Reiss, trans. H. Nisbet (Cambridge, 1970), p. 100.
10. Doyle (1986), p. 1151.
11. Ibid., p. 1161. See also Fukuyama 1992, p. xx.
12. See Doyle (1986) and M.W. Doyle, 'Liberalism and World Politics Revisited', in C.W. Kegley Jr (ed.), *Controversies in International Relations Theory* (New York, 1995), pp. 83–106.
13. J. Mueller, *Retreat From Doomsday* (New York, 1989).
14. Waltz (1991), p. 670.
15. J.L. Mearsheimer, ' "Back to the Future": Instability in Europe After the Cold War', *International Security*, vol. 15, no. 1 (Summer 1990), p. 6.
16. Waltz (1991), p. 669.
17. Ibid.

18. Mearsheimer (1990), pp. 6–7.
19. Ibid., pp. 6–7.
20. Ibid., pp. 14–19.
21. Ibid., pp. 7–8.
22. Linklater (1993), p. 33. See also pp. 33–6.
23. Ibid., p. 33.
24. Howard (1978), p. 20.
25. D. Ricardo, *The Principles of Political Economy and Taxation* (London, 1911), p. 114.
26. Paine quoted in Howard (1978), p. 29.
27. Quoted in Howard (1978), p. 37.
28. Quoted in A. Arblaster, *The Rise and Decline of Western Liberalism* (Oxford, 1984), p. 261.
29. A. Gamble, *An Introduction to Modern Social and Political Thought* (London, 1981), pp. 81–2.
30. A. Linklater, *Competing Perspectives on the State, the National Interest and Internationalism* (Australian Institute of International Affairs (Vic) and Deakin University, 1991), p. 21.
31. Doyle (1986), p. 1161.
32. D. Mitrany, 'The Functional Approach to World Organization', *International Affairs*, 24 (1948), pp. 350–63.
33. R.O. Keohane and J.S. Nye, *Power and Interdependence: World Politics in Transition* (Boston, 1977).
34. R. Rosencrance, *The Rise of the Trading State* (New York, 1986). See also S. Strange, 'New World Order: Conflict and Co-operation', *Marxism Today* (January 1991), pp. 30–1.
35. See I. Clark, *The Hierarchy of States* (Cambridge, 1989), pp. 147–8.
36. Howard (1978), p. 43.
37. Cobden quoted in M.V. Kauppi and P.R. Viotti (eds), *The Global Philosophers* (New York, 1992), pp. 208–9.
38. For a lively survey of British Liberal thinking on war, see A.J.P. Taylor, *The Troublemakers* (London, 1957).
39. H. Bull, *The Anarchical Society: A Study of Order in World Politics* (London, 1977), p. 107.
40. Ibid., pp. 106–12.
41. Howard (1983), p. 40.
42. Clark (1989), p. 23.
43. A. Giddens, *The Nation-State and Violence* (Cambridge, 1985), pp. 258.
44. R.D. McKinlay and R. Little, *Global Problems and World Order* (London, 1986), p. 186.
45. Giddens (1985), pp. 258–61.
46. E.H. Carr, *The Twenty Years' Crisis 1919–1939* (London, 1939), p. 87.
47. Clark (1989), ch.8.
48. Howard (1978), p. 132.

49. Ibid, p. 18.
50. K. Polanyi, *The Great Transformation* (Boston, 1944), pp. 137–9.
51. F. Block and M. Somers, 'Beyond the Economistic Fallacy: The Holistic Social Science of Karl Polanyi', in T. Skocpol, (ed.), *Vision and Method in Historical Sociology* (Cambridge, 1984), p. 56.
52. K. Polanyi, 'Our Obsolete Market Mentality', in G. Dalton (ed.), *Primitive, Archaic and Modern Economies*, (New York, 1968), p. 70.
53. Block and Somers (1984), p. 63.
54. Dalton (1968), p. xxvii.
55. S. George and F. Sabelli, *Faith and Credit* (Harmondsworth, 1994), p. 249.
56. Dalton (1968), pp. i and xxx.
57. Polanyi (1968), p. 70.
58. Dalton (1968), p. xxiv.
59. F. Block, *Postindustrial Possibilities* (Berkeley, 1990), p. 39.
60. E.H. Carr, *Nationalism and After* (London, 1945).
61. Carr (1939), pp. 9–10 and 146–54.
62. Polanyi (1944), pp. 139–40.
63. Ibid., p. 73.
64. Ibid., p. 150. See also D.P. Calleo and B.M Rowland, *America and the World Political Economy* (Bloomington, 1973), pp. 23–4.
65. Polanyi (1944), p. 132.
66. Ibid., p. 145.
67. N. Chomsky, *Year 501* (Boston, 1993), p. 149.
68. Ibid., p. 250.
69. A. Gramsci, *Selections From Prison Notebooks* (New York, 1971), p. 160.
70. Polanyi (1944), p. 249.
71. See Polanyi (1944), p. 73.
72. N. Chomsky, 'Notes on Nafta' (Boston, 1993), p. 2.
73. Stephen Hymer quoted in G. Hodgson, *The Democratic Economy* (Harmondsworth, 1984), p. 79.
74. See, for example, F. Pollock, 'State Capitalism', in S.E. Bronner and D.M. Kellner, (eds), *Critical Theory and Society* (New York, 1989), Polanyi (1944) and A. Gershenkron, *Economic Backwardness in Historical Perspective* (Harvard, 1962).
75. Fitzgerald (1990), p. 27.
76. Strange (1991), pp. 30–1.
77. J. Derrida, *Specters of Marx* (New York, 1994), p. 52.
78. R. Gilpin, *The Political Economy of International Relations* (Princeton, 1987), p. 183.
79. It is generally agreed that the term free trade imperialism was coined by J. Gallagher and R. Robinson, 'The Imperialism of Free Trade', *Economic History Review*, 6, 1 (1953), pp. 1–15.
80. Gamble (1981), p. 145.
81. Gilpin (1987), p. 181.

82. Chomsky (1993), p. 10. According to Robinson, free trade was 'believed in only by those who will gain an advantage from it' (J. Robinson, *The New Mercantilism* [Cambridge, 1966], p. 108).
83. K. Marx, *Grundrisse* (St Albans, 1970), p. 153.
84. Carr (1939), pp. 103 and 58.
85. P. Deane, *The First Industrial Revolution* (Cambridge, 1979), pp. 212–3 and Hobsbawm (1969), pp. 106–7 and 137–40.
86. Arblaster (1984), p. 262.
87. Carr (1939), p. 72.
88. N. Chomsky, 'Correspondence with Author' (1992a), p. 2.
89. For a definition of preponderant power see M. Leffler, *A Preponderance of Power* (Stanford, 1992), pp. 12 and 19.
90. Leffler (1992), p. 16.
91. Leffler (1992), p. 16.
92. N. Chomsky, *Necessary Illusions* (Boston, 1989), p. 25.
93. Leffler (1992), p. 63.
94. Calleo and Rowland (1973), p. 12.
95. There are many sources, in particular see G. Kolko, *Confronting the Third World* (New York, 1988).
96. Leffler (1992), p. 16.
97. See S. Strange, 'Protectionism and World Politics', *International Organization*, 39, 2, Spring 1985. See also, H.E. Daly and J.B. Cobb Jr, *For the Common Good* (1st ed., 1989, 2nd ed., Boston, 1994) and P. Bairoch, *Economic and World History* (Chicago, 1993).
98. Daly and Cobb (1989), p. 215. See more generally, pp. 209–35.
99. H.V. Emy, *Remaking Australia* (Melbourne, 1993), p. 173.
100. Chomsky (1993), p. 95.
101. The OECD has revealed that 20 of its 24 members increased their trade protection in the 1980s.
102. *Financial Times* (UK), 14.2.90.
103. In 1992 the daily electronic transfer of funds around the world reached $US 1.7 trillion, which is more than the entire money supply in the United States. Foreign Direct Investment in 1990 reached $US 232 billion. See *Australian Financial Review*, 31.8.94.
104. Karl Marx, 'Address to the Democratic Association of Brussels', 1848, quoted by E. Wheelwright, 'Free Trade?', *Arena* (February/March 1993).

CHAPTER 3

Realism and Neo-realism

Scott Burchill

Realism is widely regarded as the most influential theoretical tradition in International Relations, even by its harshest critics. Its ancient philosophical heritage, its powerful critique of liberal internationalism and its influence on the practice of international diplomacy have secured it an important, if not dominant position in the discipline. No other theory has given as much form and structure to the study of international politics. In this chapter we shall be examining the work of E. H. Carr and Hans Morgenthau, widely regarded as the founding fathers of modern or 'traditional' realism. We shall also analyse the neo-realism of Kenneth Waltz which emerged in the 1980s as arguably the most dominant theory of international relations.

Carr

E. H. Carr's *The Twenty Years' Crisis* (1939) is not a textbook of international theory, but a critique of the prevailing wisdom of its day. Published on the eve of the Second World War, it is a devastating attack on liberal 'utopianism' which had inspired the post-Great War political arrangements in Europe, most particularly the idea of collective security as it was enshrined in the institution of the League of Nations.

In response to the horrors of the First World War, liberal internationalists, or 'utopians' as Carr called them, sought to abolish war as an instrument of statecraft. Liberals were convinced that the forms of international diplomacy could be restructured to make them more peaceful. Self-determination and statehood would be available to all national groups. Secret diplomacy would be abolished and replaced by public consent in the conduct of foreign policy. The balance of power principle would give way to a system of collective security, where individual acts of aggression would be met by the collective force of world opinion and military power.

Finally, international fora such as the League of Nations would be established to act as mechanisms for the peaceful resolution of conflicts.

Carr's initial concern with the liberal-utopian position was its underlying normative character. It was dangerous, he believed, to base the study of international politics on an imaginary desire of how we would *like* the world to be. According to Carr, 'the teleological aspect of the science of international politics has been conspicuous from the outset . . . the passionate desire to prevent war determined the whole initial course and direction of the study' which, consequently, made it 'markedly and frankly utopian'. As a result of its preoccupation with the 'end to be achieved' (international peace), International Relations in its initial stage was a discipline 'in which wishing prevails over thinking, generalisation over observation, and in which little attempt is made at a critical analysis of existing facts or available means'. Until the 1930s, International Relations was, according to Carr, a discipline in which teleology preceded analysis.[1]

For Carr, although we might *wish* the world was more peaceful and harmonious, this was not a useful basis on which to erect a scientific study of world politics. 'Events which have occurred since 1931', writes Carr in 1939, 'clearly revealed the inadequacy of pure aspiration as the basis for a science of international politics, and made it possible for the first time to embark on serious critical and analytical thought about international problems'.[2] The failure of the League of Nations to prevent Japan's invasion of Manchuria and Italy's occupation of Abyssinia had dashed the hopes of many liberals who believed the world could be made peaceful simply by wishing it to be so. What was needed, according to Carr, was a more rigorous approach which emphasized the realities of power in international politics rather than one which took as its starting point, an image of how the world could be: in other words, what *is* rather than what *ought* to be.

> The impact of thinking upon wishing which, in the development of a science, follows the breakdown of its first visionary projects, and marks the end of its specifically utopian period, is commonly called realism. Representing a reaction against the wish-dreams of the initial (utopian) stage, realism is liable to assume a critical and somewhat cynical aspect. In the field of thought, it places its emphasis on the acceptance of facts and on the analysis of their causes and consequences. It tends to depreciate the role of purpose and to maintain, explicitly or implicitly, that the function of thinking is to study a sequence of events which it is powerless to influence or alter. In the field of action, realism tends to emphasise the irresistible strength of existing forces and the inevitable character of existing tendencies, and to insist that the highest wisdom lies in accepting, and adapting oneself to these forces and these tendencies.[3]

Carr believed that realism was 'a necessary corrective to the exuberance of utopianism' which had ignored the central element of power in its consideration of international politics.[4] Until the unequal distribution of

power in the international system became the central focus of a dispassionate analysis of international relations, the root causes of conflict and war
would not be properly understood. Carr believed the liberal-utopians were
so concerned with eradicating the scourge of war they had completely,
neglected its underlying rationale.

The liberals had also imputed common interests to states, interests which
were clearly not as widely shared as they hoped. They believed, for example, that every nation had an identical interest in peace and that any state
which behaved aggressively or failed to respect the peace was acting
irrationally and immorally.[5] According to Carr, this was in fact nothing
more than an expression of the 'satisfied powers' with a vested interest in
the preservation of the 'status quo'. The post-war system had been created
by the victors of the war, and it was an arrangement from which they stood
to gain the most at the expense of the 'revisionist' powers. 'The post-war
utopia became the tool of vested interests and was perverted into a bulwark
of the status quo . . . a cloak for the vested interests of the privileged'. The
rhetoric of liberal internationalism, if it were to be taken seriously, was
based on 'the illusion of a world society possessing interests and sympa-
thies in common'.[6] In reality the post-war order reflected the specific
interests of 'satisfied powers', and was therefore unlikely to receive the
support of those states, such as Germany, which clearly felt disadvantaged
by the 1918 Versailles settlement.

Carr refutes the liberals' belief that international concord could be
achieved by the widest possible application of their views. This is because
'these supposedly absolute and universal principles (peace, harmony of
interests, collective security, free trade) were not principles at all, but the
unconscious reflexions of national policy based on a particular interpretation of national interest at a particular time'.[7] These allegedly universal
principles form part of the doctrine of the *harmony of interests*, a central pillar
of liberal internationalism, which is revealed as little more than the selfish
and particular interests of the elites within the 'satisfied powers':

> the doctrine of the harmony of interests . . . is the natural assumption of a
> prosperous and privileged class, whose members have a dominant voice in the
> community and are therefore naturally prone to identify its interest with their
> own. In virtue of this identification, any assailant of the interests of the dominant
> group is made to incur the odium of assailing the alleged common interest of the
> whole community, and is told that in making this assault he is attacking his own
> higher interests. The doctrine of the harmony of interests thus serves as an
> ingenious moral device invoked, in perfect sincerity, by privileged groups in
> order to justify and maintain their dominant position.[8]

Assuming particular interests are commonly shared is not a new practice in
politics and government. 'Once industrial capitalism and the class system
had become the recognised structure of society, the doctrine of the harmony

of interests . . . became . . . the ideology of a dominant group concerned to maintain its predominance by asserting the identity of its interests with those of the community as a whole'.[9] Its adoption in the international arena by the liberal-utopians, however, resulted in the collapse of the inter-war peace. According to Carr, 'just as the ruling class in a community prays for domestic peace, which guarantees its own security and predominance, and denounces class war, which might threaten them, so international peace becomes a vested interest of predominant powers'.[10] For a state which feels aggrieved and wishes to revise its territorial boundaries or its economic and strategic power, 'international peace' is an oppressive tyranny masquerading as universal harmony. It is the slogan of those players sufficiently powerful enough to impose their will on subordinate societies. For realists, the liberal idea that every international conflict is unnecessary, if not immoral, is nothing more than an attempt to enshrine an existing economic and political order which is favourable to ruling classes within currently predominant states. There is no natural harmony of interests between states in the international system, only a temporary and transient reflection of a particular configuration of global power. War may in fact be the only way in which power can be recalibrated in the international system.

Carr cites the example of *laissez-faire* economics to refute the notion of a *harmony of interests* between states. *Laissez-faire* is the ideology of the ruling elites within dominant economic states which claims that what is good for them is, by definition, of benefit to all. In the nineteenth century, the British manufacturer and merchant, 'having discovered that laissez-faire promoted his own prosperity, was sincerely convinced that it also promoted British prosperity as a whole'. In turn, British statesmen in the same period, 'having discovered that free trade promoted British prosperity, were sincerely convinced that, in doing so, it also promoted the prosperity of the world as a whole'.[11] Carr, invoking List, points out that while free trade was the correct policy for a nation like Great Britain, which was industrially dominant at the time, only policies of protection would enable weaker nations to break the British stranglehold. There was no evidence that the economic nationalism practised by the United States and Germany had achieved anything less than enabling those states to challenge Britain's economic power.[12] 'Laissez-faire, in international relations as in those between capital and labour, is the paradise of the economically strong. State control, whether in the form of protective legislation or of protective tariffs, is the weapon of self defence invoked by the economically weak'.[13] Accordingly, there is no underlying and natural harmony of interests between nations, only asymmetrical power. Common interests between states, if they are to emerge, must be artificially harmonised by state action.[14]

The liberal-utopians had wanted to eliminate power as a consideration for states in the international system. Realists such as Carr on the other hand, believed the pursuit of national power was a natural drive which states neglected at their peril. Nation-states which eschewed the pursuit of power on principle simply endangered their own security. For Carr, the pursuit of power by individual states took the form of promoting 'national interests', a term later to be more broadly defined as the foreign policy goals of the nation but understood by realists to specifically mean strategic power. Clashes of national interests were inevitable: it was futile and dangerous to suggest otherwise. The only way to minimise such clashes, and therefore the incidence of war, was to ensure that a rough balance of power existed between the states in the international system. To put it another way, the best safeguard against international conflict was the prevention of one state emerging with preponderant power. Far from being a cause of international conflict, as the liberals had argued, the balance of power system resembled the laws of nature: it was the normal expression of international power and the best guarantee of peace. Collective security, the liberal alternative, was little more than a method of placing predominant power in the hands of the victorious states, thus institutionalizing the status quo. The League of Nations proved to be incapable of rising above the national interests of its principal members, failing to take account of the shifting differentials of power between the status quo and revisionist states.

It is a mistake to believe that Carr was dismissive of the notion of change in the international system, or that he discounted the role of utopian thought entirely. For realists, peaceful change comes with adjustments to new relations of power: that is, shifting strategic alliances between states. This is what is meant by 'the irresistible strength of existing forces and the inevitable character of existing tendencies'. Shrewd diplomacy involves accommodation and adaption to these forces, rather than the naïve neglect of them. Power has a rational flow of its own and it is pointless to attempt to swim against the tide.[15] However, although realism is an important corrective to the naivety of liberal thought, 'utopianism must (also) be invoked to counteract the barrenness of realism'. Both, therefore, have their place in 'sound political thought' – realism to expose the fact that utopianism serves the interests of the privileged and powerful, and utopianism to deny that 'altruism is an illusion' and demonstrate that 'pure realism can offer nothing but a naked struggle for power which makes any kind of international society impossible'.[16] The 'science of international politics' requires a blend of both forms of thinking.

Critics of Carr's position point to the irreconcilable antinomies between realism and idealism. Carr's response was to defend 'national policy which aimed at the extension of moral obligation and the enlargement of political community'.[17] Unlike his successors, Carr was not wedded to the belief that the state was the final evolutionary form of political community: there was no need to assume that the nation was the 'ultimate group unit of human society'. He envisaged other political units which were not necessarily territorially based, such as religion, class and ethnicity. Few things in international politics had permanent form, including the size of political communities. Carr predicted that the nation-states of the world would pass through a tumultuous period of integration and disintegration in their search for 'optimal size'. In the process, the concept of sovereignty would become 'even more blurred and indistinct than it is at the present'.[18]

Whatever its final form, Carr was convinced that a new international order would be shaped by the realities of global power rather than morality. He was not arguing that morality was an irrelevant consideration, in fact he believed that international peace was most likely when the dominant power is 'generally accepted as tolerant and unoppressive or, at any rate, as preferable to any practical alternative'.[19] But this was the closest he came to conceding that there might be a moral basis for international order. He preferred to stress that 'power is a necessary ingredient of every political order'.[20] This conviction exposed Carr to critics who claimed he was privileging power, and its pursuit by states, above all other factors. How could he explain, for example, that states often forgo their national interests (as narrowly defined by realists) in the interests of international humanitarianism? And why is it so 'wise' for smaller states to 'adapt' to 'irresistible forces and tendencies' which they are 'powerless to alter' but which perpetuate injustice and inequalities?

For Carr, as for all realists, conflict between states was inevitable in an international system without an overarching authority regulating relations between them. The absence of a compulsory jurisdiction for states – an 'anarchical' international system – confirmed the principal distinction between domestic and international politics. In civil society, an individual must submit to the rule of law or pay the consequences: voluntary compliance is not an option. In the international system on the other hand, there is no equivalent regulatory system which can enforce compliance on states. There is no binding international law or legal system which can bring states to account for their behaviour. States can 'get away' with whatever their power allows them to achieve. Carr expresses the same domestic–international distinction in another way. 'Nationalism was one of the forces by which the seemingly irreconcilable clash of interest between classes within the nation was reconciled. There is no corresponding force which can be invoked to reconcile the seemingly irreconcilable clash of interest between nations'. Moreover, appeals to the common interests of states were an 'illusion', the voice of preponderant power, and always at the expense of the weak and disadvantaged.[21]

Carr's work should be understood as primarily a critique of liberal internationalism, or what he called utopian thinking. It was not put forward as a meta-theory of international relations. It is not a comprehensive, rigorous or very sophisticated theoretical account. It is the kind of explanation one could expect from a historian who believed that history was a sequence of cause and effect which could only be properly appreciated by intellectual effort. Carr believed that the theory of international relations would emerge from the ways in which those relations were practised, and not the other way around. For him, ethics was a function of politics and morality was the product of power.[22] It is therefore not surprising that he thought it was important to defend realism and highlight its relevance in explaining the drift towards another global conflagration. In neglecting the importance of power as a consideration in international relations, Carr was convinced that the architects of the Versailles peace had set the world on an inevitable course to further conflict.

Morgenthau

Hans Morgenthau's *Politics Among Nations* (1948) comes closer to being a realist textbook. It was written in the aftermath of the Second World War as the United States was emerging as a major world economic and strategic power. It became not only an attempt to consolidate the principles of realism, which had seemingly been vindicated by the war, but it was also designed to provide intellectual support for the role the United States was to play in the post-war world. Morgenthau's most important work therefore straddled two worlds: it was an intellectual statement destined to influence generations of students in the academy and a series of guidelines for US foreign policy-makers confronted by the uncertainties of the Cold War.

From the tone and style of the book it is possible to sense the extent to which the US academic community was influenced, if not enthralled by developments in the natural sciences during this period. Morgenthau took up Carr's challenge to create a 'science of international politics' by applying the positivist methodology of the 'hard' or natural sciences to the study of international relations. The intellectual rigour of this approach would reveal the underlying 'reality' of world politics, from which certainties and predictions could be deduced. Not surprisingly, Morgenthau's writings are scattered with references to laws and principles, objectivity and science.

His definition of theory, for example, is explicitly borrowed from the natural sciences. Theories, according to Morgenthau, should be judged 'not by some pre-conceived abstract principle or concept unrelated to reality', but by their purpose which is 'to bring order and meaning to a mass of phenomena which without it would remain disconnected and unintelligible'. They must be 'consistent with the facts and within itself'. In other words, theories must be factual, independent and retrospective. Theories must also satisfy strict empirical and logical criteria: 'do the facts as they actually are lend themselves to the interpretation the theory has put on them, and do the conclusions at which the theory arrives follow with logical necessity from its premises?'.[23] Morgenthau clearly believes there is a 'knowable reality' or what he called a 'rational essence' of foreign policy which theories can reveal.[24] This is the methodological approach of positivism and its application to the study of international politics was designed to provide the field with greater coherence, rigour and intellectual respect. It later inspired the discipline's epistemological debates which erupted in the 1980s.

Morgenthau's account of world politics is underpinned by the contrast he draws between two schools of modern political thought and their conceptions of the nature of man, society and politics. The first, which closely resembles liberal-utopianism, 'believes that a rational and moral political order, derived from universally valid abstract principles' can be achieved by conscious political action. It 'assumes the essential goodness and infinite malleability of human nature, and blames the failure of the social order to measure up to the rational standards on [a] lack of knowledge and understanding, obsolescent social institutions, or the depravity of certain isolated individuals or groups. It trusts in education, reform, and the sporadic use of force to remedy these defects'. This school believes in the perfectibility of the human condition.

By contrast the second school, with which Morgenthau identifies and that he calls realism, believes the world's imperfections are 'the result of forces inherent in human nature'. According to this approach, 'to improve the world one must work with those forces, not against them'. In a world where conflicts of interest are endemic, moral principles can never be fully realised, only approximated through a temporary balancing of interests. Absolute good cannot be achieved, but a system of checks and balances can help to produce acceptable outcomes. Principles of universal relevance can be deduced from historical experience rather than abstract moral or ethical codes.[25] Like Carr, Morgenthau begins his approach by defining his position in opposition to what he sees as the influence, if not the dominance, of the liberal-utopian perspective.

From this contrast between the utopian and realist conceptions of the nature of politics, Morgenthau lists 'six principles of political realism' which, taken together, summarise his theoretical approach to the study of international relations. Below is a précis of each point.

(1) Politics is governed by *objective laws* which have their root in human nature. These laws do not change over time and are impervious to human preference. A rational theory of politics and international relations can be based on these laws, in fact any such theory should reflect these objective laws. Following this approach it is possible to distinguish between truth or facts on the one hand, and opinion on the other. These laws provide us with certainty and confidence in predicting rational political behaviour.

(2) The key to understanding international politics is the concept of *interest* defined in terms of *power*. Reference to this concept enables us to see politics as an autonomous sphere of action. It 'imposes intellectual discipline upon the observer, infuses rational order into the subject matter of politics, and thus makes the theoretical understanding of politics possible'.[26] The idea of interest defined in terms of power reveals the true behaviour of politicians and guards us against two popular misconceptions about what determines a state's foreign policy – the motives of statesmen and ideological preferences.

While political leaders will cast their policies in ideological terms (defence of democracy, and so on) they are inevitably confronted by the distinction between what is desirable and what is actually possible. There is no room for moral or ethical concerns, prejudice, political philosophy or individual preference in the determination of foreign policy because actions are constrained by the relative power of the state. The 'national interest', which ought to be the sole pursuit of statesmen, is always defined in terms of strategic and economic capability.

(3) The forms and nature of state power will vary in time, place and context but the concept of interest remains consistent. The political, cultural and strategic environment will largely determine the forms of power a state chooses to exercise, just as the types of power which feature in human relationships change over time. In addition, realists ought not to be wedded to a perennial connection between interest and the nation-state which is 'a product of history, and therefore bound to disappear'. There is no reason why 'the present division of the political world into nation states will [not] be replaced by larger units of a quite different character, more in keeping with the technical potentialities and moral requirements of the contemporary world'. Change in the international system, however, will only occur 'through the workmanlike manipulation of the perennial forces that have shaped the past as they will the future'.[27]

(4) Universal *moral principles* do not guide state behaviour, though state behaviour will certainly have moral and ethical implications. Individuals are certainly influenced by moral codes, but states are not moral agents. Any attempt to explain the international behaviour of states should not, therefore, concentrate on the stated moral principles which are said to underpin the conduct of foreign policy. Whereas ethical behaviour is judged according to whether it conforms with a set of moral principles, political behaviour is evaluated according to the political consequences which ensue: there is a tension between moral action and the expedient requirements of political action. Prudential behaviour based on a judicious assessment of the consequences arising out of alternative political choices is the guiding law for realists.

(5) There is no *universally* agreed set of moral principles. Though states from time to time will endeavour to clothe their behaviour in ethical terms

(human rights advocacy), the use of moral language to justify external behaviour is designed to confer advantage, legitimacy and further the national interests of the state. It ought not to be mistaken for political motives which in reality are restricted to the pursuit of interests defined in terms of power. Universal moral principles are not a reliable guide to state behaviour. When states proclaim these universal principles they are merely projecting their *particular* national or cultural codes onto the world as a whole. 'Interest is the perennial standard by which political action must be judged and directed'.[28]

(6) Intellectually, the political sphere is *autonomous* from every other sphere of human concern, whether they be legal, moral or economic. This enables us to see the international domain as analytically distinct from other fields of intellectual inquiry, with its own standards of thought and criteria for the analysis and evaluation of state behaviour (interest defined in terms of power). Key questions such as 'how does this policy affect the power of the nation?' are central to the concerns of this separate sphere of intellectual analysis.

Like Carr's account, Morgenthau's principles of political realism reflected the intellectual mood of the age. They were designed as an antidote to liberal utopianism which was widely held to be responsible for shaping the intellectual climate as Europe drifted towards the Second World War. For Morgenthau, international politics was a struggle for power between states: the pursuit of national interests was a normal, unavoidable and desirable activity. Above everything else, Morgenthau wanted to attack the idea that any state could attempt to universalise its own particular moral and ethical principles. This was reckless utopianism which breached the laws of politics. Although there were certain moral goals which mankind should aspire to, the exigencies of world politics render it difficult, if not futile, to attempt to realize them.[29] Human nature, however imperfect, is fixed and ought to be accepted for what it is rather than what it might be. To the extent that it can be maintained for long periods of time, peace can only be realized when the rational pursuit of power by statesmen acting according to the laws of politics is more widely understood. Radical changes to the international system will be doomed to failure and might possibly be counter-productive, if they challenge the 'laws of politics'.

Realists such as Morgenthau spoke with an air of certainty about politics because they believed it to be governed by immutable laws, 'deriving either from human nature itself, or from the dynamics of inter-state competition'.[30] After all, the concept of interest defined as power 'imposes discipline upon the observer' and 'infuses rational order into the subject matter of politics'.[31] It provides us with unshakeable knowledge about how states will behave. For Morgenthau, national interests are permanent conditions which provide policy-makers with a rational guide to action: they are fixed, politically bipartisan and always transcend changes in government. The 'national interest . . . is not defined by the whim of a man or the partisanship of party but imposes itself as an objective datum upon all men applying their rational faculties to the conduct of foreign policy'.[32] Peace, on the other hand, is never a permanent feature of the international system. It is merely a temporary truce based on a rough equilibrium of state power, between inevitable periods of tension and conflict. The balance of power system is an essential stabilising factor in international relations, and the best way of managing the tendency for states to accumulate strategic power.

It is usually taken for granted that realists regard the nation-state as the primary actor in international politics; however, neither Carr nor Morgenthau regarded it as the ultimate expression of political community. Writing in 1970, Morgenthau anticipated that the forces of globalization would render the nation-state 'no longer valid' and soon 'obsolete'. The impact of 'nuclear power, together with modern technologies of transportation and communications, which transcends the ability of any nation-state to control and harness it and render it both innocuous and beneficial, requires a principle of political organisation transcending the nation-state'.[33] It was time to think of 'novel structures and types of organization' such as a 'supranational community and a world government, a political organization and structure that transcend the nation-state'.[34] The openness of this argument stands in stark contrast to the stereotypical image of realism as the conservative realm of recurrence and repetition. Clearly neither Carr nor Morgenthau were wedded to the idea of the nation-state as an indefinite fixture on the international landscape, a position which distinguishes them from their neo-realist successors.

Morgenthau's approach to international relations has been attacked from a number of directions. His infatuation with positivism and empirical science is not surprising, given that at the time of writing *Politics Among Nations* (1948), the natural sciences (particularly in the areas of physics, biology and chemistry) appeared to be providing humankind with a degree of mastery over nature. If science could subdue the natural world, why could its methodology not do the same for international relations? As behaviourists, critical theorists and postmodernists would later demonstrate, many questions have been raised over the application of scientific methodology to the social domain. Does the social aspect of the international world really lend itself to being understood in terms of enduring, objective laws and certainties? Just how authoritative is the scientific method and is it relevant to the complexities of international relations? Morgenthau's realism was based on a priori assumptions about human nature (the rational pursuit of self-interest, utility maximization, and so on) which by definition cannot be tested or verified to any meaningful extent. What if these assumptions are flawed or do not conform in any actual sense to a shared reality? What are the implications for Morgenthau's thesis if there are no laws of politics at all, only subjective impressions? What happens to Morgenthau's thesis if, as postmodernists claim, there is no 'objective truth' or if there is no simple division between 'truth and rationality' on one hand and 'prejudice and subjective preference' on the other? Morgenthau's world is a pessimistic and sterile one. He sees strengths in a dispassionate and amoral approach to international relations when this may be little more than a cover for and rationalization of immoral and unethical behaviour.

Morgenthau's treatment of Marxism is paltry and ungenerous. His critique of theories of imperialism is simplistic and hostile. He largely ignores economic considerations in the formulation of foreign policy and says very little about the nature of capitalism and its effects on the international order. He assumes the nation-state is a unitary actor but is completely uninterested in its internal nature, including the composition of its commercial and state elites. Other international actors, such as non-governmental authorities and international markets, are almost entirely neglected. And though he rejects the prescriptive elements of liberal idealism (utopianism), his message about the immutability of the 'laws of politics' appears equally dogmatic.

Kenneth Waltz parts company with what he calls the 'traditional realism' of Morgenthau by arguing that international politics can be thought of as a system with a precisely defined structure. Realism, in his view, is unable to conceptualise the international system in this way because it is limited by its behavioural methodology which 'explains political outcomes through examining the constituent parts of political systems'. According to this approach, 'the characteristics and the interactions of behavioural units are taken to be the direct cause of political events'.[35] Morgenthau explained international outcomes by focussing on the actions and interactions of the units – the principles of human nature, the idea of interest defined in terms of power, the behaviour of statesmen – rather than highlighting the systemic constraints of international politics. He infers political outcomes from 'the salient attributes of the actors producing them' and ignores the effects of structure on state behaviour. According to Waltz traditional realists could not explain behaviour at a level above the nation-state.[36] Whereas Morgenthau argued that power is rooted in the nature of humankind, Waltz points to the anarchical condition of the international realm which he claims imposes the accumulation of power as a systemic requirement on states. The former explanation relies on a particular understanding of human nature to explain conflict in international politics. The latter abandons such a reliance, preferring to treat the international system as a separate domain which conditions the behaviour of all states within it.

Morgenthau sought to create a guidebook for students and statesmen at a time when the old conventions and understandings about the international order were under challenge. He wanted to instil certainty into the field of international politics by providing an interpretative guide which would help us to 'look over the shoulder' of a statesman, enabling us to 'read and anticipate his very thoughts'.[37] The extent of his success can be measured by the fact that *Politics Among Nations* is regularly reprinted and still widely used by students of statecraft.

Problems with Traditional Realism

The realist school, as its name suggests, formulated their views in reaction to the liberal-utopians of the 1920s and 1930s. Whereas liberals had called for the repudiation of power politics as a feature of international behaviour, realists saw power politics as a necessary and endemic feature of all relationships between sovereign states. Realists drew attention to the reality of conflict in international relations, and the lessons to be learnt from its cyclical and recurrent patterns. Unlike the idealists, realists stressed the positive functions of those features of international diplomacy normally associated with 'power politics' – state sovereignty, the balance of power and limited war.

Although realists were not the first to think and write about international relations, they were the first to offer a comprehensive account of the international system in practice. In the sense that it 'codifies practice', realism can therefore be considered the other foundational theory of the discipline. In the two decades following the First World War, when serious debates about the appropriate forms of the discipline took place, there was a growing awareness that the purpose of the study should be to develop generalizations about patterns of behaviour in international relations, and to emphazise recurring phenomena rather than unique events. The early realists brought to the fledgling discipline a variety of experiences and intellectual antecedents which contributed significantly to the theoretical longevity of the discourse. In the United States, Hans Morgenthau, Arnold Wolfers, Klaus Knorr and Henry Kissinger were European emigrés who 'suffered at first hand the operations of unchecked power operating in support of an alien value system'.[38] E. H. Carr was alternately a historian and diplomat, whose twenty years in the British foreign service included membership of that country's 1919 peace delegation to what he later called the 'fiasco' of the Versailles negotiations. George Kennan was also an academic, but one who as a senior US diplomat in Moscow during the 1950s was awarded responsibility for the authorship of the Truman Administration's policy of 'containment'.

Realists defined their own position in opposition to what Carr called 'utopian liberal internationalism' and the 'moralism' of creating a model of the international system which, however desirable, took little account of the realities of power. A number of incontrovertible assumptions formed the basis of their approach. The first concerned the reification of the state. The modern nation-state was seen as the most desirable form of political organization: conceptions of national sovereignty were regarded as the 'natural' political condition of humankind. Consequently, the international system was considered 'anarchical' – that is, without an overarching authority to regulate the behaviour of nation-states.[39] International law was regarded sceptically, particularly if states believed that it infringed on their capacity to pursue their national interests. For realists, a state's assertion of its sovereignty, and its concomitant claim for protection under the doctrine of non-intervention, came before any right the international community might assert for intervention in 'the internal affairs' of that state. Furthermore, realists argued that states are the primary actors in international relations because they retain a monopoly on the legitimate use of violence.

As a result of a growing commonality of views and methodological approaches to the subject matter in its early years, International Relations was constituted as a discrete field of study concerned with the strategic and diplomatic behaviour of states. Contemporaneously, realism, which concerned itself with concepts such as sovereignty, the state, diplomacy, the balance of power and the causes of war, established itself as the discipline's hegemonic discourse. In the first two decades after the Second World War the discipline and realism were widely regarded as one and the same thing.

Foundational texts such as those by Carr and Morgenthau ensured that realism would be concerned with a number of specific empirical and normative preoccupations, including: (a) sovereign states are both the primary actors and basic units of analysis; (b) inter-state behaviour takes place in an environment of ungoverned anarchy; and (c) the behaviour of states can be understood 'rationally' as the pursuit of power defined as interest. Taken collectively, these central concerns indicated an acceptance (however reluctant) of the present structure and operation of international relations: there was no point in denying its underlying 'reality'. Realism was an argument from necessity, based on the pursuit of national interest revealed by 'the evidence of history as our minds reflect it'.[40] It offered an account of the reproduction of the states-system, and in the sense that it contributed to the perpetuation of the international system by providing it with an intellectual defence, realism obstructed paths to alternative historical developments. Marxists have argued from this that realism is primarily concerned with the reinforcement and reproduction of capitalist relations of production, at both the domestic and international levels, and that the system of states structurally supports this mode of production. It is sometimes argued that there is a link between realism and ruling class interests in leading industrial societies.

The difficulty with this line of argument is in establishing why capitalism specifically requires a states-system and could not operate globally with some alternative form of international organization, and why a self-pro-claimed 'revolutionary state' such as the Soviet Union became a leading agent for the reproduction of the states-system. It is perhaps helpful, then, to distinguish between realism as an intended expression of dominant class interests (a Marxist contention) and realism as an ideology which has the unintended consequence of preserving structures which favour such inter-ests. Realism may well play a significant role in reproducing a world order which favours dominant classes. Cox's point that realism can be criticised for its failure to recognise how its contribution to international stability preserves social and economic inequalities within and between societies, is therefore more relevant than an axiomatic alignment between realism as discourse and ruling class ideology.

Linked with this argument is the additional criticism that, in its concern with continuity and a logic of reproduction, realism has neglected the existence of a logic of change, though as we have noted neither Carr nor Morgenthau discount the eventual possibility of alternative structures in the international system. However, in suggesting that we 'must work *with* rather than against immutable forces inherent in human nature' (Mor-genthau), that the laws of politics are 'impervious to our preferences' (Morgenthau), that the function of thinking is to study a sequence of events which we are 'powerless to influence or alter' (Carr), and that wisdom lies in 'accepting and adapting oneself' to the 'irresistible strength of existing forces and tendencies' (Carr), realism is nevertheless militating against structural change in the international system. It is effectively stifling the possibility of transforming, or at least renovating, international relations by encouraging us to accept the current reality.

Realism maintains that the search for power and security is the dominant logic in global politics, and that states as the primary actors in the arena have no choice but to accumulate the means of violence in the pursuit of self preservation: the 'international' is a self-help system. In a more recent study, Waltz draws the distinction between 'reductionist' and 'systemic' theories of international relations to emphazise the possibility of abstracting the states system or strategic interaction as 'a domain apart' from analyses that link foreign policy exclusively with the internal social and economic characteristics of states. Thus for neo-realists, the specific internal structure of states is largely irrelevant to their international behaviour. What is crucial in this 'systemic' approach is the state's location in the global power configuration. This is not to imply, however, that the pursuit of physical security through violence is completely unregulated. Through the skilful use of the balance of power, states can regulate their propensity for violence by maintaining a strategic equilibrium between the major powers. Accord-ing to realists, this can reduce, though not eliminate the incidence of war.

Clearly, if there is an identifiable ideology (here meaning the process of sustaining asymmetrical relations of power) associated with realism it is the more general idea of conservatism.[41] Ostensibly, realism purports to aim at an accurate representation of the 'reality' of global politics as opposed to a way of thinking in which some higher state is imagined or recommended as a course of action (idealism). In actual fact, realism can be both a conduit for and an expression of conservative ideology. As has been pointed out, realism seeks to resist change and foreclose alternative political practices.[42] How it encourages this process is more obvious when we look closely at its value system, ideas, and nomenclature.

As political consciousness reflecting relations of power in society, ideology provides orientations for political action. In the field of international relations, the terrain of struggle is systemic, with most political behaviour directed at either the recurrence or revision of the existing international order. The ideology of conservatism codifies a world view based on the primacy of the state as an actor in world politics, as opposed to supranational organizations, interdependent authorities or class. It highlights the existence of constraints upon the realization of alternative political orders, emphazising the necessity of working within highly restricted parameters of choice and dismissing opportunities for radical structural reform. It is also important for conservatism, as the ideology of those who benefit directly from asymmetrical power relations, to secure the consent of subordinate groups within the community by providing them with a coherent and plausible understanding of world politics. Ideology reflects economic interests, but it also organizes action through the way it is embodied in social relations and institutions and their practices. Chomsky and others have written extensively about the symbiosis between realism and foreign policy establishments – in the conduct of international diplomacy. We are less familiar, however, with the role played by the realist discourse in delimiting thinking and expression about international politics to within rigidly prescribed theoretical boundaries.

The language of realism is said to be ideologically encoded. And yet one of the most powerful factors sustaining the dominance of realism has been the capacity of its authors to project the realist nomenclature (system of states, balance of power, strategy, stability, deterrence, national interest) as politically neutral and non-ideological: the language of realism has largely become the language of International Relations.[43] To some this may not be surprising, after all realism seeks to describe 'reality'. However, it is significant that the discipline's reference points come from one theoretical approach because ideology and values are transmitted through language. Through the selection of 'appropriate words', realists ask us to consider their theory as commonsense, normal and neutral.[44] Decoding the language of realism, however, reveals what some theorists regard as a value-laden dialogue which uses a vast array of lexical and grammatical devices to conceal an ideologically conservative predisposition. Its critics argue that even a rudimentary textual analysis exposes the manner in which realism fixes the domain of debate in International Relations. As Rothstein has argued, realism

> has fostered a set of attitudes that predisposed its followers to think about international politics in a particularly narrow and ethnocentric fashion, and to set very clear bounds around the kind of policies which it seemed reasonable to contemplate.[45]

Realism is concerned with the reproduction of the international system of states. It uses notions of order, stability, deterrence and especially the balance of power, to convey its message of constraint and to reify the structure of the international system.[46] At the same time it marginalizes those theories offering alternative or contradictory accounts of the 'reality' of world politics: Morgenthau's dismissal of Marxism and theories of imperialism is a good example of this. And it is precisely because realism has set the terminological agenda within International Relations that alternative and dissenting discourses have been so effectively occluded.

Waltz

Neo-realism emerged in the 1970s, partly as a response to the challenges posed by interdependency theory and partly as a corrective to traditional realism's neglect of economic forces. In the sub-discipline of international political economy, Robert Gilpin and Stephen Krasner sought to reclaim a role for the state in a world where transnational economic players threatened to undermine its primacy. Ideas such as 'regimes' and 'hegemonic stability theory' were invented to demonstrate the continuing importance of the nation-state in the newly globalized world economy.[47]

In the more traditional provinces of International Relations, Kenneth Waltz has attempted to bring what he sees as the scientific and methodological rigour of disciplines such as anthropology and economics to the study of international politics. Waltz's 'neo-realism' or 'structural realism' is both a critique of traditional realism and a substantial intellectual extension of a theoretical tradition which was in danger of being outflanked by rapid changes in the contours of global politics. Waltz presents a more sophisticated theory than his predecessors in the realist tradition, to the extent that his account has often been referred to as occupying a position of intellectual hegemony in the discipline.

The nature of theory

A number of criticisms of Waltz's neo-realism centre on the charge that he has not produced an all encompassing account of international politics: there are said to be too many holes or omissions in his theory. However, according to Waltz his critics 'fail to understand that a theory is not a statement about everything that is important in international political life, but rather a necessarily slender explanatory construct'.[48] A number of his critics appear to have failed to understand Waltz's conception of theory, in particular his belief that theory is necessarily abstract and deliberately artificial.

Waltz cites the gains made in the understanding of political economy by the physiocrats of the seventeenth and eighteenth centuries. They were able to make important advances in their understanding of economic growth and prosperity because they invented the concept of *the economy* as distinct from the society and polity. The artificial demarcation of the economy as a separate domain meant that specific economic forces could be isolated and properly understood. For Waltz, this is the great value of the theoretical enterprise. Theory is a tool which makes the task of intellectual explanation possible. Without theory all we are left with are disconnected and randomly selected facts which tell us very little about the subject of our inquiry. According to Waltz, a theory is an intellectual construction by which we select facts and interpret them. The challenge is to bring theory to bear on facts in ways that permit explanation and prediction. That can only be achieved by distinguishing between theory and fact.[49]

The process of theorizing is therefore deliberately contrived, or as Waltz puts it, 'theory is artifice'. It becomes possible only 'if various objects and processes, movements and events, acts and interactions, are viewed as forming a domain that can be studied in its own right'.[50] The physiocrats were not claiming that an economy actually exists in isolation from society and polity, but that by treating it that way for the purpose of intellectual inquiry, it was possible to make 'radical advances' that might not otherwise have been made. By adopting this approach the rationality of human motives and the laws of supply and demand were discovered and then used as assumptions upon which broader theoretical constructions were built.

A theory selects and organises facts, processes and relationships into a separate domain so that importance and significance can be identified. The isolation of one domain from another in order to study it is artificial, but this is an intellectual strength rather than a weakness. Although the effect of such as process is to simplify complex forces and relationships, this is the only way meaningful explanations can be reached. Accordingly, Waltz applied the same approach to the study of international relations. His 'structural realism' or 'neo-realism' argues that 'by depicting an international political system as a whole, with structural and unit levels at once distinct and connected, neo-realism establishes the autonomy of international politics and thus makes a theory about it possible'.[51] If the state-system is considered as a 'domain apart' from domestic considerations such as dominant ideology, religion, mode of production and social organization, it becomes possible to make advances in our understanding of the nature of international relations. The idea that international politics can be understood as a system with a precisely defined and separate structure is both the starting point for international theory and Waltz's point of departure from traditional realism.[52] As with the approach of the physiocrats to political economy, the abstraction of the international system as a 'domain apart' by neo-realists is an equivalent distortion of reality, but it is similarly necessary to delineate the central forces and principles of international politics.

Realism and neo-realism

The key question which Waltz poses and then proceeds to answer is: why do states exhibit similar foreign policy behaviour despite their different political systems and contrasting ideologies? Waltz frequently cites the example of superpower behaviour during the Cold War to refute the argument that it is possible to infer the condition of international politics from the internal composition of states. The Soviet Union and the United States comprised quite different, if not antithetical political and social orders. And yet as Waltz points out, their behaviour during the period of East–West tension is remarkably similar. Their pursuit of military power and influence, their competition for strategic advantage and the exploitation of their respective spheres of influence were strikingly parallel. The explanation, says Waltz, can be found in the systemic constraints on each state rather than their internal composition. These systemic forces homogenize foreign policy behaviour by interposing themselves between states and their diplomatic conduct. The identification of these systemic forces is perhaps neo-realism's single greatest contribution to international theory.

Waltz advances beyond what he calls 'traditional realism' by arguing that international politics can be thought of as a system with a precisely defined structure. Realism was unable to conceptualise the international system in this way because it was limited by its behaviourist methodology which 'explains political outcomes through examining the constituent parts of political systems'. By this logic, 'the characteristics and the interactions of behavioural units are taken to be the direct cause of political events'.[53] Morgenthau attempted to understand and explain international outcomes by examining the actions and interactions of the units – the principles of human nature, the idea of interest defined in terms of power, the behaviour of statesmen – rather than focusing on the systemic constraints of international politics. He inferred political outcomes from 'the salient attributes of the actors producing them' and ignored the important effects of structure. As Waltz argues, 'realists cannot handle causation at a level above states because they fail to conceive of structure as a force that shapes and shoves the units'.[54] Whereas realists such as Morgenthau argued that power is rooted in the nature of humankind, neo-realists such as Waltz point to the anarchical condition of the international realm which imposes the accumulation of power as a systemic requirement on states. The former account relies on a particular understanding of human nature to explain conflict in international politics, always a difficult approach to substantiate. The latter abandons such a reliance on reductionism, preferring to treat the international system as a separate domain which conditions the behaviour of all states within it.

Units and structure

Before examining exactly what Waltz understands by 'structure' and the nature of the international 'system', it is important to consider what he is rejecting. Waltz's concern with traditional realism is the same as his reservations about liberal and Marxist accounts of international relations, which he labels 'second image' or 'second level' explanations in his earlier work and 'reductionist' in his most detailed analysis.[55] Waltz rejects 'unit-level' theories because they attempt to explain the whole (the global system) by examining the interactions of its parts (domestic orders). These 'reductionist' approaches assume there is a direct link between the intentions of individual actors such as nation-states, and the results of their actions. What they fail to recognize are the structural conditions which belong to the international system, which impose themselves on all the units, and which therefore ultimately determine the outcomes of the interactions between states. Other theories err by explaining the behaviour of states at the unit level rather than at the system level. Realists emphasize human nature and the intentions of statesmen, liberals stress the importance of democracy and free trade, and Marxists highlight the class struggle between capital and labour. All ignore the overriding importance of the international system which comes between the intentions of states and the results of their interactions.

For the purpose of explaining its determining properties and distinguishing it from domestic political systems, Waltz believes the international system has a precisely defined structure with three important characteristics. These are (1) the ordering principle of the system, (2) the character of the units in the system, and (3) the distribution of the capabilities of the units in the system.[56]

In domestic political systems the ordering principle is hierarchic, with power and authority exerted through the compulsory jurisdiction of political and legal processes. The ordering principle of the international system is anarchic, with an absence of any overarching authority regulating the behaviour of nation-states towards each other. Nation-states, unlike individuals in domestic society, exist in a self-help environment where the quest for survival requires them to seek security through the accretion of military power. This security dilemma is common to all states, regardless of their domestic cultural or political complexions. In other words, the ordering principle of the international system forces states to perform exactly the same primary function regardless of their capacity to do so. In the process they become 'socialized' into behaviour which centres on mutual distrust, self-reliance and the pursuit of security through the accumulation of the means to wage war against each other. This socialization to the system of power politics occurs even to non-conformist states with revolutionary regimes, because a refusal to play the political game may risk their own destruction.[57] According to Waltz, the anarchical nature of the international system has been its ordering principle for several centuries, a pattern in international relations which has withstood the extraordinary changes to the internal composition of nation-states in recent years.[58]

According to Waltz, the characters of the units in the system are identical or, to put it another way, all states in the international system are made functionally similar by the constraints of structure. The anarchic realm imposes a discipline on states: they are all required to pursue security before they can perform any other functions. In fact their concern about their own survival conditions much of their behaviour. However, although they are functionally similar, states differ vastly in their capabilities. There is an unequal and constantly shifting distribution of power across the international system. States 'are alike in the tasks that they face, though not in their abilities to perform them. The differences are of capability, not of function'.[59] The capacity of each state to pursue and achieve their common objectives varies according to their placement in the international system, and specifically their relative power. As a key to understanding the behaviour of states, the distribution of power in the international system overrides consideration of ideology or any other internal factor. Hence the important distinction neo-realists make between great and small powers.

Criticisms

As Linklater points out, a major problem with Waltz's unit-structure relationship is that it leaves little or no room for systemic change induced by the units themselves.[60] Waltz is convinced that states are virtually powerless to alter the system in which they find themselves trapped, though he concedes that under certain conditions 'virtuosos' can resist the constraints of structure.[61] Although this argument allows him to explain the persistence and longevity of the international system, it is by definition hostile to the idea that the system can be fundamentally altered by the states which comprise it. There is a contradiction and a weakness here. On the one hand Waltz argues that the values, ethics and moral aspirations of states are thwarted by the systemic constraint of anarchy. On the other he concedes to the arguments of liberal internationalists such as Doyle that 'on external as well as on internal grounds, I hope that more countries will become democratic', which suggests that states can limit the influence of structure by changing their internal dispositions.[62] He appears too willing to discount the character of the units in the system. It may be that structure is simply not as important in conditioning state behaviour as Waltz would have us believe and that the system-level properties are not as historically immutable as he suggests.

Waltz also denies that greater levels of economic interdependency amongst states pose a threat to the condition of anarchy, despite Rosencrance's claim that the 'trading state' is displacing the 'military state' in the contemporary world because competition for global market shares has become more important than territorial conquest.[63] Nevertheless it is clear that the use of force has become counter-productive in the post-Second World War period because it threatens the stability of the global trading and finance system, despite neo-realist incantations about strategic primacy. Doyle's argument that liberal democracies have transcended their violent instincts – and the insecurities engendered by anarchy – and have learnt to resolve their differences peacefully, is relevant here. The pacification of a core of liberal-democracies and the increasing number of states choosing liberal democratic orders poses a challenge for neo-realism's contention that the units can do little to alter the structure of the system.[64]

Waltz also discounts the rationalist view that though it is anarchic in structure, the international system is also normatively regulated. The idea of international society with common interests and values, rules and institutions, where conflict is mollified by mutually recognized requirements for co-existence undermines the neo-realist view that states are incapable of altruistic behaviour. Waltz appears to be suggesting that states cannot widen their conception of self-interest beyond the egoism of strategic interaction, despite the gains that can be made through co-operation, submission to the rules of a diplomatic culture, and membership of international organizations. For him, states will not subordinate the pursuit of their national interests for the sake of international order.

The epistemological critiques of neo-realism by Ashley and Cox expose the conservative ideology which underwrites Waltz's theoretical approach.[65] Both adopt a critical approach to neo-realism, highlighting the extent to which it naturalizes or reifies the international system by treating structures which have a specific and transitory history as if they were 'permanent', 'normal' or 'given' political fixtures. This not only has the effect of legitimizing the status quo, it also occludes arguments for alternative forms of political community which are more sensitive to changing social and ethnic identities and the exclusionary character of political boundaries. As Linklater argues, by emphasizing recurrence and repetition in the international system, 'neo-realism cannot envisage a form of statecraft which transcends the calculus of power and control'.[66] Cox places neorealism in the category of 'problem-solving theory' which 'takes the world as it finds it, with the prevailing social and political relations and institutions into which they are organised, as the given framework for action.[67] The general aim of problem-solving theory is to make these relationships and institutions work smoothly by dealing effectively with particular sources of trouble'. Problem solving theory fails to question the pattern of relationships and institutions in question and can 'fix limits or parameters to a problem area' which in turn limits 'the number of variables which are amenable to relatively close and precise examination'.[68] For Cox, neorealism reduces international relations to great power management by legitimating a political order which favours the powerful and is hostile to change.

Critical theory, on the other hand, 'stands apart from the prevailing order of the world and asks how that order came about. Critical theory, unlike problem-solving theory, does not take institutions and social and power relations for granted but calls them into question by concerning itself with their origins and how and whether they might be in the process of changing. It is directed towards an appraisal of the very framework of action . . . which problem-solving theory accepts as its parameters'. Whereas problem-solving theory is 'a guide to tactical actions which, intended or unintended, sustain the existing order', critical theory provides a 'a guide to strategic action for bringing about an alternative order'.[69] This is an approach which would directly undermine neo-realism's faith in recurrence, repetition, and the cyclical pattern of international politics.

Conclusion

The strength of the realist tradition is its capacity to argue from necessity. It seeks to describe reality, solve problems and understand the continuities of world politics. To accomplish this task it invokes a philosophical tradition, with Hobbes, Rousseau, Machiavelli re-employed to provide the theory with the authority of classicism. By reclaiming its intellectual antecedents realism again emphasizes its timelessness and the importance of continuity in theoretical research. A normative concern with the causes of war and the conditions of peace, security and order will continue to guide research and teaching in International Relations because they are centrally important issues. Realism speaks to these concerns directly by privileging strategic interaction and the distribution of global power above other considerations. It explains the inevitability of competition and conflict between states by highlighting the insecure and anarchical nature of the international environment.

Neo-realism provides a convincing account of why the foreign policies of nation-states are so familiar, despite their very diverse internal natures. It also provides a more sophisticated explanation for the persistence of the international system. However, it exaggerates the autonomy states enjoy from their domestic conditions, overstates the importance of structure and underestimates the potential for states to transform the international system. Neo-realism implies that, in its present form, the nation-state is a permanent fixture in the international system and that the prospects for alternative expressions of political community are limited.[70] This claim is now under considerable challenge from more critically orientated accounts of international relations. The extent to which neo-realism can provide answers to its growing number of critics will determine its future value as international theory.

Notes

1. E. H. Carr, *The Twenty Years' Crisis* (London, 1939), pp. 11–12.
2. Ibid., p. 13.
3. Ibid., p. 14.
4. Ibid., p. 14.
5. Ibid., p. 67.
6. Ibid., pp. 289 and 297.
7. Ibid., p. 111.
8. Ibid., p. 102.
9. Ibid., p. 58.
10. Ibid., p. 104.
11. Ibid., p. 103.
12. Ibid., pp. 61 and 72. See also E. H. Carr, *Nationalism and After* (London, 1945), p. 17.
13. Ibid., p. 77.
14. Ibid., p. 66.
15. Ibid., pp. 283 and 14.

16. Ibid., pp. 14, 93 and 97.
17. A. Linklater, *Beyond Realism and Marxism: Critical Theory and International Relations* (Basingstoke, 1990), p. 7.
18. Carr (1939), pp. 292–6.
19. Ibid., pp. 301–2.
20. Ibid., p. 297.
21. Ibid., p. 297.
22. M. Hollis and S. Smith, *Explaining and Understanding International Relations* (Oxford, 1990), pp. 63–4.
23. H. J. Morgenthau, *Politics Among Nations* (6th edn, New York, 1985), p. 3.
24. Ibid., p. 7.
25. Ibid., pp. 3–4.
26. Ibid., p. 5.
27. Ibid., p. 12.
28. Ibid., p. 12.
29. I. Clark, *The Hierarchy of States* (Cambridge, 1989), p. 84.
30. Ibid., p. 87.
31. Morgenthau (1985), p. 5.
32. H. Morgenthau in *The New Republic*, 22.1.77.
33. H. Morgenthau, 'The Intellectual and Political Functions of Theory (1970)', in J. Der Derian (ed.), *International Theory: Critical Investigations* (Basingstoke, 1995), p. 50.
34. Morgenthau (in Der Derian) (1970), p. 52.
35. K. N. Waltz, 'Realist Thought and Neo-Realist Theory', *Journal of International Affairs*, vol.44, no.1 (1990), p. 33.
36. Ibid., p. 34.
37. Morgenthau (1985), p. 5.
38. M. Howard, *The Causes of Wars* (London, 1983), p. 41.
39. There were exceptions such as Morgenthau, who believed in the long-term need for some form of world government.
40. Morgenthau, cited in N. Chomsky, *Towards a New Cold War* (New York, 1982), p. 74.
41. See J. Rosenberg, 'What's the matter with realism?', in *Review of International Studies*, vol.16 (1990), pp. 296–9.
42. R. D. McKinlay and R. Little, *Global Problems and World Order* (London, 1986), p. 5.
43. Thompson calls this process 'disimulation': see J. B. Thompson, *Ideology and Modern Culture* (Oxford, 1990), p. 61.
44. This is what Thompson calls the 'legitimation' mode of ideological operation'.
45. R. L. Rothstein, 'On the costs of Realism', in M. Smith, R. Little and M. Shackleton (eds), *Perspectives on World Politics* (London, 1981), pp. 388–97.
46. Reification here meaning that 'relations of domination may be established and sustained by representing a transitory, historical state of affairs as if it were permanent, natural [and] outside of time' (Thompson 1990, p. 65).

47. See, for example, S. D. Krasner, *Defending the National Interest* (Princeton, 1978) and R. Gilpin, The *Political Economy of International Relations* (Princeton, 1987).
48. Waltz (1990), p. 32.
49. Ibid., p. 22.
50. ibid., p. 23.
    For an expansion of Waltz's conception of theory, see Waltz, K., *Theory of International Politics* (New York, 1979), pp. 1–17 and 116–23.
51. Waltz (1990), p. 29.
52. Ibid., pp. 29–30.
53. Ibid., p. 33.
54. Ibid., p. 34.
55. 'Theories of international politics that concentrate causes at the individual or national level are reductionist; theories that conceive of causes operating at the international level as well are systemic' (Waltz, 1979, p. 19).
56. Waltz (1979), pp. 88–97, 104.
57. Ibid., p. 128.
58. Waltz (1979), p. 66; Waltz (1990), p. 34.
59. Waltz (1979), p. 96.
60. A. Linklater, 'Neo-realism in Theory and Practice', in K. Booth and S. Smith (eds), *International Relations Theory Today* (Cambridge, 1995), pp. 251–4.
61. K. 'Waltz, Reflections on Theory of International Politics: A Response to My Critics', in R. O. Keohane (ed.), *Neorealism and its Critics* (New York, 1986), p. 343.
62. K. Waltz, 'America as a Model for the World?', in *PS: Political Science and Politics*, vol.24, no.4 (1991), p. 670
63. R. Rosencrance, *The Rise of the Trading State* (New York, 1986). See also S. Strange, 'New World Order: Conflict and Co-operation', *Marxism Today* (January 1991), pp. 30–1.
64. See M. Doyle, 'Liberalism and World Politics', *American Political Science Review*, vol.80, no.4 (1986), pp. 1151–69.
65. R. K. 'Ashley, The Poverty of Neorealism', *International Organisation*, 38 (1984), pp. 225–86; R. W. Cox, 'Social Forces, States and World Order: Beyond International Relations Theory', *Millennium: Journal of International Studies*, 10 (1989), pp. 126–55.
66. Linklater (1995), p. 256.
67. For a discussion of both Horkheimer's and Habermas' theoretical constructions, see R. Bernstein, *The Restructuring of Social and Political Theory* (London, 1976), pp. 191–200.
68. Cox (1981), pp. 128–9.
69. Ibid., pp. 128–30.
70. Linklater (1995), pp. 258–9.

CHAPTER 4

Rationalism

Andrew Linklater

Realism was first systematically developed by twentieth-century thinkers such as Carr, Morgenthau and Waltz although it is often associated with a great tradition of political thinkers including Thucydides, Hobbes and Machiavelli. Long the dominant perspective within the discipline, realism stresses the endless competition for power and security in the world of states. Sovereignty, anarchy and the security dilemma are crucial terms in its lexicon whereas the idea of progress and morality are absent from most realist accounts of relations between states. Moral principles and social progress are thought to be relevant in many domestic political systems where trust exists, security being provided by the state, but moral projects have little impact in international politics where states have to provide for their own security and trust few of their neighbours. In foreign policy, universal moral principles serve to legitimate national interests and stigmatize principal competitors rather than foreshadow a post-sovereign international community.

The unbridgeable gulf between domestic and international politics is a central theme in realist thought. Cosmopolitan approaches as defended by philosophers from Kant to Beitz envisage a form of world political organisation – but not necessarily a form of world government – in which universal moral principles are taken seriously. Cosmopolitans believe that the gulf between domestic and international politics can be reduced, even eliminated, and that projects of reform are not only feasible but of vital importance in the context of anarchy. The opposition between these two perspectives has been crucial to the history of thought about international relations and was central to the first great debate between the realists and the idealists.

This debate was essentially about the possibility of pacifying international society through the development of a strong sense of moral obligation to human beings everywhere. Cosmopolitans argued that realism was not only unjustifiably pessimistic about the possibility of a peaceful world but a serious obstacle to the exercise of political imagination to promote international political change. Realism regarded cosmopolitanism as not only naïvely optimistic about the prospects for a new world order based on the rule of law, open diplomacy and collective security but dangerous if taken seriously by foreign policy elites. Ignorant of the basic realities of international politics, idealists distracted attention from the primary task of ensuring national security and rendered the state vulnerable to its more sinister competitors. The experience of the inter-war years secured the victory of realism.

The rationalist approach which is associated with Grotius and Vattel and with more recent thinkers such as Wight, Bull, Watson and Vincent suggests there is another way of thinking about international relations which overlaps with realism and idealism to some degree. Certain rationalist formulations clearly owe no small debt to the realist tradition. In an influential essay entitled 'Why is there no International Theory?' Martin Wight claimed that domestic politics is the sphere of the good life while international politics is the sphere of security and survival.[1] Similarly realist is his claim that international relations is 'incompatible with progressivist theory'. In a strikingly realist statement Wight maintained that Sir Thomas More would recognise the basic features of international politics in the 1960s.[2]

Like realism, then, rationalism begins with anarchy but unlike realism it acknowledges that the sense of belonging to the community of humankind has left its civilizing mark upon the state and international relations. Rationalism shares the cosmopolitan concern that the international system stubbornly fails to accommodate the principles of freedom and equality. It takes moral arguments for change seriously although it is invariably sceptical about grand visions of global reform. Like any doctrine rationalism contains a number of different inclinations, some favouring realism, others leaning towards cosmopolitanism, yet never wholly reconciling itself to either point of view. It has its own particular object of analysis. Rationalism focuses neither on the system of states nor upon the community of humankind but upon what it regards as the basic reality which realism and idealism ignore, this being the phenomenon of international order.

To some degree rationalism is attracted towards elements of realism and idealism, yet occupies a mid-point between these polar extremes. This is how Wight described rationalism in his series of lectures delivered at the London School of Economics in the 1950s. Rationalism, Wight claimed, was the *via media* between realism and revolutionism, the latter term being Wight's expression for idealist or cosmopolitan modes of thought.[3] Rationalism recognises that the condition of anarchy forces states to provide their own security and acknowledges that notions of a universal morality continue to check the egoism of the sovereign state but emphasizes the high level of international order which exists even in the context of anarchy where there is no higher authority or sovereign power equipped with the legal right to govern the actions of states. Later, Hedley Bull neatly captured this apparently paradoxical feature of the sovereign states-system in the title of his most famous work, *The Anarchical Society*.

Rationalism argues that there is more to international relations than the realist suggests but less than the cosmopolitan desires. The position which rationalism occupies as the *via media* raises the important question of how order and change are conceptualized by members of the rationalist school. There are two main points to make in this context.

First, rationalism departs from realism by seeking to explain how states control the quest for power in the context of anarchy. It is less concerned than realism with how states outmanoeuvre, control and defeat each other and more concerned than realism with how states acquire and employ the careful art of accommodation and compromise without which international order would be impossible. At times rationalists encroach upon notions of historical inevitability. Adam Watson has argued that: 'A strong case can be made out, on the evidence of past systems as well as the present one, that the regulatory rules and institutions of a system usually, and perhaps inexorably, develop to the point where the members become conscious of common values and the system becomes an international society.'[4] Realists focus on the nature of the international system and believe that rationalists overestimate the importance of society in international relations.[5] By contrast, the transition from an international system (in which states interact with one another and calculate each other's economic and military capacities and political intentions) to an international society (in which they have shared purposes and rely on common institutions) is crucially important for rationalism.[6] Having noted a possibly universal tendency for systems of states to become societies of states, Watson adds that the important question to ask is where the ethical component in international societies comes from. Put differently, rationalists are specifically interested in explaining the puzzle of international order.[7]

Second, rationalism insists that international order should not be taken for granted – it is a precarious achievement which can be destroyed by the emergence of aggressive powers – but rationalism raises the question of how far a secure international order can be transformed further to satisfy demands for morality and justice. Wight encourages this consideration of further possibilities by noting that 'the fundamental political task at all times [is] to provide order, or security, from which law, justice and prosperity may afterwards develop'.[8] This insightful formulation resembles Kant's understanding of the political project as establishing the condition of civility in which freedom and justice could then advance, and invites consideration of the question of how international order might come to accommodate cosmopolitan moral principles. It is arguable that rationalism in the 1980s and 1990s began to act as an advocate for greater justice in international relations whereas earlier it tended to emphasize the achievement of international order. This is an important theme to be considered later in this chapter.

The remainder of this chapter is in four parts. Part I focuses on order and society in rationalist writings. Part II considers the place of justice within the traditional European society of states. Part III analyses the significance of the 'revolt against the West' and the emergence of a universal society of states. Part IV returns to the central question of whether rationalism is committed to a notion of international progress in which the quest for power is tamed by the need for order, and order is revised to admit cosmopolitan principles; in this context, Part IV briefly considers rationalism in the context of recent debates within the field and stresses its distinctiveness and continuing importance for the future of the discipline. The chapter ends with some brief comments about the main strengths and weaknesses of the rationalist position.

I   From Power to Order: International Society

Explaining the surprisingly high level of order which exists between political entities which refuse to submit to a higher political authority is the key to the rationalist project. Some rationalists such as Wight expressed fascination with the small number of international societies which have existed in human history and with their relatively short life-span, all previous societies of states having been destroyed by empire after only a few centuries.[9] Wight also noted their propensity for internal schism in the form of international revolutions which brought transnational political forces and ideologies rather than sovereign states into conflict.[10] Wight posed the question of whether commerce first brought different societies into contact and provided the context within which a society of states could develop.[11] But when reflecting upon the three international societies about which a great deal is known (the Ancient Chinese, the Graeco-Roman and the modern society of states) Wight maintained that they had emerged in areas in which there was already a common language and culture. Of equivalent importance, the constituent parts felt that they belonged to a great civilization which was vastly superior to the other cultures with which they had contact.[12] This keen awareness of their 'cultural differentiation' from the allegedly semi-civilized and barbaric peoples living elsewhere made it easier for political systems to communicate to determine the rights and duties which would link them together in a bounded international society.

Wight's protégé, Hedley Bull, adopted a similar position at times. Writing of the evolution of the modern society of states Bull observed that in 'the form of the doctrine of natural law, ideas of human justice historically preceded the development of ideas of interstate or international justice and provided perhaps the principal intellectual foundations upon which these latter ideas at first rested'.[13] However, Bull immediately added that European states subsequently weakened the medieval conception of a human society which had facilitated the emergence of society between them. The more pronounced theme in his work is that international societies can exist without there being a culture which is common to all members. Bull was careful to distinguish between an international system and an international society, a distinction which Wight did not introduce in his own work. On the subject of systems of states, Bull noted that a 'system of states (or international system) is formed when two or more states have sufficient contact between them, and have sufficient impact on one another's decisions to cause them to behave – at least in some measure – as parts of a whole'.[14] As for societies of states: a 'society of states . . . exists when a group of states, conscious of certain common interests and common values, form a society in the sense that they conceive themselves to be bound by a common set of rules in their relations with one another, and share in the working of common institutions'.[15] This is an important distinction because it highlights the need to explain precisely how international societies have evolved and how the element of society in international relations has increased and decreased over time.

As noted, Bull believed that order can exist between states which do not feel that they belong to a common civilization. John Vincent later observed in an essay on Edmund Burke that the basic theme which ensures the working of international society is 'functional' rather than 'cultural', or utilitarian rather than moral, in configuration.[16] The pragmatic need to co-exist is sufficient to produce what Bull called a 'diplomatic culture' – a system of rules, conventions and institutions which preserves order between political associations with diverse cultures and ideologies.[17] Bull added that the diplomatic culture will be stronger if the political units are broadly committed to a similar form of life and therefore have an 'international political culture' in common. To illustrate these themes, Bull argued that the modern universal society of states is not founded upon one international political culture as the European society of states was in the nineteenth century, although a cosmopolitan culture of modernity may now be uniting elites across the world.[18] This is a crucial theme in Bull and Watson's pathbreaking book, *The Expansion of International Society*, which considers whether the order which existed when the society of states was limited to Europe will endure now that membership of international society has been conferred upon the non-European cultures which constitute the majority of states in the modern world. As we shall see later, Bull and Watson answered this question in the affirmative. They added that international order can exist even though states do not share an international political culture but one is more likely to survive and function reasonably well if states and, just as importantly, peoples have some basic political values in common.

The most detailed analysis of the basic preconditions of international order is to be found in Bull's *The Anarchical Society*, which emphasizes certain similarities between domestic and international society. Bull argues that before any society can be said to exist members must co-operate to secure three 'primary goals': placing constraints on violence, respecting property and ensuring that agreements are kept.[19] Rationalists are opposed to 'the domestic analogy' which is the idea that the centralized institutions which make domestic political order possible are equally necessary to ensure order between states.[20] As we have seen, rationalists stress the ability of sovereign states to create society without any overarching power – without abolishing anarchy understood as the absence of government rather than violence and chaos. Nevertheless, the fact that all societies share three primary goals means that when they do enter into relations with one another they can draw upon existing political resources in order to contrive order among themselves. In Bull's analysis, the need to ensure that the use of force is limited, that sovereignty is respected and that treaties are kept, rather than any common culture, forms the basis of international order.

Yet international society and domestic society are not the same, and the absence of a higher sovereign power is the key feature which sets the former apart. In domestic societies individuals are governed by 'primary rules' which concern right conduct and by 'secondary rules' which determine how these primary rules are made, interpreted and enforced.[21] The salient point is that domestic societies are highly institutionalized and centralized whereas in international society states administer the primary rules which govern proper conduct and resist efforts to give centralized institutions control over secondary rules. International society, moreover, is distinguished from domestic society by the existence of a unique set of primary goals.[22] The principle that sovereignty is necessary to acquire membership of the society of states distinguishes international society; the conviction that the society of states is the only legitimate form of world political organization is a primary goal peculiar to the international realm; the belief that the sovereignty of every member of the society of states should be defended also illustrates the uniqueness of the society of states. These goals are not always compatible, as Bull observed in his writings on order and justice which are considered in the next section.

The society of states arises because states learn the need to control force and to bring civility to their relations but the question arises of whether any particular kind of society is especially likely to be drawn towards membership of international society, to care for its institutions and to resist challenges to order. Rationalism argues that states with different cultures and ideologies can come together in a society of states because they have primary goals in common. It therefore affirms its confidence in diplomacy as the activity through which the different, the suspicious and the hostile reach some common ground. It strongly denies that international society can only exist between states which have the same ideology or philosophy of government.

Another theme in rationalism, however, suggests that while a commitment to the domestic rule of law on the part of the great powers is not a necessary condition of international society it was an important factor in the evolution of the modern European society of states. This theme is evident in the comments on constitutionalism which have largely been ignored in analyses of rationalism.[23] Martin Wight observed that the countries which contributed most to the development of the balance of power in the eighteenth and nineteenth centuries were England, Germany and the Netherlands, the societies which were most deeply involved in the struggle against absolutism.[24] The values which were enshrined in the European society of states were intimately connected with 'the political philosophy of constitutional government'.[25] The multiple balance of power was the international counterpart of 'liberal constitutionalism'.[26] Echoing the point, Bull maintained that the rise of constitutionalism in the Middle Ages prepared the way for an international society of states.[27]

It is worth considering this theme in the light of some recent debates about the relationship between the unit (the state) and the international system. The neo-realist perspective taken by Waltz stresses the respects in which the international system constrains the units and almost no attention is paid to the respects in which the units can influence the system.[28] The liberal perspective argued by Michael Doyle argues, *contra* neo-realism, that liberal states incline towards peaceful relations with each other though not necessarily with non-liberal states.[29] When compared with these perspectives it becomes apparent that rationalism has some affinities with the liberal perspective because it believes that it is necessary to take account of domestic structures and beliefs to understand the nature of international relations. Rationalism does not lend support to Doyle's thesis as such but its comments on constitutionalism reveal that it is clearly concerned to understand how the domestic moral and political preferences of the units shape the functioning of international society (and are shaped by it).

Wight's essay on international legitimacy, in which he considered how the criteria for defining membership of the society of states change over time (from the dynastic principle to the national principle, for example), illustrate this very clearly: 'these principles of legitimacy mark the region of approximation between international and domestic politics. They are principles that prevail (or are at least proclaimed) *within* a majority of the states that form international society, as well as in the relations *between* them'.[30] Whereas realism and neo-realism more specifically often refer to an international system in quasi-mechanistic terms, rationalism highlights the cultural dimensions of world politics, and specifically the national and international ideas and beliefs which weave societies together in a greater society of states. This focus upon the 'normative' and 'institutional' dimensions which give international politics its separate 'logic' distinguishes rationalism from other perspectives.[31]

II   From Order to Justice?

To summarise the discussion to this point, rationalism considers the processes by which systems of states are transformed into international societies and focuses upon the normative and institutional expressions of society between states. It also poses the question of how far international order might undergo further patterns of change which result in efforts to secure justice for the individual members of a world society. In addition to distinguishing international societies from international systems, rationalism therefore distinguishes between types of international society.

In an early essay Bull distinguished between two approaches to international society which he labelled the Grotian and the pluralist views. For Bull the 'central Grotian assumption is that of the solidarity, or potential solidarity, of the states comprising international society, with respect to the enforcement of the law'.[32] The solidarity of international society has been manifested in the belief that there is a clear distinction between just and unjust wars and in the broader assumption 'from which [the] right of humanitarian intervention is derived: that individual human beings are subjects of international law and members of international society in their own right'.[33] The opposing pluralist conception of international society argues that 'states do not exhibit solidarity of this kind, but are capable of agreeing only for certain minimum purposes which fall short of that of the enforcement of the law'.[34] According to the pluralist perspective exemplified by the work of Oppenheim, the members of that society are states rather than individuals.[35] Having distinguished the pluralist from the solidarist form of international society Bull asked whether there was any evidence that the pluralist international society of the 1950s and 1960s might be developing a more solidarist character. In *The Anarchical Society*, Bull's answer was that the expectation of greater solidarity was significantly 'premature'.[36]

Bull's analysis of the difficulties of moving from pluralism to solidarism is evident in his writings on the conflicts which can arise between the primary goals of international society and in his more general consideration of the tension between order and justice.[37] Bull argued that the preservation of the sovereignty of the state was one such primary goal but noted that the great powers would sacrifice the independence of a small power in order to preserve the global balance of power and to uphold the greater peace. The sacrifice of Poland in the eighteenth century and the failure of the League of Nations to defend Abyssinia from Italian aggression in the 1930s indicate how order which depends upon a balance of power between the great powers can clash with justice which requires that states should be treated equally. Bull added that in contemporary international society the principle of justice which requires that all states have an equal right to own the instruments of mass destruction clashes with the claims of order which require the raising of barriers to membership of the nuclear club.[38]

The danger of the selective application of moral principles is ever-present in the society of states, as the trial of war criminals at the end of the Second World War indicates.[39] Crucially important, states have different, even conflicting, interpretations of justice which can damage the fabric of international society if they are pressed too far. Bull's writings reveal a relativism about morals and his reminder to Western readers that liberal conceptions of human rights may not strike a chord in other parts of the world advises against assuming that there are ready-made moral universals.[40] No philosophical system has emerged which transcends the horizons of epoch and culture and resolves fundamental moral differences. Diplomacy has yet to succeed where philosophy has so obviously failed. States do not agree about the meaning of justice but they can agree on the basic legal and moral conventions which will preserve order between themselves. International order in the context of moral controversy and cultural diversity is maintained by a general agreement that grand projects of moral and political reform should be contained within the boundaries of states which are firmly committed to sovereignty and non-intervention.

Bull argued that the requirements of order and justice can clash but added that international order has moral value not only because it contains violence between states but 'because it is instrumental to the goal of order in human society as a whole', and 'order among all mankind . . . [is] of primary value, not order within the society of states'.[41] Moreover, Bull argued that 'a world society or community' is a goal which all 'intelligent and sensitive persons' should take seriously.[42] This cosmopolitan theme is accompanied by the conviction that there is very little evidence that different states and cultures will agree about the purposes of a world community. This scepticism partly reflects the influence of the realist claim that anarchy prohibits fundamental change in international relations but the rationalist concern with the different cultural preferences and moral codes which clash in international society is the main ingredient in its recipe for scepticism. In this context the claim that it is the *via media* between realism and cosmopolitanism is worth repeating. From the vantage-point of rationalism there is more to international relations than the struggle for power though far less than the cosmopolitan search for a world community. A limited progressivist interpretation of world politics is offered, despite Wight's apparent claim to the contrary, but the tension between order and justice reveals that this interpretation does not extend very far although it is desirable that it extend further.

Given this often understated moral concern, rationalism is especially interested in whether international order might come to embrace cosmo-politan principles and sentiments which pertain to the well-being of individuals and of social arrangements other than sovereign states. Although it is frequently concerned with possible threats to the survival of society and order it also considers what the members of a rather different intellectual tradition – critical theory – call the immanent possibility of progressive development. In this context rationalism stresses the exclusionary character of many traditional principles of international society and the existence of moral and political forces opening up the society of states to moral con-siderations which have generally been shown little sympathy. Over the last few decades resistance to the traditional exclusion of the rights of indivi-duals and to the exclusion of non-Western peoples from the society of states has transformed the constitutive norms of international society. It is useful to consider these dimensions of change in greater detail.

Bull argued that in the modern society of states the notion of the rights and duties of individuals 'has survived but it has gone underground'. There appears to have been 'a conspiracy of silence entered into by governments about the rights and duties of their respective citizens', although the in-dividual is granted legal status in the norms governing the conduct of war, political asylum, the right of emigration etc.[43] States have feared that a vigorous human rights doctrine would create unwelcome possibilities of interference and intervention in their sovereign internal affairs. Third World states in particular have feared that the dominant Western states would employ European notions of human rights to undermine their recently-acquired sovereignty.

Scepticism concerning future progress in the international protection of human rights is less marked in Bull's later work, especially in his last publications which return to the long-standing theme of order and justice in international relations. There Bull comments on the improved status of the individual in international law reflecting stronger cosmopolitan senti-ments in world society.[44] In *Human Rights and International Relations*, John Vincent argued that the most basic human right, the right to be free from starvation, was the sole human right upon which states could agree despite their various ideological differences.[45] Collective action to ensure human survival was necessary to combat one of the great offences in international society but it was also the common ground which could strengthen the post-European society of states. In one of his last essays Vincent reaffirms Bull's point that the idea of human rights has made important advances over the last decade. Sovereign states are increasingly open to scrutiny and under pressure to live up to international standards of performance.[46] What is true of individual human rights, it might be added, is also increasingly true of the rights of minorities and indigenous peoples.

The 'revolt against the West' will be considered further in the next section but one aspect of the revolt, namely the demand for racial equality, overlaps with the themes discussed in the last few paragraphs. The rejection of white supremacism has been one of the most important themes in the great transition from a European to a universal society of states and one example of the growing realization that international order now depends upon the greater satisfaction of Third World claims for justice. Clearly, regional order was insecure as long as white supremacist regimes governed Southern Africa but the crucial stake in the debate about white supremacist rule was the immorality of the system of government rather than the threat posed to regional order. The nature of the struggle is a reminder of Wight's claim that the modern European society of states has come nearer than any other to making the legitimacy of domestic systems of government a matter of importance for the entire international community.[47] States have disagreed profoundly about the rights of the international community to determine questions of domestic legitimacy although virtually all were agreed that an international order which accepted apartheid in any one of its constituent parts did not deserve to command legitimacy. In his essay on the West and South Africa Bull noted that the agreement regarding the evils of apartheid was about as far as a universal moral consensus extended in contemporary international society.[48]

What Bull concluded from this episode was that order can be strengthened by efforts to create justice between the Western and the non-Western powers but only if there is general agreement, especially among the great powers, about the most desirable forms of change: if 'there is overwhelming evidence of a consensus in international society as a whole in favour of change held to be just, especially if the consensus embraces all the great powers, the change may take place without causing other than a local and temporary disorder, after which the international order as a whole may emerge unscathed or even appear in a stronger position than before'.[49] Quite how far Bull and Watson thought a global moral consensus could extend is unclear. Watson has noted that Bull and he 'inclined' towards the 'optimistic view' that states in the contemporary system were 'consciously working out, for the first time, a set of transcultural values and ethical standards'.[50] Against this judgement must be set Bull's pessimism in the early 1980s that neither of the superpowers seemed to possess the requisite 'moral vision' for tackling the central problems in North–South relations.[51]

It is therefore difficult to judge whether the rationalist position takes the view that the expansion of international society has generated greater solidarism and cosmopolitanism between states. Although an emerging elite cosmopolitanism is noted in Bull's writings, he adds that this 'nascent cosmopolitan culture . . . is weighted in favour of the dominant cultures of the West'.[52] Greater account of non-Western ideas in international law could help to overcome the gulf between the West and other cultures yet there is already evidence that the latter might be increasingly attracted by social and political ideas which are unattractive in the West:

> we have to remember that when these demands for justice were first put forward, the leaders of Third World peoples spoke as supplicants in a world in which the Western powers were still in a dominant position. The demands that were put forward had necessarily to be justified in terms of . . . conventions of which the Western powers were the principal authors; the moral appeal had to be cast in terms that would have most resonance in Western societies. But as . .. non-Western peoples have become stronger . .. and as the Westernised leaders of the early years of independence have been replaced in many countries by new leaders more representative of local or indigenous forces, Third World spokesmen have become freer to adopt a rhetoric that sets Western values aside, or . .. places different interpretations upon them. Today there is legitimate doubt as to how far the demands emanating from the Third World coalition are compatible with the moral ideas of the West.[53]

Intriguing questions about the possibility of a progressivist interpretation of international society are posed by such claims. Rationalism eschews doctrines of inevitable progress associated with the great European philosophies of history of the nineteenth century and it doubts that a moral consensus can extend very far given the diverse political interests and cultural forces which exist in an international society. Its emphasis is on how states can universalise norms for preserving international order and perhaps even reach an agreement about basic moral principles which all states should uphold. Scepticism and pessimism at times are present in rationalism but just as it eschews utopianism so does it eschew the fatalistic interpretation of international politics which is present within, for example, neo-realism. Rationalists are cautiously optimistic that states with their very different interests and cultures can agree on the rules and conventions which will preserve order between themselves. For rationalists the function of political activity is to stake out this common ground so striking a balance between universalizable norms and particular cultures and interests.

III   The Revolt against the West and the Expansion of International Society

The impact of the revolt against the West upon the modern society of states was central to rationalist writing in the 1980s. The key issue in the discussion was whether the diverse civilizations which have been brought together in the modern world have reached an agreement about the basic rules of co-existence and therefore belong to an international society as opposed to an international system. To answer this question it was necessary to recall the world of the late eighteenth century. In that era, the European, Chinese, Islamic and Indian worlds comprised the four main regional international systems and 'most of the governments in each group had a sense of being part of a common civilization superior to that of the others'.[54] The European society of states, which would dominate these systems in the nineteenth century, was committed to the principle of sovereign equality within Europe but denied that non-European peoples possessed this right. The correct relationship between the West and other civilizations was keenly debated in the West, some favouring the enslavement or annihilation of the non-European peoples, others pleading that all peoples are equally human and potential members of the one society of states. Some doctrines of imperialism argued that the West had the duty to assume a trusteeship role in its dealing with non-Western peoples. The League of Nations mandates system and the United Nations trusteeship system reflected the emerging pattern of thought in which the West was obliged to prepare non-European peoples for admission into the society of states.

The Europeans believed that this incremental process would take several centuries to complete because other civilizations placed themselves at the centre of the world and possessed a hierarchical rather than egalitarian conception of international society. The Chinese, for example, distinguished the Middle Kingdom from tribute-paying societies at a lower stage of social and political development. Traditional Islamic conceptions of the world divided the House of Islam (*Dar al Islam*) from the House of War (*Dar al Harb*), the world of the believer from the world of the infidel, though they allowed for a temporary truce with non-Islamic powers (*Dar al Suhl*). The different regional international societies formed an international system before they became the equal members of a universal international society.[55] Membership of the European society of states was barred to those who had failed to reach the European standard of civilization.[56] The non-European civilizations were obliged to fit within the legal and political framework established by an expansionist Europe with its deeply-entrenched views about the inferiority of other cultures and civilizations. Non-European societies accepted Western conceptions of sovereignty, diplomacy and law after enduring a long and painful process of domestic change in which they reconciled themselves to conducting international relations according to Western rules. The West also had to make serious adjustments to its world-view given the revolt against the West which hastened the transition from a European to a universal society of states.

The revolt against the West consisted of five main struggles against Western practices of exclusion.[57] The first revolt was 'the struggle for equal sovereignty' by societies such as China and Japan which had 'retained their formal independence' but possessed an 'inferior status'. These societies were governed by unequal treaties 'concluded under duress' and they were, as a consequence of the principle of extra-territoriality, unable to bring disputes involving Western citizens under the jurisdiction of their domestic law. As a result of the struggle for legal equality Japan joined the society of states in 1900, Turkey in 1923, Egypt in 1936 and China in 1943. The second revolt was the national assault upon Western colonialism in which the colonies demanded the same sovereign rights as their imperial overlords. The third revolt was the critique of racial exclusion and white supremacism; the fourth revolt challenged the biases inherent within the Western trade and financial system and called for compensation for colonial exploitation. The fifth revolt, the cultural revolt, protested against forms of Western cultural imperialism and the West's assumed right to set the standards for judging other societies. The first four elements of the revolt against the West employed the moral vocabulary of the West and appeared to signify a desire to follow its trajectory of development. As already noted, the cultural revolt provides a new point of departure since often it is 'a revolt against Western values as such'.[58]

Bull and Watson posed the crucial question of whether the rise of a universal society of states would usher in a new era of estrangement between different cultures and civilizations or produce an unprecedented agreement on transcultural values. This question remains at the heart of current debates and it is useful to compare rationalism with three other theses adopted in recent times. The first thesis supposes that civilizational conflicts are likely to intensify in the aftermath of bipolarity.[59] Bull and Watson also drew attention to the revival of traditional patterns of belief and concomitant resistance to the intrusion of Western values. The second thesis emphasizes the growth of a universal consensus about the normative superiority of liberal democracy.[60] There are parallels between this thesis and Bull and Watson's remarks about an emerging elite 'cosmopolitan culture of modernity'. The third thesis maintains that cultural diversity has increased with the rise of the post-European world and the West can no longer claim to possess some moral truths which all other societies are bound to observe.[61] According to this thesis the sovereign state has been accepted by non-European peoples and there is a basic consensus about the need to uphold basic rules of co-existence though not to promote any particular set of moral standards. Pluralism has been accepted and solidarism resisted.

The claim that the revolt against the West has resulted in the triumph of a pluralist conception of international society has some support from Bull and Watson's writings although it is qualified by their observation that the culture of modernity now links many elites across the world.[62] More importantly, Bull and Watson argued that while an international order reflecting the interests of non-Western states was 'in some measure constructed' further changes would be required before international society could command the legitimacy of the majority of the world's peoples.[63] For that legitimacy to exist it will be essential to 'absorb non-Western elements to a much greater degree' within international law and to encourage a radical redistribution of the world's wealth.[64]

The tension between order and justice was a central theme in rationalism in the 1970s but in the early 1980s an important shift occurs. Bull continues to insist that 'justice is best realised in the context of order' but adds that it is increasingly true that the 'measures that are necessary to achieve justice for peoples of the Third World are the same measures that will maximise the prospects of international order or stability, at least in the long run'.[65] Greater moral advocacy and an inclination towards the solidarist rather than the pluralist approach is evident as the issue of who benefits most from the existing international order assumes more central importance in Bull's later work.[66]

The tension between order and justice has acquired renewed importance in international relations with the fragmentation of state-socialist societies in Eastern Europe. In *Unspoken Rules and Superpower Dominance*, Paul Keal argued that the superpower spheres of influence contributed to order but were 'intrinsically unjust' because they frustrated claims to self-determination on the part of subordinated peoples.[67] Fragmentation in socialist societies demonstrates the point that 'often justice can be purchased only at the price of order'.[68] The reopening of old territorial disputes and the risk that states will intervene to protect minorities in other societies further illustrates this point without endorsing the view that order must always take precedence over justice. As Keal argues, no defence of order transcends the preoccupations of particular interests.[69] Even so, the members of international society cannot avoid difficult questions about the conditions which need to be met by groups seeking admission into international society as sovereign states.

No less complex is the question of how international society should behave towards states which retain their sovereignty but lack viability because of famine or civil war. The 'failed state'[70] or the 'quasi-state'[71] raises complex questions about the extent to which international society should intervene to assist vulnerable populations. Whether the principle of non-intervention should be sacrificed in such instances to ensure justice for individuals caught up in famine and civil war is one of the issues to which contemporary international society has yet to find an answer.

In *Quasi-States in International Relations*, Robert Jackson argues that the failed state is a symptom of a sea-change in international society in which many colonies were admitted into the society of states as equal sovereign members despite the evidence that they might be ill-equipped to govern themselves. The convention that a people had to demonstrate a capacity for good government before they could make a reasonable claim for self-government was abolished by Resolution 1514 of the United Nations General Assembly Resolution in 1960. By accepting that the right to self-government was more important than evidence of a capacity for good government the society of states allowed the admission of societies which would have been denied entry a few decades earlier. 'Juridical statehood' was bestowed where 'empirical statehood' (possession of the economic and political prerequisites of viability) simply did not exist. States acquired negative sovereignty – the right to be free from external interference – when they lacked positive sovereignty – the capacity to satisfy the economic and political needs of their citizens. The rise of the quasi-state following a relaxation of the conventions governing admission into the society of states led to calls for an ethic of redistribution in which the rich acknowledged their obligation to enable weaker governments to acquire positive sovereignty.

The problem of the quasi-state may require more drastic measures. Jackson maintains that a smoother transition to the post-colonial world could have resulted had a system of global trusteeship been responsible for preparing the colonies for sovereign independence. Although such a proposal might have commanded little support among nationalist movements the plight of the quasi-state may require a bold experiment with forms of international government which assume temporary responsibility for the welfare of vulnerable populations. A similar invitation to consider the need for new instruments of global stewardship can be found in the essay by Helman and Ratner on failed states. A crucial issue in this discussion is whether the international community must secure the consent of the sovereign government before intervening in the failed state.

This question is linked, as Jackson points out, with whether sovereignty enables governing elites to terrorise their subjects while claiming the protection of international law. Sovereignty has given political elites the international legal right to do more or less what they please within their national territories. Since political elites have often benefited from having legal rights which are supposed to benefit the community as a whole the issue arises of whether international society has the right to override the sovereignty claims of particular regimes. Two questions arise here. The first is whether the society of states has the authority to demand that governments which request admission into their ranks must grant their citizens an array of constitutional safeguards and rights. The European Community made such a demand of the governments of Greece, Portugal and Spain, as has the Council of Europe in its dealings with the new states of Eastern Europe. The second question is whether a society which has gained membership of international society may be said to relinquish its sovereignty when it systematically abuses its citizenry. The West is firmer in its resolve to spread human rights and democracy and is more prepared to contemplate humanitarian intervention on the grounds that sovereignty wrongly privileges order over justice. Whether there is a consistent rationalist position on this issue is unclear although there is evidence of a greater willingness to endorse humanitarian intervention in certain cases[72] while remaining 'critical of any general undermining of non-intervention'.[73]

IV   A Progressivist Interpretation of International Relations?

Quite how far progress in international relations is possible remains the central problem of the field. Realism and rationalism often seem agreed that international relations is 'the realm of recurrence and repetition' but a more accurate view is that rationalists believe that a limited progressivist account of international relations is indeed possible.[74] As the *via media* between realism and revolutionism it identifies civilizing processes which contain the struggle for power and security by involving states in the co-operative venture of maintaining order. Rationalists believe that international order should be judged by its capacity to bring order to the lives of individual human beings but where order conflicts with justice, agonising choices have to be made.[75] Rationalists such as Bull clearly have sympathy with the cosmopolitan project but they doubt that human reason can ascertain moral principles which will command the consent of the whole of the human race. They recognise that order often falls tragically short of satisfying the desire for human justice (however it is defined) but they are troubled by measures to realize justice which jeopardise the precarious achievement of order.

As the *via media* rationalism is attracted towards the poles of realism and revolutionism. Bull's distinction between the pluralist and solidarist conceptions of international society demonstrates that rationalism is Janus-faced. Wight divided rationalism into the 'realist' and 'idealist' wings and suggested that realism and revolutionism could be further sub-divided.[76] Far from having clearly-defined boundaries the three perspectives are blurred at the edges.[77] Bull's last writings reveal the considerable overlap which Wight had stressed between the 'idealist' rationalism of Gladstone and the 'evolutionary' revolutionism of Wilson.[78]

This fusion of horizons occurs because of Bull's cosmopolitan turn which is evident in the lectures he gave at the University of Waterloo in 1983. In these lectures Bull argued that 'the idea of sovereign rights existing apart from the rules laid down by international society itself and enjoyed without qualification has to be rejected in principle'.[79] The move beyond absolute sovereignty was in part a function of increased support for the doctrine of human rights: 'within the system, the idea of the rights and duties of the individual person has come to have a place, albeit an insecure one, and it is our responsibility to seek to extend it'.[80] The 'moral concern with welfare on a world scale' demonstrated 'the growth of a cosmopolitan moral aware-ness' and 'a major change in our sensibilities'.[81] Increasingly nation-states were required to be 'local agents of a world common good'.[82] Similarly cosmopolitan themes are evident in Vincent's argument that the principle of non-intervention no longer sums up the morality of states in a world which is broadly committed to the international protection of human rights.[83]

These expressions of cosmopolitanism are accompanied by the deeply-entrenched rationalist impulse to warn against assuming that there are simple moral solutions to the troubled affairs of states. Reference has already been made to Bull's claim that even in the more cosmopolitan world agonizing choices still have to be made. Vincent cautioned that grand cosmopolitan projects may always falter on the rocky ground of implemen-tation.[84] This dualism is also apparent in Bull's comments about the ade-quacy of the state as a mode of political organization. *The Anarchical Society* claims that the time may be ripe for the enunciation of new principles of world political organization in which sub-national, national and supra-national loyalties have political voice but none can claim exclusive sover-eign jurisdiction.[85] Neo-medievalism 'promises to avoid the classic dangers of the system of sovereign states by a structure of overlapping structures and criss-crossing loyalties that hold all peoples together in a universal society while at the same time avoiding the concentration inherent in a world government'.[86] But this cosmopolitanism is quickly combined with caution and scepticism: the experience of the Christian world reveals that a network of overlapping jurisdictions and multiple loyalties could 'contain more ubiquitous and continuous violence and insecurity than does the modern states system'.[87] Rationalism therefore offers a qualified defence of the states-system and emphasizes 'the state's positive role in world affairs'.[88]

An assessment of the claim that rationalism occupies the middle ground between realism and revolutionism should note that it provides an imbal-anced account of what exists at each end of the spectrum of approaches to international relations. While it provides a clear account of the gravitational attraction of realism, rationalism offers a deeply-flawed analysis of the possibilities inherent in some forms of revolutionism and fails to consider their ability to strengthen its own position on order and justice. In *The Anarchical Society* Bull maintains that the Kantian view posits 'a horizontal conflict of ideology that cuts across the boundaries of states and divides human society into two camps – the trustees of the immanent community of mankind and those who stand in its way, those who are of the true faith and the heretics, the liberators and the oppressed'.[89] The Kantian approach assumes that the rules of the society of states can be sacrificed for the sake of realising a community of humankind: 'Good faith with heretics has no meaning, except in terms of tactical convenience; between the elect and the damned, the liberators and the oppressed, the question of mutual accep-

tance of rights to sovereignty or independence does not arise'.[90] Stanley
Hoffmann argues that Bull is guilty of misreading Kant 'who was much less
cosmopolitan and universalist in his writings on international affairs than
Bull suggests' and who shared much of Bull's perspective on the mutual
rights and duties which constitute the society of states.[91] Closer analysis of
Kant's cosmopolitan approach to the society of states could have accelerated the radicalisation of rationalism.

A more accurate portrayal of Kant's position is provided by Wight, who
was nevertheless critical of the liberal cosmopolitanism which Kant advocated for the society of states. Wight argued that Kant was committed to
'doctrinal uniformity' by maintaining that peace could only occur through
the universalization of republican principles of government.[92] Kant defends
a republican society of states because republican government is committed
to the protection of the liberty of citizens and to the domestic rule of law.
These domestic commitments have international implications since they
strongly predispose republican states to resolving disputes by peaceful
means rather than by war.

Rationalism does not make the universalization of republicanism a precondition of peace between states – hence Wight's criticisms of Kantian
doctrinal uniformity. There are nevertheless important similarities between
Kant and the Grotian tradition since both assume that the existence of a
society of states depends upon the international acceptance and projection
of domestic notions of civility. Bull argues that a society of states depends
upon primary goals which are already understood and protected within the
constituent parts. Bull and Wight argue that the modern European society
of states has been deeply influenced by notions of constitutional government. Kant's political project is to extend the realm of constitutionalism in
international relations by peaceful means. Wight argued that the least
dangerous form of revolutionism is to be found in Kantian thought. Kant
resembles the rationalist who is first and foremost 'a reformist, the practi-
tioner of piecemeal social engineering'.[93] Moreover, both Kant and Grotius
understood the world as comprising three concentric circles. As Wight
observes, the three circles in the thought of Grotius are the state, the society
of states and the community of humankind.[94] Kant offers three images of
law: the law of the state (*ius civitatis*); the law of the society of states (*ius
gentium*) and the law of the community of humankind (*ius cosmopoliticum*).[95]
Ius gentium and *ius cosmopoliticum* represent the advance of the constitutional idea into the sphere of relations between states although Kant
thought that civility should also obtain in the relations between European
states and indigenous peoples.[96] Rationalism similarly upholds the need for
civility not only between societies which are similarly organized as sovereign states but also between societies which take different political forms.
As noted earlier it would be erroneous to suppose that rationalism is
committed to civility between independent states whereas Kant's thought

extends further to encompass the rights of individuals. Each defends sovereignty and each has a place for the individual, although Kant is the more obviously committed to extending the influence of the cosmopolitan idea and the more optimistic that states will agree on the content of a cosmopolitan ethic.

Parallels exist yet differences remain which are specifically concerned with the prospects for extending the sense of community beyond the sovereign state. Questions concerning community are central to recent work in international relations, and Bull went some way towards foreshadowing this development in his comments on Karl Deutsch's work on security communities. Though underdeveloped, Deutsch's writings were 'pregnant with implications of a general theory of international relations'.[97] The important theme in Deutsch's work is the nature of political community, the nature of the bond which unites a community and separates it from the rest of the world. Specifically, Deutsch aimed 'to think out the distinguishing features of a community, the different sorts of community that obtain, the elements that make up the cohesion of a community, the determinants of mutual responsiveness between one people and another'.[98]

Focusing as it does on how systems of states become societies of states rationalism is inevitably interested in how communities become more open to considering the interests of others. This is evident in the comment by Wight that an international society can only exist if communities are prepared to modify their particular conceptions of their interests in the light of the legitimate interests of others and therefore inclined towards the tolerance of other points of view.[99] The analysis of the expansion of international society stressed the shift from hierarchical to egalitarian conceptions of relations between states, thereby drawing attention to the sense in which a society of states presupposes political communities which are not closed in upon themselves. The question of whether order can be revised to admit cosmopolitan morality and justice further probes the issue of how far political communities are prepared to acknowledge what Bull described as 'purposes beyond ourselves'.[100] An interest in the way in which the sense of political community contracts and expands should be central to the rationalist project but it is not developed in any detail. A more sympathetic analysis of some main strands of revolutionist thought would have broadened the rationalist project.

Many of the important questions about political community which are missing from rationalism arise in perspectives which are rarely linked with rationalism but are relevant to it. The perspectives are postmodernism, critical theory and feminism. The connections here have been overlooked for many different reasons. The assumption that rationalism is a distinctively British realism, an interpretation which Wheeler and Dunne reject[101] and the conviction that it belongs to an intellectual orthodoxy which new perspectives aim to undermine[102] are two reasons for this neglect. These characterizations of rationalism fail to bring out the pronounced rationalist interest in the role of culture and cultural differences. What is already evident in the rationalist consideration of the expansion of the society of states is a concern with otherness and cultural difference, and an emphasis on the possibility of a dialogue between very different cultures from which some basic agreement about order and justice may develop. Similar concerns, often more sharply focused, arise within a number of more recent critical-theoretical points of departure.

A detailed analysis of areas of affinities between rationalism and these perspectives is beyond the scope of this chapter. Suffice it to note that affinities with philosophical hermeneutics have been noted in the recent literature.[103] Parallels with the project of reconstructing historical materialism have also been stressed. Rationalism and critical theory are both concerned with the processes by which human groups learn to create order and devise moral principles which can command the consent of all.[104] Although there are fundamental differences between them, rationalism and postmodernism address conceptions of otherness and modes of exclusion involving political communities. They invite greater empathy with the other and they react against the supposition that universal moral truths reside in any one civilization. Recent feminist literature is critical of universalist ethical positions which assume that the same set of rules can govern all human beings. There is a powerful defence in this literature of forms of dialogue which take account of concrete differences and aim for an agreement which takes account of all points of view. This conception of dialogue does not assume that any one form of life can be true for all but it puts forward the cosmopolitan ideal that all human beings have an equal right to take part in open dialogue.[105]

The extent to which such notions of dialogue form a cosmopolitanism which rationalists might find congenial is an issue worthy of exploration in future research. Rationalism has stressed the importance of an order based on dialogue which does justice to different cultures and beliefs. It has argued for a new balance in the relationship between Western and non-Western states, a theme central to recent discussions about widening the membership of the Security Council to include such societies as Nigeria, India and Brazil. However, a cosmopolitanism which does not exclude any particular voice needs to expand the range of discussants to include political associations and communities which have been inadequately represented within the society of states. Widening the discussion to include nongovernmental organizations, sub-national minorities and indigenous peoples is one means of evolving towards the rationalist goal of creating an international order which commands the consent of peoples as well as sovereign states.

Conclusion

What, finally, are the main strengths and weaknesses of the rationalist position? By way of strengths, rationalism avoids what E. H. Carr called the 'sterility' of realism and the 'naivety and exuberance' of idealism.[106] Rationalism should be distinguished from realism because of its emphasis on how states learn the art of accommodating the interests of others and create a civil order even in the context of anarchy. Rationalists are keen to stress the importance of tolerance as a principle of international relations and the need to recognise that the moral and political preferences of one state or group of states may command little loyalty elsewhere. Order depends upon a careful balance of universal norms and particular cultures and interests. Order is a precarious achievement which can always be undermined by the policies of aggressive powers but it is the context in which morality and justice can develop. Order between states is not an absolute: it is to be valued because of the order which it brings to human beings and it should be extended where a consensus exists about international political change. By affirming the capacity of states to establish basic order between themselves and by doubting their capacity to develop a universal moral consensus very far rationalists argue that they provide the *via media* between realism and revolutionism.

The main weakness in rationalism is its curious portrayal of revolutionist thinking, its neglect of connections with moral and political theory and its ensuing failure to develop an adequate normative stance. Vincent is right that Bull's claim that Walzer failed to establish his own normative principles applies to Bull himself.[107] Part of this failure to offer a bolder moral standpoint arises because of a distrust of abstract ethical reflections with little immediate relevance for the central problems of states; this failure is compounded by its tendency to emphasize one form of revolutionism which advocates the violent overthrow of existing political institutions as a means of reaching a single universal community.

The compelling instances of revolutionism (exemplified by Kant's writings, for example) do not make this assumption. They are closer to rationalism and more relevant to its development than is generally realized. In this context it is worth noting that Kant sought to give normative direction to the currents leading beyond the existing order, as rationalism begins to do when addressing the ramifications of the emergence of the first universal society of states. The nature of the sociological project which is implicit here would have been more clearly understood had rationalism been engaged with modern social and political theory and especially with critical theory, which seeks to identify processes of change immanent within existing orders. This method is clearly present in Marxism, which rationalists dismissed as marginal to the study of international relations. Recent strands of international relations theory offer ways of developing a normative stand-point which enlarges rationalist concerns. The need to be open to forms of dialogue from which no one and no view is excluded prima facie is one such theme.

Rationalism is the branch of international relations theory which seeks to understand how culturally different states can agree on the principles of international order and justice. Creating a world community which promotes the well-being of individuals and their primary social groups in the context of increasing cultural difference requires modes of analysis which preserve the strengths of rationalism and build specifically upon its more radicalised form. The logic of the argument is to weaken the rationalist's claim to provide the *via media* and to incorporate its strengths within critical interpretations of world politics previously misconstrued as revolutionist.

Notes

1. M. Wight, 'Why is there no International Theory', in H. Butterfield and M. Wight (eds), *Diplomatic Investigations: Essays in the Theory of International Politics* (London, 1966a), p. 33.
2. Wight (1966a), p. 26.
3. M. Wight, 'Western Values in International Relations', in H. Butterfield and M. Wight (eds), *Diplomatic Investigations: Essays in the Theory of International Politics*, (London, 1966b), p. 91.
4. A. Watson, 'Hedley Bull, States Systems and International Societies', *Review of International Studies*, 13 (1987), p. 151.
5. J. D. B. Miller, 'The Third World', in J. D. B. Miller and R. J. Vincent (eds), *Order and Violence: Hedley Bull and International Relations* (Oxford, 1990), pp. 77–80.
6. Buzan, B., 'From International System to International Society: Structural Realism and Regime Theory Meet the English School', *International Organization*, 47 (1993), 335–52.
7. Watson (1987), p. 151.
8. M. Wight, *Systems of States* (Leicester, 1977), p. 192.
9. Ibid. p. 43.
10. Ibid., pp. 35–9.
11. Ibid., p. 33.
12. Ibid., pp. 33–5.
13. H. Bull, *The Anarchical Society: A Study of Order in World Politics* (London, 1977), p. 82.
14. Ibid., pp. 9–10.
15. Ibid., p. 13.
16. R. J. Vincent, 'Edmund Burke and the Theory of International Relations', *Review of International Studies*, 10 (1984), p. 213.

17. Ibid., p. 316.
18. Ibid., p. 317.
19. Ibid., pp. 53–5.
20. H. Suganami, *The Domestic Analogy and World Order Proposals* (Cambridge, 1989).
21. Bull (1977), p. 133.
22. Ibid., pp. 16–20.
23. A. Linklater, 'Liberal Democracy, Constitutionalism and the New World Order', in R. Leaver and J. L. Richardson (eds), *Charting the Post-Cold War Order* (Colorado, 1993).
24. M. Wight, 'The Balance of Power and International Order', in A. James (ed), *The Bases of International Order: Essays in Memory of C. A. W. Manning* (London, 1973), pp. 96–97.
25. Wight (1966b), p. 91.
26. Wight (1973), p. 111.
27. H. Bull *et al.* (eds) *Hugo Grotius and International Relations* (Oxford, 1990), pp. 73–4.
28. K. Waltz, *Theory of International Politics* (New York, 1979).
29. M. Doyle, 'Liberalism and World Politics', *American Political Science Review*, 80, 1986, 1151–69.
30. Wight (1977), p. 153; author's italics.
31. H. Bull and A. Watson (eds), *The Expansion of International Society* (Oxford, 1984), p. 9.
32. H. Bull, 'The Grotian Conception of International Society', in H. Butterfield and M. Wight (eds), *Diplomatic Investigations: Essays in the Theory of International Politics* (London, 1966b), p. 52.
33. Ibid., p. 64.
34. Ibid., p. 52.
35. Ibid., p. 68.
36. Bull 1977, p. 73.
37. Ibid., pp. 16–18 and ch.4.
38. Ibid., pp. 227–8.
39. Ibid., p. 89.
40. Ibid., p. 126; H. Bull, 'Human Rights and World Politics', in R. Pettman (ed.), *Moral Claims in World Affairs* (London, 1979a), p. 90.
41. Bull (1977), p. 22.
42. Ibid., p. 289.
43. Ibid., p. 83.
44. H. Bull, *The Hagey Lectures*, University of Waterloo (1984).
45. R. J. Vincent, Human Rights and International Relations (Cambridge, 1986).
46. R. J. Vincent, and P. Wilson, 'Beyond Non-Intervention', in I. Forbes and M. Hoffman (eds), *Political Theory, International Relations and the Ethics of Intervention* (London, 1994), pp. 128–9.
47. Wight (1977), p. 41.

48. H. Bull, 'The West and South Africa', *Daedalus*, 11, 1982, p. 266.
49. Bull (1977), p. 95.
50. Watson (1987), p. 152.
51. H. Bull, 'The International Anarchy in the 1980s', *Australian Outlook*, 37 (1983), pp. 127–31.
52. Bull (1977), p. 317.
53. Bull (1984), p. 6.
54. Bull and Watson (1984), p. 87.
55. Bull (1977), p. 14.
56. G. Gong, *The Standard of Civilisation in International Society* (Oxford, 1984).
57. Bull and Watson (1984), pp. 220–4.
58. Ibid., p. 223.
59. S. Huntington, 'The Clash of Civilisations', *Foreign Affairs*, 72 (1993), pp. 22–49.
60. F. Fukuyama, *The End of History and the Last Man* (London, 1992).
61. C. Brown, 'The Modern Requirement: Reflections on Normative International Theory in a Post-European World', *Millennium*, 17 (1988), pp. 339–48.
62. Bull and Watson (1984), p. 435.
63. Ibid, p. 429.
64. Bull (1977), pp. 316–17.
65. Bull (1984), p. 18.
66. R. J. Vincent, 'Order in International Politics', in J. D. B. Miller and R. J. Vincent (eds), *Order and Violence: Hedley Bull and International Relations* (Oxford, 1990), pp. 41–4.
67. P. Keal, *Unspoken Rules and Superpower Dominance* (London, 1983), ch.8.
68. Ibid., p. 210.
69. Ibid.
70. G. B. Helman, and S. R. Ratner, 'Saving Failed States', *Foreign Policy*, 89 (1992–93), pp. 3–20.
71. R. Jackson, *Quasi-States: Sovereignty, International Relations and the Third World* (Cambridge, 1990).
72. Vincent (1994); N. Wheeler, 'Order, Justice, Statecraft and Humanitarian Intervention', unpublished paper, 1994.
73. A. Roberts, 'Humanitarian War: Military Intervention and Human Rights', *International Affairs*, 69 (1993), p. 449.
74. Wight (1966a), p. 26; Waltz (1979), p. 66.
75. Bull (1984), p. 18.
76. M. Wight, *International Theory: The Three Traditions* (Leicester, 1991), p. 159.
77. Ibid., p. 158.
78. Ibid., p. 160.
79. Bull (1984), pp. 11–12.
80. Ibid.
81. Ibid, p. 13.
82. Ibid, p. 14.
83. Vincent (1994), p. 129.

84. Ibid., p. 124.
85. Bull (1977), p. 267.
86. Ibid., pp. 254–5.
87. Ibid., p. 255.
88. H. Bull, 'The State's Positive Role in World Affairs', *Daedalus*, 108 (1979b), pp. 111–24.
89. Bull (1977), p. 26.
90. Ibid., p. 26.
91. S. Hoffmann, 'International Society', in J. D. B. Miller and R. J. Vincent (eds), *Order and Violence: Hedley Bull and International Relations* (Oxford, 1990), pp. 23–4; Harris, I. 'Order and Justice in the Anarchical Society', *International Affairs*, 69 (1993), p. 738.
92. Wight (1991), pp. 41–2.
93. Ibid., p. 29.
94. Ibid., p. 73.
95. I. Kant, *Perpetual Peace*, in M. G. Forsyth *et al.* (eds), *The Theory of International Relations: Selected Texts from Gentili to Treitschke* (London, 1970), p. 206.
96. Kant (1970), p. 215.
97. H. Bull, 'The Theory of International Politics, 1919–1969', in B. Porter (ed.), *The Aberystwyth Papers* (London, 1969), pp. 42–3.
98. H. Bull, 'International Theory: The Case for a Classical Approach', in *World Politics*, 18 (1966a), 361–77, p. 365.
99. Wight (1991), pp. 120 and 248.
100. H. Bull, 'Foreign Policy of Australia', in *Proceedings of Australian Institute of Political Science* (Sydney, 1973), p. 137.
101. N. Wheeler and T. Dunne 'Hedley Bull's Pluralism of the Intellect and Solidarism of the Will', unpublished paper, 1994.
102. J. George, *Discourses of Global Politics: A Critical (Re)Introduction to International Relations* (Boulder, 1994), pp. 80–2.
103. R. Shapcott, 'Conversation and Co-existence: Gadamer and the Interpretation of International Society', Millennium, 23 (1994), pp. 57–83.
104. A. Linklater, *Men and Citizens in the Theory of International Relations* (2nd edn, London, 1990).
105. A. Linklater, 'The Achievents of Critical Theory', in S. Smith *et al.* (eds) *After Positivism* (Cambridge, 1995).
106. E. H. Carr, *The Twenty Years' Crisis 1919–1939* (London, 1949) p. 12.
107. Vincent (1990), p. 48.

CHAPTER 5

Marxism

Andrew Linklater

In the mid-1840s Marx believed that the expansion of capitalism was eliminating the classical divisions between sovereign nation-states and replacing the international states-system with a world capitalist society in which the principal form of conflict was centred on two antagonistic social classes: the bourgeoisies of the world and the international proletariat. Marx was confident at that juncture that political revolution would overthrow the capitalist order and create a world socialist society in which the principles of freedom and equality enshrined in capitalist ideology but frustrated by capitalist structures would be realised to improve the circumstances of human beings everywhere.

Until quite recently the essence of the Marxist approach to international relations was thought to be contained in these few propositions. Rationalists such as Hedley Bull regarded Marxism as a form of revolutionist thought whose focus on the allegedly horizontal clash between two great social movements wholly underestimated the tenacity of the nation-state and the robust structure of international society.[1] Earlier Martin Wight had maintained that Lenin's *Imperialism: The Highest Stage of Capitalism* seemed to deal with relations between societies but was too concerned with the economic aspects of human life, as was the Marxist tradition more generally, to deserve to be taken seriously as a work of International Relations.[2]

In recent years more subtle and sophisticated interpretations of Marxism have circulated within International Relations. A more balanced view of the strengths and weaknesses of Marxism has replaced the stereotypical representations of the doctrine which once prevailed.[3] Marxism remains an essential resource in the literature which is concerned with developing a critical theory of international relations. Its impact is also clearly evident in efforts to construct a political economy of international relations which analyses the interplay between states and markets, the states-system and the capitalist world economy, the spheres of power and production. The relevance of Marxism for the present epoch has increased with the passing of the age of bipolarity and with the heightened impact of globalization and ethnic fragmentation on contemporary state structures and international affairs. As already noted, Marxism was intrigued by the processes which are unifying the human race – by globalization in the current parlance – and rightly identified capitalism as the main driving force behind the unprecedented level of international interdependence. Yet capitalism accelerated and dramatized a process with a long prehistory and Marx in particular was keen to stress how commerce and conquest had steadily widened the sphere of human interaction and intercourse in pre-capitalist epochs. Marx's writings therefore analysed the processes by which human beings moved beyond small-scale societies which were estranged from one another, came to be entangled in an alienating world economic system and finally reached the threshold of a universal socialist society committed to upholding the freedom and equality of all.

In the study of international relations Marx's enthusiastic prediction of the unification of the whole human race in one socialist society has often been criticized for neglecting the deeper logic of fragmentation powered by the endless rivalries between nation-states. The anticipation of universal socialism was dismissed for its utopianism by the realists. That the Marxist tradition was slow to appreciate the continuing importance of the nation-state and violence is beyond doubt but key strands of Marxist thought identified national fragmentation as the essential counterpart of capitalist globalization.[4] Indeed the tension between globalization and fragmentation which is at the heart of much contemporary thinking about international relations was crucial in the thinking of Marx and Engels and it has remained central in later Marxist reflections on nationalism, imperialism and the stratified capitalist world-system.[5] In this context it is imperative to reconsider Marxism, to appreciate its considerable strengths and learn from its undoubted weaknesses in order to develop the critical theory of world politics.

The analysis of globalization and fragmentation in the Marxist tradition is anchored in the paradigm of class and production and many have argued that its reductionist focus upon the economic dimensions of social existence prevented a deeper understanding of the main contours of modern history and hindered the development of a normatively and politically sound response to the problems of world politics. To assess the value of Marxism in the light of these accusations Part I of this chapter outlines the key elements in the doctrine of historical materialism and describes how Marx and Engels developed their views of international relations within this framework. Part II considers the Marxist literature on nationalism and imperialism. Part III offers a brief overview of the orthodox critique of Marxism within the field of International Relations and explains its rehabilitation in the 1980s as political economy and critical theory acquired prominence within the field. Part IV considers the place of Marxism in the light of some recent developments in the theory of international relations. The conclusion offers some brief comments about the principal strengths and weaknesses of Marxist approaches to international relations.

I Class, Production and International Relations in Marx and Engels' Writings

Human history for Marx is a laborious struggle to satisfy basic material needs, to understand and tame natural forces, to gain control over alienating and exploitative social systems and to overcome estrangement from the members of other societies. Human history entails the conquest of forces beyond human understanding and control, the elimination of superstition, fear and ignorance, the abolition of crippling material scarcity in the context of exploitation and the creation of a society in which human beings are free to develop a range of creative powers possessed by no other species. Human history unfolds tragically, enhancing the collective power of society *vis-à-vis* the natural world but simultaneously placing individuals within the confines of an international social division of labour, an unregulated world market and networks of class subordination which diminish their lives and limit their freedom. Alienation describes the condition in which the human race is at the mercy of the structures and forces which are its own creation. Exploitation refers to the condition in which particular groups directly control and profit from the labour-power of others. Estrangement describes the world of suspicion and hostility between separate national or cultural groups. Transforming global society to eradicate alienation, exploitation and estrangement has been the fundamental political aspiration of the Marxist tradition.

Marx and Engels believed that the impact of production upon the structure of society and the shifting patterns of history had been seriously neglected in earlier strands of political theory. Their thought was specifically concerned with correcting the idealist modes of explanation present within Hegelian thinking which considered the multitudinous images of self, society and history through which the human race had passed in its long struggle to characterize and comprehend itself. The Left Hegelians believed that religious alienation was the chief instance of human ignorance and superstition but, for Marx, religion did not reveal an error in cognition but expressed frustrations and aspirations born from the everyday material existence of human beings. Since, as Marx put it, religion was the 'sigh of an oppressed creature' the critical-theoretical project had to address the deeper social relations and material conditions which were at the root of human misery.

The pivotal theme in Marxist thought is that throughout history human beings have acted on the physical world within exploitative class-based societies in which the mass of humanity has been compelled to labour for the enrichment of others. Class antagonism has been the dominant form of conflict in history and the engine of social transformation. Through their labour human beings have modified the natural environment but they have also produced themselves as a species by developing unique powers and needs. Marx believed that the species had been formed by passing through a series of modes of production and forms of class struggle which destroyed the isolation of societies and finally brought the whole human race within the grim confines of global capitalism. The universalizing processes inherent in capitalism enabled the great mass of humanity – led by the industrial proletariat – to mobilize to realise the promise of freedom contained within capitalist ideology. The conquest of nature produced by capitalist technological development created the real possibility that human beings could enter 'a kingdom of freedom' in which they would escape laborious work and enjoy the social and economic conditions in which they would be able to cultivate the full range of their creative powers. Marxism sought to understand the expanding circle of human interconnectedness and, crucially, the deep forces which frustrated the extension of human sociability.[6] To release the potential for universal co-operation and freedom which had been so greatly expanded by capitalism it was essential to bring an end to class-divided societies. The continuous technological revolution which had occurred under capitalism could then become the agent of human emancipation rather than the instrument of capitalist accumulation.

Clearly Marx and Engels were not concerned with developing simply a disengaged sociological description of the history of modes of production. Although they declined to rest their analysis on explicitly moral claims, their chief purpose was to give sociological explanation a critical purpose.[7] This purpose is most clearly illustrated in the introductory remarks to *The Eighteenth Brumaire of Louis Bonaparte* where Marx argued that human beings make their own history but not under conditions of their own choosing.[8] Humans make their own history because they possess the power of self-determination which other species do not possess, but they do not make history just as they please because they act within terrible constraints inherited from the past. For Marx human beings emerged from the animal kingdom and their capacity for self-determination evolved from a complex process of species development, as did their comprehension of how the social and natural environment constrained their freedom and might be changed. Early societies were unaware that social arrangements were their own product and were capable of being reformed. Yet the history of the formation of the species which is a history of the labour process reveals the development of the capacity and desire to transform social arrangements so that human beings can realize their potential for greater self-determination.

The meaning of history is the quest for freedom and the purpose of understanding society is to show how its further development is possible – hence Marx's immensely important observation in the *Theses on Feuerbach* that the philosophers have only interpreted the world whereas the significant point is to change it.[9]

Marx and Engels echoed Kant's conviction that the effort to realize freedom within the state would be shattered by the sudden impact of unpredictable and calamitous external events. Like Kant they believed that in the new circumstances of globalization human freedom could only be realized by developing a system of universal co-operation. They were not especially concerned with international relations understood as relations between states but with capitalist globalization which introduced the social conditions in which higher levels of freedom could be possessed by the whole of humanity. For Marx and Engels globalization has not been produced by relations between states but by the internal dynamics of the dominant capitalist system of production. They noted the importance of relations between states in the past and the role of conquest in creating larger political associations but they concluded that globalization under capitalism overshadowed the role played by relations between states in the period in which they were writing. Although it was accompanied by many profound weaknesses which will be considered below, this emphasis upon the revolutionary impact of capitalist globalization upon human society is one of their main contributions to the history of international thought.[10]

Some of the most striking passages in Marx and Engels' writings reveal the importance of inside-out analysis for their explanation of the unprecedented integration of the species in the age of capitalism. The essence of capitalism is to 'strive to tear down every barrier to intercourse', to 'conquer the whole earth for its market' and to annihilate the tyranny of distance by reducing 'to a minimum the time spent in motion from óne place to another'.[11] For Marx and Engels analysing the bourgeois system of production reveals the rhythm and direction of global change. In *The Communist Manifesto* they argued that:

> The bourgeoisie has through its exploitation of the world-market given a cosmopolitan character to production and consumption in every country . . . In place of the old local and national seclusion and self-sufficiency, we have intercourse in every direction, universal interdependence of nations . . . National one-sidedness and narrow-mindedness become more and more impossible, and from the numerous national and local literatures, there arises a world literature . . . The bourgeoisie . . . draws all, even the most barbarian nations, into civilisation. The cheap prices of its commodities are the heavy artillery with which it batters down all Chinese walls, with which it forces the barbarians' intensely obstinate hatred of foreigners to capitulate. It compels all nations, on pain of extinction, to adopt the bourgeois mode of production . . . In one word, it creates a world after its own image.[12]

Globalization had very definite implications for revolutionary strategy. According to Marx's early writings 'nationality is already dead' among the proletariat but the world remains divided into nation-states and the bourgeoisie of each nation retains control of the repressive apparatus of the state. In *The Communist Manifesto*, Marx and Engels maintained that the proletariat must first settle scores with the national bourgeoisie. But only the form of the revolutionary struggle is national and transforming global society was the paramount goal.[13]

It may therefore appear that the explanation of globalization replaced the analysis of international relations in Marx and Engels' thought. Three points need to be made in this context. First, there is little doubt that in the period up to 1848 Marx and Engels believed that the classical world of statecraft and diplomacy was being dismantled forever by advancing capitalist globalization. Second, the importance of nationalism in the 1848 revolutions and its widening appeal later in the century forced Marx and Engels to reconsider their initial point of departure and led Engels in particular to reflect deeply on the role of war in history and its potential for accelerating the transition from capitalism to socialism. Third, despite the reconsideration of war and international relations towards the end of the century, Marxism failed to appreciate the significance of this domain for its critical orientation to society and politics. The upshot was that Marxism failed to broaden its range to analyse the manifold patterns of alienation, exploitation and estrangement based on ethnicity, race and gender as well as class which block the development of universal co-operation and freedom. Each point is worth considering in turn.

First, Marx and Engels displayed a penchant for endogenous explanations of society since, for the most part, they thought that societies were relatively bounded entities moved by internal logics of change.[14] They did not deny the importance of relations between states although Marx argued that these were of secondary or tertiary importance when compared with the dynamics issuing from spheres of production.[15] Globalization and the relatively peaceful nature of the international system in the middle of the nineteenth century meant that the economy and society rather than the state and war became the principal object of analysis.[16] Theories of society and the economy displaced theories of the state. Marxism reflected the dominant tendency of the epoch. In a letter to Annenkov Marx posed the question of whether 'the whole organisation of nations, and all their international relations [is] anything else than the expression of a particular division of labour. And must not these change when the division of labour changes?'.[17] This analytic focus seemed to discount the possibility of exploring the state and violence as autonomous forces in human history.

Turning to the second point, the resurgence of nationalism nevertheless provoked some serious rethinking on their part. Marx and Engels recognized that the Irish and the Poles were the victims of national as opposed to class oppression and proceeded to argue that freedom from national dominance was the necessary first step which these nationalist movements would have to take before close involvement with the international proletarian movement would become possible.[18] This theme that national liberation from colonial and neo-colonial rule may be the prelude to socialist internationalism has been a primary theme in twentieth-century Marxism although in a more radical departure some influential strands of Third World Marxism tended to favour nationalism rather than internationalism on the grounds that the struggle against national domination has replaced the struggle against class domination in importance.[19]

These reflections on nationalism demonstrated Marx and Engels' efforts to respond not only to capitalist alienation and exploitation but to the older phenomenon of estrangement between national groups. Similar revisions were prompted by the growing threat of violence between states in the last few years of the nineteenth century. Engels' writings emphasised the role of war throughout human history, anticipated unprecedented suffering in the next major interstate conflict and asserted that war rather than capitalist crisis might be the spark to ignite the proletarian revolution. These writings also stressed the need for the socialist movement to reflect on matters of national security and to take the defence of the homeland seriously.[20]

Third, these developments reveal that Marx and Engels had begun to consider the significance of the tenacity of national communities and the continuing and deepening estrangement between national groups for socialist theory and practice. But as Gallie has noted, these intriguing comments about nationalism, the state and war did not lead to a systematic recasting of the early statements about historical materialism which continued to stress the centrality of class and production and reaffirmed the belief that the task of transforming society was primarily one of eradicating class domination. What was required was a new historical sociology alert to the existence of the multiple tracks of social and political development. An unhelpful distinction between the economic base of society and the legal, political and ideological superstructure should have been laid to rest. This distinction presented the state as a passive instrument of ruling class forces which could only acquire the power of independent initiative under extraordinary historical circumstances. Marx and Engels developed a profound analysis of capitalist alienation but failed to reflect systematically on other axes of alienation, exploitation and estrangement in global society. A more comprehensive account of the constraints on extending human co-operation and autonomy would have contained more systematic reflections on estrangement between national groups and alienation in international relations – alienation in that the world of statecraft is, like capitalism, humanly-produced but eludes communal control.[21]

As a mode of sociological inquiry Marxism needed to bring the world of bounded communities within its field of vision and as a critical sociology committed to the goal of human emancipation it was necessary to reflect deeply on what role, if any, bounded national communities might play in improving human society. Engels' comments on the need for socialists to accept the principle of defending the homeland invited awkward questions about whether internationalism could be advanced at all by states which are constrained by domestic class structures and a powerful global economy. These vital questions were simply not asked. In addition, Marx and Engels were notoriously vague about whether or not national differences and groupings would flourish – indeed survive at all – in the future world socialist society.[22]

A more subtle and complex response to capitalist globalization and national differences emerged in the writings of the Austro-Marxists. Writing at the beginning of the twentieth century the Austro-Marxists such as Karl Renner and Otto Bauer argued that Marx and Engels greatly underestimated the importance of cultural differences in history and the strength of national identity in the modern world.[23] The Austro-Marxists defended the cosmopolitan ideal found in earlier Marxist texts but they envisaged a socialist world order in which national groupings would have an influential role. They developed Marx's key insights by arguing that the achievement of higher levels of human co-operation and freedom required not only the abolition of capitalist forms of alienation and exploitation but also the supersession of estrangement between different national-cultural groups.

In the Austro-Marxist writings the political response to the twin forces of globalization and fragmentation advocated higher levels of universality and difference than the citizens of capitalist states had ever known – higher indeed than the citizens of the future socialist society might enjoy if the dominant visions of socialism were realized. These were controversial proposals to which we shall return but they were among the more promising ways of ensuring the continuing dynamism of Marxism as a mode of critical theory. With the emergence of Marxism–Leninism in the Soviet Union, what Alvin Gouldner once described as the anomalies, contradictions and latent possibilities within the Marxist tradition gave way to a closed, quasi-scientific system of supposed truths which suppressed the latent potential for further development and growth.[24] Numerous encrustations formed around the doctrine, as Perry Anderson noted in his overview of Marxism in the early 1980s, but earlier themes about capitalist globalization and national fragmentation were taken further in interesting ways in the literature on nationalism and imperialism.[25]

II   Nationalism and Imperialism

Although Marx and Engels were primarily interested in the sphere of domestic class relations and modes of production they analysed the movement towards the economic and technological unification of the human race and raised key questions about the relationship between centrifugal and centripetal processes, especially in the context of modern capitalism. Their analysis of globalization and fragmentation identified stages in the evolution of the social bond which ties members of a society together and separates them from the rest of the world.[26] Within this philosophy of history early capitalism was understood to have forged a scattered population with local loyalties into a single nation sharing a common territory. In its early phase capitalism created national bonds which inhibited the formation of class identifications and loyalties but, as it matured, capitalism tore these national bonds apart and created the possibility of internationalist sentiments and alliances among the proletariat. These early assumptions about the intimate relationship between capitalism and internationalism had to be rethought in the light of the revival of nationalism and the drift towards inter-state war at the end of the nineteenth century.

Lenin and Bukharin developed the theory of imperialism to explain the causes of the First World War.[27] They argued that the war was caused by the urgent need for outlets for surplus capital which had accumulated within the most powerful capitalist states. The theory of capitalist imperialism has been discredited but often the accusation of economic reductionism has overlooked its tentative efforts to explain the closure of political communities in the early twentieth century.[28] Interpreted in this way the Marxist doctrine of imperialism developed Marx and Engels' observations about the intensification of exclusionary national bonds and the apparent demise of internationalism.

The theory of imperialism provided a critique of the liberal proposition that late capitalism necessarily encouraged free trade strategies and fostered peaceful interdependence between nations. Lenin and Bukharin argued that the dominant tendency of the age destroyed *laissez-faire* ideology and created new mercantilist states which were increasingly willing to use force to achieve their economic and political objectives. The accumulation of surplus capital was stressed as the primary cause of the decline of a relatively peaceful international climate but Lenin argued that other factors including the decline of British hegemony and the emergence of a new configuration of military power had contributed, albeit to a secondary degree, to weakening the constraints on the use of force in international relations.

Lenin and Bukharin argued that class loyalties and class antagonisms lost their centrality in this epoch as a result of the increased power of nationalist and militarist ideologies. In *Imperialism: The Highest Stage of Capitalism* Lenin argued that no 'Chinese wall separates the [working class] from the other classes' not least because of the existence of a labour aristocracy bribed by colonial profits to align itself with the bourgeoisie.[29] Consequently with the outbreak of the First World War the working classes, which had become 'chained to the chariot of . . . bourgeois state power' immediately rallied to the call to defend the homeland.[30] Yet the shift of the 'centre of gravity' from class conflict to inter-state rivalry would not last indefinitely and the horrors of war would demonstrate to the working classes that their 'share in the imperialist policy is nothing compared with the wounds inflicted by the war'.[31] Instead of 'clinging to the narrowness of the national state' and of being seduced by the patriotic ideal of 'defending or extending the boundaries of the bourgeois state' the proletariat would resume its class project of 'abolishing state boundaries and merging all the peoples into one Socialist family'.[32]

The fact that capitalism created the preconditions for the extension of community from the nation to the species had been a dominant theme in Marx and Engels' thought. Clearly Lenin and Bukharin argued that the prising apart of national boundaries and the rediscovery of cosmopolitan aspirations would occur albeit after a brief digression along the disastrous path of nationalism and war. Although placed within a conceptual framework which exaggerated the importance of production and the supposed superabundance of finance capital their remarks on the tenacity of the nation-state and the greater possibility of inter-state war after several decades of relative peace dealt with the intriguing question of how the interplay between universalizing forces and particularistic identities shaped the boundaries of political communities and influenced their interaction.[33]

Deep tensions between the agents of universalization and particularistic loyalties are equally important in the Marxist analysis of nationalism. Lenin argued that globalization and fragmentation were two sides of the coin of capitalist development: 'Developing capitalism knows two historical tendencies in the national question. The first is the awakening of national life and national movements, the struggle against all national oppression, and the creation of national states. The second is the development and growing frequency of international intercourse in every form, the breakdown of national barriers, the creation of the international unity of capital, of economic life in general, of politics, science etc'.[34] Lenin's explanation of nationalism emphasized the uneven development of world capitalism in which the metropolitan core exploited the periphery which responded in the form of national struggles for independence.

Lenin recognized that particular groups such as the Jews were oppressed by virtue of their religion or ethnicity and that the politics of national self-determination was their unsurprising riposte. Estrangement between national groups was therefore taken seriously as a phenomenon inhibiting freedom and co-operation. Although Lenin believed that socialist support for the national struggle was vital to win the respect of nationalist movements he firmly opposed the Austro-Marxist federalist approach to national cultures which proposed to grant minorities real autonomy within existing nation-states. National movements, in Lenin's thought, should choose between complete secession and continued membership of the state. Most, he thought, would opt for the latter because small-scale societies would be unable to generate the levels of economic growth which were possible in large capitalist states. Those movements which opted for secession would free themselves from the international conditions which had generated national animosity and distrust. New circumstances would result in which alliances between different national proletariats would then become possible. The compromise with nationalism was designed to avoid 'adapting socialism to nationalism' and dividing the proletariat into 'separate national rivulets'.[35] The literature on nationalism and imperialism recognized that capitalist globalization brought about national fragmentation. But so powerful was the emphasis on class inequality that the cosmopolitanism espoused by the leading Marxists – Austro-Marxism aside – failed to issue an adequate response to claims for the recognition of cultural differences.

Marx's belief that capitalism would bring industrialization to the world as a whole was later echoed in the theory of imperialism. Lenin's analysis of capitalist globalization embodied the prevalent assumption in the nineteenth century that the West would remake the non-Western world entirely in its own image. Alternative possibilities were advanced in Trotsky's law of combined and uneven development, which maintained that new social formations would arise from the encounter between the capitalist and pre-capitalist worlds.[36] More recent theories of imperialism have developed this theme. Dependency theory in the writings of Gunder Frank argued that the alliance between the dominant class interests in the core and the periphery obstructed the economic development of peripheral regions.[37] Only the act of national secession from the world capitalist economy would give peripheral societies the capacity to industrialize autonomously. World-systems theory as developed by Wallerstein also denies that capitalism brings about the industrialization of the world as a whole.[38] The world-systems perspective stresses the role of peripheral and semi-peripheral states and movements in challenging the political principles of the capitalist world economy and the cultural hegemony of Western scientific culture. These approaches are often described as neo-Marxist because they deny that capitalism has the inevitable developmental impact which Western Marxism once imputed to it.

Neo-Marxist approaches also argue that capitalism brings all societies within a single world history yet fosters nationalist revolts against economic exploitation and inequality.[39] Recent neo-Marxist commentaries reiterate the Marxist theme that uneven capitalist development engenders fierce nationalist resentments and they frequently regard the national revolt as more important than the struggle between social classes.[40] Support for national movements has created considerable controversy between neo-Marxists and classical Marxists, who fear the abandonment of the internationalist legacy. Although lamenting past failures to take national domination seriously many Marxists have doubted whether support for national secession is compatible with the aim of creating a universal society.[41] Marxism framed its cosmopolitanism in an age of Western ascendancy when it seemed safe to assume that the non-European world would imitate Western forms of modernisation. The observation that world history is not Western history writ large is true of cultural shifts as well as models of economic development and many non-European societies clearly reject the emphasis on individualism, materialism and secularism within Western societies. The complexity of the exchange between Western and non-Western societies demonstrates not only that internationalization and internationalism are different phenomena[42] but that serious doubts about the virtues of cosmopolitanism arise in the transition to the post-European age.[43]

III   The Place of Marxism in International Relations

To recapitulate the argument thus far: Marxist approaches to international relations reflected on the processes which have unified the human race and stressed the unprecedented role of capitalism in this development. The dominant strands of thought analysed the prospects for replacing alienation, exploitation and estrangement with a system of universal co-operation and freedom. In Marx's and Engels' early writings the international proletariat was assigned the leading role in promoting this transition but the prospects for universal social co-operation had to be reviewed in the light of rising nationalism and the drift towards war in Europe. The question of nationalism has remained at the heart of more recent Marxist accounts of core exploitation of the periphery in the world economy. The idea of a global revolutionary proletariat has been abandoned. Marxism remains concerned with the classical agenda of alienation, exploitation and estrangement although the commitment to a cosmopolitan society no longer unifies its many branches.

Until recently, the study of international relations and realism especially was deeply sceptical of Marxist modes of explanation and harshly critical of the moral commitment to socialist internationalism. The realist tradition has long argued that Marx and Marxism stressed how societies interact with nature but overlooked the basic reality of their strategic and political interaction with each other. According to realists Marxism was preoccupied with the dynamics of capitalism and neglected the vital trilogy of nationalism, the state and war. Its vision of an international socialist society failed to realize how the struggle for power and security in the context of anarchy could destroy its preferred economistic mode of analysis and its moral vision of a community of humankind committed to realizing socialism.[44]

The interpretation of Marxism as a legitimate influence within the field has therefore had to surmount deep resistance, especially from realists and neo-realists. Realists denied that capitalism would unify the world in the manner predicted by Marxists and rejected the claim that a global revolutionary proletariat could emerge in a world divided into separate nation-states. Waltz argued that if the nation-state was the vessel in which socialism developed then socialists would first have to ensure its survival.[45] Trotsky's claim that he would issue a few revolutionary proclamations as Commissar for Foreign Affairs before closing shop has frequently been cited as evidence of a serious failure to grasp the allegedly perennial characteristics of the international system of states. The pace with which Marxism in power succumbed to traditional methods of diplomacy to maintain the survival and security of the nation-state reinforced realist views. Stalin's pact with Hitler and abandonment of the Chinese Communists in the inter-war years when the Soviet Union required a viable, if anti-communist, China to balance the growing military power of Japan strengthened the realist's conviction that anarchy repeatedly dashes the reformist aspirations of nation-states. Instead of transforming the international system Marxism was transformed by it. Instead of acting as an agent of the transformation of the international system Marxism became an instrument of its reproduction. The Soviet domination of Eastern Europe, for example, fostered the nationalist aim of acquiring sovereign independence. Border disputes between China and the Soviet Union, the Vietnamese invasion of Cambodia and the war between China and Vietnam further demonstrated the failure of Marxism to make a significant dent upon the international system of states.[46]

Realism identified one of the fundamental weaknesses in Marxist thought, which was its reductionist interpretation of the state. Too often Marxists stressed the role which the state played in protecting ruling class interests from external competitors and subordinate classes. What they underestimated was the importance of the state's monopoly control of the instruments of violence and its ability to act autonomously of class forces in the course of pacifying society, resisting external threats and preparing for, and participating in, war. During the 1960s and 1970s Marxist writers began to deal with earlier omissions by acknowledging the autonomy of the state but often they regarded the relative autonomy of the state as a functional requirement of capitalism. Without the restraining hand of the state, they argued, the ruling class would exploit human labour to the extent that the long-term survival of capitalism would be placed in jeopardy. These efforts to revise Marxism ultimately failed because they relied on an endogenous account of the state and its behaviour. Locating the state in international anarchy and emphasizing the significance of competition and conflict between states was the more radical step required to answer the critics, and in the 1970s and 1980s the Marxist literature conceded the point that Marxism had to rethink its assumptions about nationalism, the state and war.[47] The writings of Anderson, Block, Brucan, Nairn and Skocpol were influential in redirecting Marxism away from the orthodox focus upon the state's location in the mode of production towards an appreciation of its additional position within the international system of states.[48]

The need to reconstruct critical theory in the light of this reassessment of the nation-state and violence figured prominently in the sociological literature and particularly in the work of Giddens who argued that critical theory had to address the separate but interrelated logics of state-building, geopolitics, capitalist development and industrialization.[49] Earlier, Habermas, the foremost critical theorist of modern times, embarked on reconstructing historical materialism and revising the emancipatory project of Marxism. Habermas's principal claim was that Marx and Marxism had believed that technical-instrumental learning (learning how to master natural forces and increase technological power) was the essential prerequisite for the establishment of socialism. What this neglected according to Habermas was the independent sphere of moral-practical learning in which human beings develop the ethical skill of creating social orders which command the consent of human agents.[50] Such efforts to rearticulate the critical project within a modified Marxism or post-Marxist framework recall the Frankfurt School's plea for 'a movement to a new problematic, in the tradition of Marx and his spirit, but not of his word' or for the transition to a new standpoint which is no longer 'simply Marxist'.[51] In this new problematic greater importance was attached to nationalism, the state and war.

While Marxism was being redefined in the light of themes which are at the core of realism the classical study of international relations was being reconsidered to take account of themes which have long been vital to Marxism. Growing disenchantment with the explanatory range and moral stance of realism was the primary reason for the reassessment of Marxism within the field. The first major challenge to realism occurred in the 1970s as liberal international political economy began to focus on the rise of transnational relations and global interdependence. Apart from taking issue with realist explanation liberal international political economy contested realist pessimism by emphasising the declining utility of force and the greater role for multilateral diplomacy and global institutions.[52] The analysis of global patterns of social and economic change linked with a muted normative interest in the possibilities for alternative principles of international relations created an environment which was more receptive to Marxist approaches and ideas.

Writers influenced by radical approaches to international political economy, including dependency theory, argued that the analysts of interdependence overlooked the unequal distribution of wealth within the capitalist world-system. The study of global inequality was the initial conduit for the admission of Marxist approaches into the study of international relations. Subsequent developments argued that Marxism was significant not only for the question of dependency and development (which tended to limit its significance to the realm of North–South relations) but for the entire field. The key point is made by Halliday, who argues that 'the modern inter-state system emerged in the context of the spread of capitalism across the globe, and the subjugation of pre-capitalist societies. This socio-economic system has underpinned both the character of individual states and of their relations with each other: no analysis of international relations is possible without reference to capitalism, the social formations it generated and the world system they comprise'.[53] Although Marxism neglected the realm of strategic interaction between states, realism abstracted this domain from the wider context of global social and economic change shaped by modern capitalism.

Robert Cox's attempt to supersede conventional international relations theory by focusing upon the interactions between social forces, states and world orders is the most ambitious attempt to use historical materialism within the discipline. Cox traces the development of modes of production, states and the world system, stressing how production shapes other realms such as strategic interaction and is shaped by them. Particular emphasis is placed in Cox's writings upon the internationalization of relations of production, on the rise of a global as opposed to an international economy and upon the forms of global hegemony combining coercion and consent which perpetuate inequalities of power and wealth. The notion of global hegemony has been developed further in the emerging neo-Gramscian school of international political economy.[54] Global hegemony exists when 'the dominant state and dominant social forces sustain their position through adherence to universalised principles which are accepted or acquiesced in by a sufficient proportion of subordinate states and social forces'.[55] Global hegemony operates through alliances between elites in core and industrializing societies and through the mechanisms of control afforded by global economic and political institutions.[56] By claiming that a system of transnational governance already exists the approach rejects the opposition between anarchy and hierarchy which is fundamental to neo-realism.[57]

By seeking to identify counter-hegemonic forces (nationalist movements, socialist groups and cultural movements) within the global order the neo-Gramscian perspective challenges the neo-realist claim that explaining the reproduction of international anarchy is the primary task of international theory. Cox's writings therefore link international political economy with critical social theory. In an oft-quoted passage Cox argued that knowledge is always for someone and for some purpose: it is never value-free.[58] Two forms of knowledge are identified in Cox's work: problem-solving theory which takes the existing order for granted and asks how it may be made to function more smoothly, and critical theory which asks how the existing order came into existence and whether it might be changing. Neo-realism is the problem-solving approach which has dominated the field. Critical theory is the approach which challenges neo-realism by highlighting tendencies towards new principles and models of political organization emerging within the prevailing world order. Critical social theory is concerned then with the possibilities, however slight at present, which are immanent within existing global social and political relations.

Cox's distinction between problem-solving and critical theory revealed that the traditional critique of Marxism rested upon a superficial understanding of the nature and purpose of Marxism. Marxism was thought to combine economic reductionism, historical teleology and utopianism. Orthodox perspectives within the field were held to be politically-neutral interpretations of the basic realities of world politics. Questions about what knowledge was and who it was for were not raised within the realist tradition. That such questions are now integral to the study of international relations is very largely a consequence of its belated engagement with Marxism.

The contribution of Marxism in this respect is especially evident in its critique of bourgeois economics. Marx argued that the liberal conviction that private property is a feature of all social orders gave the class-based inequalities of the capitalist order the illusory authority of natural law. The liberal idea of private property did not mirror an unchanging reality but helped to reproduce an order which was biased towards particular class interests. The contention that certain modes of inquiry are not innocent interpretations of an immutable reality but possess the ideological function of underpinning mutable and unjust social orders is essential to many contemporary debates in International Relations. Habermas's analysis of the relationship between knowledge and human interests which explores the philosophical dimensions of these issues has been especially influential in the critique of neo-realism.[59] In the 1980s and 1990s this critique has exposed its problem-solving character and ideological functions[60] and replaced its weary emphasis on the supposedly immutable character of international relations with a critical enquiry into the prospects for new principles and forms of social and political organization.[61]

Marxism has been influential in opening up new areas of discussion about the purpose of knowledge to which two other approaches, feminism and postmodernism, have also contributed. Reflecting past concerns Marx-

ist writings stress the rivalries within the sphere of production and exchange to alter the conditions under which human beings produce. But the
emphasis on relations of production is no longer exclusive and much of the
current literature takes account of the counter-hegemonic role of new social
movements which are concerned with ecological issues, gender and minority rights. Reflecting recent concerns with the politics of culture and
civilizational identity Cox argues that 'a post-hegemonic order would be
one in which different traditions of civilisation could co-exist, each based on
a different intersubjectivity defining a distinct set of values and a distinct
path towards development'.[62] A process of 'mutual recognition and mutual
understanding' involving these different cultures and weaving them into
new webs of significance is one precondition of a post-hegemonic order.
These themes mark the upsurge of interest in recent social theory with the
problem of estrangement between groups as distinct from the traditional
Marxist preoccupation with alienation and exploitation. In the Marxist
literature they reveal subtle movements beyond the traditional agenda of
emancipation to more recent concerns with promoting greater understanding between different social groups.[63] The stress on promoting a rationality
which 'unites without effacing separation' or without 'depriving the other
of otherness' reveals a more serious interest on the part of Marxists with
culture, otherness and estrangement.[64]

Culture and morality have long been at the centre of Habermas's
thought. As previously noted, in a pathbreaking essay on reconstructing
historical materialism Habermas argues that the Marxist emphasis on how
human societies acquired technical mastery of nature had to be comple-
mented by an analysis of social learning in the moral-practical sphere.[65]
Whereas classical Marxism had focused on the tendencies immanent within
modes of production, Habermas shifts to potentialities inherent in human
communication. In a complex and controversial line of argument he maintains that through the development of language human beings acquire
more sophisticated means of judging social arrangements. In the advanced
moral codes human beings do not appeal to tradition, authority or convention to defend their claims about how societies should be organized. Recognizing the partiality of their individual views and their inevitably
limited cultural horizons they retreat from arguments that there is a single
moral code to which everyone must submit. Acknowledging that there can
be no certainty about who will learn from whom they engage one another in
dialogue to establish how far they can reach an agreement which rests quite
simply on the force of the better argument. No specific vision of the good
society – such as a world-wide socialist society espoused by Marx – is
posited as the universal which all human beings should recognize as valid.
Habermas therefore attempts to recover the cosmopolitan moment in
Marx's thought by arguing that the ideal of universal dialogue which treats
all human beings as equal is inherent in the use of language.[66]

Three points are worth noting about Habermas's efforts to open historical materialism to insights drawn from the paradigm of communication. First, the cosmopolitan goal of Marx and Marxism is reaffirmed but within a framework which defends the moral right of every human being to take part in dialogue. There is a striking contrast between the analysis of discourse ethics in Habermas's thought and the tendency in earlier Marxism to dismiss morality as an epiphenomenal aspect of society. Second, the reconstruction of historical materialism does not assert the primacy of class and production but recognizes a plurality of social and political movements (concerned with ecology, national rights and the rights of women) which resist various forms of alienation, exploitation and estrangement.[67] Third, despite these advances, discourse ethics is specifically concerned with the philosophy of language and omits the substantive analysis of power and inequality which was at the heart of classical Marxism. Attempts to reconstruct historical materialism have the peculiar effect of emptying the doctrine of much of its classical focus although, as Cohen and Apel argue, the ideal of the 'communication community' involves 'neo-Marxism' in the project of analysing and seeking to eradicate all 'asymmetries' which obstruct open dialogue.[68] Echoes of classical Marxism can be detected in this formulation but the possibilities which are charted owe more to the spirit than to the letter of Marxism since they break with the traditional belief in the primacy of class and production and the centrality of the socialist vision.

IV   Marxism in the Context of the Current Debate

The metamorphosis which Marxism has undergone in recent years raises the question of whether it is likely to play a determining role in furthering the development of critical international theory. Not only have several alternative critical positions emerged in the last few years but, as the nature of Habermas's argument reveals, those who locate their work within Marxist tradition now draw many of their primary themes from intellectual realms which previously fell outside the scope of traditional analysis.

Marxism was the most powerful tradition of critical theory because it denied that the basic structure of capitalism was natural or immutable. However, its preoccupation with class-based exclusion left it open to the accusation of failing to take other forms of exclusion based on language, ethnicity, gender or race seriously. Perspectives such as feminism and postmodernism have extended the critique of allegedly immutable structures beyond the realms of Marxism. Of equal importance, alternative critical perspectives are wary of, or firmly opposed to, the cosmopolitan aspirations of the classical Marxist tradition. As noted above, Marxism argued that the division of human society into competing nation-states would be replaced by new forms of political community which would bring the whole human race within the embrace of global socialism. This vision of a humanity united to advance international socialism finds little support within alternative critical perspectives. Feminism and postmodernism have questioned and opposed the universalism which is present in Marxism and in other strands of Enlightenment thinking. Some exponents of these positions are supportive of the politics of dialogue but they are troubled by the Habermasian claim that its primary purpose is to establish universal ethical principles. The problem of universalism is the key to much of the current debate between different modes of critical theory.[69]

Many contemporary writers who adopt a critical approach to society and politics oppose the overarching emancipatory project associated with Marxism. The French postmodernist, Lyotard, has been influential in arguing for a move beyond the grand narrative which Marxism defended in which the whole of human history is thought to be a process of gradual ascent towards the summit of universal freedom and equality. For Lyotard, Marx and others misplaced their faith in the Western idea of reason and scientific progress.[70] The emancipatory project which was carried out in the name of reason and science had its dark side, which is evident in the rise of totalitarian society and the destruction of groups deemed less than completely rational. In particular, the European domination and destruction of non-European peoples displayed the other side of what the postmodernists have called the Enlightenment project. Bringing an end to the Enlightenment project has been one of the main ambitions of the postmodern turn in recent social and political theory. Greater difference or diversity is one of the latter's concrete political goals.

Interpreted in this context Marxism stands out as a doctrine which was frequently condescending towards, or contemptuous of, societies and religions in the non-Western territories – those 'historyless peoples' as Engels once described them – which the West would prepare for emancipation. There can be little doubt that Marx and the different strands of Marxist thought adopted a Eurocentric view of the world in which the West was the higher destination which the entire human race would eventually reach. Within the traditional Marxist grand narrative the West was on the verge of transcending the religious world-views in which other alienated civilizations were still embedded. Habermas's reconstruction of historical materialism is intriguing by way of contrast because it rejects the supposition that any moral code, Western or otherwise, has validity for all. Some of the critics of Habermas's perspective argue that the Enlightenment commitment to a universal consensus remains at the heart of this project[71] but this interpretation cannot be sustained.[72] It is not assumed that dialogue will necessarily conclude in a universal moral consensus and, as already noted,

Habermas in his recent work stresses the goal of understanding between social groups as much as the classical notion of emancipation.

Some of the postmodern critics of Enlightenment universalism support the cosmopolitan idea of human equality but contest its traditional foundations.[73] For example, Lyotard argues that all human beings have an equal right to take part in dialogue and to 'establish their community by contract' using 'reason and debate'.[74] The argument is reminiscent of the defence of dialogue in Habermasian critical theory. Edward Said defends 'a new universality' which escapes the particularistic agendas of the dominant powers.[75] Jacques Derrida argues that *The Communist Manifesto* is relevant to current political debates since, to return to the theme with which this chapter began, globalization has acquired the importance which Marx and Engels imputed to it and political action reveals a marked tendency to become 'world-wide'.[76] Opposing Francis Fukuyama's quaint thesis that history ends with the triumph of liberal democracy Derrida defends a 'new international' on the grounds that 'violence, inequality, exclusion, famine, and thus economic oppression [have never] affected as many human beings in the history of the Earth and of humanity'. Derrida refers to a 'new International' which breaks with the dictatorship of the proletariat and socialist internationalism, criticizes 'the state of international law, the concepts of state and nation' and transcends conventional assumptions about community and citizenship.[77] Deconstruction advances the 'spirit of Marxism' and argues for a new version of the withering away of the state in which the state no longer possesses a 'a space which it . . . dominates' and which 'it never dominated without division'.[78] Such statements redirect traditional Marxist concerns towards greater engagement with the sovereign state, nation and community, international law and citizenship.

No doubt major differences exist between Habermas, Derrida, Said and Lyotard but it is striking how far the various strands of contemporary social and political thought are either reworking the cosmopolitan spirit which animated so much of Marx's thought or, more frequently, continuing the critique of a world organized around the exclusionary principle of sovereignty. No modern universalism, with the possible exception of Fukuyama's recent triumphalism, accepts Marx's thesis that the principles of Western modernity are universally valid. Respect for the cultural difference of others is a universal principle espoused by the varied strands of modern social and political thought. The new universalism which respects difference points towards forms of political community which, to employ Derrida's terminology, no longer dominate a bounded political space and dominate it with division. What such communities would allow is more freedom for the sub-national groups which have traditionally been marginalized by the sovereign state and greater opportunity for human beings to develop transnational solidarities and create stronger international linkages and associations.

Marxist reflections on globalization and fragmentation have acquired renewed significance in the present context. They are especially relevant to efforts to transcend neo-realism with its supposition that international anarchy is the basic immutable reality of world politics which ensures the reproduction of separate, sovereign states. Many realist and neo-realist writers criticized the Marxist idea that globalization would extinguish international relations. These were forceful criticisms but it is striking that with the end of the bipolar era there is fresh support for the thesis that globalization is pacifying core states and eroding traditional national boundaries and for the argument that strong claims for cultural recognition have been intensified by this very process. That globalization would have this double effect was a central theme in the Marxist tradition. For over fifty years realists have argued that the main trends in world politics demonstrate the tenacity of the nation-state but as the century comes to an end the challenging question is how to complete the unfinished Marxist project of problematizing the state and its boundaries.[79]

In this context images of alternative forms of community which encourage greater universality and diversity also have renewed importance.[80] The Austro-Marxist answer to the challenge of globalization and fragmentation was to articulate a vision of new forms of political community which embraced both cosmopolitanism and respect for cultural difference. Internationalism in Marx and Engels' writings envisaged a society in which human beings would enjoy equal access to the material and cultural resources of the world and co-operate to satisfy one another's needs and increase each other's powers. Marx and Engels regarded the eradication of class-based exclusion as the key to realizing this vision partly because they assumed that capitalism was undermining hierarchical conceptions of ethnicity and race, and partly because they believed that the proletarian struggle for class emancipation would secure freedom for all. The failure of their perspective to stress the value of cultural difference has been noted but what remains most valuable to critical theory is the critique of alienation, exploitation and the boundaries and divisions which estrange human beings from one another and prevent their collaboration to realize universal freedom. As the single most comprehensive study of alienation, exploitation and estrangement Marxism remains crucial for the project of developing the critical theory of international relations.

Conclusion

Marxism offered a broad historical vision of the development of the human race from an original condition in which small-scale societies interacted with one another to the modern condition in which the human race is integrated by, and exposed to, the rigours of global capitalism. This conception of history remains valid in the contemporary age of globalization. Marx and Marxism ensured that the role of production in transforming the physical environment and the social conditions in which human beings lived became central to the study of society and politics. Marxism offered a critical account of modes of production which aimed to explain the nature and dynamics of class exploitation and enlighten human subjects about the prospects for new social relations which would increase their freedom. Marx and Marxism drew out the connections between knowledge and power, revealing how claims about the immutability of structures had the ideological effect of reproducing constraints upon human freedom. As the analysis of the logics of globalization and fragmentation reveal, Marxism was not concerned with promoting the freedom of the citizens of any particular state or civilization but with promoting the freedom of the whole human race. These are among its greatest achievements.

As a critical theory Marxism possessed a moral vision of a world in which the barriers between human beings and the constraints upon co-operation had broken down. Many limitations and weaknesses surrounded this vision: too much emphasis on class and production at the expense of other phenomena such as nationalism, the state, geopolitics and war; a misplaced confidence that the class struggle would release all human beings from alienation, exploitation and estrangement; a naïve faith that advanced technology would create the essential preconditions of human emancipation; too complacent a belief in the superiority of Western civilization; too cramped a vision of the good society and too little analysis of what the vision of universal freedom would mean and how it might be realized in a world of different cultures and states.

Finally, throughout its short history the discipline has taken bounded political communities for granted and it has concentrated on how they interact in the context of international anarchy. The study of international relations developed as a response to liberal and Marxist strands of thought which assumed that commerce or capitalism would replace the nation-state with new and more internationalist forms of political community. The discipline acquired its distinctive identity against the background of several decades of war and international tension. However, the combined effect of globalization and fragmentation has created new historical circumstances in which the continuation of traditional bounded political communities can no longer be taken as given and in which the discipline cannot be confined to analysing the ways in which bounded communities conduct their external relations within the unchanging circumstances of international anarchy. The question of how bounded communities are being transformed by the pincer effect of globalization and fragmentation is increasingly fundamental to the discipline. In this context it becomes essential to advance the critical enquiry developed by Marxism into the prospects for extending community to represent outsiders and for deepening community to represent insider groups which have long been marginal. Marx and Marxism aimed to understand the possibility of communities which will replace alienation, exploitation and estrangement with freedom, co-operation and understanding in a world characterized by extraordinary levels of globalization and fragmentation. These remain the most pressing issues of the age.

Notes

1. H. Bull, *The Anarchical Society: A Study of Order in World Politics* (London, 1977).
2. M. Wight, 'Why is there no International Theory', in H. Butterfield and M. Wight (eds), *Diplomatic Investigations* (London, 1966), p. 25.
3. V. Kubalkova and A. Cruickshank, *Marxism-Leninism and the Theory of International Relations* (London, 1980); V. Kubalkova and A. Cruickshank, *Marxism and International Relations* (London, 1985); R. W. Cox, 'Social Forces, States and World Orders: Beyond International Relations Theory', *Millennium*, 10 (1981), 126–55; R. W. Cox, 'Gramsci, Hegemony and International Relations', *Millennium*, 12 (1983), 162–75; R. W. Cox, *Production, Power and World History: Social Forces in the Making of History* (New York, 1987); R. W. Cox, 'Production, the State and Change in World Order', in E.-O. Czempiel and J. Rosenau (eds), *Global Change and Theoretical Challenges: Approaches to World Politics* (Lexington, 1989), ch. 3; R. W. Cox, 'Multilateralism and World Order', *Review of International Studies*, 18 (1992), 161–80; R. W. Cox, 'Structural Issues of Global Governance: Implications for Europe' in S. Gill (ed.), *Gramsci, Historical Materialism and International Relations* (Cambridge, 1993), ch 10.; J. MacLean, 'Marxism and International Relations: A Strange Case of Mutual Neglect', *Millennium*, 17 (1988), 295–319.; A. Linklater, 'Realism, Marxism and Critical International Theory', *Review of International Studies*, 12 (1986), 301–12; A. Linklater, *Beyond Realism and Marxism: Critical Theory and International Relations* (London, 1990a); A. Linklater, 'Marxism and International Relations: Antithesis, Reconciliation and Transcendence' in R. Higgott and J. L. Richardson (eds), *International Relations: Global and Australian Perspectives on an Evolving Discipline* (Canberra, 1991); C. Brown, 'Marxism and International Ethics', in T. Nardin and D. R. Napel (eds), *Traditions of International Ethics* (Cambridge, 1992), ch. 11.; J. Rosenberg, *The Empire of Civil Society: A Critique of the Realist Theory of International Relations* (London, 1994); F. Halliday, *Rethinking International Relations* (London, 1994); H. Smith, 'Marxism and International Relations Theory', in A. J. R. Groom and M. Light (eds), *Contemporary International Relations: A Guide to Theory* (London, 1994).
4. A. Giddens, *A Contemporary Critique of Historical Materialism* (London, 1981).

5. M. Cochran, 'Cosmopolitanism and Communitarianism in a Post-Cold War World' in J. MacMillan and A. Linklater (eds), *Boundaries in Question: New Directions in International Relations* (London, 1995), ch. 2.
6. S. Gill, 'Gramsci and Global Politics: Towards a Post-Hegemonic Research Agenda' in S. Gill (ed.), *Gramsci, Historical Materialism and International Relations* (Cambridge, 1993).
7. Brown (1992).
8. K. Marx, *The Eighteenth Brumaire of Louis Bonaparte*, in D. McLennan (ed.), *Karl Marx: Selected Writings* (Oxford 1977), p. 300.
9. Ibid., p. 158.
10. Halliday (1994), ch. 2
11. K. Marx, *Grundrisse* (Harmondsworth, 1973), p. 539.
12. Marx (1977), pp. 224–5.
13. Ibid., pp. 230 and 235.
14. Giddens (1981).
15. Marx (1973), p. 109.
16. W. B. Gallie, *Philosophers of Peace and War* (Cambridge, 1978).
17. K. Marx, *The Poverty of Philosophy* (Moscow, 1966), p. 159.
18. K. Marx and F. Engels, *Ireland and the Irish Question* (London, 1971), p. 332; E. Benner, 'Marx and Engels on Nationalism and National Identity: A Reappraisal', *Millennium*, 17 (1988), 1–23.
19. A. Emmanuel, *Unequal Exchange: A Study of the Imperialism of Trade* (New York, 1972).
20. Gallie (1978).
21. Ibid.; and M. Rupert, 'Alienation, Capitalism and the Inter-State System: Towards a Marxian/Gramscian Critique' in S. Gill (ed.), *Gramsci, Historical Materialism and International Relations* (Cambridge, 1993), ch. 3.
22. I. Cummins, *Marx, Engels and National Movements* (London, 1980).
23. T. B. Bottomore and P. Goode (eds), *Austro-Marxism* (Oxford 1978).
24. A. Gouldner, *The Two Marxisms: Contradictions and Anomalies in the Development of Theory* (York, 1980).
25. P. Anderson, *In the Tracks of Historical Materialism* (London, 1983).
26. Linklater (1990a), ch. 2; A. Linklater, *Men and Citizens in the Theory of International Relations* (London, 1990b).
27. V. Lenin, *Imperialism: The Highest Stage of Capitalism* (Moscow 1968); N. Bukharin, *Imperialism and World Economy* (London, 1972).
28. Linklater (1990a), ch. 4.
29. Lenin (1968), p. 102.
30. Bukharin (1972), p. 166.
31. Ibid., p. 167.
32. Ibid., p. 167.
33. Linklater (1990a).
34. V. Lenin, *Collected Works*, vol. 20 (Moscow, 1964), p. 27.

35. J. Stalin, 'Marxism and the National Question', *Collected Works* (Moscow, 1953), pp. 343 and 354.

36. B. Knei-Paz, *The Social and Political Thought of Leon Trotsky* (Oxford 1978).

37. A. G. Frank, *Capitalism and Underdevelopment in Latin America* (New York, 1967).

38. I. Wallerstein, *The Capitalist World Economy* (Cambridge, 1979).

39. Frank (1967); Wallerstein (1979).

40. Emmanuel (1972).

41. B. Warren, *Imperialism: Pioneer of Capitalism* (London, 1980); T. Nairn, *The Break-up of Britain* (London, 1981).

42. F. Halliday, 'Three Concepts of International Relations', *International Affairs*, 64 (1988), 187–98.

43. Brown (1986).

44. K. N. Waltz, *Man, the State and War* (New York, 1959).

45. Ibid., ch.5.

46. Giddens (1981), p. 250; Kubalkova and Cruickshank (1980; 1985).

47. Linklater (1990a).

48. P. Anderson, *Lineages of the Absolutist State* (London, 1974); F. Block, 'Beyond State Autonomy: State Managers as Historical Subjects', *Socialist Register* (1980), 227–42; S. Brucan, *The Dialectic of World Politics* (New York, 1978); Nairn (1981) and T. Skocpol, *States and Social Revolutions* (Cambridge, 1979).

49. Giddens (1981); A. Giddens, *The Nation-State and Violence* (Cambridge, 1985); Linklater (1986).

50. J. Habermas, *Communication and the Evolution of Society* (Boston, 1979).

51. G. Friedman, *The Political Philosophy of the Frankfurt School* (London, 1981), pp. 35–6.

52. R. O. Keohane and J. S. Nye, *Power and Interdependence* (London, 1989).

53. Halliday (1994), p. 61.

54. Gill (1993).

55. Cox (1993), p. 264.

56. Cox (1983); Gill (1993).

57. K. N. Waltz, *Theory of International Politics* (Reading, Mass., 1979).

58. Cox (1981), p. 128.

59. J. Habermas, *Knowledge and Human Interests* (London, 1972).; R. Ashley, 'Political Realism and Human Interests', *International Studies Quarterly*, 25 (1981), 204–36; M. Hoffman, 'Critical Theory and the Inter-Paradigm Debate', *Millennium*, 16 (1987), 231–49; Linklater (1986, 1990a).

60. Cox (1981).

61. A. Linklater, 'The Achievements of Critical Theory', in M. Zalewski, S. Smith and K. Booth (eds), *After Positivism* (Cambridge, 1996).

62. Cox (1992); (1993), p. 265.

63. J. Habermas, *The Past as Future* (Cambridge, 1994), p. 104.

64. Ibid., pp. 119–20.

65. Habermas (1979).

66. J. Habermas, *Moral Consciousness and Communicative Action* (Cambridge, 1990).
67. L. J. Ray, *Rethinking Critical Theory: Emancipation in the Age of Global Social Movements* (London, 1993).
68. J. Cohen, 'Discourse Ethics and Civil Society', in Rasmussen, D. (ed.), *Universalism vs Communitarianism* (Cambridge, Mass., 1990); K.-O. Apel, *Towards a Transformation of Philosophy* (London, 1980), p. 283.
69. Linklater (1996).
70. J-F. Lyotard, *The Postmodern Condition: A Report on Knowledge* (Manchester, 1984).
71. J. George, *Discourses of World Politics: A (Re)Introduction to International Relations*, (Boulder, 1994).
72. S. Benhabib, *Situating the Self: Gender, Community and Postmodernism in Contemporary Ethics* (Cambridge, 1992); Linklater (1996).
73. P. Dews, *Logics of Disintegration: Post Structuralist Thought and the Claims of Critical Theory* (London, 1987), p. 208; Linklater (1990b).
74. J.-F. Lyotard, 'The Other's Rights' in S. Shute and S. Hurley, (eds), *On Human Rights: The Oxford Amnesty Lectures* (New York, 1993) p. 138.
75. E. Said, 'Nationalism, Human Rights and Interpretation', in B. Johnson (ed.), *Freedom and Interpretation: The Oxford Amnesty Lectures 1992* (New York, 1993).
76. J. Derrida, 'Spectres of Marx', *New Left Review*, 205 (May/June, 1994), pp. 31–58. p.32.
77. Ibid., p. 53.
78. Ibid., pp. 56 and 58.
79. Linklater (1990a); E. Augelli and C. Murphy, 'Gramsci and International Relations: A General Perspective and Example from Recent US Foreign Policy Toward the Third World' in S. Gill (ed.), *Gramsci, Historical Materialism and International Relations* (Cambridge, 1993), ch. 5. pp.141–6.
80. Cox (1993), p. 263; Linklater (1996).

CHAPTER 6

Critical Theory

Richard Devetak

Ever since its inception after the First World War, the discipline of international relations has guarded its identity and boundaries as vigilantly as a state patrols its frontiers. There have been occasional debates about purpose (realism versus idealism) and methodology (behaviourism versus classical theory), but none has posed a challenge to the fundamental ground on which the discipline of International Relations stands. It was not until the 1980s that International Relations was submitted to radical critique. Questions of purpose and methodology were raised once again, but further questions pertaining to deeper epistemological and ontological assumptions were also advanced. The most basic, unquestioned assumptions about knowledge claims and the order of things were now placed under scrutiny as International Relations felt the impact of critical theory. Behind critical international theory lies the conviction that 'international relations could be other than it is at both the theoretical and practical levels'.[1] It is the aim of this chapter to flesh out the alternative theory and practice promised by critical international theory.

This chapter is divided into four main parts: firstly, a sketch of the origins of critical theory; secondly, an examination of the connection between knowledge and values in international relations; thirdly, an explanation of critical international theory's reconstruction of historical materialism; and fourthly, an outline of the concept of emancipation used by critical international theory.

Origins of Critical Theory

Critical theory has its roots in a strand of thought which is often traced back to the Enlightenment and connected to the writings of Kant, Hegel and Marx. While this is an important lineage in the birth of critical theory it is

145

not the only possible one that can be traced, as there is also the imprint of classical Greek thought on autonomy and democracy to be considered, as well as the thinking of Nietzsche and Weber. However, in the twentieth century critical theory became most closely associated with a distinct body of thought known as the Frankfurt School. It is in the work of Max Horkheimer, Theodor Adorno, Walter Benjamin, Herbert Marcuse, Erich Fromm, Leo Lowenthal and, more recently, Jurgen Habermas that critical theory acquired a renewed potency, in which the term *critical theory* came to be used as the emblem of a philosophy which questions the prevailing order of social and political modernity through a method of immanent critique. It was largely an attempt to recover a critical potential that had been overrun by recent intellectual, social, cultural, economic and techno-logical trends.

Essential to the Frankfurt School's critical theory was a concern to comprehend the central features of contemporary society by understanding its historical and social development, and tracing contradictions in the present which may open up the possibility of transcending contemporary society and its built-in pathologies and forms of domination. Critical theory intended 'not simply to eliminate one or other abuse', but to analyse the underlying social structures which result in these abuses, with the intention of overcoming them.[2] It is not difficult to notice the presence here of the theme advanced by Marx in his eleventh thesis on Feuerbach: 'philosophers have only interpreted the world in various ways; the point is to change it'.[3] This normative interest in identifying immanent possibilities for social transformation is a defining characteristic of a line of thought which ex-tends, at least, from Kant, through Marx, to contemporary critical theorists such as Habermas. This intention to analyse the possibilities of realizing emancipation in the modern world entailed critical analyses of both ob-structions to, and immanent tendencies towards 'the rational organization of human activity'.[4] Indeed, this concern extends the line of thought back beyond Kant to the classical Greek conviction that the rational constitution of the *polis* finds its expression in individual autonomy and the establish-ment of justice and democracy. Politics, on this understanding, is the realm concerned with realizing the just life.

There is, however, an important difference between critical theory and the Greeks which is suggested by the Hegelian and Marxist critiques of knowledge and ideology. This relates to the conditions under which know-ledge claims can be made regarding social and political life. There are two points worth recalling in this regard: firstly, that reflection on the limits of what we can know is a fundamental part of theorizing, and secondly, knowledge is always, and irreducibly, conditioned by historical and mate-rial contexts. Since critical theory takes society itself as its object of analysis, and since theories and acts of theorizing are never independent of society, critical theory's scope of analysis must necessarily include reflection on theory. In short, critical theory must be self-reflective theory; it must include an account of its own genesis and application in society. As expressed by McCarthy critical theory attempts to 'radicalize epistemology by unearthing the roots of knowledge in life'.[5] It draws attention to the relationship between knowledge and society (the object of knowledge) which is so frequently excluded from theoretical analysis.

It was on the basis of this relationship that Horkheimer distinguished between two conceptions of theory, which he referred to as traditional and critical theories. Traditional conceptions of theory picture the theorist at a remove from the object of analysis. By analogy with the natural sciences, they claim that subject and object must be strictly separated in order to theorize properly. Traditional conceptions of theory assume there is an external world out there to study, and that an inquiring subject can study this world in a balanced and objective manner by withdrawing from the world it investigates, and leaving behind any ideological beliefs, values, or opinions which would invalidate the enquiry. To qualify as theory it must at least be value-free. On this view, theory is only possible on condition that an inquiring subject can withdraw from the world it studies (and in which it exists) and rid itself of all biases. This contrasts with critical conceptions which view theory as irreducibly related to social and political life.

By recognizing that theories are always embedded in social and political life, critical conceptions of theory allow for an examination of the purposes and functions served by particular theories. However, while such conceptions of theory recognize the unavoidability of taking their orientation from the social matrix in which they are situated, their guiding interest is one of emancipation from, rather than legitimation and consolidation of, existing society. The purpose underlying critical, as opposed to traditional, conceptions of theory is to improve human existence by abolishing injustice.[6] In sum, critical conceptions of theory accept that knowledge is unavoidably entangled in the purposes and functions that shape social and political life, and therefore can be a force in that shaping process. As articulated by Horkheimer, this conception of theory does not simply present an expression of the 'concrete historical situation', it also acts as 'a force within [that situation] to stimulate change'.[7] It allows for the intervention of humans in the making of their history.

It should be noted that though critical theory has not directly addressed the international level, this in no way implies that international relations is beyond the limits of its concern. The writings of Kant, Hegel, and Marx in particular have demonstrated that what happens at the international level is of immense significance to the achievement of universal emancipation. It is the continuation of this project in which critical international theory is engaged. The Frankfurt School, however, never addressed international relations in its critiques of the modern world, and Habermas makes only scant reference to it. The main tendency of critical theory is to take society as the focus and to neglect the dimension of relations between and across societies. For critical international theory, however, the task is to extend the trajectory of Frankfurt School critical theory beyond the domestic realm to the international, or more accurately, global, realm. It makes a case for a theory of global or world politics which is 'committed to the emancipation of the species'.[8] Such a theory would no longer be confined to an individual *polis*, but would examine relations between and across them, and reflect on the possibility of extending the rational, just and democratic organization of politics to the entire species.

To summarise, critical theory draws upon various strands of Western social, political, and philosophical thought in order to erect a theoretical framework capable of reflecting on the nature and purposes of theory and revealing both obvious and subtle forms of injustice and domination in society. As Thomas McCarthy remarks, critical theory promises 'both a reflection on the conditions of knowledge and a critical-reflective dissolution of dogmatic forms of life'.[9] Critical theory not only challenges and dismantles traditional forms of theorizing, it also problematizes and seeks to dismantle entrenched forms of social life that constrain human freedom. Critical international theory is an extension of this critique to the international domain. The next part of the chapter focuses on the attempt by critical international theorists to dismantle traditional forms of theorizing by promoting more self-reflective theory.

Knowledge and Values in International Relations Theory

Traditional approaches to the study of international relations rarely, if ever, inquired into the important relationship between knowledge and values. On the rare occasions that the relationship was mentioned at all, it was normally to issue warnings about the dangers of allowing values to influence enquiry. Despite the fact that social and political theory were beginning to realize the importance of taking serious account of epistemology, international relations theory tended to leave it aside. The status of knowledge, the justification of knowledge claims, the methodology applied, and the scope and purpose of enquiry, were fundamental epistemological issues that International Relations ignored to its own detriment. The so-called 'second great debate' which took place in the 1960s between behaviouralism and classical theory, and most famously between Kaplan and Bull, was but a brief and underdeveloped debate about the fundamental questions of methodology and epistemology. It was not until the 1980s that such questions would be taken seriously in International Relations.

The 1980s is often characterized as having witnessed the 'third great debate', and it is largely thanks to critical theory that the debate was to 'get off the ground' at all. One of the important contributions of critical international theory was to widen the object domain of international relations to include epistemological issues. This is precisely what Maclean was getting at when he claimed that the *'real objects of enquiry* can be other than empirically observable phenomena'.[10] In the following section critical theory's concern with interests in knowledge formation is examined.

Traditional and critical conceptions of international relations theory

This section outlines the way in which critical international theory brought knowledge claims in international relations under critical scrutiny. First, it considers the question of epistemology by describing how Horkheimer's distinction between traditional and critical conceptions of theory has been taken up in International Relations; and secondly, it describes how a tripartite division of knowledge-types devised by Habermas has been employed in International Relations. The result of this scrutinizing was to place the connection between knowledge and values at the centre of theoretical analyses of international relations.

In many ways it was in response to Waltz's neo-realism that critical international theory emerged. In his landmark text, *Theory of International Politics* (1979), Waltz attempted to place realism, or the balance-of-power theory, on more secure, scientific ground. There is no need to go into the content of Waltz's argument in detail. However, the conception of theory advanced by Waltz, with its rules of theory-construction, its purpose, and criteria for appraisal, are definitely pertinent. After briefly reviewing Waltz's conception of theory consideration is given to Cox's Horkheimer-like distinction between problem-solving and critical theories.

The conception of theory advanced by Waltz corresponds to that which Horkheimer calls 'traditional'. This conception shares its epistemology with the natural sciences. It begins by making a radical separation between subject and object, and, as explained by another proponent of neo-realism, then proceeds to identify 'the objective laws of international relations while excluding subjective and intersubjective phenomena such as behaviour motivated by norms, values, or consent'.[11] A fundamental aspect of this epistemology is the expunging of values and normative commitments. A prior distinction between facts and values, and subject and object is made on the supposition that it is both possible and necessary for theoretical enquiry. Following from this basic rule of theory-construction, and again in line with the natural sciences, Waltz's purpose is to explain why certain patterns remain constant in international politics. The task of theory, says Waltz, is 'to single out the propelling principle even though other principles operate'.[12] Waltz makes clear right from the beginning that on his conception of theory, 'the urge to explain is not born of idle curiosity alone. It is produced also by the desire to control, or at least to know if control is possible'.[13] The criteria by which theory is judged on the traditional conception are utility and technical applicability. Waltz affirms that 'questions of truth and falsity are somehow involved, but so are questions of usefulness and uselessness'.[14] The ultimate test of a theory is its usefulness in guiding policy towards given ends, in this case, orientating foreign policy to obtain power and security under international anarchy.

It is precisely this conception of theory that Cox has in mind with the label 'problem-solving'. Problem-solving theory 'takes the world as it finds it, with the prevailing social and power relationships and the institutions into which they are organized, as the given framework for action'.[15] It does not question the present order, but has the effect of legitimizing and reifying it. Its general aim, says Cox, is to make the existing order 'work smoothly by dealing effectively with particular sources of trouble'.[16] Neo-realism, *qua* problem-solving theory, takes seriously the realist dictum to work with, rather than against, prevailing international forces. By working within the given system it tends to preserve the existing global structure of social and political relations; it has a stabilizing effect. Cox points out that neo-liberal institutionalism also partakes of problem-solving. Its objective, as explained by its foremost exponent, is to 'facilitate the smooth operation of decentralized international political systems'.[17] Situating itself between the states-system and the liberal capitalist global economy, neo-liberalism's main concern is to ensure that the two systems function smoothly in their co-existence. It seeks to render the two global systems compatible and stable by diffusing any conflicts, tensions, or crises that might arise between them.[18]

To summarize, traditional conceptions of theory tend to work in favour of stabilizing prevailing structures of world order and their accompanying inequalities of power and wealth. The main point that Cox wishes to make about problem-solving theory is that its failure to reflect on the prior framework within which it theorizes means that it can have no other effect than a conservative one. Its claims to value-neutrality notwithstanding, problem-solving theory is plainly 'value-bound by virtue of the fact that it implicitly accepts the prevailing order as its own framework'.[19]

In contrast, critical theory starts from the premiss that theory is always situated in a particular time and place. Theory, like all knowledge, is necessarily conditioned by social, cultural and ideological influence, and one of the main tasks of critical theory is to reveal the effect of this conditioning. It seeks to bring to consciousness latent perspectives, interests, or values that give rise to, and orientate, any theory. By adopting this self-reflective attitude critical theory takes its point of departure in the connection between knowledge and values. It is more like a meta-theoretical attempt to examine how theories are situated in prevailing social and political orders, how this situatedness impacts on theorizing, and, most importantly, the possibilities for theorizing in a manner that challenges injustices and inequalities built into the prevailing world order.

Critical theory's relation to the prevailing order needs to be explained with some care. For although it refuses to take the prevailing order as it finds it, critical theory does not simply ignore it. It accepts that humans do not make history under conditions of their own choosing, as Marx observed in *The Eighteenth Brumaire of Louis Bonaparte*, and so a detailed examination of present conditions must necessarily be undertaken. Nevertheless, the order which has been 'given' to us is by no means natural, necessary or historically invariable. Critical theory views the prevailing order of social and political relations as a historical production which must be explained. Of crucial importance for critical theory is an understanding of the origin and development of social and political configurations that have culminated in the present. Critical *international* theory takes the global configuration of power relations as its object and asks how that configuration came about, what costs it brings with it, and what other possibilities remain immanent in history. For critical international theory the prevailing order is shot through with injustices and inequalities on a global scale and it is on this basis that it favours alternative visions of world order.

Critical international theory is not only concerned with providing explanations of the existing realities of world politics, it also intends to criticise in order to transform them. It is an attempt to comprehend essential social processes for the purpose of inaugurating change, or at least knowing whether change is possible. In Hoffman's words, it is 'not merely an expression of the concrete realities of the historical situation, but also a force for change within those conditions'.[20] The knowledge critical international theory seeks is not neutral; it is politically and ethically charged by an interest in social and political transformation. It affirms, as Cox says, 'a normative choice in favour of a social and political order different from the prevailing order'.[21]

The debt to Horkheimer in Cox's assessment of problem-solving and critical theories is plain to see. Most of the inspiration behind Cox's analysis, however, is drawn from Giambattista Vico and Karl Marx. Both thinkers reject the thesis that the existing order is immutable, arguing instead that it should be understood in genetic and developmental terms; the existing order has a history which needs to be accounted for. Moreover, the existing order cannot be understood without taking account of the historically changing interaction between ideas, consciousness, ideologies and analytical concepts on the one hand, and concrete social, economic, and political circumstances on the other. In Cox's view, the foremost source of such an understanding is Marx's method of historical materialism. Historical materialism will be examined in more detail in the next part of the chapter, for now it will be enough to note that Cox favours this method because, among other things, it includes the interplay of consciousness and material circumstances in its dialectical account of social conflict and the possibility of transformation that such conflict generates.[22]

This concern with identifying transformational possibilities in the present order also finds expression in the critical international theories of Ashley and Linklater. Both theorists adopt Habermas's tripartite division between forms of knowledge with the intention of developing theories guided by an interest in emancipation.

Ashley's immediate concern is to delineate different strands of realist thought. Realism is not the homogeneous tradition that it might at first appear. According to Ashley's Habermasian reading it is possible to distinguish technical and practical forms of realism. The basis on which this distinction is made is the interest which guides the theory. Ashley asserts that 'knowledge is always constituted in reflection of interests', and his intention is to map out the different strands of realist thought by revealing the underlying interest.[23]

Technical realism is guided by an interest in obtaining knowledge to expand a subject's control over an objectified environment. Waltz's neo-realism provides the starkest expression of technical realism. It forges together *raison d'état* and *raison de science positive*, as Ashley says, producing a 'scientific' version of power politics.[24] Ashley argues that the very method employed by neo-realism, positivism, leads to a view of politics defined in terms of technical efficiency. The focus is on the means with which to achieve a given end rather than the validity of the end itself. As a result statecraft is reduced to figuring out technical adjustments states can make in order to take full advantage of their position in the international system irrespective of their impact on other states. Constituted by a technical interest neo-realism provides a theory of and for the state and for extending its power, security and control in the international environment.

Practical realism, on the other hand, is guided by an interest in obtaining knowledge to maintain and further develop communication and mutual understandings. In contrast to neo-realism, practical realism's logic of enquiry, which Ashley finds expressed in some of Morgenthau's writings, is more hermeneutic or interpretative. It eschews positivism in favour of an approach which takes account of history, law and morality. The focus is on principles and practices which maintain international order by orientating actors to respect common traditions, institutions, rules and norms in order to avoid the outbreak of conflict and war wherever possible. Constituted by a practical interest this form of realism provides a theory of and for international order and for sustaining the intersubjective background which makes possible dialogue between states.[25]

It is important to note that though these two strands of realism are analytically distinguishable, Ashley believes that they are closely related and mutually reinforcing. Ultimately practical realism cannot break free of technical realism. Although it has 'partial autonomy' it remains anchored in a problematique set by an interest in control.[26] The upshot of this relationship is that questions of change or moral progress cannot be posed. Indeed, the 'impossibility theorem', as Ashley calls it, denies the possibility of global transformation whereby moral and political co-operation or community is extended universally. Realists must fall back on the axiom that 'there exists no actual or immanent universal consensus that will or can for a long time satisfy the real and emerging wants and needs of all states and peoples'.[27] Commitment to extending the rational, just and democratic organization of politics beyond the level of the state is deflected in realism by the impossibility theorem, or 'immutability thesis' as Linklater calls it.[28]

In an attempt to revive this commitment, Ashley draws out an emancipatory interest which, he argues, can be found in the unique realism of John Herz. The emancipatory interest is concerned with 'securing freedom from unacknowledged constraints, relations of domination, and conditions of distorted communication and understanding that deny humans the capacity to make their future through full will and consciousness'.[29] It plainly runs against the grain of the immutability thesis and demands an alternative theoretical method which can reflect on the ideological and conceptual constraints built into technical and practical realism. The way ahead offered by Ashley is to adopt critical theory *à la* Frankfurt School. It should be noted that Ashley's critical theory does not denigrate technical and practical realism but argues for a perspective which can incorporate them into a higher synthesis.[30] To understand the nature of this synthesis Linklater's critical international theory will be considered.

Like Ashley, Linklater adopts Habermas's division between technical, practical and emancipatory interests. But whereas Ashley confines these interests to the tradition of realism, Linklater applies them to three separate traditions of international relations theory: realism, rationalism, and revolutionism.[31] The technical interest finds expression in realism, practical interest in rationalism, and the emancipatory interest in revolutionism, according to Linklater's schema. The task of critical international theory as proposed by Linklater is to absorb the strengths of these theories into a reconstructed problematique. While this reconstructed problematic takes its orientation from revolutionism it is by no means reducible to the tradition of thought known in international relations theory as revolutionism or idealism. Revolutionism offers the guiding interest of emancipation, but it also contains weaknesses which can only be overcome by dialectically playing it off against realism and rationalism. In particular, revolutionism suffers from two main problems. First, it has not always taken sufficient account of the capacity of the states-system to reproduce itself and, secondly, it has not always heeded the Hegelian and Marxist point that moral principles are socially and historically produced rather than immutable or transcendental laws. With this in mind, how does Linklater dialectically sublate these three theories?

Linklater's critical international theory accepts that an adequate account of emancipatory prospects must account for the forces which work against emancipation or thwart its realization. In neo-realism a case is made for explaining the recurrence and repetition of war and power politics on the basis of international anarchy. Focusing on states' struggles for power, security and control under the condition of anarchy, neo-realism concludes that the peaceful transformation of world politics is virtually impossible. Where neo-realism, like any traditional or problem-solving theory, fails is in its incapacity to reflect on its own complicity with the international system. It fails to recognize its embeddedness in social and political life and its contribution to the prevailing order of things by accepting this order as its framework. Neo-realism, and realism in general, makes no allowance for political action guided by interests other than technical ones.

Rationalism, on the other hand, reveals that the condition of international anarchy does not preclude statecraft informed by non-technical interests. For rationalists, states do not exist in an international anarchy exclusively, they also inhabit an international society, hence Bull's cleverly paradoxical notion of 'anarchical society'.[32] In contrast to neo-realism, rationalism argues that an exclusive focus on struggles for power, security and control among states cannot account for the important manifestation of international order. The rationalist is predisposed by a practical interest in maintaining the institutions of international order which orientate states to develop common principles, practices, and purposes. According to Linklater, rationalism sublates neo-realism because it 'highlights the state's practical commitment to consensus and order without underestimating the importance of its technical interest in power and control'.[33] Despite its insistence on historical development and the importance of the normative dimension, especially its focus on principles of legitimacy and institutions of order, rationalism is to be found deficient because it does not adequately resolve the tensions between order and justice, and has an ill-equipped theoretical framework to criticise injustices and inequalities built into international society. Only a critical theory can correct these deficiencies in rationalism, but Linklater is careful to point out that rationalism marks a crucial stage in the development of critical international theory.

There are two key thinkers whom Linklater identifies with revolutionism: Immanuel Kant and Karl Marx. Kant's approach is instructive because it seeks to incorporate the themes of power, order, and emancipation.[34] As expressed by Linklater, Kant 'considered the possibility that state power would be tamed by principles of international order and that, in time, international order would be modified until it conformed with principles of cosmopolitan justice'.[35] Kant's theory of international relations is an early attempt to map out a critical international theory by absorbing the insights and criticising the weaknesses in realist and rationalist thought under an interest in universal freedom and justice.

While Marx's approach is deficient in several respects it nevertheless provides the basis of a social theory on which much critical international theory has evolved. As Linklater observed in an early work, both Marx and Kant share 'the desire for a universal society of free individuals, a universal kingdom of ends'.[36] Both held strong attachment to the Enlightenment themes of freedom and universalism, and both launched strong critiques of particularistic lifeforms with the intention of expanding community.

To conclude this part of the chapter, it can be seen that critical international theory has made a strong case for paying closer attention to the relations between knowledge and values. One of the main contributions that critical international theory has made in this regard is to disclose the interests which guide realism and neo-realism and the practical political implications that follow from this, particularly on questions of history and political change. Underlying all this is an explicit interest in challenging and removing socially produced constraints on human freedom, thereby contributing to the possible transformation of international relations.[37]

Reconstructing Historical Materialism and the Prevailing World Order

'To change the world', Cox says, 'we have to begin with an understanding of the world as it is'.[38] A critical international theory must be able to provide a critical, historical account of the prevailing order's origin and evolution if it is to present a sound assessment of transformational possibilities. It is this historical anchoring which prevents critical international theory's normative interest in progressive change from sliding into sheer fantasy. 'Its utopianism is constrained by its comprehension of historical processes'.[39]

The practical use of critical international theory, *qua* political theory, is to consider the social and political forces which would have to be mobilized in order to bring about one or another 'feasible outcome'.[40] The same view informs Booth's notion of 'utopian realism' which combines a normative and empirical dimension. The normative dimension refers to a 'universal appeal, based on reason, to various world order principles', while the empirical dimension offers a 'fuller understanding of the forces shaping "Who gets what, when, and how", to use Harold Lasswell's phrase'.[41] The empirical dimension is crucial to critical international theory's attempt to identify immanent tendencies in the present order which might facilitate progressive change. Linklater suggests that an 'empirical philosophy of history', as outlined by Habermas in his reconstruction of historical materialism, offers the best reconciliation of the normative and empirical dimensions.[42]

If the point of critical international theory is to inquire into the potentials for progressive social and political transformation it must be able to explain the nature of the present order and the way in which it came into being. Indeed if critical international theory is to remain distinct from traditional forms of theory it must, as Cox says, 'stand apart from the prevailing order of the world and ask how that order came about'.[43] For critical international theory accounting for the present order, its origins, and development, warrants a much broader approach than any theory that has thus far been offered in International Relations. The notion of the 'present order' is broadened to encompass processes and structures beyond the limits of traditional theoretical frameworks, that is, beyond the 'anarchy problematique'. This has important methodological implications which should be clarified before continuing.

Implicit in the approach tendered by critical international theory is a focus on the 'social totality'. It insists on a holistic methodology as employed by Hegel and Marx alike. This method comprises a moment of abstraction, where a specific structure or object is temporarily lifted from its context in order to be studied in isolation, and a moment of reconstruction, where that which is abstracted is re-inserted into the whole. 'Only when the whole had been understood would the [Hegelian or Marxist] analysis be complete'.[44] It is this reconstructive moment which methodologically distinguishes critical from traditional theories. It 'leads towards the construction of a larger picture of the whole of which the initially contemplated [or abstracted] part is just one component'.[45] It is the failure of traditional theories (and this includes Marxism) to account for the totality of modern social relations which critical international theory sets out to overcome.

Moving beyond both realism and Marxism, Cox argues for a focus on the full range of modernity's 'global power relations'.[46] The object is to provide both a historical and structural explanation of the power relations which frame the prevailing world order. In other words, Cox directs attention to relations of domination and subordination which cut across the globe. Maclean argues for a similar focus. The task of a critical international theory, in his view, is to provide a critical, historical explanation of global stratification and inequality.[47] Linklater, Cox and Maclean agree that critical international theory's focus should not be restricted to an analysis of relations between states, but should broaden its scope to take account of the full impact of modernity, especially those structures formed and sustained under processes of globalization. Added to this empirical focus is a normative concern with forms of domination and inequality, or, as Linklater puts

it, unnecessary constraints on the human capacity for freedom and autonomy. This two-pronged analysis (empirical and normative) is intended to
offer a critical, historical account of the present order and immanent trends
towards the removal of socially-created constraints on human freedom.

The following section outlines critical international theory's attempt at
accounting for the present order. After briefly reviewing realism and neo-
realism it considers historical materialism and its rehabilitation within
critical international theory's revised international relations problematic.

Realism and Marxism on the present order

For traditional theories of international relations such as realism and neo-
realism the present order is equivalent to past and future orders. International relations is understood as a necessitous realm of recurrence and
repetition, as Wight famously stated, and the main explanatory task is to
account for the reproduction, and apparent permanence, of the condition of
international anarchy. The best accounts, according to realists, will focus on
the interaction of self-interested states in their pursuit of power and security. This would be a specifically political study and could omit reference to
morality, culture, and the economy. The upshot of realist approaches is that
accounting for the present order is simply a matter of invoking the permanent condition of anarchy and self-helping, self-interested states.

Marxist accounts of the present order, on the other hand, tend to emphasise the role of capitalism; in particular, they focus on modes of production and class antagonism as the determining features of modernity. Within
Marxism it is, of course, possible to distinguish different strands of thought,
some of which are more historical, others which are more 'structuralist.
Generally, however, Marxism tends to underestimate the impact of the
state, states-system, nationalism and war on the present order.[48] It is no
surprise then that Linklater finds Marxism deficient as a critical international theory as it cannot account for the principles and practices by which
international relations move from power to order to emancipation.[49]

In similar fashion to the realist assertion of the autonomy of the political,
Marxists tends to assert the autonomy of the economic. The political phenomena that realists emphasize are relegated, by Marxism, to effects of the
deeper economic forces at work in history. Furthermore, while Marxism has
an interest in the emancipation of the species it has been mainly concerned
with overcoming alienating and exploitative relations of production, and
has, as a consequence, neglected other forms of alienation, exploitation and
estrangement based on gender, race, nationalism, and state sovereignty.[50]

From the perspective of critical international theory realism and Marxism
are, in many ways, mirror images of each other. They both neglect crucial

dimensions of the present order and underestimate the vitality and significance of structures and processes beyond the scope of their theoretical
frameworks. As a correction to both realism and Marxism, critical international theory seeks to absorb their strengths at the same time that it seeks
'their joint transcendence'.[51] Critical international theory would mark a step
beyond realism and Marxism if it could articulate the relationship between
the capitalist world economy and the system of sovereign states within a
single theoretical perspective. The following section reviews the attempts
by Cox and Linklater to explain this relationship within a revised historical
materialism.

Cox on social forces, states, and world orders

Cox offers a version of political economy which utilises the concepts of
production, social forces, hegemony, and the state drawn from Antonio
Gramsci, the Italian Marxist political thinker. These concepts contribute to
what Cox calls a historical structures approach. After explaining the purpose and method of this approach, some consideration is given to Cox's
assessment of prospects for building alternative world orders.

An important methodological shift underlies Cox's focus on historical
structure. Against the positivism of realism and neo-realism Cox adopts a
more hermeneutic approach which conceives of social structures as having
an intersubjective existence. 'Structures are socially constructed', that is,
says Cox, 'they become a part of the objective world by virtue of their
existence in the intersubjectivity of relevant groups of people'.[52] Allowing
for the active role of human minds in the constitution of the social world
does not lead to a denial of reality, it simply gives it a different ontological
status. Although structures, as intersubjective products, do not have a
physical existence like tables or chairs, they nevertheless have real, concrete
effects.[53] Structures produce concrete effects because humans act *as if* they
were real.[54] It is this view of ontology which underlies Cox's and critical
international theory's attempts to comprehend the present order and, most
distinctively, potentials for world-order change.

The question of world-order change is a constant theme in Cox's writing.
It seems to constitute one of the central methodological issues for Cox.
Indeed he goes so far as to say that 'any fresh approach to theory should . . .
confront the question of change in world order'.[55] His essential concern is
with the structural transformation of world order, that is, how the structural
characteristics of world orders emerge, are consolidated, and break down.
The purpose is not simply to reveal the structural characteristics of world
order at any given time, but to explain the transition from one order to

another. He seeks to understand and explain 'what the constituent elements of world order are (or were at any given time) and how and why the relationship among these elements has changed'.[56]

In short, the key issue for Cox is how to account for the transition from one world order to another. He devotes much of his attention to explaining 'how structural transformations have come about in the past'.[57] For example, he has analysed the structural transformation that took place in the late nineteenth century from a period characterized by craft manufacture, the liberal state, and *pax Britannica*, to a period characterized by mass production, the emerging welfare-nationalist state, and imperial rivalry.[58] He has also endorsed John Ruggie's analysis of the structural transformation from the medieval to modern system.[59] Again, the point of studying these transformations is to consider whether or not the prevailing order is irretrievably breaking down. It is with the express purpose of analysing world-order structures and the potential for structural transformation that Cox deploys his method of historical structures.[60]

Cox distinguishes his historical structures approach from the traditional realist approach which focuses on individual actors and the interests which drive their interactions.[61] In contrast to the individualist approach of realism Cox's approach is more interested in explaining how individual actors emerge in, and are conditioned by, history. Against realist dogma that the state is a state is a state, Cox views the state and its functions, roles, and responsibilities as socially and historically determined.[62] The key to rethinking international relations lies in examining the relationship between state and civil society, thereby recognizing that the state takes different forms, not only in different historical periods, but also within the same period. The point is to historicize the state and to locate it in the full array of social relations rather than reify it as a singular entity unrelated to the changing nature of social forces. Whereas the state is taken for granted by realism, critical international theory seeks to provide a social theory of the state.

There are two fundamental and intertwined presuppositions upon which Cox founds his arguments. The first reflects the Gramscian assertion that 'world orders . . . are grounded in social relations'.[63] This means that observable changes in military and geopolitical balances, 'can be traced to fundamental changes in social relations'.[64] The second presupposition stems from Vico's argument that institutions such as the state are historical products. The state cannot be abstracted from history as if its essence could be defined or understood as *prior to* history.[65] The end result is that the definition of the state is enlarged to encompass 'the underpinnings of the political structure in civil society'.[66] The influence of the church, press, education system, culture, and so on, has to be incorporated into an analysis of the state, as these 'institutions' help to produce the attitudes, dispositions, and behaviours consistent with, and conducive to, the state's arrangement of power relations in society. In short, for Gramsci and Cox alike, the state is thought to be absolutely inseparable from civil society as together they constitute and reflect the 'hegemonic social order'.[67]

To recapitulate Cox's argument thus far: whereas realism presupposes the state as an actor in international relations, Cox takes a step back in order to examine how the state is produced in history. The account of the state offered by Cox is based on an analysis of social forces. Lest it be thought that Cox is simply interested in producing a theory of the state, it should be remembered that the state is but one force which shapes the present world order. Cox argues that a comprehensive understanding of the present order and its structural characteristics must account for the interaction between social forces, states, and world orders.[68] Within Cox's approach the state plays an 'intermediate though autonomous role' between, on the one hand, social forces shaped by productive forces, and on the other hand, a world order which embodies a particular configuration of power determined by the states-system and the global economy.[69]

To analyse this configuration of power Cox employs the Gramscian concept of hegemony. Hegemony is 'represented as a fit between material power, ideology and institutions'[70] which 'frames thought and thereby circumscribes action'.[71] It is more than just order among states for it also includes order within a world economy. By combining military, political, economic, ideological and cultural forces, hegemony permeates the whole order. The concept of hegemonic world order as employed by Cox 'is founded not only upon the regulation of inter-state conflict but also upon a globally-conceived civil society'.[72] It is a form of dominance woven from many interlacing threads of social and cultural power which assumes the form of a legitimate intersubjective consensus.

Most importantly, the Gramscian notion of hegemony involves concessions on the part of dominant classes to induce subordinate classes to acquiesce to prevailing distributions of power. In other words, it passes off existing social structures as normal or natural at the same time that it tries to convince subordinate classes that they are not being exploited. To facilitate this, hegemonic leadership is expressed 'in terms of universal or general interests, rather than just serving their own interests'.[73] It is a form of domination where a particular interest parades itself as universal.

As a critical theorist Cox is also interested in the forces which work to undermine hegemony. Such forces, which bring about fundamental changes in the structure of world order, Cox calls 'counter-hegemonic'. Counter-hegemonic forces could be states, such as a coalition of Third World states which struggles to undo the dominance of 'core' countries,[74] or non-state actors such as classes, or new social movements.[75] While the impact of counter-hegemonic movements will be transnational, Cox firmly believes that the source of these movements can only be national or domestic.[76]

Linklater on rationalization processes

The task of critical international theory as conceived by Linklater is to provide a social theory of modern world politics. This enlarges the scope of enquiry beyond the limits of traditional international relations requiring 'what Bull has called "a general historical analysis" of the evolution of the "political structure of the world as a whole"'.[77] Beyond this analysis Linklater also posits an interest in social and political transformation. To meet these requirements Linklater follows Habermas in reconstructing historical materialism. The following section provides a brief sketch of Habermas's reconstruction of historical materialism before turning to Linklater's appropriation of this reconstruction and its implications for a historical analysis of the political structure of the world.

Habermas and Marx

The reconstruction of historical materialism offered by Habermas accepts the critiques of Marx's overemphasis on modes of production, but seeks to retrieve the theory of social evolution that remains implicit in it. On Habermas's account, the theory of capitalism and capitalist development worked out by Marx in the *Grundrisse* and *Capital* rests on a deeper and more fundamental 'theory of social evolution that, owing to its reflective status, is also informative for processes of political action'.[78] However this theory of social evolution is constrained in Marx by a preoccupation with the development of productive forces, that is, the more effective mobilization of labour power, technological improvements, increased industrialization, and so on, all of which contribute to the material reproduction of social life.

Habermas argues that Marx's emphasis on modes of production as the key to social evolution was too narrow as it neglected the important dimension of the symbolic reproduction of social life. Marx focused on forces of production at the expense of relations of production, that is, the intersubjective rules, norms, and institutions which structure social interaction. He tended to represent relations of production as simply reflecting changes in the mode of production. By emphasizing the impact on society of changes in the mode of production Marx underestimated the impact of rationalization processes that took place at the level of relations of production. According to Habermas Marx failed to contemplate 'whether *other* rationalization processes are just as important or even more important for the explanation of social evolution' than productive forces.[79] The implication of Habermas's argument is that a more differentiated and complex analysis of rationalization processes is required than that which Marx offers. Marx rightly pointed out the importance that improvements or rationalizations in productive forces can have on society, but he neglected the autonomous capacity of society to rationalize normative structures in order to accommodate and mitigate the rationalization of these productive forces. In short, relations of production, to use Marx's terms, are not impotent or inconsequential in the development of modern societies. Indeed Habermas goes so far as to argue that 'the development of . . . normative structures is the pacemaker of social evolution'.[80]

The key to Habermas's reconstruction of historical materialism is the shift from the paradigms of production and consciousness to a paradigm of language or, as Habermas was to call it later, a theory of communicative action.[81] Underlying this shift was, among other things, a general effort to differentiate between forms of rationality, and a more specific effort to come to grips with the development of communicative rationality or moral-practical forms of reasoning in social life.

Habermas dispenses with Marx's distinction between forces and relations of production and moves to a distinction between cognitive-instrumental and communicative rationality.[82] The basis of this distinction lies in the different ways in which knowledge is translated into action, which leads back, in many respects, to Habermas's earlier distinction between technical and practical interests. In line with this distinction Habermas says that social actions can be distinguished according to whether the participants adopt either a success-orientated or cognitive-instrumental attitude, on the one hand, or consent-orientated or communicative attitude which is concerned with mutual understanding, on the other.[83] Within success-orientated actions a further distinction can be made between those actions taken in non-social situations – instrumental actions; and those taken in social situations – strategic actions.[84] To summarize, Habermas distinguishes three types of action and corresponding rationalities: instrumental, strategic and communicative or moral-practical.

A sociology of the state

Linklater follows Habermas by distinguishing three types of rationality. 'Whereas technical-instrumental rationalization refers to learning how to control nature, and moral-practical rationalization refers to learning how to construct order and social consensus, strategic rationalization refers to learning how to manipulate and control others under conditions of actual or potential conflict'.[85] Linklater makes a further sub-division within moral-practical rationality in order to distinguish between rationalization of principles of co-existence and rationalization of a universal moral code. Link-later ends up then with four types of rationality or action each of which corresponds to a tradition of thought within International Relations: tech-nical-instrumental rationalization which correlates with Marxism's enquiry; strategic rationalization with realism and neo-realism; diplomatic rationa-lization with rationalism; and ethical rationalization with revolutionism.

As Linklater states on the final page of *Beyond Realism and Marxism*, the interplay between these four rationalization processes marks the starting point for a critical international theory.[86] Although he introduces this classification only in the conclusion, it is possible to read the main argument of the book as an attempt to weave these processes into a single theoretical perspective.

The primary concern of this theory, in Linklater's view, is to inquire into the expansion and contraction of community as a consequence of the inter-play of the four rationalization processes.[87] By focusing on class, production and the world economy Marxism makes a crucial contribution to this analysis. By the same token, by focusing on states, war and international anarchy realism and neo-realism also make an important contribution. However, two important qualifications must be made, each of which re-cognizes rationalism and revolutionism as correctives to realism and Marx-ism.

First, the relationship between the capitalist world economy and the states-system must also be dialectically related to international society and the development (or obstruction) of universal moral principles. Sec-ondly, because the sovereign state has defined the modern form of moral and political community, a theory of the state must be developed which takes account of the changing ways in which states and their citizens determine the principles which, by virtue of binding them into a commu-nity, separate them from the rest of the world.[88] Linklater refers to this as the need to develop, *pace* Waltz, a 'fourth image' of international relations.[89] The main concern here deviates from the traditional study of relations between bounded states and instead focuses on the originary constitution of boundedness as a result of competing rationalization processes. Linklater laments that 'too little is known about the ways in which communities come to be bounded and distinct from one another and too little is known about how boundedness and separateness change over time'.[90] Though the state has been a central theme in the study of international relations it has been inadequately analysed because there exists virtually no examination of how societies interpret the social bond which unites some and separates others from moral and political community.[91] According to this view the state remains a central theme in alternative narratives of world politics not because it is the most important actor, but because the nature and future of the state is closely related to the changing boundaries of moral and political community in modernity.

It is clear that, like Cox, Linklater rejects the realist view that a state is a state is a state. For Linklater the state's function as a form of moral and political community is historically and socially determined. Egotism, which realism and neo-realism take as a starting assumption, is a socially produced and historically contingent feature of the state for critical international theory, it 'is acquired rather than given in anarchy itself'.[92] Taking a cue from Wendt's memorable claim that anarchy is what states make of it, critical international theorists regard the meaning and institution of state sovereignty as a historical and social construct.[93] Consequently, 'sovereignty does not have a fixed meaning or characterization, . . . instead, it constitutes the site of continual political struggle over the meaning of the boundaries and constitution of identities'.[94] It is the impossibility of freezing any social construct, including the sovereign state, that compels critical international theory to undertake historical-sociological inquiries. It is in this regard that Linklater calls for 'a sociology of state structures which explains how states construct their legal or moral rights and duties and how these cultural inventions change over time'.[95] This necessarily leads to an analysis of the dominant principles which govern relations between states in different historical periods, but its core concern is with 'changes affecting the social bond which unites members of the sovereign state and separates them from the outside world'.[96] In terms of the Habermasian concern with rationalization processes it leads to a focus on the moral-practical rationalization of boundaries.

Elsewhere Linklater has formulated this concern with the 'fourth image' in terms of the dialectics of inclusion and exclusion.[97] In a similar vein Hoffman also identifies the dialectics of inclusion and exclusion in world politics as the primary focus of critical international theory.[98] The nature and future of the modern social bond and the dialectic of inclusion and exclusion it brings with it is emerging as a fundamental theme of critical international theory.

Linklater has suggested that a concern with this dialectic can be found in most critical approaches to the study of international relations.[99] Critical theory, postmodernism, feminism, Marxism and rationalism all include a concern with various forms of exclusion, whether it takes the shape of exclusion based on gender, race, ethnicity, civilization, culture. The point for Linklater is that a comprehensive account of world politics requires analysis of the 'multiple axes of exclusion'.[100] There are three dimensions to this comprehensive account: the philosophical, the historical, and the political. The philosophical or normative task is to reflect on criteria for determining the validity of modes of inclusion and exclusion. The historical-sociological task is to 'examine the origins, reproduction and transformation of the moral boundaries which separate the societies which comprise specific intersocietal systems'.[101] The political task is to strike a just balance between the universal and particular in the practical application of any mode of inclusion and exclusion. In the next part of the chapter the philosophical and political dimensions of critical international theory's account of exclusion will be clarified.

To summarize this part of the chapter, although Cox and Linklater use different theoretical sources, they both make a case for the rehabilitation of Marxist theory in the study of world politics. More substantively, both Cox and Linklater argue for the inclusion of class, production, and the world economy in any analysis of world politics. No theory of world politics would be complete without contemplating the relationship between these forces and the traditional objects of international relations theory such as the state, nationalism, the states-system, war, and international society. The object of enquiry, as critical international theory understands it, must be extended to encompass the full range of power relations that shape world politics. This necessarily leads to normative issues regarding the justifiability of unequal or exploitative relations in world politics. The overall result of Cox and Linklater's individual efforts is to pave the way for a critical enquiry into world politics that combines empirical and normative concerns. Cox and Linklater have a common theoretical interest in the development of a social theory which can provide a historical account of the present order, a critique of injustices and inequalities, and an assessment of immanent possibilities of change. It is the fact that the prevailing world order is shot through with inequalities and injustices which makes social and political transformation, or emancipation, imperative. It is to this defining feature of critical international relations that we now turn.

Emancipation and the Reconstruction of World Politics

This chapter has argued that critical international theory radically differs from traditional theories. It offers a different conception of theory, it employs a different methodology, and it is guided by an emancipatory interest. However, while it disagrees with much of realist theoretical analysis it accepts realism's general description of world politics as a domain shaped predominantly by various particularistic and exclusionary practices and institutions. Whereas realism accepts this as the given framework, critical international theory seeks to bring about radical change; it seeks to remove these unnecessary constraints on universal freedom. This brings critical international theory back to the task set out most powerfully by Kant in *Perpetual Peace*: how to bring peace and freedom to a world divided by particularistic forces? Linklater implies a return to this project when he says, critical international theory inquires into 'the possibility of realizing the moral life in an international system of states'.[102] In other words critical international theory sets itself the task of understanding the conditions under which emancipation in world politics is possible.[103]

The following section aims to describe and explain the themes which lie behind the conception of emancipation as expressed by critical international theorists. It begins by sketching the basis of emancipation in autonomy before considering the implications this has for thinking about security and community. It then outlines Habermas's discourse ethics as a procedure for clarifying the normative grounds on which world politics can be reconstructed.

Autonomy, security, community

The conception of emancipation promoted by critical international theory is largely derived from a strand of thought which finds its origin in the Enlightenment project. This project was generally concerned with breaking with past forms of injustice to foster the conditions necessary for universal freedom.[104] To begin with, emancipation as understood by Enlightenment thinkers and critical international theorists expresses a negative conception of freedom which consists in the removal of unnecessary, socially-created constraints. This understanding is manifest in Booth's definition of emancipation as 'freeing people from those constraints that stop them carrying out what freely they would choose to do'.[105] The emphasis in this understanding is on dislodging those impediments or impositions which unnecessarily curtail individual or collective freedom. More substantively, Ashley defines emancipation as the securing of 'freedom from unacknowledged constraints, relations of domination, and conditions of distorted communication and understanding that deny humans the capacity to make their own future through full will and consciousness'.[106] The common thrust of these understandings is that emancipation implies a quest for autonomy. 'To be free', says Linklater, is 'to be self-determining or to have the capacity to initiate action'.[107] Emancipation begins with autonomy. Autonomy on its own is not enough however. For critical international theory, exploring the prospects 'for extending the human capacity for self-determination' must also include an exploration of security; the quest for autonomy must also be a quest for security.[108]

Security, which Booth defines as 'the absence of threats' is necessarily implicated in emancipation because autonomy rests, to a certain degree, on the absence of incapacitating threats.[109] Security is that which protects or guards autonomy. There is no autonomy without security; for without security individuals or groups would not be safe in their pursuit of freedom, hence Booth's assertion that 'security and emancipation are two sides of the same coin'.[110] Violence, war, poverty, political oppression, and poor

education are just some of the constraints Booth cites which threaten the
well-being of individuals and groups, thereby jeopardizing their capacity to
act freely. Security has the effect of holding at bay threats to freedom and
autonomy. It is in this regard that the concept of emancipation unavoidably
involves security.

Booth's argument holds significant implications for the study of international relations. Though security has been one of the key terms in the study
of international relations it has suffered the same fate as terms such as state
and power; rarely has there been any critical analysis of its meaning.
Booth's argument continues in more radical fashion an examination of
security initiated by Barry Buzan.[111] Booth deals a critical blow to traditional assumptions about security, particularly realist ones about achieving
security for the state through violence and the accumulation of the instruments of violence. The upshot of Booth's approach was to inaugurate a
strand of thought now referred to as 'critical security studies'.

As a form, or perhaps dimension, of critical international theory, critical
security studies signifies a reaction to traditional security and strategic
studies. It objects to the problem-solving approach taken by traditional
approaches preferring, as Richard Wyn Jones says, to challenge the 'hegemonic security discourse and the prevailing practices of global (in)security'.[112] It seeks to do this by posing three basic questions: 'first, what is
security? Second, who is being secured by the prevailing order, and who or
what are they being secured against? Third, ... [with] whose security
should we be concerning ourselves, and by which agents and through
which strategies should this security be attained?'.[113] The second and third
questions which are rarely, if ever, posed in traditional security studies are
the starting point for critical security studies which makes no effort to
conceal its discontent with prevailing regimes of security and its preference
for change. The obvious consequence of taking this starting point is to bring
into question the orthodox view that states are the primary or exclusive
subjects of security. 'Eschewing the statism of mainstream security discourse, proponents of Critical Security Studies recognise that, globally,
the sovereign state is one of the main causes of insecurity: it is part of the
problem rather than the solution'.[114]

Critical security studies thus shifts the focus of security from the sovereign state to humanity. In a sense it revives the Kantian idea of a 'cosmopolitan system of general political security' which takes humans rather than
states as the subjects of security.[115] Security, in this definition, is not confined to particular sovereign states – indeed, it cannot be exclusive or
particularistic at all, it must be generalized across all human social relations
and all communities. This means that security cannot be understood in the
traditional strategic sense which, Booth says, rests on a notion of security as
'ethnocentric self-interest writ large'.[116] It cannot be purchased at the
expense of others, whether states or people. Ultimately, security, as Booth

defines it, requires submitting to Kant's practical imperative always to treat others as ends in themselves and never as means.[117] 'True security', says Booth, 'can only be achieved by people and groups if they do not deprive others of it'.[118] There is an essential universality or reciprocity built-in to the revised concept of security such that one can only be secure if others are also secure. Security depends on mutual interdependence.

By appealing to this Kantian categorical imperative in his revision of the concept of security Booth directs attention to the connection between security and community. If security is to be generalized, as Kant and Booth insist, it unavoidably entails the expansion of moral and political community. The concept of security as revised by critical security studies rests, like critical theory in general, on a critique of exclusion and particularism. This critique leads to an inevitable concern with the fundamental concept of community and a critique of the sovereign state as repository of moral and political community.

Critical international theory reacts against the conventional tendency to associate community with the state or nation. It challenges the practice of limiting community to 'the confines of the state's authoritative domain'.[119] By refusing to take the sovereign state as an idealised form of community it challenges the state's role as sole constructor of identity, and invites rethinking the nature and limits of moral and political community under changing global conditions.[120]

The impact on states from countervailing pressures of globalisation and fragmentation has forced a rethinking of moral and political community.[121] As Linklater has pointed out, it is doubtful whether the conditions under which sovereign states have regulated political community and identity in the past remain intact.[122] The basis of this doubt is not just the facts of globalization, mass migration, the rise of sub-national groups, and so on, but normative reasons concerning the state's claim to determine political community and identity. An essential problem with the state is that, as a 'limited moral community', it promotes a form of particularism which generates insecurity and intersocietal estrangement by imposing, as Linklater says, rigid boundaries between insiders and outsiders, 'us' and 'them'.[123] On this basis sovereign states purchase moral and political community by sacrificing internal dissenters, outsiders, and other states' security.

Eschewing the particularism associated with the state, critical international theory defends a theoretical position which is committed to the goal of emancipating the species. It seeks to facilitate moral and political community not just by extending it beyond the frontiers of the sovereign state, but also by deepening it within those frontiers. It is concerned with overcoming intersocietal estrangement and establishing a system of general political security based on universal emancipation. Such a system would require forms of political organization which were 'less insistent on sovereignty and more tolerant of the sub-national and transnational loyalties on which future sites of organizational power may come to rest'.[124]

Underlying critical international theory's critique of the sovereign state is a critique of all forms of exclusion or particularistic association because of the estrangement they produce. Critical international theory undertakes its critique of the sovereign state by deploying a philosophical critique of particularism inherited from Kant and Marx but advanced by more recent strands of thought such as feminism and postmodernism.

As Linklater asserts, Marxism contains the resources for undertaking a critique of all forms of particularism.[125] However, while Marx rightly emphasized class-based particularism, he underestimated the importance of national-based and state-based particularism. It is also necessary, following Kant, to recognize the particularism fostered by the state and states-system, as they are crucial 'obstacles to the universal recognition of men as species-beings'.[126] However, as feminist theorists have pointed out, what is missing from both Kant and Marx is recognition of gender-based particularism. Postmodernism has also taken issue with forms of exclusion or closure which attempt dogmatically to circumscribe moral, political and cultural limits. In view of this, Linklater insists that a critical international theory must develop a 'comprehensive account of the multiple axes of exclusion' that pervade the modern world and prevent the realization of universal emancipation.[127]

The above section has attempted to outline critical international theory's understanding of emancipation by considering the themes of autonomy, security, and community. Underlying the treatment of these themes was a critique of particularism or exclusion. Emancipation, then, can be understood as the establishment of a community which allows, and protects, the development of universal autonomy. Such a community would reject unnecessary, socially-created forms of exclusion. The question arises at this point as to how non-exclusionary forms of community can be achieved, or in other words, how to reconstruct world politics so as to extend to the entire species a rational, just and democratic organization of politics. The final section deals with Habermas's suggestion that such a reconstruction should adopt a discourse-ethical approach.

Discourse ethics: the moral point of view in pluralistic contexts

It has already been noted that for critical international theory emancipation necessarily involves the evolution of more inclusionary, less particularistic, forms of political association; but how is particularism to be overcome? By what means can particularistic and exclusionary practices be transcended? Furthermore, what forms of community would displace attitudes and institutions of exclusion? These have become central questions in contemporary international relations theory which direct attention to the complex problem of striking the right, or just, balance between principles of universalism and the value of difference.[128] In other words, how is it possible to realize the 'moral life' in world politics given the tremendous pluralism that exists? This has become the most important question for recent normative theories of international relations as theorists have come to recognize the fact of cultural difference and the moral claims attached to these cultures. Although general agreement exists that the world consists of great diversity, none exists as to the desirability or possibility of establishing universal moral principles.

Critical international theorists take this question very seriously. Cox reflects on the possibility of a post-hegemonic order which would be forced to 'derive its normative content in a search for common ground among constituent traditions of civilisation'.[129] Such an order would accept Chris Brown's point that no way of life can be used as a standard, and no single culture or state could legitimately lay down the normative foundations for such an order.[130] Cox wants to consider whether it would be possible for 'alternative intersubjective worlds' to co-exist 'without one coming to dominate and absorb the others . . .'.[131] Hoffman advances a similar argument in his commitment to a cosmopolitan ethic. Such an ethic would seek to avoid ethnocentric and imperialist meta-narratives and recognize 'the reality and desirability of diversity'.[132] At the same time, however, it maintains a commitment to a 'cautious and contingent' universalism.[133] Most importantly, Hoffman's notion of 'ironic cosmopolitanism' addresses the tensions between universalism and particularism without giving a priori privilege to either. In similar vein, much of Linklater's recent work has been dominated by a concern with balancing universalism with cultural diversity.[134] Crucially, for Linklater this is precisely a question of justice. But on what basis does critical international theory decide questions of justice in a pluralistic context? The following section turns to Habermas's notion of discourse ethics as an attempt to deal with this issue.

Habermas and discourse ethics

The resort to discourse ethics is meant to provide a means of resolving situations of social conflict in a just and impartial manner. It offers a basis for advancing the moral point of view wherever there are clashes of culture or morality, that is, wherever there is politics. Against sceptical views which capitulate to the apparent incommensurability of values, discourse ethics remains committed to the promotion of the Kantian principle of generalisability.

To understand discourse ethics it is necessary to recall that it comes out of Habermas's 'consent-orientated' theory of communicative action. This theory builds on the need for communicating subjects to rationalize or account for their beliefs and actions in terms which are intelligible to others and which they can then accept or contest.[135] Similarly, social norms and institutions must also be submitted to scrutiny and argumentation if they are to maintain legitimacy. At such moments when a principle, social norm, or institution loses legitimacy or when consensus breaks down, then discourse ethics enters the fray as a means of consensually deciding upon new principles or institutional arrangements. According to discourse ethics, newly-arrived-at political principles, norm, or institutional arrangements can only be said to be valid if they can meet with the approval of all those who would be affected by them.[136]

There are three features worthy of note for our purposes. First, discourse ethics is universalist. It is orientated to the establishment and maintenance of the conditions necessary for open and non-exclusionary dialogue. No individual or group which will be affected by the principle, norm, or institution under deliberation should be excluded from participation in dialogue. Secondly, discourse ethics is democratic. It builds on a model of the public sphere which is bound to intersubjective recognition and consent and where participants retain the 'uninfringeable freedom to respond with a "yes" or "no" to criticizable validity claims'.[137] Combining the universalist and democratic impulses, discourse ethics provides a mechanism that can test which principles, norms, or institutional arrangements would be 'equally good for all'.[138] Thirdly, discourse ethics is a form of moral-practical reasoning. As such it is not simply guided by utilitarian calculations or expediency, nor is it guided by an imposed concept of the 'good life'.[139] Rather, it is guided by justice. It is concerned with the 'justification and application of norms that stipulate reciprocal rights and duties' in situations of disagreement or conflict.[140]

It is possible to identify three general implications of discourse ethics for the reconstruction of world politics; these can only be briefly outlined here. First, by virtue of its democratic, consent-orientated approach, discourse ethics offers normative guidance regarding issues of globalization and global governance. In light of social and material changes such as the globalization of trade and finance, the movement of peoples, the rise of indigenous peoples and sub-national groups, environmental degradation, and so on, the 'viability and accountability of national decision-making entities' is being brought into question.[141] Held highlights the democratically-deficient nature of the sovereign state when he asks: 'whose consent is necessary and whose participation is justified in decisions concerning, for instance, AIDS, or acid rain, or the use of non-renewable resources? What is the relevant constituency: national, regional or international?'.[142] In the range of issues which involve relations across, between, and within communities, the sovereign state, because of its monopolising tendency, is inadequate by the standards of discourse ethics.

Secondly, discourse ethics offers a procedure for regulating social conflict and arriving at resolutions which are acceptable to all affected parties. Hoffman believes that the practice of third-party facilitation offers a discourse-ethical approach to the resolution of conflict. Third-party facilitation aims at achieving a non-hierarchical, non-coercive resolution of conflict by including both or all affected parties as participants in the dialogue.[143] The dialogue fostered by third-party facilitation involves the conflicting parties in the reversing of perspectives and encourages them to reason from the other's point of view. As Hoffman observes, third-party facilitation seeks 'to promote a self-generated and self-sustaining resolution to the conflict'.[144] Because the outcome must be acceptable to all concerned it is more likely to promote compliance.[145] In plainly Habermasian language Hoffman says that 'third-party facilitation could be characterized as the promotion of consensual decision-making towards the resolution of conflict via a process of undistorted communication'.[146]

Thirdly, discourse ethics offers a means of criticising and justifying the principles by which the species organizes itself politically, that is, it reflects on the principles of inclusion and exclusion. To begin with, discourse ethics runs against the grain of state sovereignty which is particularistic and exclusionary. As Linklater observes, the sovereign state 'restricts the capacity of outsiders to participate in discourse to consider issues which concern them'.[147] It is characteristic of discourse ethics to call into question the dogmatic imposition of all exclusionary, bounded communities.[148] From the moral point of view contained within discourse ethics the sovereign state as a form of community is unjust because the principles of inclusion and exclusion are not the outcome of open dialogue and deliberation where all who stand to be affected by the arrangement have been able to participate in discussion. Against the exclusionary nature of the social bond underlying the sovereign state, discourse ethics has the universalist aim 'to secure the social bond of all with all'.[149] In sum, discourse ethics promotes a cosmopolitan ideal where the political organization of humanity is decided by a process of dialogue in which participation is open to all who stand to be affected by the decision. As Linklater observes, 'the principles of political life should be agreed, as far as possible, by all'.[150]

To conclude this part, critical international theory's understanding of emancipation involves rethinking and reconstructing security and community in modern political life. The achievement of a rational, just, and democratic organization of global politics cannot be advanced, however, without first taking account of the procedures by which political principles, social norms, and institutions are decided upon. Critical international theory argues that discourse ethics provides just the sort of procedure necessary for emancipation. Of course, by recognizing the importance of giving equal respect for universality and diversity, critical international theory opts for a revised version of cosmopolitanism. As Booth remarks, this would lead to what has been called 'sensitive universalism'.[151]

Conclusion

This chapter has been concerned with explaining the contribution of critical theory to the study of international relations. It considered the relationship of knowledge to interests and values, the influence of Marxism, and, in particular, Habermas's reconstruction of historical materialism, and the question of emancipation in world politics.

Critical international theory has made an important contribution to the study of international relations simply by posing fundamental questions regarding epistemology and ontology in the early 1980s. To be sure, other theoretical perspectives such as feminism and postmodernism have since dealt with these issues as well. But the distinctive contribution of critical international theory relates to three broad areas: (1) the historical-sociological analysis of the structures of modern world politics; (2) the philosophical critique of particularism and exclusion, and (3) the philosophical enquiry into the conditions under which emancipation in world politics is possible. The theme common to all three areas is the sovereign state. The sovereign state is a central actor on the world stage which must be accounted for in social and historical terms; it is the foremost example of a particularistic or exclusionary political institution; and, as a result, it is a formidable obstacle to emancipation. Critical international theory's aim of achieving an alternative theory and practice of international relations centers on the possibility of overcoming the sovereign state and inaugurating post-sovereign world politics. It is this critical analysis of state sovereignty which is emerging as the central object of critical international theory just as it is for postmodernism.

Finally, a note on its future. As Linklater warns in his closing sentence to *Beyond Realism and Marxism*, the success of critical international theory will not be determined by its performance in the spheres of philosophy and historical sociology alone, but 'by the amount of light cast on present possibilities'.[152] This is an exacting test for any theory and the question of whether critical international theory can pass this test in the future will depend on its ability to develop analyses which advance the practical political task of reconstructing world politics. For the moment, however, there can be little doubt that the theoretical study of international relations has been transformed by the entry of critical international theory.

Notes

1. J. Maclean, 'Political Theory, International Theory, and Problems of Ideology', *Millennium*, vol. 10, no. 2 (1981), p. 103.
2. M. Horkheimer, *Critical Theory* (New York, 1972), p. 206.
3. K. Marx, *Selected Writings* (Oxford, 1977), p. 158.
4. Horkheimer (1972), p. 223.
5. T. McCarthy, *The Critical Theory of Jürgen Habermas* (Cambridge, Mass., 1978), p. 55.
6. Horkheimer (1972).
7. Horkheimer (1972), p. 215.
8. A. Linklater, *Beyond Realism and Marxism: Critical Theory and International Relations* (London, 1990a), p. 8.
9. McCarthy (1978), p. 96.
10. Maclean (1981), p. 113
11. M. Fischer, 'Feudal Europe, 800–1300: Communal Discourse and Conflictual Practices', *International Organization*, vol. 46, no. 2 (1992), p. 429.
12. K. Waltz, *Theory of International Politics* (New York, 1979), p. 10.
13. Ibid., p. 6.
14. Ibid., p. 124.
15. R. W. Cox 'Social Forces, States and World Orders: Beyond International Relations Theory', *Millennium*, vol. 10, no. 2 (1981), p. 128.
16. Ibid., p. 129.
17. R. O. Keohane, *After Hegemony: Cooperation and Discord in the World Political Economy* (Princeton, 1984), p. 63.
18. R. W. Cox 'Multilateralism and World Order', *Review of International Studies*, vol. 18 (1992a), p. 173.
19. Cox (1981), p. 130.
20. M. Hoffman, 'Critical Theory and the Inter-Paradigm Debate', *Millennium*, vol. 16, no. 2 (1987), p. 233.
21. Cox (1981), p. 130.
22. Ibid., pp. 133–4.
23. R. K. Ashley, 'Political Realism and Human Interests', *International Studies Quarterly*, vol. 25 (1981), p. 207.
24. Ibid., p. 221.
25. See Linklater's chapter on rationalism in this volume.
26. Ashley (1981), pp. 221–6.
27. Ibid., p. 219.
28. A. Linklater, 'The Achivements of Critical Theory', in K. Booth, S. Smith and M. Zalewski (eds), *International Political Theory: Positivism and After* (Cambridge, 1996).
29. Ashley (1981), p. 227.

30. Hoffman (1987), p. 236; K. Booth, 'Security and Emancipation', *Review of International Studies*, vol. 17, no. 4 (1991b), p. 321.
31. Linklater (1990a), ch.1.
32. H. Bull, *The Anarchical Society: A Study of Order in World Politics* (London, 1977).
33. Linklater (1990a), p. 21.
34. Ibid., pp. 21–22.
35. A. Linklater, 'What is a Good International Citizen?' in P. Keal (ed.), *Ethics and Foreign Policy* (Canberra, 1992a) p. 36.
36. A. Linklater, *Men and Citizens in the Theory of International Relations* (2nd edn, London, 1990b), p. 159.
37. Linklater (1990a), p. 1.
38. R. W. Cox 'Postscript 1985', in R. O. Keohane (ed.), *Neo-realism and its Critics* (New York, 1986), p. 242.
39. Cox (1981), p. 130.
40. Cox (1986), p. 245.
41. K. Booth, 'Security in Anarchy: Utopian Realism in Theory and Practice', *International Affairs*, vol. 67, no. 3 (1991a), p. 534.
42. Linklater (1990a).
43. Cox (1981), p. 129.
44. Linklater (1990a), p. 42.
45. Cox (1981), p. 129.
46. Ibid., p. 128.
47. Maclean (1981), p. 113.
48. Linklater (1990a).
49. Ibid., p. 148.
50. Linklater in this volume, pp. 119–44.
51. Linklater (1990a), p. 5.
52. R. W. Cox 'Towards a Post-Hegemonic Conceptualization of World Order: Reflections on the Relevancy of Ibn Khaldun' in E.-O. Czempiel and J. N. Rosenau (eds), *Governance Without Government* (Cambridge, 1992b), p. 138.
53. Cox (1992b), p. 133.
54. Cox (1986), p. 242.
55. R. W. Cox 'Production, the State, and Change in World Order', in E.-O. Czempiel and J. N. Rosenau (eds), *Global Change and Theoretical Challenges* (Cambridge, 1989), p. 37.
56. Cox (1992b), p. 157.
57. Cox (1986), p. 244.
58. Cox (1989).
59. Cox (1986), pp. 244–4; J. G. Ruggie, 'Continuity and Transformation in the World Polity: Toward a Neo-Realist Synthesis', *World Politics*, vol. 35, no. 2 (January 1983), pp. 261–85.
60. Cox (1981), p. 135ff.
61. Cox (1989), p. 37.

62. Cox (1981), p. 127.
63. R. W. Cox 'Gramsci, Hegemony and International Relations: An Essay on Method', *Millennium*, vol. 12, no. 2 (1983), p. 173.
64. Ibid., p. 169.
65. Cox (1981), p. 133.
66. Cox (1983), p. 164.
67. Ibid., p. 164.
68. Cox (1981), pp. 137–8.
69. Ibid., p. 141.
70. Ibid., p. 141.
71. Cox (1992a), p. 179.
72. Cox (1983), p. 171.
73. Cox (1981), p. 137.
74. Ibid..
75. Cox (1989).
76. Cox (1983).
77. Linklater (1990a), p. 163.
78. J. Habermas, *Communication and the Evolution of Society* (Boston, 1979), p. 130.
79. Habermas (1979), p. 118.
80. Ibid., p. 120.
81. J. Habermas, *The Theory of Communicative Action, vol. 1: Reason and the Rationalization of Society* (Cambridge, 1984).
82. Ibid., p. 10.
83. Ibid., p. 286.
84. Ibid., p. 285.
85. A. Linklater, 'Rationalization Processes and International History: Critical Theory, Poststructuralism and International Relations', in M. Hoffman and N. J. Rengger (eds), *Beyond the Inter-Paradigm Debate: Critical Theory and International Relations* (forthcoming).
86. Linklater (1990a), p. 172.
87. Ibid., p. 171.
88. Ibid., p. 143; (1995b).
89. Linklater (1992a), p. 37; (1995b), p. 255.
90. A. Linklater, 'Community', in A. Danchev, *Fin de Siècle: The Meaning of the Twentieth Century* (London, 1995a), p. 183.
91. A. Linklater and J. MacMillan, 'Introduction: Boundaries in Question', in J. MacMillan and A. Linklater (eds), *Boundaries in Question* (London, 1995), pp. 12–3.
92. A. Linklater, 'Neo-Realism in Theory and Practice', in K. Booth and S. Smith (eds), *International Political Theory Today* (Cambridge, 1995b), p. 254.
93. Linklater (1995b); M. Hoffman, 'Agency, Identity and Intervention', in I. Forbes and M. Hoffman (eds), *Political Theory, International Relations and the Ethics of Intervention* (London, 1993), p. 200.
94. Hoffman (1993), p. 202.

95. Linklater (1995b), p. 255.
96. Linklater (1996); Linklater (1990b), pp. 220–1.
97. Linklater (1990b), postscript; (1992a); (1992b).
98. Hoffman (1993), p. 198.
99. A. Linklater, 'The Question of the Next Stage in International Relations Theory: A Critical-Theoretical Point of View', *Millennium*, vol. 21, no. 1 (1992b), p. 85.
100. Linklater, forthcoming.
101. Linklater (1990b), p. 223.
102. Linklater (1990a), p. 138.
103. See R. Devetak, 'The Project of Modernity and International Relations Theory', *Millennium*, vol. 24, no. 1 (1995), pp. 27–51.
104. Ibid., pp. 29–35.
105. Booth (1991a), p. 539.
106. Ashley (1981), p. 227.
107. Linklater (1990b), p. 135.
108. Linklater (1990a), p. 10.
109. Booth (1991b), p. 319.
110. Ibid., p. 319.
111. B. Buzan, *People, States and Fear: An Agenda for International Security Studies in the Post-Cold War Era* (Hemel Hempstead, 1991).
112. R. Wyn Jones, '"Message in a Bottle"? Theory and Praxis in Critical Security Studies', *Contemporary Security Policy*, vol. 16, no. 3 (1995), p. 309.
113. Ibid., p. 309.
114. Ibid., p. 310.
115. I. Kant, *Kant's Political Writings* (Cambridge, 1970), p. 49.
116. Booth (1991a), p. 537.
117. I. Kant, *Fundamental Principles of the Metaphysic of Morals* (New York, 1987), p. 58; Booth (1991b), p. 319; (1991a), p. 539.
118. Booth (1991a), p. 539.
119. Hoffman (1993), p. 202.
120. Ibid., p. 207.
121. Ibid., M. Cochran, 'Cosmopolitanism and Communitarianism in a Post-Cold War World', in J. MacMillan and A. Linklater (eds), *Boundaries in Question* (London, 1995).
122. Linklater (1995a).
123. Linklater (1990b), p. 28.
124. Linklater (1995a), p. 195.
125. Linklater (1990b), p. 159.
126. Ibid.
127. Linklater, forthcoming.
128. Linklater (1990b), postscript.
129. Cox (1992b), p. 141.
130. C. Brown, 'The Modern Requirement? Reflections on Normative International Theory in a Post-Western World', *Millennium*, vol. 17, no. 2 (1988), p. 346.

131. Cox (1992b), p. 159.
132. Hoffman (1993), p. 199.
133. M. Hoffman, 'Conversations on Critical International Relations Theory', *Millennium*, vol. 17, no. 1 (1988), p. 93.
134. Linklater (1990b), postscript; (1992b); (1995a); (1995c).
135. Habermas (1984), p. 99.
136. J. Habermas, *Moral Consciousness and Communicative Action* (Cambridge, 1990), pp. 65–6.
137. Habermas (1990), p. 202.
138. J. Habermas, *Justification and Application: Remarks on Discourse Ethics* (Cambridge, 1993), p. 151.
139. Habermas (1993), ch.1.
140. Habermas (1993), p. 9.
141. D. Held, 'Democracy: From City-States to Cosmopolitan Order', in D. Held (ed.), *Prospects for Democracy: North, South, East, West* (Cambridge, 1993), p. 26.
142. Held (1993), pp. 26–7.
143. M. Hoffman, 'Third-Party Mediation and Conflict-Resolution in the Post-Cold War World', in J. Bayliss and N. J. Rengger (eds), *Dilemmas of World Politics* (Oxford, 1992), p. 265.
144. Hoffman (1993), p. 206.
145. Hoffman (1992), p. 270.
146. Ibid., p. 273.
147. Linklater (1995c).
148. Ibid.
149. J. Habermas, *The Philosophical Discourse of Modernity: Twelve Lectures* (Cambridge, 1987), p. 346.
150. A. Linklater, 'Community, Citizenship and Global Politics', *Oxford International Review*, vol. 5, no. 1 (1993), p. 9.
151. K. Booth, 'Human Wrongs and International Relations', *International Affairs*, vol. 71, no. 1 (1995), pp. 103–26, p. 119.
152. Linklater (1990a), p. 172.

CHAPTER 7

Postmodernism

Richard Devetak

It was in the mid-1980s that the discipline of International Relations came under serious challenge from various critical theories. Frankfurt School critical theory and, subsequently, postmodernism, dealt telling blows to a discipline that for so long had managed more or less successfully to hide its severe limitations. A central figure in this challenge was Richard K. Ashley. While his writings in the early 1980s were plainly inspired by Habermas and the Frankfurt School, his writings in the mid-1980s no longer drew inspiration from the same source, but increasingly drew from French thinkers such as Pierre Bourdieu and Michel Foucault. By 1987 Ashley had completely departed from Frankfurt School critical theory as practised by Robert Cox, Andrew Linklater and Mark Hoffman, and was now, like Rob Walker and James Der Derian, firmly committed to a postmodern approach. It was Der Derian's *On Diplomacy* and Walker's *One World/Many Worlds: Struggles for a Just World Peace*, published in 1987 and 1988 respectively, which inaugurated book-length inquiries into international relations with a clear postmodern slant. By 1989 the first collection of explicitly postmodern essays appeared – *International/Intertextual Relations: Postmodern Readings of World Politics*, edited by James Der Derian and Michael J. Shapiro. This was followed in 1990 by a special issue of *International Studies Quarterly* entitled, 'Speaking the Language of Exile: Dissidence in International Studies', edited by Ashley and Walker, which included contributions by Shapiro, Der Derian, Bradley Klein, Jim George and David Campbell, Cynthia Weber and the editors, all of whom have continued to theorise international relations from a postmodern perspective.

But why did these theorists adopt a postmodern approach to the study of international relations? And what is it that binds these thinkers together, making them postmodern? A straightforward response to these questions depends on clearly defining postmodernism. Unfortunately a clear definition of postmodernism that will meet with general agreement is precisely what is not possible. Not only is the definition and meaning of postmodernism in dispute between proponents and critics, but also among proponents.

Sometimes the different understandings of postmodernism amount to fairly minor differences of emphasis, sometimes they result in significantly divergent theoretical trajectories and conclusions. If there is anything clear about postmodernism it is that its meaning and definition is a source of great contention. In lieu of a definition of postmodernism, this chapter adopts a pragmatic and nominalistic approach. Theorists who are referred to, or who regard their own writing, as postmodern will be included here as postmodern. So too will be those who make no explicit reference to postmodernism, but who theorise in a manner which is informed by ideas associated with postmodernism. The intention of this chapter is therefore not so much to portray postmodernism as a coherent or unified theory, as it is to make intelligible some of the different problematique, focii, and theoretical strategies which can loosely be gathered together under the name postmodernism.

The chapter is divided into four main parts. The first part deals with the relationship between power and knowledge in the study of international relations. The second part outlines the textual strategies employed by postmodern approaches to this study. The third part is concerned with how postmodernism deals with the state. And the final part of the chapter outlines the ethical orientation of postmodernism.

Power and Knowledge in International Relations

In the study of international relations there is no shortage of references to the concept of 'power'. Indeed, power is normally taken to be one of the key concepts in the subject that is commonly known as 'power politics'. It has shared centre-stage with the concept of 'state' since the discipline's inception, and is viewed as the basic currency of international relations. Despite this centrality it has remained largely an underdeveloped concept. More worrying than the underdevelopment of the concept of power has been the virtual silence regarding questions of knowledge in the study of international relations until recently.

It was not until the 1980s that a focus on knowledge was treated seriously. With the advent of critical theory and postmodernism the silence was lifted on questions of knowledge. Reflection on the interests and metaphysical suppositions which guide and frame knowledge became fundamental aspects of international relations theory. As Der Derian noted as late as 1988, 'international relations is undergoing an epistemological critique which calls into question the very language, concepts, methods, and history (that is, the dominant discourse) which constitutes and governs a "tradition" of thought'.[1] Instead of taking for granted issues of epistemology (knowledge claims) and ontology (claims about being or thinghood), it was now seen as essential to investigate how such issues had been dealt with by the competing 'traditions' of thought. The consequences of the orthodox divorce between knowledge and values, knowledge and reality, and knowledge and power now had to be examined. Such issues were not considered to be secondary in importance to the so-called 'real' issues. Indeed, one consequence of this new focus was to inquire into the ways that some issues were framed as serious, legitimate or real, whereas others were sidelined as unimportant, the subject of another discipline, or far too abstract for serious consideration within International Relations. It is under the rubric of power-knowledge that postmodernism makes some important observations regarding these issues. In the following section Foucault's understanding of the connection between power and knowledge will be outlined before turning to consider his notion of genealogy and its implications for the study of international relations.

Foucault, power, knowledge

Within orthodox social scientific accounts, knowledge should be immune from the influence of power. The study of international relations, or any scholarly study for that matter, requires the suspension of values, interests and power relations in the pursuit of balanced (objective) knowledge – knowledge uncontaminated by external influences and based on (pure) reason. Kant's caution that 'the possession of power inevitably corrupts the free judgement of reason', stands as a classic example of this view.[2] It is this view that Foucault, and postmodernism generally, have begun to problematize. Foucault asks whether 'we should abandon a whole tradition that allows us to imagine that knowledge can exist only where the power relations are suspended and that knowledge can develop only outside its injunctions, its demands and its interests'.[3] Perhaps we should 'admit rather that power produces knowledge (and not simply by encouraging it because it serves power or by applying it because it is useful); that power and knowledge directly imply one another; that there is no power relation without the correlative constitution of a field of knowledge, nor any knowledge that does not presuppose and constitute at the same time power relations'.[4]

This suggests a critical recasting of the relationship between knowledge and power, between ideas and the material world, and between reason and violence. It sees in the theory of knowledge a crucial reserve of political power, that is, its 'specifically symbolic power to impose principles of the construction of reality'.[5] Against empiricism it recognises the importance of ideas, knowledge, representation and ideology in the constitution of social

and political realities. But against abstract philosophical idealism it emphasises that the realm of knowledge is already shaped by, and to a degree, in
the service of, prevailing power relations. In sum, 'truth is a thing of this
world', said Foucault, and 'it induces regular effects of power'.[6] One of
Foucault's concerns was to situate the production of knowledge and truth at
the centre of historical and political analysis, and not, in any way, to divorce
the production of knowledge from the production of power.

The upshot is that, 'between techniques of knowledge and strategies of
power, there is no exteriority'.[7] Foucault calls this the 'rule of immanence'.[8]
According to this 'rule' there is a general consistency (which cannot be
reduced to an identity) between modes of interpretation and operations of
power. They are mutually supportive. The task is to see how operations of
power fit in with the wider social and political matrices of the modern
world. What kinds of knowledge follow from, give rise to, and legitimize
prevailing configurations of power? How is knowledge implicated in the
constitution of dominant modes of subjectivity and fields of action? Such
are the questions made possible by a focus on power–knowledge relations.

Instead of treating knowledge and power as if they occupied two separate fields, Foucault wanted to see if there was not some common matrix
which hooked them together. For example, in *Discipline and Punish* Foucault
investigates the possibility that the evolution of the penal system is intimately connected to the human sciences. His argument is that a 'single
process of "epistemologico-juridical" formation' underlies the history of the
prison on the one hand, and the knowledge of 'man' on the other.[9] In other
words, the prison is consistent with modern society and modern modes of
apprehending 'man's' world. The knowledge produced by this single process is not objective or neutral, but determined by the prevailing conceptions of what is required in the social domain. There is, Foucault argues, a
rule of immanence between knowledge of man and knowledge regarding
prisons.

This type of analysis has been attempted in International Relations by
various thinkers. Ashley has exposed one dimension of the power–knowledge nexus by indicating the rule of immanence between knowledge of the
state and knowledge of 'man'. His argument, stated simply, is that, 'modern
statecraft is modern mancraft'.[10] Ashley seeks to demonstrate how the
'paradigm of sovereignty' simultaneously gives rise to a certain epistemological disposition and a certain account of modern political life. On the one
hand, knowledge is thought to depend on the sovereignty of 'the heroic
figure of reasoning man who knows that the order of the world is not God-
given, that man is the origin of all knowledge, that responsibility for supply-
ing meaning to history resides with man himself, and that, through reason,
man may achieve total knowledge, total autonomy, and total power'.[11] This
idea of knowledge is driven by what Bernstein calls the 'Cartesian anxiety'.[12]
It longs for a firm foundation on which 'man' can ground his knowledge after

the dissolution of Christendom and God-given guarantees. On the other hand, modern political life finds in sovereignty its constitutive principle. The state is conceived by analogy with sovereign man as a pre-given, bounded entity which enters into relations with other sovereign presences. Sovereignty is the key here, or at least, the paradigm of sovereignty turns on the ability to determine the presence or absence of sovereignty over political space. The state is marked by the presence of sovereignty, which contrasts with international relations which is marked, and violently so, by the absence of sovereignty (or alternatively stated, the presence of multiple sovereignties). In short, international relations as either a field of knowledge or a domain of politics is conditioned by the unexamined constitutive principle of sovereignty.

Bartelson attempts in *A Genealogy of Sovereignty* to trace the historical relationship between sovereignty and truth.[13] In Foucaultian fashion he treats sovereignty and truth as, respectively, two mutually determining fields (of power and knowledge). 'Without a proper mode of knowledge to render it intelligible, sovereignty cannot exist, and loses its power to organize political reality through a demarcation of inside from outside, of Same from Other'.[14] By the same token, 'without a proper form of sovereignty, knowledge loses its power to organize reality, and to constitute objects and fields of enquiry as well as criteria of validity and truth'.[15] Bartelson's stated purpose is to map the connections between knowledge and power in three historical periods, namely: the Renaissance, the Classical Age, and Modernity. Each period is mapped according to the relationship between the specific criteria of truth and specific arrangements of sovereignty. But it should not be assumed that the relationship between knowledge and power is the same throughout history. Instead, the discourse of sovereignty binds together knowledge and power in historically contingent ways. Borrowing further from Foucault, Bartelson implies that the history which bears and determines us is intelligible by reference to war and battle.[16] There are 'battles over sovereignty within knowledge, and battles of different knowledges within the discourse on sovereignty'.[17] The changing nature of these battles makes for historical shifts in politics and international relations. One of the main points advanced by Bartelson is that the political implications of state sovereignty cannot be separated from the ways in which it has been studied and understood in history. Knowledge is inextricably tied up with power to the extent that it produces the discourse of sovereignty as the primary means of arranging political relations in modernity; this is the rule of immanence.

Similarly, in *Simulating Sovereignty* Cynthia Weber provides an account of how different configurations of power and knowledge give rise to different conceptions of sovereignty, statehood and intervention. One of the questions central to her enquiry is: How are practices of power and knowledge organized to ground the notion of the sovereign state?[18] According to

Weber, state sovereignty is not a fixed concept. Rather, like any political concept or institution, its functions, competences, and legitimate privileges change over time. There is a degree of 'slippage in the notion of sovereignty' which needs to be recognized.[19] In particular Weber is concerned with how changes in the notion of state sovereignty have been shaped by changing conceptions of intervention and modalities of punishment. She reads the historicity of state sovereignty in terms of its transgression and corrective practices. Historical configurations of power–knowledge are presented by Weber through three episodes, each of which is defined by a particular modality of punishment. The point of this is to suggest that the concept of state sovereignty as currently used wipes out the historicity of the concept by arbitrarily fixing its meaning; it loses a sense of the historical nature of sovereignty's meaning and function. Furthermore, the concept of state sovereignty depends not on the presence of a foundational political community but on practices of power–knowledge which help to constitute this apparent foundation.

As the above examples of Foucault, Ashley, Bartelson and Weber illustrate, power–knowledge relations are historically contingent. But how is historical enquiry to proceed? The following section outlines the genealogical approach to history which seeks to take account of power–knowledge relations in history.

Genealogy

It is important to grasp the notion of genealogy as it has become crucial to many postmodern perspectives in international relations. Genealogy is, put simply, a style of historical thought which exposes and registers the significance of power–knowledge relations. It is perhaps best known through Nietzsche's radical assault on the concept of truth and moral values in *Beyond Good and Evil* and *On the Genealogy of Morals*. Nietzsche sought to expose, contra philosophy, how something can be contaminated at its origin by that to which it appears antithetical. Moreover, for Nietzsche truth is but an error or untruth that has hardened into truth over the long baking process of history. It is in these connections between knowledge, power, history and values that genealogy focuses its critical attention.

Genealogy is a form of history which historicizes those things which are thought to be beyond history, including those things or thoughts which have been buried, covered over, or excluded from view in the writing and making of history. In a sense it is concerned with writing counter-histories which expose the processes of exclusion and covering which make possible the idea of history as a unified, unfolding story, with a clear beginning, middle and end. History, from a genealogical perspective, does not evidence a gradual disclosure of truth and meaning. Rather, it stages 'the endlessly repeated play of dominations'.[20] History proceeds as a series of dominations and impositions in knowledge and power, and the task of the genealogist is to unravel history to reveal the multifarious trajectories that have been fostered or closed off in the constitution of subjects, objects, fields of action and domains of knowledge. Moreover, from a genealogical perspective there is not one single, grand history, but many interwoven histories varied in their rhythm, tempo, and power–knowledge effects.

Rather than engage in a form of positivism which seeks to identify general laws to explain continuity over time, or a hermeneutics of recovery which seeks to identify original meanings and self-understandings of actors in history, or even a hermeneutics of suspicion which hopes to penetrate ideologically distorted or repressed self-understandings in order to uncover the deeper meanings and structures behind history, genealogy affirms a perspectivism which denies the capacity to identify origins and meanings in history objectively. A genealogical approach is anti-essentialist in orientation, affirming the idea that all knowledge is situated in a particular time and place and issues from a particular perspective. The subject of knowledge is situated in, and conditioned by, a political and historical context, and constrained to function with particular concepts and categories of knowledge. Knowledge is never unconditioned. As a consequence of the heterogeneity of possible contexts and positions, there can be no single, archimedean perspective which trumps all others. There is no 'truth', only competing perspectives and 'régimes of truth'.

Foucault coined the phrase 'régime of truth' as a shorthand for the way in which truth and power are mutually produced and sustained. It focuses attention on what is believed to be true, on the rules or criteria which determine truthful propositions as against false ones, and reveal how beliefs given the status of truth shape social practices and institutions. This concern with 'régimes of truth' is to be clearly distinguished from a search for truth itself, as it emphasises how any given regimes of truth prevail only by subjugating alternative regimes. There are battles between and within régimes of truth, whereby hierarchies are established and rules are imposed on knowledge claims. Postmodernism is concerned with the ways in which a perspective produces representations which attain dominance and monopolise legitimacy by marginalising others.

International Relations as a field of knowledge is not immune to the various battles surrounding régimes of truth. International Relations remains a battlefield of contending representations, where some representations attain hegemony over others. The point of postmodernism is not to provide the 'true' representation of international relations, but to provide a critical account of how particular representations circulate and take hold to produce practical political effects.

In genealogical style, Steve Smith reminds us that disciplines are 'fields of battle between rival interpretations'.[21] Although there is a dominant 'self-image' of the discipline of International Relations, it only obtains dominance by excluding alternatives, and covering over the power struggles that installed one image as the dominant 'self-image'. There is no single self-image, only competing self-images of the discipline. 'Rather than being a "natural" and "autonomous" discipline with a series of unfolding debates which get ever closer to explaining reality, from a genealogical perspective international theory appears as a historical manifestation of a series of conflicting interpretations, whose unity and identity are the product of a victory in this conflict'.[22] The differences between International Relations and its many 'others' (for example, political theory, sociology, history, philosophy) depends on a repression of differences within. The discipline is never fully at one with itself, though it might be said to be at war with itself.

Metaphors of war and battle are central to genealogy. It has already been noted that Bartelson follows Foucault by employing such metaphors in his genealogy of sovereignty. This is clearly another Nietzschean tactic. Rather than view agonism as secondary or contingent, genealogy views it as structurally necessary in history. Genealogy is a reminder of the essential agonism in the historical constitution of identities, unities, disciplines, subjects and objects. From this perspective, 'all history, including the production of order, [is comprehended] in terms of the endless power political clash of multiple wills'.[23] Furthermore, Foucault claims as one of genealogy's express purposes the 'systematic dissociation of identity'.[24] There are two dimensions to this purpose. Firstly, it has a purpose at the ontological level: to avoid substituting causes for effects (*metalepsis*). It does not take unity as given but seeks to account for the forces which underwrite this apparent unity. Unity is an effect to be explained, not assumed. This means resisting the temptation to attribute essences to things or events in history, and requires a transformation of the question 'what is . . .?' into 'how is . . .?' For Nietzsche (and postmodernism) it is more important to determine the forces that give shape to an event or a thing than to attempt to identify its hidden, fixed essence. Ashley demonstrates an affinity with this type of question by asking, 'how, by way of what practices, are structures of history produced, differentiated, reified and transformed'?[25] Secondly, it has an ethico-political purpose to problematize prevailing identity formations which appear normal or natural. It refuses to use history for the purpose of confirming present identities, preferring to use it instead to disturb identities that have become dogmatized, conventionalized or normalized.

An example of how the present might problematize or systematically dissociate identity in international relations would be to ask: is sovereignty an adequate resolution to the political problems that exist in the world today? In view of multiculturalism, ethnic diversity and interpenetration,

minority and indigenous rights, diasporic peoples, environmental degradation, migration and the general movement of peoples, globalization, interdependence, and so on, is the sovereign state an effective form of political
organization? From these questions which arise from present political
circumstances, a genealogy would seek to retrace the career of the sovereign
state as an answer to pressing political problems across history. Though
state sovereignty has plainly hardened into a political 'truth' over the
baking process of history, and represents a form of identity, postmodernism
examines how state sovereignty was forged into an identity, and whether
the cracks in this political concept are rendering it anachronistic or dysfunctional.

As this example demonstrates, the questions posed by postmodernism
no longer demand the determination of an essence, nor do they presume
the permanence of political problems, or the transhistorical validity of
political practices and responses. Indeed, a genealogical approach would
be sceptical of transhistorical answers to historically specific problems. As
Veyne notes in his reflections on Foucault, 'the solution to a contemporary
problem will never be found in a problem raised in another era, which is
not the same problem except through a false resemblance'.[26]

It is in this sense that Foucault described his work as an attempt at
'writing the history of the present'.[27] He seeks to question the status of
the present, most especially, to problematize conventional histories and
their constitutive subjects and objects which are presumed to be natural
or necessary in the present.[28] Unavoidably, however, genealogy must necessarily begin with the present at the same time that it questions it. A
history of the present asks: how have we made the present seem like a
normal or natural point of arrival? What has been forgotten or buried in
history in order to legitimize the present? How do we select and differentiate what is necessary and what can be passed over in silence when
trying to make the present intelligible?

There is a clear normative impulse behind this form of enquiry which is
to challenge present constraints on freedom and to open up alternative
future possibilities. The 'function of any diagnosis concerning the nature of
the present', says Foucault, 'does not consist in a simple characterization of
what we are, but, instead – by following lines of fragility in the present – in
managing to grasp why and how that-which-is might no longer be that-
which-is'.[29] The present is never quite at one with itself, or at least with
representations of itself, and the task of the postmodern theorist (*qua*
genealogist) is to apply pressure on those points which offer the possibility
of transforming the present.

In sum, the study of international relations can no longer exclude questions concerning the connections between knowledge and power, and their
import for the study of history. The above section has outlined some of the
ways that postmodernism has dealt with these questions. One of the

important insights of the genealogical approach is that many of the problems and issues studied in International Relations are not just matters of
epistemology and ontology, but of authority, and struggles to impose
authoritative interpretations of international relations. The following section outlines a strategy which is concerned with destabilising these dominant interpretations by showing how every interpretation systematically
depends on that for which it cannot account.

Textual Strategies of Postmodernism

Der Derian contends that postmodernism is concerned with exposing the
'textual interplay behind power politics'.[30] To be sure, it is concerned with
exposing the textual interplay *within* power politics, for the effects of
textuality do not remain behind politics, but are intrinsic to them. The
'reality' of power politics (like any social reality) is always already constituted through textuality and inscribed modes of representation. It is in
this sense that David Campbell refers to 'writing' security, and Cynthia
Weber refers to 'writing' the state.[31] Two questions arise: (1) what is meant
by textual interplay? and (2) how, by using what methods and strategies,
does postmodernism seek to expose this textual interplay?

Textuality is a common postmodern theme. It stems mainly from Derrida's redefinition of 'text' in *Of Grammatology*. It is important to clarify what
Derrida means by text. Derrida is not restricting its meaning to literature
and the realm of ideas, as some have mistakenly thought. Rather, he is
implying that the world is *also* a text, or better, the 'real' world is constituted
like a text, and 'one cannot refer to this 'real' except in an interpretive
experience'.[32] Derrida and postmodernism firmly regard interpretation as
necessary and fundamental to the constitution of the social world. It is
worth recalling that in an essay on interpretation Derrida quotes Mon-
taigne: 'we need to interpret interpretations more than to interpret things'.[33]
Textual interplay refers to the supplementary and mutually constitutive
relationship between different interpretations in the representation and
constitution of the world. In order to tease out the textual interplay postmodernism deploys the strategies of deconstruction and double reading.

Deconstruction

Deconstruction is a general mode of radically unsettling what are taken to
be stable concepts and conceptual oppositions. Its main point is to demon-

strate the effects and costs produced by the settled oppositions, to disclose the parasitical relationship between opposed terms, and to attempt a displacement of them. According to Derrida conceptual oppositions are never simply neutral but are inevitably hierarchical. One of the two terms in the opposition is privileged over the other. This privileged term supposedly connotes a presence, propriety, fullness, purity or identity which the other lacks (for example, sovereignty as opposed to anarchy). Deconstruction attempts to show that such oppositions are untenable, as each term always already depends on the other. Indeed, the prized term only gains its privilege by disavowing its dependence on the subordinate term.

From a postmodern perspective, the apparently clear opposition between two terms is neither clear nor oppositional. Derrida often speaks of this relationship in terms of a structural parasitism and contamination, as each term is structurally related to, and already harbours, the other. Difference *between* the two opposed concepts or terms is always accompanied by a veiled difference *within* each term. Neither term is pure, self-same, complete in itself, or completely closed off from the other, though as much is feigned.

This implies that totalities, whether conceptual or social, are never fully present and properly established. Moreover, there is no pure stability, only more or less successful stabilizations as there is a certain amount of 'play', or 'give', in the structure of the opposition. The logic of this structural parasitism means that no term can claim transcendental privilege as it is constantly threatened with destabilization by the parasite. It is in this sense that deconstruction is a strategy of interpretation and criticism that shakes up theoretical concepts and social institutions which attempt totalisation and total stability.

As a general mode of unsettling, deconstruction is particularly concerned with locating those elements of instability or 'give' which ineradicably threaten any totality. Nevertheless, it must still account for stabilizations (or stability-*effects*). It is this equal concern with undoing or deconstitution (or at least their ever-present possibility) which marks off deconstruction from other more familiar modes of interpretation. To summarise then, deconstruction is concerned with both the constitution and deconstitution of any totality, whether a text, theory, discourse, structure, edifice, assemblage or institution.

Double reading

Derrida seeks to expose this relationship between stability-effects and destabilizations by passing through two readings in any analysis. As expressed by Derrida, double reading is essentially a duplicitous strategy which is 'simultaneously faithful and violent'.[34] The first reading is a commentary or repetition of the dominant interpretation or 'régime of truth', that is, a reading which demonstrates how a text, discourse or institution achieves the stability-effect. It faithfully repeats or mimics the dominant story by building on the same foundational assumptions, and repeating conventional steps in the argument. The point here is to demonstrate how the text, discourse or institution appears coherent and consistent with itself. It is concerned, in short, to elaborate how the identity or homogeneity of a text, discourse or institution is put together or constituted. Rather than yield to the monologic first reading, the second, counter-memorialising reading unsettles it by applying pressure to those points of instability within a text, discourse or institution. It exposes the internal tensions and how they are (incompletely) covered over or expelled. The text, discourse or institution is never completely at one with itself, but always carries within it elements of tension and crisis which render the whole thing less than stable. The point of this second reading is to demonstrate how the dominant reading always risks being undone.

The task of double reading as a mode of deconstruction is to understand how a discourse or edifice is assembled or put together, but at the same time to show how it is always already threatened with its undoing. It is important to note that there is no attempt in deconstruction to arrive at a single, conclusive reading. The two mutually inconsistent readings, which are in a performative (rather than logical) contradiction, remain permanently in tension. The point is not to demonstrate the truthfulness or otherwise of a story, but to expose how any story depends on the repression of internal tensions in order to produce a stable effect of homogeneity and continuity.

Ashley's double reading of the anarchy problematique

Ashley's main target is the conception of anarchy and the theoretical and practical effects it produces in international relations. The anarchy problematique is Ashley's name for what he believes is the defining moment of most inquiries in International Relations. The anarchy problematique is exemplified by Oye's assertion that 'nations dwell in perpetual anarchy, for no central authority imposes limits on the pursuit of sovereign interests', or Waltz's that 'the essential structural quality of the [international] system is anarchy – the absence of a central monopoly of legitimate force'.[35] Most importantly, the anarchy problematique deduces from the absence of central, global authority, not just an empty concept of anarchy, but a description of international relations as power politics, characterised by self-interest, *raison d'état*, the routine resort to force, territoriality, and so on.

The main brunt of Ashley's analysis is to problematize the deduction of power politics from the lack of central rule. Ashley's many analyses of the anarchy problematique can be understood in terms of double reading. The first reading assembles the constitutive features, or 'hard core' of the anarchy problematique, while the second reading disassembles the constitutive elements of the anarchy problematique, showing how the anarchy problematique rests on a series of questionable suppositions or *non sequiturs*.

In the first reading Ashley outlines the anarchy problematique in conventional terms. He describes not just the absence of any overarching authority, but the presence of a multiplicity of states in the international system, none of which can lay down the law to the individual states. Further, the states which comprise this system have their own identifiable interests, capabilities, resources and territory. The second reading questions the self-evidence of international relations as an anarchical realm of power politics. The initial target in this double reading is the opposition between sovereignty and anarchy where sovereignty is valorised as a regulative ideal, and anarchy is regarded as the absence or negation of sovereignty. Anarchy takes on meaning only as the antithesis of sovereignty. Moreover, sovereignty and anarchy are taken to be mutually exclusive and mutually exhaustive. Ashley demonstrates, however, that the anarchy problematique works only by making certain assumptions regarding sovereign states. If the dichotomy between sovereignty and anarchy is to be tenable at all, then inside the sovereign state must be found a domestic realm of identity, homogeneity, order and progress guaranteed by legitimate force; and outside must lie an anarchical realm of difference, heterogeneity, disorder and threat, recurrence and repetition. But to represent sovereignty and anarchy in this way (that is, as mutually exclusive and exhaustive), depends on converting differences *within* sovereign states into differences *between* sovereign states.[36] Sovereign states must expunge any traces of anarchy that reside within them in order to make good on the distinction between sovereignty and anarchy. Internal dissent and what Ashley calls 'transversal struggles' which cast doubt over the idea of a clearly identifiable and demarcated sovereign identity must be repressed or denied to make the anarchy problematique meaningful.[37] In particular, the opposition between sovereignty and anarchy rests on the possibility of determining a 'well-bounded sovereign entity possessing its own "internal" hegemonic centre of decision-making capable of reconciling "internal" conflicts and capable, therefore, of projecting a singular presence'.[38]

The general effect of the anarchy problematic is to confirm the opposition between sovereignty and anarchy as mutually exclusive and exhaustive. This has two particular effects: (1) to represent a domestic domain of sovereignty as a stable, legitimate foundation of modern political community, and (2) to represent the domain beyond sovereignty as dangerous and anarchical. These effects depend on what Ashley calls a 'double exclusion'.[39] They are possible only if, on the one hand, a single representation of sovereign identity can be imposed, and on the other hand, if this representation can be made to appear natural and indisputable. The double reading problematizes the anarchy problematique by posing two questions: firstly, what happens to the anarchy problematique if it is not so clear that fully present and completed sovereign states are ontologically primary? And secondly, what happens to the anarchy problematique if the lack of central global rule is not overwritten with assumptions about a domain 'populated by a number of states, each an identical subject . . . that has its own identifiable set of interests, and that controls some significant set of social resources, including the means of violence'.[40] That is, should anarchy necessarily be interpreted as power politics?

Double readings of the discipline of international relations

The strategy of double reading has also been deployed to problematize narratives of how the discipline of International Relations has evolved around a set of (apparently) permanent problems, themes, and questions. In particular it has focused on references to the realist tradition as the guiding thread in the evolution of the study of international relations from Thucydides through, *inter alia*, Machiavelli, Hobbes, and Rousseau, to the twentieth-century realists and neorealists. However, the tradition is not so coherent as realists would like to believe. Contrary to realist claims that there is a unifying thread which ties these thinkers together in contraposition to others, such as idealists, liberals, Marxists, and so on, postmodernism is concerned with exposing the tensions which render appeals to a realist tradition problematic.

To represent realism as a tradition depends on the possibility of differentiating realism from these other traditions, and this is possible only if internal differences are overlooked or covered over. Walker has developed this argument most fully.[41] One of his main focuses is the differences between Machiavelli and Hobbes, who are uncritically invoked as examples of the same tradition of realism. Walker argues that placing Machiavelli and Hobbes 'in the same undifferentiated category of political realism is seriously misleading, particularly with respect to the issue of change'.[42] Despite the different views of time, space, structure, and political action that shape the political thought of these thinkers, and the distinctive normative trajectories that each thinker takes, realism still appeals to a tradition.

Postmodernism reads the tradition 'against the grain', highlighting those points where the tradition must remain blind to tensions or differences that would put the continuity and coherence of the tradition in doubt. The import of this strategy is to bring into focus the way in which 'accounts of tradition serve to legitimize and circumscribe what counts as proper scholarship'.[43] The meaning, purpose, and scope of International Relations is not an objectively determined, neutral matter. More importantly, the prevailing idea of the discipline of International Relations is not the only one conceivable. Ashley and Walker have pointed out the irreducibly contested nature of the discipline, and the ever-present 'crisis' that confronts it.[44] The work of 'dissident' or postmodern thinkers, as Ashley and Walker argue, is to intensify and exploit this crisis, by making more evident the artificial construction of the discipline in its present form, and the ambiguity and uncertainty that plague the discipline's boundaries.

The above section has attempted to sketch out the key textual strategies deployed by postmodernism. The main concern of these strategies is to question prevailing interpretations of international relations by exposing instabilities and tensions which render any interpretation unstable. At this level, postmodernism remains largely a second-order discourse. In the following part, however, postmodernism's quasi-phenomenological enquiry into patterns of human existence, especially the state, is explained, before consideration is given to the ethical dimensions of postmodernism.

Theorising States of Violence

International Relations has long been concerned with states, sovereignty and violence. These are standard, long-standing themes which draw on established traditions of international relations thinking. They are also central themes in postmodern approaches to the study of international relations. Rather than adopt them uncritically from traditional approaches, postmodernism revises them in view of insights gained from genealogy and deconstruction.

Lest it be thought that that postmodern theories of international relations mark a return to realist state-centrism, some clarification will be needed to explain its concern with the sovereign state. Postmodernism does not seek to explain international relations by focusing on the state, nor does it take the state as given or primary. Instead, as Ashley's double reading of the anarchy problematique testifies, it seeks to explain the conditions which make possible such an explanation and the costs consequent on such an approach. What is lost by taking a state-centric perspective? And most importantly, to which aspects of the state does state-centrism remain blind?

State-centrism assumes the very thing that postmodernism seeks to account for: the state. In particular, postmodernism seeks to address a crucial issue regarding interpretations and explanations of the sovereign state that state-centrism has obscured, namely, its historical constitution and reconstitution as the primary mode of subjectivity in world politics.

This returns us to the type of question posed by Foucault's genealogy: how, by virtue of what political practices and representations, is the sovereign state instituted as the normal mode of international subjectivity? Posing the question in this manner directs attention, in Nietzschean fashion, less to what is the essence of the sovereign state, than to how the sovereign state is made possible, how it is naturalized, and how it is made to appear as if it had an essence.

To the extent that postmodernism seeks to account for the conditions which make possible the phenomenon of the state as something which concretely affects the experience of everyday life, it is phenomenological. Yet this is no ordinary phenomenology. It might best be called a 'quasi-phenomenology' for, as already noted, it is equally concerned with accounting for those conditions which destabilise the phenomenon or defer its complete actualisation. In the following section the postmodern quasi-phenomenology of the state will be explained. This comprises four main elements: (1) a genealogical analysis of the modern state's 'origins' in violence, (2) an account of boundary inscription, (3) a deconstruction of identity as it is defined in security and foreign policy discourses, and (4) a revised interpretation of statecraft. The overall result is to rethink the ontological structure of the state in order to respond properly to the question of how the sovereign state is (re)constituted as the normal mode of subjectivity in international relations.

(1) Violence

Modern political thought has attempted to transcend illegitimate forms of rule (such as tyranny and despotism) where power is unconstrained, un-checked, arbitrary and violent, by founding legitimate, democratic forms of government where authority is subject to law. In modern politics, it is reason, not power or violence, which is the measure of legitimacy. How-ever, as Campbell and Dillon point out, the relationship between politics and violence in modernity is deeply ambivalent, for on the one hand, violence 'constructs the refuge of the sovereign community', and on the other hand, it is 'the condition from which the citizens of that community must be protected'.[45] The paradox here is that violence is both poison and cure. It is simultaneously, the thing which the modern state is designed to protect citizens against, but also that which makes possible the modern state as a shelter from violence.

Walker draws upon a rereading of Max Weber to capture this paradox-ical relationship between violence and the modern state, and to expose the spatial exclusion which gives rise to the state. Modern states have displaced violence to the 'water's edge', so to speak. There, in the space known as international relations, violence seems natural and unavoidable, and is used legitimately as an instrument by states in their encounters with each other. As a consequence, it seems natural for the strategic, war-making state to be the normal mode of subjectivity in international relations.

This same concern is found in Klein's genealogy of the state as strategic subject. Klein's general purpose in *Strategic Studies and World Order* is to open up an analysis into 'the violent making and remaking of the modern world'.[46] His more particular purpose is to explain the historical emergence of war-making states. Rather than assume their existence, as many realists and neo-realists tend to do, Klein is interested in examining how political units which are capable of relying upon force to distinguish a domestic political space from a foreign one emerge in history. Consonant with other postmoderns, he argues that 'states rely upon violence to constitute them-selves as states', and in the process, 'impose differentiations between the internal and external'.[47] Strategic violence does not merely 'patrol the frontiers' of the state, it 'helps constitute them as well'. 'Strategic violence is an ongoing process of defining state boundaries, excluding that which differs from its domain, and punishing those who would challenge it'.[48]

Ashley, too, exposes the intimate relationship between violence and the modern state. He argues that the state is a supplement of modernity.[49] To speak of the state in this way is to suggest not only that the state is an addition to modernity, but that it is also essential to that which it supple-ments. Following Derrida, Ashley plays on the ambiguity in the word supplement. It is more than just an addition, it also compensates for a lack or flaw in what it supplements. Therefore it supplies a necessary condition, and there would be no modern state without the supplement of violence. The implication is that it cannot be supposed that there has been a pro-gressive humanisation in politics as violence is constitutive of modern political life.

The point made by postmodernism regarding violence in modern politics needs to be clearly differentiated from traditional approaches. In general, traditional accounts begin by accepting the distinction between domestic and international politics, which is in hock to the sovereignty/anarchy opposition. The distinction is thought to turn on the way in which violence is managed in the two realms. Domestically, by virtue of the presence of sovereignty, there is a monopoly over the legitimate use of violence. Inter-nationally, by virtue of anarchy, violence is decentralized. There is, inter-nationally, a multiplicity of actors who can, with some legitimacy, resort to the use of violence (war). Indeed, violent confrontation is taken to be a normal and regular occurrence in international relations. In many ways, international relations is about the ways in which international affairs have been shaped by the threat, preparation for, and waging of war. Certainly the condition of anarchy is thought, by realists, to incline states to war, as there is nothing to stop wars from occurring. In traditional accounts, then, violence is an act undertaken by states as a means to an end.

Violence is not constitutive in such accounts as these, but is 'configurative' or 'positional'.[50] The ontological structure of the states is taken to be set-up already before violence is undertaken. The violence merely modifies the territorial configuration, or is an instrument for power-political, strategic manoeuvres in the distribution or hierarchy of power. Postmodernism, however, exposes the constitutive role of violence in modern political life. As expressed by Campbell and Dillon, 'war makes the body politic (the political subject) that is invoked to sanction it'.[51] It is fundamental to the ontological structuring of states, and is not merely something to which fully formed states resort for power-political reasons. Violence is, according to postmodernism, inaugural as well as augmentative. It is possible to find traces of Nietzsche here, as he asserted that 'the welding of a hitherto unchecked and shapeless populace into a firm form was not only instituted by an act of violence but also carried to its conclusion by nothing but acts of violence'.[52]

A related issue which must be examined is the violence implicated in the division of political space. The role of violence in the constitution and reconstitution of the state is closely linked to the marking of boundaries. Boundaries are highly ambiguous, however, as Connolly points out, as they 'form an indispensable protection against violation and violence; but divisions they sustain in doing so also carry cruelty and violence'.[53]

(2)   Boundaries

To inquire into the state's (re)constitution, as postmodernism does, is partly to inquire into the ways in which global political space is partitioned. The world is not naturally divided into differentiated political spaces, and there is no single authority to carve up the world either. This necessarily leads to a focus on the 'boundary question', as Dillon and Everard call it, because any political subject is constituted by the marking of physical, symbolic and ideological boundaries.[54] The question is: How is a particular mode of subjectivity instituted and copied throughout the world? Postmodernism is less concerned with *what* is sovereignty, than *how* it is spatially and temporally produced and how it is circulated. How is a certain configuration of space and power instituted? And with what consequences?

The obvious implication of these questions is that the prevailing mode of subjectivity (the sovereign state) is neither natural nor necessary. There is no necessary reason why global political space has to be divided as it is and with the same bearing. Of crucial importance in this differentiation of political space is the inscription of boundaries. Marking boundaries is not an innocent, pre-political act. It is a political act with profound political implications as it is fundamental to the production and delimitation of political space. There is no political space in advance of boundary inscription. Boundaries function in the modern world to divide an interior, sovereign space from an exterior, pluralistic, anarchical space. The opposition between sovereignty and anarchy rests on the possibility of clearly dividing a domesticated political space from an undomesticated outside. It is in this sense that boundary inscription is a defining moment of the sovereign state. Indeed, neither sovereignty nor anarchy would be possible without the inscription of a boundary to divide political space. Furthermore, the boundary produces the effect of a completed, bounded state.

At stake is a series of questions regarding boundaries: how boundaries are constituted, how they operate, what they simultaneously include and exclude, what moral and political status they are accorded, and what general and particular effects they produce? Clearly, it is not just a concern with the location of cartographic boundaries, but with how these cartographic boundaries serve to represent, limit, and legitimate a political identity. But how, through which political practices and representations, are boundaries inscribed? And what implications does this hold for the mode of subjectivity produced?

(3)   Identity

By differentiating political spaces, boundaries are fundamental to the modern world which is predicated on discrete containers for politics. It is in this regard that Dalby rightly asserts that 'formulations of identity and difference are fundamental to the structuring of the state system'.[55] Postmodernism asks: how has political identity been imposed by practices and representations of domestication and exclusion? And how has the concept of a territorially defined self been constructed in opposition to a threatening other? It is in this regard that postmodernism has inquired into discourses and practices of security and foreign policy in the constitution of political identity.

In traditional accounts of international relations, security policy and foreign policy are viewed as actions taken by fully formed states to pursue their own goals. The boundaries and identity of the sovereign state are taken to be pre-established and settled. Security and foreign policy are viewed, in consequence, as activities states undertake to protect and advance their interests as they negotiate the dangers of international anarchy. In contrast, postmodernism is interested in how these discourses and practices shape international anarchy and the mode of subjectivity.

Of utmost importance here is the definition and articulation of threats and dangers. The political problem of facing and dealing with threats and dangers is a long-standing concern in the study of international relations. There is a need, however, to focus on how 'threats' and 'dangers' are defined and interpreted, giving rise to particular conceptions of the state as moral and political subject. Postmodernism focuses on the discourses and practices which substitute threat for difference. Simon Dalby, for instance, explains how cold wars result from the application of a geopolitical reasoning which defines security in terms of spatial exclusion and the specification of a threatening other. 'Geopolitical discourse constructs worlds in terms of Self and Others, in terms of cartographically specifiable sections of political space, and in terms of military threats'.[56] The geopolitical creation of the external other is integral to the constitution of a political identity (self) which is to be made secure. But to constitute a coherent, singular political identity often demands the silencing of internal dissent. There can be internal others that endanger a certain conception of the self, and must be necessarily expelled, disciplined, or contained. Identity, it can be surmised, is an effect forged, on the one hand, by disciplinary practices which attempt to normalize a population, giving it a sense of unity, and on the other, by exclusionary practices which attempt to secure the domestic identity through processes of spatial differentiation, and various diplomatic, military, and defence practices. There is a supplementary relationship between containment of domestic and foreign others, which helps to constitute political identity.[57]

If it is plain that identity is defined through difference, and that a self requires an other, it is not so plain that difference or otherness necessarily equates with threat or danger. Nevertheless, as Campbell points out, the sovereign state is predicated on discourses of danger. 'The constant articulation of danger through foreign policy is thus not a threat to a state's identity or existence', says Campbell, 'it is its condition of possibility'.[58] The possibility of identifying the USA as a political subject, for example, rested, during the Cold War, on the ability to impose an interpretation of the Soviet Union as an external threat, and the capacity of the US government to contain internal threats.[59] Indeed, the pivotal concept of containment takes on a Janus-faced quality as it is simultaneously turned inwards and outwards to deal with threatening others, as Campbell suggests.[60] The end result of the strategies of containment was to conflate the territorial borders of the state with the boundaries of American political and cultural identity, or more specifically, to ground identity in a territorial state.

It is important to recognise that political identities do not exist prior to the differentiation of self and other. The main issue is how something which is different becomes conceptualized as a threat or danger to be contained, disciplined, negated or excluded. There may be an irreducible possibility that difference will slide into opposition, danger, or threat, but there is no necessity. Political identity need not be constituted against, and at the expense of, others, but the prevailing discourses and practices of security

and foreign policy tend to reproduce this reasoning. Moreover, this relation
to others must be recognized as a morally and politically loaded relation.
The effect is to allocate the other to an inferior moral space, and to arrogate
the self to a superior one. As Campbell puts it, 'the social space of inside/
outside is both made possible by and helps constitute a moral space of
superior/inferior'.[61]. By coding the spatial exclusion in moral terms it
becomes easier to legitimize certain politico-military practices and inter-
ventions which advance national security interests at the same time as they
reconstitute political identities. As Shapiro puts it, 'to the extent that the
Other is regarded as something not occupying the same moral space as the
self, conduct toward the Other becomes more exploitative'.[62] This is especially so in an international system where political identity is so frequently
defined in terms of territorial exclusion.

(4) Statecraft

The above section has sketched how violence, boundaries and identity
function to make possible the sovereign state. This only partly deals with
the main genealogical issue of how the sovereign state is (re)constituted as a
normal mode of subjectivity. Two questions remain if the genealogical
approach is to be pursued: how is the sovereign state naturalised and
disseminated? And how is it made to appear as if it had an essence?

Postmodernism is interested in how prevailing modes of subjectivity
neutralize or conceal their arbitrariness by projecting an image of normalcy,
naturalness, or necessity. Ashley has explored the very difficult question of
how the dominant mode of subjectivity is normalized by utilizing the
concept of hegemony. By hegemony Ashley means not an 'overarching
ideology or cultural matrix', but 'an ensemble of normalized knowledge-
able practices, identified with a particular state and domestic society . . .
that is regarded as a practical paradigm of sovereign political subjectivity
and conduct'.[63] Hegemony refers to the projection and circulation of an
'exemplary' model, which functions as a regulative ideal. Of course the
distinguishing characteristics of the exemplary model are not fixed but are
historically and politically conditioned. The sovereign state, as the currently
dominant mode of subjectivity, is by no means natural. As Ashley remarks,
sovereignty is fused to certain 'historically normalized interpretations of the
state, its competencies, and the conditions and limits of its recognition and
empowerment'.[64] The fusion of the state to sovereignty is, therefore, conditioned by changing historical and cultural representations and practices
which serve to produce a political identity.

A primary function of the exemplary model is to negate alternative
conceptions of subjectivity or to devalue them as underdeveloped, inade-

quate or incomplete. Anomalies are contrasted with the 'proper', 'normal', or 'exemplary' model. For instance, 'quasi-states' or 'failed states' represent empirical cases of states which deviate from the model by failing to display the recognizable signs of sovereign statehood. In this failure they help to reinforce the hegemonic mode of subjectivity as the norm, and to reconfirm the sovereignty/anarchy opposition which underwrites it. In order for the model to have any power at all though, it must be replicable; it must be seen as a universally effective mode of subjectivity which can be invoked and instituted at any site. The pressures applied on states to conform to normalized modes of subjectivity are complex and various, and emanate both internally and externally. Some pressures are quite explicit, such as military intervention, others less so, such as conditions attached to foreign aid, diplomatic recognition, and general processes of socialisation. The point is that modes of subjectivity do not naturally become dominant, they achieve dominance in space and time through power and imposition.

How has the state been made to appear as if it had an essence? The short answer to this question is that the state is made to appear as if it had an essence by performative enactment of various domestic and foreign policies, or what might more simply be called 'statecraft'. Traditionally, statecraft refers to the various policies and practices undertaken by states to pursue their objectives in the international arena. The assumption underlying this definition is that the state is already a fully formed, or bounded, entity before it negotiates its way in this arena. The revised notion of statecraft advanced by postmodernism stresses the ongoing political practices which found and maintain the state, having the effect of keeping the state in perpetual motion.[65] The upshot is that, for postmodernism, there is statecraft, but there is no completed state. This leads to an interpretation of the state as always in the process of being constituted, but never quite achieving that final moment of completion. The state is never constituted once and for all time; it is an ongoing political task.

The above section has explained postmodernism's quasi-phenomenological analysis of the sovereign state by focusing on issues of violence, boundaries, identity, and statecraft. The consequence of this analysis is to raise a number of important ethical questions; most crucially, postmodernism focuses on the sovereign state as an ethical problem.

Sovereignty, Exclusion and Ethics

There is more to postmodernism than simply challenging the ontological assumptions at work in international relations theory. It also has an abiding ethical concern which hinges on state sovereignty. State sovereignty, as the dominant mode of subjectivity in international relations, holds significant ethico-political implications, for, as Walker says, it 'expresses a theory of ethics'.[66] It is in this respect that Ashley and Walker identify the 'question of sovereignty' as crucial and Campbell identifies it as the source of our impoverished political imagination.[67] It is at the heart of both ontological and ethical problems in modern political life. The ethical problems associated with state sovereignty will be outlined in this section.

Sovereignty and the ethics of exclusion

The ethical critique of state sovereignty needs to be understood in relation to the deconstructive critique of totalization. Deconstruction has already been explained as a strategy of interpretation and criticism that targets theoretical concepts and social institutions which attempt totalization or total stability. It is important to note that the postmodern critique of state sovereignty focuses on *sovereignty*. It is not the state *per se* which is under challenge by postmodernism but the claim of sovereignty which brings to the state assumptions of boundedness and supremacy, thereby designating an 'ultimate marker of certainty', as Lefort would say.[68]

State sovereignty is the foremost target in international relations because it is predicated on an exclusionary political space (territoriality) ruled by a single, supreme centre of decision-making which claims to represent a single political community or identity. Sovereign statehood means that the state is exclusive and monopolistic. Furthermore, the sovereign state claims to trump all other competing levels of political decision-making or representation. The sovereign state may well be the dominant mode of subjectivity in international relations today, but it is questionable whether its claim to be the primary and exclusive ethical and political subject is justified.

The most thorough-going account of state sovereignty's ethico-political costs is offered by Rob Walker in *Inside/Outside*. He sets out there the context in which state sovereignty has been mobilised as an analytical category with which to understand international relations, and as the primary expression of moral and political community. Walker's critique suggests that state sovereignty is best understood as a constitutive political practice which gives rise to a series of oppositions or dichotomies: inside and outside, domestic and foreign, self and other, one and many, unity and diversity, identity and difference, and the traditions of political theory and international theory, among others. In deconstructive fashion, Walker's concern is to 'destabilise [these] seemingly opposed categories by showing how they are at once mutually constitutive and yet always in the process of dissolving into each other'.[69] The overall effect of Walker's enquiry into state sovereignty is to question whether it is any longer a useful descriptive category, and an effective response to the problems that confront humanity in modern political life.

The analysis offered by Walker suggests that it is becoming increasingly difficult to organize modern political life in terms of sovereign states and sovereign boundaries. He argues that there are 'spatiotemporal processes that are radically at odds with the resolution expressed by the principle of state sovereignty'.[70] So for both material reasons and normative ones, Walker refuses to accept state sovereignty as the only, or best, possible means of organizing modern political life. Dividing humanity according to the principle of state sovereignty is not the only possibility. Modern political life need not be caught between mutually exclusive and exhaustive oppositions such as: inside and outside, one and many, identity and difference. For example, identity need not be exclusionary, and difference need not be interpreted as antithetical to identity. In short, humanity need not be divided according to an 'ethics of absolute exclusion'.[71]

To rethink questions of political identity and community without succumbing to binary oppositions is to contemplate a political life beyond the constraints of sovereign states. It is to take seriously the possibility that new forms of political identity and community can emerge which are not predicated on absolute exclusion. The practical political task is to move towards forms of state which do without the claims of territorial exclusion and supremacy as necessary constitutive features of modern politics. The practical political problems which stem from state sovereignty are brought into stark relief when considering the limited scope of democracy in modern political life.

Connolly delivers a postmodern critique which brings the question of democracy to bear on sovereignty. His argument is that the notion of state sovereignty is incompatible with democracy, especially in a globalized late modernity. The point of his critique is to challenge the sovereign state's 'monopoly over the allegiances, identifications and energies of its members'.[72] The multiple modes of belonging and interdependence, and the multiplication of global risk, that exist in late modernity complicate the neat simplicity of binary divisions between inside and outside. His point is that obligations and duties constantly overrun the boundaries of sovereign states. Sovereignty, he says, 'poses too stringent a limitation to identifications and loyalties extending beyond it' and so it is necessary to promote an ethos of democracy which exceeds territorialization by cutting across the state at all levels.[73] He calls this a 'disaggregation of democracy' or what might better be called a 'deterritorialization of democracy'.[74] Fundamental to the ethos of democracy advanced by Connolly is that it seeks to maintain a 'productive tension between the functions of governance and disturbance'.[75] Democracy is not to be mistaken for an 'ultimate marker of certainty', but is to be understood as a form of political deliberation and negotiation which perpetually destabilizes such markers by periodically unsettling 'cultural presumptions about true religious faith, gender relations, nature, territory, the essence of civilisation'.[76]

The consequence of taking a postmodern stance is that central political concepts such as community, identity, democracy and the state are rethought without being anchored in 'ultimate markers of certainty' like sovereignty. Indeed, de-linking these concepts from sovereignty underlies the practical task of a postmodernism politics. It should be understood that while postmodernism brings with it a 'loss of faith in the moment of identity as a guarantee of progress', it is not against identity or community as such, it is only against their dogmatization.[77] Postmodernism, as a critique of ultimate markers, is against concepts of identity and community only to the extent that they are tied dogmatically to notions of totality, boundedness and exclusion. For postmodernism, any examination of the conditions under which emancipation would be possible, must confront these notions. It is in this sense that postmodernism articulates an ethics and can be related to the project of modernity.[78]

Postmodern ethics

There is a common perception that postmodernism lacks an ethics and is self-annihilating because of its relativism, anti-universalism and nihilism. Postmodernism, or, as Habermas prefers, the 'radical critique of reason, exacts a high price for taking leave of modernity'.[79] The issue at stake, according to Habermas, is whether or not postmodernism can offer a politics or ethics. According to Habermas, postmodernism cannot explain why resistance should be mustered against prevailing injustices. In short, he rebukes postmodernism for being unable or unwilling to account for its normative foundations.[80] There have been attempts, however, to account for postmodernism's ethics. This final section provides a brief description of traditional understandings of ethics before outlining the ethical approach of postmodernism.

The treatment of ethics in international relations usually begins with a description of how international relations is structured. It begins with an ontological description of state sovereignty, territoriality, and the distinction between inside and outside. This gives rise to an ethics based on distinguishing between fellow citizens and outsiders. Moral obligation is determined by the boundary that separates 'us' from 'them'. Ethics is therefore understood as something which is more readily applicable to relations within a sovereign state rather than relations between them. Nevertheless, there is recognised in the traditional study of international relations a degree of ethical responsibility. This ethical responsibility is usually couched as a limited duty owed to those beyond our borders.[81] Noteworthy features of the ontology that underlies the traditional understanding of ethics include an unquestioned acceptance of the boundary that separates inside from outside, and a conception of identity which corresponds to a delimited territory. Postmodernism asks: what might ethics come to mean if these ontological assumptions were not made? There are two strands of ethics which develop out of postmodernism's reflections on international relations. Though the strands are distinguishable, they are by no means incompatible or unconnected. One strand challenges the ontological description on which traditional ethical arguments are grounded. It advances a notion of ethics which is not predicated on a rigid, fixed boundary between inside and outside. The other strand focuses on the relation between ontological grounds and ethical arguments. It questions whether ethics ought to begin with ontology before moving to ethics.

The first strand is put forward most fully by Ashley and Walker, and Connolly. Fundamental to their writing is a critique of the faith invested in boundaries. Again, the main target of postmodernism here is the sovereign state's defence of rigid boundaries. Territorial boundaries, which are thought to mark the limits of political identity or community, are taken by postmodernism to be historically contingent and highly ambiguous products.[82] As such, they hold no transcendental status. As a challenge to the ethical delimitations imposed by state sovereignty, postmodern ethics, or the 'diplomatic ethos' as Ashley and Walker call it, is not confined by any spatial or territorial limits. It is a transgressive ethics based on a trespass of sovereignty. It seeks to 'enable the rigorous practice of this ethics in the widest possible compass'.[83] No demarcatory boundaries should obstruct the universalization of this ethics which overruns boundaries (both imagined and territorial). Furthermore,

> where such an ethics is rigorously practiced, no voice can effectively claim to stand heroically upon some exclusionary ground, offering this ground as a source of a necessary truth that human beings must violently project in the name of a citizenry, people, nation, class, gender, race, golden age, or historical cause of any sort. Where this ethics is rigorously practiced, no totalitarian order could ever be.[84]

In breaking with the ethics of sovereign exclusion, postmodernism offers an understanding of ethics which is detached from territorial limitations. The diplomatic ethos is a 'deterritorialized' ethics which unfolds by transgressing sovereign limits. This transgressive ethics complements the deterritorialized notion of democracy advanced by Connolly. Underlying both ideas is a critique of state sovereignty as a basis for conducting, organising and limiting political and ethical relations.

The other ethical strand is advanced by Campbell. He follows Derrida and Levinas by questioning traditional approaches which deduce ethics from ontology (specifically an ontology or metaphysics of presence). It does not begin with an empirical account of the world as a necessary prelude to ethical consideration. Rather, it gives primacy to ethics as, in a sense, 'first philosophy'. The key thinker in this ethical approach is Emmanuel Levinas who has been more influenced by Jewish thought than Greek philosophy. Indeed, the differences between these two styles of thought are constantly worked through in Levinas's thought as a difference between a philosophy of alterity and a philosophy of identity or totality.

Levinas overturns the hierarchy between ontology and ethics, giving primacy to ethics as the starting point. Ethics seems to function as a condition which makes possible the world of beings. Levinas offers a redescription of ontology such that it is inextricably tied up with, and indebted to, ethics, and is free of totalising impulses. In Levinas's schema, subjectivity is constituted through (and as) an ethical relation. The effect of the Levinasian approach is to recast notions of subjectivity and responsibility in light of an ethics of otherness or alterity. 'Ethics redefines subjectivity as . . . heteronomous responsibility'.[85]

This gives rise to a notion of ethics which diverges from the Kantian principle of generalizability and symmetry. Rather than begin with the self and then generalize the imperative universally to a community of equals, Levinas begins with the other. The other places certain demands on the self, hence there is an asymmetrical relationship between self and other. The end result is to advance a 'different figuration of politics, one in which its purpose is the struggle *for* – or *on behalf of* – alterity, and not a struggle to efface, erase, or eradicate alterity'.[86]

Once again, however, the brunt of this ethical approach is a critique of state sovereignty. If an important political purpose is to defend alterity, then the sovereign state seems increasingly incapable of carrying out this purpose. Present demands for justice are being made both above and below the level of the sovereign state, and in direct challenge to its ability to accommodate them. If such voices are to be given a hearing then it would appear crucial to question the sovereign state as a vehicle for a non-exclusionary ethics. To confine ethics to the sovereign state would be to subjugate many voices. If justice is to be done, all who are affected by it must be capable of understanding and interpreting it. 'It is unjust to judge someone who does not understand the language in which the law is inscribed or the judgement pronounced'.[87] This means rethinking notions of subjectivity, political identity and community, and ethics beyond the constraints of sovereignty as Campbell has advocated.[88] This would make necessary revised notions of ethics and responsibility which could hold non-totalising relations to others.

This final part of the chapter has attempted to outline some of the ethical themes developed in postmodern international relations theory. The thrust of postmodernism has always been to challenge claims to totality and sovereignty. The key to understanding much of the ethical argument is a critique of the sovereign state as a constitutive political practice which is premissed on exclusion. For postmodern international relations theory the main issue is to destabilize the forms and practices associated with state sovereignty in order to allow ethical relations between self and other, insiders and outsiders, to develop. This would involve a generalized delegitimation of boundaries and the possibility of deterritorialized political relations. It would, of necessity, involve undoing the assumed correspondence between territory and political identity that underlies much traditional international relations theory.

Conclusion

This chapter has been concerned with explaining the contribution of postmodernism to international relations theory. It considered issues of power–knowledge relations, textual and interpretative strategies, theorizing the sovereign state, and questions of exclusion and ethics. The input of postmodernism to research in these areas is already high, and is growing steadily. Future research will no doubt continue along similar lines. It is worth pausing, in conclusion, to ask what the contribution of postmodernism has been to international relations theory.

It is possible to identify three significant contributions to international relations theory: (1) the problematization of state sovereignty, which is essentially a *critique* of the sovereign state for both material and, most especially, normative reasons; (2) the problematization of the sovereignty/anarchy opposition, which is a *deconstruction* of a fundamental opposition in international relations theory; and (3) theorizing the historical constitution and reconstitution of sovereign states, which is a *genealogical* analysis of how states are reproduced as the primary mode of subjectivity in international relations. By combining these moments of critique, deconstruction and genealogy, postmodernism has opened the study of international relations to much more rigorous self-reflection, and advanced the understanding of important themes in world politics. If there is an area which will need further development in the future it is postmodernism's ethical account, which remains rather underdeveloped at the moment, but the possible contours of a postmodern ethics are clearly emerging.

Notes

1. J. Der Derian, 'Philosophical Traditions in International Relations', *Millennium*, vol. 12, no. 2 (1988), p. 189.
2. I. Kant, *Kant's Political Writings* (Cambridge, 1970), p. 115.
3. M. Foucault, *Discipline and Punish: The Birth of the Prison* (Middlesex, 1977), p. 27.
4. Ibid., p. 27.
5. P. Bourdieu, *Outline of a Theory of Practice* (Cambridge, 1977), p. 165.
6. M. Foucault, *Power/Knowledge: Selected Interviews and Other Writings 1972–1977* (New York, 1980), p. 131.
7. M. Foucault, *The History of Sexuality: An Introduction* (Middlesex, 1978), p. 98.
8. Ibid., p. 98.
9. Ibid., p. 23.
10. R. K. Ashley, 'Living on Border Lines: Man, Poststructuralism and War', in J. Der Derian and M. J. Shapiro (eds), *International/Intertextual Relations: Postmodern Readings of World Politics* (Massachusetts, 1989a), p. 303.
11. Ashley (1989a), pp. 264–5.
12. R. J. Bernstein, *Beyond Relativism and Objectivism* (Philadelphia, 1983), p. 18.
13. J. Bartelson, *A Genealogy of Sovereignty* (Cambridge, 1995), p. 2.
14. Ibid., p. 83.
15. Ibid., p. 83.
16. Foucault (1980), p. 114.
17. Bartelson (1995), pp. 83–4.
18. C. Weber, *Simulating Sovereignty: Intervention, the State and Symbolic Exchange* (Cambridge, 1995), p. 30.
19. Weber (1995), p. 16.
20. M. Foucault, 'Nietzsche, Genealogy, History', in M. Gibbons (ed.), *Interpreting Politics* (London, 1987), p. 228.
21. S. Smith, 'The Self-Images of a Discipline: A Genealogy of International Relations', in S. Smith and K. Booth (eds), *International Relations Theory Today* (Cambridge, 1995), p. 6.
22. Smith (1995), p. 6.
23. R. K. Ashley, 'The Geopolitics of Geopolitical Space: Toward a Critical Social Theory of International Politics', *Alternatives*, vol. 12 (1987), pp. 403–34, p. 409.
24. Foucault (1987), p. 236.
25. Ashley (1987), p. 409.
26. P. Veyne, 'The Final Foucault and His Ethics', *Critical Inquiry*, vol. 20, no. 1 (1993), p. 2.
27. Foucault (1977), p.31.
28. C. Gordon, 'Afterword', in Foucault, *Power/Knowledge* (London, 1980), p. 241.
29. M. Foucault, *Politics, Philosophy, Culture: Interviews and Other Writings 1977–1984* (London, 1988) p. 36.

30. J. Der Derian 'The boundaries of knowledge and power in International Relations', in J. Der Derian and M. J. Shapiro (eds), *International/Intertextual Relations: Postmodern Readings of World Politics* (Massachusetts, 1989a), p. 6.

31. D. Campbell, *Writing Security: United States Foreign Policy and the Politics of Identity* (Minneapolis, 1992); Weber (1995).

32. J. Derrida, *Limited Inc* (Evanston, 1988), p. 148.

33. J. Derrida, *Writing and Difference* (Henley, 1978), p. 278.

34. J. Derrida, *Positions* (Chicago, 1981), p. 6.

35. K. Oye, 'Explaining Cooperation Under Anarchy: Hypotheses and Strategies', *World Politics*, vol. 38, no. 1 (1985), p. 1; K. Waltz, *Theory of International Politics* (New York, 1979), p. 42.

36. R. K. Ashley, 'Untying the Sovereign State: A Double Reading of the Anarchy Problematique', *Millennium*, vol. 17, no. 2 (1988b), p. 257.

37. Ashley (1987), p. 423; (1989a), p. 299.

38. Ashley (1988b), p. 245.

39. Ibid., p. 256.

40. Ibid., p. 239.

41. R. B. J. Walker, *Inside/Outside: International Relations as Political Theory* (Cambridge, 1993).

42. Ibid., p. 112.

43. Ibid., p. 29.

44. R. K. Ashley and R. B. J. Walker, 'Speaking the Language of Exile: Dissidence in International Studies' in *International Studies Quarterly*, vol. 34, no. 3 (1990), pp. 259–417.

45. D. Campbell and M. Dillon, 'Introduction', in Campbell and Dillon (eds), *The Political Subject of Violence* (Manchester, 1993a), p. 161.

46. B. Klein, *Strategic Studies and World Order: The Global Politics of Deterrence* (Cambridge, 1994), p. 139.

47. Ibid., p. 38.

48. Ibid., pp. 3 and 7.

49. R. K. Ashley, 'Geopolitics, Supplementary Criticism: A Reply to Professors Roy and Walker', *Alternatives*, vol. 13 (1988a), p. 100.

50. The distinction between constitutive, configurative and positional violence is borrowed from J. G. Ruggie, 'Territoriality and Beyond: Problematizing Modernity in International Relations', *International Organization*, vol. 47, no. 1 (1993), pp. 162–3.

51. Campbell and Dillon (1993a), p. 16.

52. F. Nietzsche, *On the Genealogy of Morals* (New York, 1969), second essay, section 17.

53. W. Connolly, 'Tocqueville, Territory and Violence', *Theory, Culture and Society*, vol. 11 (1994), pp. 19–40, p. 19.

54. M. Dillon and J. Everard, 'Stat(e)ing Australia: Squid Jigging and the Masque of State', *Alternatives*, vol. 17, no. 3 (1992), p. 282.

55. S. Dalby, *Creating the Second Cold War: The Discourse of Politics* (London, 1993), p. 19.

56. Ibid., p. 29.
57. Campbell (1992), chs 5 and 6.
58. Ibid., p. 12.
59. Ibid., ch. 6.
60. Ibid., p. 175.
61. Ibid., p. 85.
62. M. Shapiro, *The Politics of Representation* (Madison, 1988), p. 102.
63. R. K. Ashley, 'Imposing International Purpose: Notes on a Problematic of Governance', in E.-O. Czempiel and J. Rosenau (eds), *Global Changes and Theoretical Challenges: Approaches to World Politics for the 1990s* (Massachusetts, 1989b), p. 269.
64. Ibid., p. 267.
65. Campbell (1992); Dillon and Everard (1992).
66. Walker (1993), p. 64.
67. Ashley and Walker (1990); Campbell (1992), p. 252.
68. C. Lefort, *Democracy and Political Theory* (Cambridge, 1988), p. 228.
69. Walker (1993), p. 25.
70. Ibid., p. 155.
71. Ibid., p. 66.
72. W. Connolly, 'Democracy and Territoriality', *Millennium*, vol. 20, no. 3 (1991), p. 479.
73. Ibid., p. 480.
74. Ibid., p. 476.
75. Ibid., p. 478.
76. Connolly (1994), p. 33.
77. R. B. J. Walker, *One World, Many Worlds: Struggles for a Just World Peace* (Colorado, 1988), p. 87.
78. Devetak, R. 'The Project of Modernity and International Relations Theory', *Millennium*, vol. 24, no. 1 (1995b), pp. 27–51.
79. Habermas, J. *The Philosophical Discourse of Modernity* (Cambridge, 1987), p. 336.
80. Habermas (1987), p. 276.
81. See for example, S. Hoffmann, *Duties Beyond Borders: On the Limits and Possibilities of Ethical International Politics* (New York, 1987).
82. Ashley and Walker (1990); Connolly (1994).
83. Ashley and Walker (1990), p. 395.
84. Ibid., p. 395.
85. Levinas, quoted in D. Campbell, 'The Deterritorialization of Responsibility: Levinas, Derrida and Ethics after the End of Philosophy', *Alternatives*, vol. 19, no. 4 (1994), p. 463.
86. Ibid., p. 477.
87. J. Derrida, 'Force of Law', in D. Cornell, M. Rosenfeld and D. Gray (eds), *Deconstruction and the Possibility of Justice* (New York, 1992), p. 18.
87. Campbell (1994).

CHAPTER 8

Feminism

Jacqui True

The twentieth-century field of International Relations has for the most part been concerned with studying the causes of war and conflict, the development of diplomacy and international law, and the global expansion of trade and commerce with no particular reference to people called 'men' or 'women' *per se*. Indeed the centering of abstract categories such as 'the state', 'the market', 'the system', predominance of strategic discourses of national interest and national security, military defense and nuclear deterrence, and research approaches such as methodological individualism and inductive reasoning have effectively removed people as agents embedded in social and historical contexts from theories of international relations. The 'international' has come to be characterized in this discipline as the impersonal and perilous realm of 'high (faluting) politics' among states. And 'the actions of states or more accurately of men acting for states' have come to dominate the substance of 'relations'.[1] So where does the study of people called 'women' or the social construction of (masculine–feminine) gender and subjectivity fit into this picture? How is the international system and the study of international relations gendered? To what extent do understandings of the co-constitution of sovereign man and gendered states help us to understand and ultimately transform the reproductive practices of international relations? This chapter will endeavour to explore these questions and others as they have been addressed in the rich and diverse work of feminist international relations scholars.

It goes without saying that feminism is a relatively recent and highly provocative intervention in the theory and practice of international relations. This is not surprising given that 'the absence of a moment of critique' in International Relations (IR) is its distinguishing feature.[2] Just as the contemporary entry of women into military combat roles has dismantled the last bastion of male-privileged citizenship within some nation-states, and global economic shifts evidence transformations in traditional gendered divisions of labour with the introduction of feminist perspectives on world politics over the past decade, challenging the ontological and epistemological foundations of International Relations, one of the last disciplinary preserves of men and masculinity. These are significant and related developments in IR, in light of Christine Sylvester's analysis that women and their association with the private sphere of domesticity, morality, subjectivity, passion, and femininity, 'stand for what the [IR] field is not'; not least in the context of disciplinary fragmentation and postmodern challenges to boundaries, when IR is not sure what exactly it is.[3] Indeed, the representation of IR as 'high politics' is implicitly gendered in so far as 'its crucial importance and public power, the reasons for and the fact of its highest authority' are established precisely by the 'exclusion of women from its work'.[4] However, feminists, together with non-feminist critical and postmodern IR scholars, claim that we can learn much about world politics by paying attention to the disciplines' empirical, theoretical and political exclusions which make possible and give meaning to those agents, characteristics and outcomes that are ostensibly included in IR. As Jean Elshtain has said, in malestream IR theory 'what gets left out is often as important as what is put in and assumed'.[5] It has not been easy, however, to erase the common-sensical feeling that international politics is not for 'womenchildren',[6] and yet if IR is, as Scott Burchill states in the introduction to this volume, 'fundamentally concerned with asking questions about . . . prior assumptions' then it must take feminist challenges seriously. Conceptualizing new ways to understand the dynamics of international conflict and human relations at the global level while contributing to their improvement, demands criticism of the normative and constitutive foundations of existing theories and world orders.

One should not assume that just because IR has not integrated the insights of feminism that there is not a tremendous history and wealth of scholarship pertaining to women's studies, gender studies and feminist theory. Indeed, as Rebecca Grant notes, feminist theory has actually developed alongside IR theory in the twentieth century since the end of the First World War and the successful movement for women's suffrage in the UK and USA in particular.[7] Feminist theory, it could be argued, is a critical practice within 'men's studies' to transform structural oppressions, starting with our experience of oppression as women. There is a counter-canon of women philosophers reaching from Sappho in classical Greece, to Christine Pisan in Medieval Europe and Mary Wollestonecraft in modern Western Europe who have engaged in social and political debates on the nature of authority, legitimacy, democracy, and universal rights, from the perspective of women. Thus, feminism, unlike non-feminist postmodernism, is not merely a contemporary development in the sociology of knowledge, but is embedded in a rich and varied history of women's struggle and women theorising from the experience of struggle. Feminism today is part of the 'so-called heritage of the European Enlightenment' and its universalizing projects of emancipation, truth, and rationality, though 'within the enclosure of this heritage it is often inscribed in a contestatory role'.[8] There is no one feminism, no single approach to the construction of feminist theory, but multiple varieties of feminism which often embrace very contradictory and overlapping positions, discourses and practices. There are conservative feminisms, liberal feminisms, Marxist feminisms and socialist feminisms which have attempted to fit with universal malestream theories. There are and radical feminisms, eco-feminisms, cultural feminisms that have forged distinctive 'women's' positions. There are also lesbian feminisms, women of colour/ Third World feminisms, and a complex group of postmodern critical feminist theories which draw variously on poststructuralist, French continental theory, psychoanalysis, postpositivist epistemologies and non-Western, multicultural feminisms. The recognition that there are multiple feminisms has arisen out of the feminist movement itself, as different groups of women have challenged a singular, representational feminism and homogeneous category of 'woman' that do not take account of differences among women.

Over the past decade feminist international relations has developed as a distinctive contribution to theorizing world politics. In the 1990s at professional conferences, in teaching curricula and in academic publishing, feminism is considered a topical sub-field of IR which indicates the partial inclusion, rather than the serious integration of feminist perspectives in IR. For feminist scholars the disciplinary state of IR is not separate from the exclusionary practices of gendered states and the real world of gender hierarchies: women and feminists have been just as excluded from the theory of IR as they have from the practice of realpolitik. As Spike Peterson has articulated, the IR discipline continues to avoid conversing with feminist approaches.[9] Despite this marginalization, there is a fast growing and invigorating body of scholarship committed to specifically feminist approaches to IR.

Within feminist theory and gender studies there is an increasing realization that we can no longer understand or explain the varying yet remarkably persistent inequality of women compared with men without a global view of the diverse geo-political and economic conditions that have gender-differentiated causes and consequences. Feminist IR scholars therefore perform a dual meta-disciplinary task. They make IR 'gender sensitive' and at the same time they bring global perspectives to the study of women which involves elucidating the heterogeneity among women, differentiated by hierarchies of race, class, ethnicity, nationality and sexuality, and embedded in global structures and processes.[10] The latter task is essential if feminists are to *deconstruct* the multiple oppressions, including gender, sustaining the structural and direct violence of the global political-economic system; and to reconstruct practices of feminist solidarity and resistance in the face of the increased fragmentation of labour and identities and the increased mobility of capital and people.

In this chapter I have chosen to present three interrelated feminist challenges to the authority of IR knowledge, as it has been conventionally constructed: including women and gender as a variable in empirical IR studies, rendering the hidden masculine gender of IR theory and practice visible, and demonstrating the difference that feminism makes to the politics of knowing world politics. These challenges form the basis for the three sections of this chapter, gender as a variable in international relations, gender as theoretically-constitutive of international relations, and gender as a transformative of ways of knowing and doing international relations. These sections map onto the three epistemologies commonly referred to in the feminist IR literature as feminist empiricism, feminist standpoint, and feminist postmodernism. But first, in order to grasp the significance of feminist contributions to international relations, we must examine the concept of gender and the shift from including women's lives in accounts of IR and assuming a generic standpoint of 'woman', to illuminating gender as a category of analysis and as a critical lens for theorizing world politics.

Boundaries of Gender

Wendy Brown expresses the global scope of feminist theorizing by arguing that everything in the human world is a gendered construction.[11] That is, knowledge which establishes the meaning of bodily sexual difference as binary confers meaning on power relationships and social orderings in general. Specifically, *gender* structures institutions and identities through the assymetrical social constructs of masculinity and femininity, as opposed to ostensibly biological male–female sex differences. Hegemonic masculinity is associated with autonomy, sovereignty, objectivity, universalism, the capacity for reason/abstraction, and hegemonic femininity with the absence or absolute lack of these qualities. In this construction, to be masculine is not to be feminine: men are therefore, 'emasculated' when shown to embody effeminate/feminine characteristics that are associated with women, the second sex. In more abstract terms, masculine identity is achieved by demonstrating its difference from and superiority to a feminine 'other'.

Feminists argue that theory which does not pay attention to the ubiquity of gender assumes the 'naturalness' of gender hierarchy in social reality and the poverty of gender as a unit of analysis. Typically, the assumption that something is natural or 'human nature' and not subject to human construction or agency has political effects in terms of reproducing status-quo power relations.[12] In this way, Joan Scott argues that 'the binary opposition and the social process of gender relationships both become part of the meaning of power itself: to question or alter any aspect threatens the entire system'.[13] Throughout history it has been strikingly mundane for political authority to legitimize itself and its concomitant hierarchical structures through the gendered symbolic relationship between male and female sexes.

In international relations we can see the construction of gendered sub-jectivities at work in the training of soldiers and in the routine practices of militaries, historically institutions for men only and a requirement for full citizenship. Military training, in Barbara Roberts' words 'is socialization into masculinity carried to the extremes'.[14] Typically, soldiers are taught not only to deride the presence of women (and gays/homosexuals whose bodies are labelled feminine/effeminate) but to achieve manhood by virtue of their autonomy from women, their suppression of emotions associated with (feminized) caregiving and bodily pain, and their 'protection' of womenchildren. When Vietnam veteran and writer Tim O'Brien confessed that he was a coward not a 'man' to go to the war on the 48th parallel instead of crossing the US–Canada border, he exposed the dependence of the achievement of US cultural constructions of masculinity on killing and expressions of domination over other men, women and children. O'Brien knew only too well that extreme personal courage is required to resist such 'taken for granted' masculinist constructions of what it means to be a citizen and even a 'human'. Cynthia Enloe quotes a former South African soldier who testifies that in post-apartheid, democratic South Africa the most difficult but 'the more manly thing to do is not be a soldier'.[15]

Feminists have attempted to undermine the power of gender and the domination of associated binary constructs in three theoretical-political moves which have ontological and epistemological consequences for the study of IR. The initial liberal feminist empiricist move demonstrates the falsity of gender ascriptions on the basis that women have the same capacities as men, and can acquire masculine characteristics suitable for positions as statesmen and commanders in chief, like men. This establishes men-masculinity as the unquestioned impartial standard from which to judge the equality of women – equal to whom? equal to men of course. Here, the 'difference' of female embodiment is regarded as deviant excess, but in the public arena it is the excess which must be made explicit. Margaret Thatcher was presented to Great Britain and the world as the *Iron* Lady but also as the daughter of a shopkeeper. Contesting elections as Pakistani Prime Minister second time around, Benazir Bhutto assumed the image of a traditional feminine Islamic woman and wife to increase her popularity as a *woman* leader. At the same time, feminine characteristics signify inferiority and are used to discredit women in power. Questions actually asked by women qua (embodied as) woman as subjects are si-lenced within this framework of 'equality', or 'e-man-cipation'. For liberal feminist empiricists, the category of gender is hardly different from the category of sex, in so far as it refers to what is explicitly said about men and women rather than the mutual, powerful construction of masculinity and femininity.[16] Rebecca Grant and Kathleen Newland argue that when this liberal perspective is applied to feminist contributions to IR 'it runs the risk of encouraging the view that the subject of women is just one of many possible, optional add-ons to IR; something akin to an area specialization'.[17]

In contrast to the first, the second feminist move valorizes femaleness. In short, it inverts the gender hierarchy of male-masculine over female-feminine. For example, some feminists celebrate characteristics associated with femaleness within patriarchal relations as superior. Maternal feminists have suggested that the experience of mothering, of caring for others could serve as an important ethical model for civic participation as well as a corrective to citizenship based on military service.[18] In particular, Sara Ruddick argues that the rationality of care and care-giving activities usually, but not exclusively, carried out by women, is necessary to antimilitarist protest and to a positive politics of peace. Similarly, the association of women with peacemaking in Peace Research, a subfield of IR, emphasises women's socialisation as promoting particularly feminine, non-violent forms of conflict resolution.[19] However, by, associating women's nature with different, more peaceful, ethical, and co-operative ways of being than men's, these positions tend to reinforce oppressive binary gender identities and structures as opposed to explaining how gender hierarchies and other forms of superordination are reproduced and how they can be transformed.

Related to this perspective, feminist IR standpoint perspectives argue that knowledge which emerges from women's experiences 'on the margins' of world politics is actually more neutral and critical because it is not as complicit with, or blinded by, existing institutions and power relations.[20] In this view, women's political struggles against marginalisation and exclusion from status-quo public power impart a strong objectivity to knowing because women often have the most to gain from developing critical understandings of exactly how the world which oppresses them is constructed, and how it might be reconstructed.[21] For some feminist IR theorists, analysis of gender begins from this standpoint of women and their experiences of exclusion and subordination in social and political life. They expose the foundations of knowledge and politics in the particular standpoints of men, rather than the universal perspective of disinterested and generic observers. Feminist standpointers argue that we can only 'make sense of men's gendered reactions if we take women's experiences seriously'.[22]

Third, postmodern feminists have questioned the oppressive effects of the masculine-feminine dichotomy and dichotomous classification generally.[23] In this third move, the feminist deconstruction of dichotomies, the problematic of gender as a filter of knowledge – and therefore an epistemological category – in the context of power relations is illuminated. Contemporary postmodern feminist attempts to *unman* the hold of binary gender arise out of the feminist deconstructionist insight that metaphysical dichotomies powerfully frame our thinking as well as our bodies. Moira Gatens and Judith Butler, together with other postmodern feminists, argue that gender is not simply the socially-constructed category imposed on natural sex, but that sex itself is a socially-constructed, gendered category and gender is its 'apparatus of production'.[24] The conventional idea of sex as natural and gender as cultural, and the intervention of feminist movements of the 1960s and 1970s, is criticized for depoliticizing gendered identities and relations, to the extent that gender differences are reduced to sex difference and sexual difference is rendered wholly binary and biological. Out of these feminist postmodern theoretical insights many feminisms have emerged which analyse politically and culturally specific constructions of sex/gender difference.

Consistent with the three feminist moves above, when gender is made central as a category of analysis in IR, relationships are drawn between the observations that few women have been visible as subjects or scholars of international relations and that women's lives and experiences have rarely been integrated into the mainstream study of world politics. The study of gender in international relations makes explicit links between empirical, theoretical and epistemological dimensions of feminist work. In the following three sections I shall review the ontological starting points and the major theoretical arguments which take gender as a category of analysis, and epistemological challenges that feminist scholars have brought to bear on the study of IR.

Gender as a Variable

The first empirical-ontological challenge proceeds from the insights of liberal feminist empiricism that, until very recently, International Relations has excluded women's lives and experiences from its substantive knowing and female scholars from the status of IR 'knowers'. This 'sexist' exclusion has resulted in research which presents only a partial 'malestream' view of international reality in an academic field in which the dominant theories claim to explain the universal 'reality' of world politics. It is not that women have not been present or their experiences relevant to IR because as Cynthia Enloe's work demonstrates, women are always (already) inside IR – if we choose to see them there.[25] However, because women's lives and experiences have not been empirically researched in the context of world politics, Rebecca Grant and Kathleen Newland argue that IR has been 'excessively focused on conflict and anarchy and a way of practicing statecraft and formulating strategy that is excessively focused on competition and fear'.[26]

Studies of 'relations international', of the diplomatic, intersubjective processes that make the reproduction of the state-system possible and analysis of the 'structural violence' which underpins the 'perennial presence' of international violence are seen as secondary to the manly study of war and conflict in IR, in part because of their association with domestic 'low politics', feminized subjectivity, everyday reproduction and the work of women. IR continues to theorize politics and the international 'in a way that guarantees that women will be absent from their enquiry [and] their research agendas remain unaltered'.[27] Taking gender seriously involves 'recognising over fifty percent of the world's population', correcting the denial or misrepresentation of women in world politics due to the false assumption that certain male experiences can count for men and women universally, and/or that women are simply absent from political activities and not relevant to political-economic processes, especially those at an international level.[28] Globally, women are a disadvantaged group: they own one percent of the world's property and resources, perform 60 per cent of the labour, are the majority of refugees, illiterate and poor persons, and yet women are central to the social and material survival of families and communities and also at the forefront of environmental, peace, indigenous, nationalist and other critical social movements. International processes and interactions have gender-differentiated causes and consequences, but more importantly the worldwide failure to resolve dilemmas of poverty, pollution, and nuclear proliferation is inseparable from our failure to understand the contributions and situation of women globally – as well as the prevalence and stability of global gender hierarchies.[29]

In recent years, gender-sensitive research has taken a variety of forms in IR. Studies of international development in the context of the 'North–South' divide expose the gender-differentiated consequences of policies designed to promote economic growth and social advancement and demonstrate the importance of taking gender into account.[30] Analyses of women's positions in development recount the historical imposition of Western models and practices of modernization, overwhelmingly based on the opinions of elite male experts from industrialized or colonizing countries. These models advocated gendered households as the basic unit of accumulation, private property and reproduction for 'development' or imperial resource and labour extraction. Where they did not exist before, these modernizing models created public and private hierarchical gendered divisions of men and women's labour, resources and power, with generally deleterious effects on the social status and economic livelihood of women.[31] As Birgit Brock-Utne argues 'men's work gets organised into paid labour while women's work is kept invisible and unpaid'.[32]

The field of 'women in development' (commonly referred to as WID), as it emerged in the 1970s and 1980s, made visible the central role of women as subsistence producers and providers of basic needs in 'developing' countries and 'developed' communities. In this sense, WID was motivated less by a concern to 'integrate' women into processes of development than by the need to recognize and support women's already integral and necessary role in economic and societal development. In practice, however, integrating women into the 'development process' has meant that aid donors have targeted women for special projects, as if women were a self-contained identity, without bringing women's concerns to mainstream male development activities, or challenging their unequal role in the actual planning process. All over the world, Kathleen Newland claims, 'male development planners have seen WID as an instrument not a goal, as a means for lower population growth, higher economic growth and more successful political mobilisation'.[33] 'Women's interests' in development are associated with their primary responsibility for health, family planning, nutrition, gardening and childcare, and development aid typically only helps women to fulfil practical interests and needs in their subordinate roles. It rarely gives them the skills to understand or influence the social, economic and political system under which they live. As a consequence, existing inequalities between men and women are reinforced by international development assistance. WID policy studies within IR show that the most efficient allocation of development assistance is the provision of appropriate agricultural technology, community income-generating projects, education and health resources for women – because they play central roles in the social reproduction of their communities. These studies continue to reform gender-blind international agencies (multilateral) and governmental (bilateral) aid policies, that have taken men as the normative agents and distributors of development, and have failed to effectively address the basic needs of developing countries and even exacerbated their problems of malnutrition-hunger, pauperization, disease, and 'overpopulation'.[34] At the national and international level of development policy and assistance women are typically not considered, other than as add-ons to malestream priorities, just as the goal of their production 'the well-being of the community' is all too frequently forgotten.

Feminist research on macroeconomic restructuring illuminates the engendering of growth, poverty and structural inequality in the global political economy.[35] This research documents the expanding gender gap in work hours, income, resources and power intensified by Third World debt crises, structural adjustment policies (SAPs), the fiscal squeezing and privatization of welfare states, and the globalization of production, finance, labor and economic management.[36] As state economic policies are increasingly governed by the 'global' imperatives of export earnings, international financial markets and comparative labour costs, states fail to deliver social welfare services and to maintain their commitment to full employment and the general well being of national populations. Gender-sensitive research reveals the disproportionate and growing burden imposed on women due to these structural shifts in the nature and relationship of (domestic) states and (global) markets, politics and economics. Such research shows that women as the majority of primary caregivers, domestic servicers and state employees, are most dependent on state services to share the burden of social reproduction and are therefore expected to pick up the state's slack voluntarily, for the survival of their families and communities. SAPs and state budget cuts assume that the market and individual families will privately fulfil the functions of what were formerly public services. They do not, however, specify *who* does this work and how it gets done when macroeconomic theories expect that people will act as rational agents, choosing to pursue their self-interest autonomously in market transactions. Only feminists theorise the power of gender identities and structures which determine that women will bear the costs of 'counting for nothing', while forgoing the monetary gains of providing a market-based service. And only feminists analyse the gender-specific consequences of this public-private shift, in terms of the costs and burdens of social and economic reproduction in the context of global restructuring.[37]

As the cheapest source of flexible paid labour, the reserve army of labour, women, especially poor women oppressed by race, ethnicity, nationality and class, are also disproportionately vulnerable to the deregulation of labour markets and the privatization of state public sectors in particular. Empirical feminist studies reveal the increasing feminization of poverty worldwide and the gendered nature of the new international division of labour – heavily reliant on women's labour in the export processing zones of developing countries, the growth of sex-tourism, migrant domestic la-bour and male-order brides in attracting foreign exchange in subordinate states, as well as the growing number of female-headed households and never-married mothers, and triply burdened (by childcare, domestic and wage labour) women workers worldwide.[38] Growth in the use of female labour, Guy Standing observes, is accompanied by the 'global feminization' and flexibilization of many occupations and tasks formerly dominated by men.[39] This means there is a turn to low cost, insecure, often part-time or contract-based temporary female employment with few social benefits. These changes in the international and gendered divisions of labour have acutely exploited women workers in developing and industrialized coun-tries. They have been constructed, supported and encouraged by multi-national corporations and governments everywhere.

More theoretical feminist studies expose the gendered constitution of international organizations and international economic management: their elite male dominance of decision-making and their masculine privileging of priorities such as growth, rational competitiveness and individual enter-prise which have gendered exclusionary effects.[40] Sandra Whitworth and Catherine Hoskyns look at how particular and changing assumptions about gender relations – women's equality with men in the labour-force, or women's difference as reproducers of the labour force who need special employment protections – are institutionalized in the International Labour Organisation and the organizations of the European Union respectively.[41] They analyse the consequences of these gendered assumptions for the involvement of women in International Organisations (IOs) and the structure and legitimization of unequal gender relations in the workforce and family, and in the order of production and reproduction globally. IOs develop policies which both sustain and challenge the inequality of men and women. For example, Catherine Hoskyns discusses the EU's European Court of Justice's precedent laws on the equal status of pregnant women in paid employment which exceed the more status-quo prerogatives of national jurisdictions. More recently, Sandra Whitworth argues that the ILO has begun to reflect upon the degree to which its own policies have gender-discriminatory effects. Further, Whitworth and Hoskyns discuss women's influence in political processes inside and outside of these male-dominated IOs. They investigate the presence of women in IOs, largely as the secretarial servicers of male bureaucratic politics and also women's organising around specific issues salient to particular IOs. As feminist scholars, they question the institutional structures that continue to ensure women's absence from their decision-making ranks.

The sheer invisibility of women is manifest in the undervaluing of their labour in male-constructed macroeconomic indicators, such as the Gross National Product, which are used to judge the economic progress of states in international policy-making. United Nations agencies and other International Organisations fall short of their virtuous decrees on human-rights and recognizing human effort when they make policy from these aggregate and mean indicators which obscure the social distribution of resources, the poverty and injustice felt by many women and their children, and the production of wealth by women. Statistical estimations which count women's unwaged work reveal not only the social and economic value of this work but just how dependent individuals, the private sector and governments are on women. These studies reverse the conventional direction of dependency by emphasizing the interdependency of production and reproduction, formal and informal economies, public and private spheres, men and women. Marilyn Waring calls for a global reassessment of the role of women, to count women's work and for the reframing of the concept of value, so that production is assessed according to its creative value as opposed to its destructive value.[42]

Interconnected with gender-sensitive research on international development and political economy, feminists have examined the gendered implications of global environmental crises, a growing concentration in the IR discipline.[43] Various studies expose women's unequal responsibility for sustaining the ecological resource balance necessary for daily subsistence and sustainable development. They point out that women are the first to suffer the effects of resource depletion and environmental degradation and are the chief caretakers in times of scarcity, hunger and natural disaster. Maria Mies contends that what women, colonies and natural resources have in common is their systematic exploitation as expendable resources by men and First-World capitalists.[44] Feminists argue that gender ideologies of 'nature as woman and woman as nature' underlie masculine quests to control and subjugate her to grander projects of civilization/culture.[45] The 'feminine principle' of ecology which formerly mediated our sustainable relation with nature – and connotes women's creative management of active processes of nature – has been regressively displaced by the 'masculinist principle' of man alienated from 'nature', including his own.[46] Beyond the empirical, Joni Seager, in her book *Earth Follies* (1993), asserts that it is masculinist institutions dominated by instrumental rationality, including science, the state, and the eco-conservationist establishment, that structure our relationship (of domination) to the environment and which are most responsible for environmental calamities. Eco-feminist critiques deconstruct the masculine gender bias of these institutions and suggest environmentally sustainable alternatives which stress women's autonomy and local self-reliance within and in relation to eco-systems.[47]

Feminist analyses reveal gender as a variable in foreign policy-making by exposing the dominant male gender of conventional practitioners and their exhibition of masculine characteristics as strategically rational actors who make life and death decisions in the name of an abstract conception of the 'national interest'. As Nancy McGlen and Meredith Sarkees have argued in their study of the foreign-policy and defence establishment, women are rarely 'insiders' of the actual institutions that make and implement foreign policy, and conduct war.[48] However, a preoccupation with the masculinity of statesmen prevents us from seeing the multiple non-state actors such as women who also play constitutive roles in international relations: in Cynthia Enloe's research, women are providers of a whole range of military support services (domestic, psychological, medical, and sexual), they are reserve armies in home industries, transnational peace activists, soldiers and mothers of soldiers, and revolutionary actors in national liberation struggles and civil wars.[49] If we see militarization as a social process consisting of many gendered assignments that make possible those ultimate acts of state violence then, she argues, the official provision of sexual services on military bases, for instance, is made central, and not peripheral to our studies of military policy and foreign intervention.

Thus, feminist insights expose the gendered foundations of militaristic foreign policies: men sacrifice their lives in war to protect the motherland as home and the home as a mothering space. Indeed, the gender dichotomies of 'just warrior–beautiful soul' and militarized masculinity–domesticated femininity, authorise violence, especially in defence of national boundaries.[50] Women, however, are being increasingly recruited into armies worldwide, although they are usually excluded from combat and decision-making roles.[51] When women are actually accepted into military combat roles, they subvert the realist association of masculine citizenship with soldiering but are co-opted into the same militarized mindset and are penalized as women within one of the most male-dominated and masculinist institutions.[52] As civilians, women and children are victims of rape, abuse and murder during war, while they bear the social opportunity costs of military build-up and the escalation of domestic violence that is usually associated with the external use of military force. The establishment of domestic violence hotlines across the former states of the Federal Republic of Yugoslavia, for example, has documented the gross increase in violence against women since the war began in 1992. There is also evidence of much higher physical and sexual abuse within the military, as compared with civilian families due to the inherently aggressive value system and lifestyles of men in the service. As a result of this militarism, and the international conflicts and forms of gender persecution that are its starkest expression, women and children also make up more than two-thirds of the world's official refugee population.[53]

Feminist foreign policy analyses open up new substantive areas of policy-making and research in the relations between 'gendered states'.[54] For instance, empirical researchers analyse the persistent 'gender-gap' in the foreign policy beliefs of men and women; women are much more likely to oppose the use of force in international actions. They compare different country's public policies on the inclusion/exclusion of gays and lesbians in the military and interpret the gendered symbolism and narratives of war and nationalism.[55] The international recognition of women's, gay and lesbian rights as human rights has consequences for state foreign policies, just as individual state policies which acknowledge the gender-specificity of human rights have influenced women's, gay and lesbian human rights instruments and declarations at the global level.[56] Only in 1990 did Amnesty International recognize women's human rights by adding gender-persecution to its list of forms of political persecution in states. In part due to its widespread media coverage as a specific war strategy in Yugoslavia, rape has now been included as a Geneva war crime – as if it did not systematically occur before this historical moment. Gender was not named as a ground of persecution in the 'Geneva Convention Against War Crimes' until the current Yugoslavian conflict because states and international agencies have ignored the political nature of private activities and interpreted the persecution of women as matters of personal privacy and cultural tradition.[57] Canada is the first state to give asylum to women refugees who fear persecution for not conforming to their society's 'traditions'; such as forced marriage, bride-burning, dowry deaths, sexual abuse, domestic violence, genital-mutilation, rape, forced sterilisation and abortion, practices of purdah and veiling. However, the problem is that human

rights is a Western androcentric construction premised on the rights-bear-
ing autonomous, male individual and moreover, that the internationally-
institutionalized status of women's human rights is a process driven by
western 'civilized' states reflecting their hegemonic moral high ground:[58]
for instance, the symbolism of the protected Arab woman versus the
liberated US woman soldier consolidates hostile national identities in difference. Some analysts have suggested that 'good states' and the international community should make the recognition of women's human rights a
condition of free-trade and diplomatic relations between states. However,
such a sanction has the tendency to further instrumentalize woman/wo-
men as symbols of the struggles between elite men across international
terrain: in fact, women's lives may be more harmed than helped by international conditions that stigmatise their position.

Recent exploration in feminist international relations research include
theoretical and regional studies of gender, nationalism, and citizenship. In
general, they argue that gender is a constitutive dimension of political
identity because politics has been associated exclusively with the masculine
public sphere and the activities of men, separated from the private sphere
identified with femininity and women's activities. Nationalisms and national identities are gendered in so far as they privilege masculine representations of the nation in war/sacrifice/heroism, and legitimize men's
control over women's bodies on the basis that they are the mothers of the
nation and the embodiment of male national honour. Women are biological
and social reproducers, as well as cultural signifiers of group identity. They
are thus central to the construction of national boundaries and vulnerable to
masculine control over their sexuality and reproductive labour.[59] The
naturalization of gender hierarchy inside nations commonly prefigures
the legitimate domination of 'others'/foreigners outside national boundaries.

Post-Cold War studies which focus on the changing positions of women
in East-Central Europe and the former Soviet Union graphically document
the post-communist remasculinisation of the public sphere and the re-
institutionalisation of rigid gender divisions of public and private spheres,
where women are routinely subordinated.[60] To varying degrees across
these regions, women are instrumentalized as reproducers of the nation
in highly militarized societies, sexually objectified in new and thriving
pornography and sex industries, and encouraged to return to the private
household due to the new capitalist democracies rescinding former socialist
rights to work, employment protection, childcare, contraception, abortion –
all of which are fundamentally threatening women's former citizenship
rights.[61]

Finally, women are significant activists in critical social movements,
organising for peace, environmental justice and women's liberation trans-
nationally. As Deborah Stienstra states 'women have been organising

[autonomously] at the global level for at least 150 years':[62] the suffrage movement, the international women's peace movement, the United Nations decade conferences which bring together governments and non-governmental organisations to discuss and devise strategies to support women's rights, and women's regional networking for post-colonial sustainable development, are all examples. Also relevant to international politics are local women activists who theorize the relationship between the impact of international processes, such as economic liberalisation, militarisation, modernisation and local community self-determination, and quality of life. Thus, in the Pacific Islands region, women speak out about 'nuclear colonialism': French Polynesian and Micronesian women have expressed their solidarity by protesting against French colonization and their nuclear testing programme, the health deformities and stress-related diseases they suffer, and the displacement of their traditional homelands by the continued military and colonial presence of superpowers within their region. Pacific women have challenged the way that economic, social and cultural life is being dangerously swept up by processes of militarization that are now global in scale. In many different actions these women have crusaded to halt nuclear testing in the Pacific, mediate harmful development policies, and to create meaningful indigenous independence and economic sustainability. Women activists are very often the strength of the peace movement in troubled conflict zones of the world. Women in Black, for instance in Israel/Palestine and in Yugoslavia, protest against the escalation of militarism, weaponry and war, and articulate their direct relationship with sexism and violence against women and children. While the dislocation and social turmoil associated with war is borne in the last instance by women caregivers and household managers, their collective activism supports and creates alternative values that motivate broad community resistance and empower people to take control over their everyday lives.[63]

Making women's lives visible in gender-sensitive research has policy-relevant and material effects: feminists argue that only when women are recognised as fundamental to economic and political processes will they share an equal part of societal decision-making. Feminist empiricist epistemology acknowledges that the absence of women scholars in IR has led to IR knowledge that is largely concerned with men's lives, but aim to correct this imbalance. Unlike feminist standpointers, they do not explain women's absence from IR in terms of the field's masculinist concepts. However, feminist empirical IR research is not separate from more theoretical and epistemological feminist scholarship. Indeed the inclusion of women in IR has rested on the political insurgency of gender as an analytic category. Finding out where women are situated globally is dependent upon criticism of IR's key concepts, to which we now turn, and the development of new concepts which render women's agency and victimization visible.

Gender as Constitutive

The second feminist challenge to the IR canon contends that 'women' have not been studied in IR because the conceptual framework of the entire field is 'gendered' in so far as it is derived from a social and political context where 'the problem of patriarchy is repressed'.[64] Feminists argue, for instance, that key IR concepts such as power, sovereignty, autonomy, anarchy, security, and core units of analysis such as man, the state and the international system are inseparable from the patriarchal division of public and private. They are identified with men's experiences and forms of knowledge inside the former masculine, male-dominated public sphere, as opposed to the private sphere where women have been historically located. According to this view, IR is not merely gender-biased, that is, premised on its very exclusion of women and feminine attributes, but gender is world-constitutive.[65] Dominant malestream theories of IR such as realism and neo-realism which claim to describe or explain the world 'as it is' 'shape our behaviours with concrete consequences for the real world of actors and events'.[66] They are responsible for making the world 'as it is', for the reproduction of global hierarchies of gender and other social hierarchies such as race, class, and ethnicity. Theorizing, as Burchill articulates in the introduction to this volume, is 'the process by which we give meaning to an allegedly objectified world "out there"'. The conceptual framework and levels of analysis prevalent in IR are thus essentially-contested attempts to make sense of world politics. From feminist perspectives, however, their failure to see the mutually historical, cultural and politically constructed boundaries of gender, the state and international relations limits their ability to explain historical change and continuity in world politics.[67]

International Relations theory claims to theorize those behaviours and processes which occur beyond the nation-state, in the space in-between states, referred to as the 'international system' and sometimes as 'international society'. For this reason, R. B. J. Walker suggests that IR theory is a constitutive political practice, in so far as the division between political theory – the study of the inside working of states, of domestic issues such as justice, legitimacy, rights, community – and International Relations theory – the study of the relations outside states, of foreign issues of security, violence, war and alliances – reifies the territoriality of the sovereign state. For Walker, the study of IR is not separate from the particular modern universalist resolution of spatio-temporal relations in the sovereign state. The principle of sovereignty he says 'resolve[s] all claims to unity and diversity, and thus all possibilities in space and time, in a moment of autonomy' in the gendered political identity of sovereign man or the rational individual.[68] It is the very assumption of this self-helping, competitive and atomistic subject which is constitutive of the autonomous sovereign state and permits an account international relations to be constructed.

Feminist theorists, however, go further in their disciplinary deconstruction. They argue that International Relations theory and practice are political acts that render invisible both the presence of women agents in international structures and the power of gender as a structuring principle in global social and economic life.[69] The discursive separation of domestic politics from international politics, and concomitant neo-realist aversion to the 'domestic analogy' obscures the prior gendered division of public and private within states and masculine aversion to the latter associated with emotion, the body, women and femininity. Both conventional problem-solving (realism, neo-realism, rationalism, neo-liberal institutionalism) and critical non-feminist (Marxism, critical theory, postmodernism) theories of world politics overlook this private sphere of the family/household, because it is submerged within the 'domestic analogy' itself.[70]

From feminist perspectives the independence of domestic politics from international politics begins to break down as the definitive disciplinary boundary, when we notice how 'anarchy outside supports [gender] hierarchy at home'[71] and how the international has been very much about the management of change in domestic political orders. Throughout modern history, for example, women have been told that they will receive equal human rights, even equality with men after the war, after liberation or after the national economy has been rebuilt. But after all of these 'outside' forces are allayed, we find the domestic (masculine) demand for things to go back to normal, and women to their traditionally subordinate place.[72] More recently in this current phase of global economic restructuring, states summon the deterministic discourse of all-encompassing 'outside' international market forces to legitimize their neo-liberal social and economic policies 'inside'. Such widespread internationalized policies are implemented by manipulating gendered ideologies and divisions of labour and by separating economic from social policy, public from private responsibility, at the expense of most citizens' security and welfare.

As Cynthia Enloe observes 'states depend upon particular constructions of the domestic and private spheres in order to foster smoother relationships at the public/international level'.[73] There is a precarious balance, however, between these oppositional spaces. Laura McEnaney analyses the gender struggles between domestic and international spheres in the America First movement and its conservative women members who advocated the isolationism/anti-interventionism of the USA during the Second World War.[74] From the perspective of these mostly white, middle-class American women, US involvement in the war was a threat to their female domestic power and their control over husbands and breadwinners. They feared that servicemen abroad would evade their breadwinner responsibilities, desert their wives and children, and engage in affairs with other women or prefer bonding with other soldiers, to their families back home. Emily Rosenburg traces these same masculine–feminine themes of international versus domestic spaces of power in the post-war Hollywood film industry, which as a site of cultural-discursive production helped to normalize domestic gender relations and nuclear families after the war.[75]

However, these relationships between domestic and international, masculine and feminine agents are mystified by the levels of analysis schema, that separates the individual, the state, and the international system. This theoretical device has become 'the most influential way of classifying explanations of war, and indeed of organising our understanding of inter-state relations in general'.[76] Several feminists IR scholars have, with the risk of reinforcing its overt power, taken the deconstruction of each level of analysis as a starting point for reconstructing a relational gender-sensitive theory of world politics.[77] Through a feminist lens, the traditional generic actors and units of analysis in IR, statesmen and nation-states in the context of an international system are revealed as gendered social constructions which take specifically masculine ways of being and knowing in the world as universal. Moreover, they are shown to depend upon men's co-operative autonomy from women, and the denigration of characteristics and actors associated with femininity and feminized others. Taking gender as a unit of analysis or even women as an identity group renders the divisions between the individual, state, and international system not only less potent because, as Sylvester argues, women are left out at all levels and each level is preconditioned by the assertion and analogy of generic man, but as simply one way to represent the world.[78] This is a representation which is arguably more evocative of hegemonic masculinity. Feminist analyses of the gendered agency of man and the state in IR expose the patriarchal logic of each and the (feminine) differences, in particular the diversity of women's agency which is absolutely essential to but theoretically and politically repressed in each bounded conception.

Man

Sovereign man constitutes the dominant model of agency in conventional IR theories and is typically extrapolated by analogy to explain inter-state behaviour. The concepts of anarchy and sovereignty – the foundational 'givens' in the field – are based on this understanding of rational, autonomous agency. Specifically, the ontology of sovereign man, Richard Ashley argues 'betokens a "rational identity" a homogeneous and continuous presence that is hierarchically ordered, that has a unique centre of decision presiding over a coherent self, and that is demarcated from, and in opposition to, an external domain of difference and change that resists assimilation to its identical being'.[79] The external domain of difference against which this self is defined, is as much the feminine 'other' inside the domestic sphere as it is an abstract conception of international 'anarchy' outside. Feminists such as J. Ann Tickner and Christine Sylvester claim that this is not a generic, generalizable ontology of human nature and behaviour, but rather an exclusionary masculine model of agency derived from a context of unequal gender relations, where women's childrearing and caregiving work supports the development of autonomous male selves.[80] People or groups of people, like women, some men or social relationships that cannot be interpreted in this way as coherent rational selves, are denied agency in international politics and history. International Relations theory, Kathleen Newland and Rebecca Grant argue, is 'constructed overwhelmingly by men working with mental models of human activity seen through a[n elite] male eye and apprehended through a[n elite] male sensibility'.[81]

This understanding of human agency is imposed by taking the standpoint of men-masculinity as generic. Rational man as metaphor for human nature is presented as self-interested and autonomous with the capacity for instrumental reason. Moreover, he is abstracted from situatedness in the concrete world, from a place in time and space, from particular prejudices, interests and needs. The workings of the inter-state system are explained by reference to the egoistic behaviour of this Hobbesian or Waltzian man in the 'state of nature'. Rousseau's stag hunt allegory, the prisoners dilemma, chicken and other game theory allow the fiction of these presocial abstract individuals to persist for the purposes of logical postulation on the nature of the abstract international system. The naturalization of gender hierarchy is inextricably tied to the assumption that the state of nature is competitive, egoistic, rapacious and violent and therefore that anarchy is not what states make of it, but is essentially power and conflict-ridden.[82] Feminist theorists are suspicious of such theoretical models which deny the centrality of human relatedness, and repress the way affective relations constitute distinctive subjectivities.

Some feminists posit a female model of the individual as connected, interdependent and interrelated. Carol Gilligan, for instance, has suggested that women can approximate either a human nature model as both connected and autonomous individuals, whereas men can only fulfil the model of the autonomous and separate individual.[83] Moreover, Joan Tronto has argued that there is a fundamentally different conception of the self and the relation between the self and others in feminine and masculine images.[84] Pitting female experience and feminine models of agency against male-masculine ones, however, runs the risk of reinforcing the power of gender dichotomies, such as idealism–realism and 'beautiful souls–just warriors', in IR. Although an oppositional feminine model exposes the partial and gendered depiction of agency in IR theories, it does not disrupt the binary framework which essentialises male–female identities and privileges masculine power politics. Most feminists in IR do not argue that adding a nurturing account of feminine nature will correct the gender-bias of generic man. In contrast, by exposing the gender-specific nature of the ontological givens of the field – man and the state – feminists open up the relationship between the domestic and the international and the conceptual field of IR more generally, which has been fixed to gendered conceptions of autonomous agency. IR theories evade other accounts of human nature, that proffer non-essential, non-unitary conceptions of agency: thus, feminist standpointers suggest looking for models of human agency emanating from marginalised sites and sites of women, the colonised, and people of colour's resistance. According to Ann Tickner, a feminist perspective needs to achieve this transformation of IR by posing richer, alternative models that take account of both production and reproduction, redefine rationality to be less exclusive and instrumental, and respect human relationships (across all levels) as well as our interdependent relation with nature.[85] Such models, Tickner stresses, would better conceptualise individuals and states as both autonomous and connected, and as having multiple identities, sovereignties and relations. In other words, feminist alternatives to the levels of analysis in IR do not promote more universal abstractions, but demand greater contextualisation in order to map more adequately the complexity and indeterminacy of agency and structure.

Reductionist arguments that draw upon conceptions of 'evil' human nature as leading inevitably to conflictual international relations, are endemic to variants of classical and neo-realism in particular. Hans Morgenthau argued that the objective national interest is rooted deeply in human nature and thus in the actions of statesmen.[86] Despite his advocacy of a systemic theory of IR, Kenneth Waltz frequently refers to the analogy between man and the state as proof of the hostile reality that he observes in the anarchical system as a whole: '[a]mong men as among states there is no automatic adjustment of interests. In the absence of a supreme authority there is then the constant possibility that conflicts will be solved by force'.[87] Similarly, while Waltz prefers international anarchy as the most potent explanation for war, he embraces Alexander Hamilton's polemic set forth in the Federalist papers: 'to presume a lack of hostile motives among states is to forget that men are ambitious, vindictive and rapacious'.[88] The upshot of the man/state analogy for feminist analysis, Sylvester argues, is that if man is rational – or rather, rationality is equated with men's behaviour – and the social institutions he creates are also rational, then the state itself bears a male-masculine identity.[89]

The state

According to the constitutive principle of territoriality the modern state is simultaneously differentiated along two axes, inside-outside and public-private.[90] Sovereignty is the formal principle which institutionalises *public* authority in mutually exclusive domains: it assumes boundaries between us and them, order and anarchy, domestic and international, public and private.[91] Andrew Linklater theorizes the problem of political obligation with the rise of the modern state and the formation of territorial boundaries that divide men from citizens, insiders from outsiders and differentiate men's private morality as members of humanity from public morality between citizens.[92] While critical of IR theories which assume the centralised state as an ontological given, these historicised accounts of state-formation within a system of states nevertheless ignore the political gendered differentiation of public-private spaces and moralities, and their implications for conceptualising shifts and consistency in state forms and global relations.

As argued above, the boundaries of the discipline of IR are marked by the boundaries of 'the state' and in the tendency to stigmatize or avoid the domestic analogy. They are also marked as IR theorists evade all reflection on states of gender and gendered states. The state, which Spike Peterson coins an 'ongoing project' in its structural origins and contemporary manifestations, is the centralised, main organiser of gendered power, working in part through the manipulation of 'public and private'.[93] It is not a 'coherent identity subordinate to the gaze of a single interpretative centre,' but rather the idealised model of Western manhood that mystifies the state's patriarchal public–private division.[94] Briefly, feminists argue that the state invades the emotional life of citizens through their identification as masculine and feminine, and that the state manipulates gender for its own project of unity in hierarchy. Men are socialised to identify with constructions of masculinity which emphasise autonomy, male superiority, fraternity, strength, protector roles, and ultimately the bearing of arms. Women on the other hand are taught to defer as wives and daughters to the protection and stronger will of men, while providing the emotional, economic and social support systems for men's activities. The state legitimises and regulates this 'naturalised' gender order for its own authority purposes: sovereign relations with other states outside, as well as man's relation to woman inside, define the internal constitution of sovereign man and sovereign state.

Masculinist domination is thus integral to and institutionalized within the state-system. Spike Peterson argues that there was an intersection of domination practices with modern state-formation involving capitalist accumulation, the rise of Western science and objectivist dualistic metaphysics.[95] Together, she says, these historical processes marginalized women in a private, exclusively reproductive realm of necessity and supported men's citizenship in a public realm defined by the political apparatuses of the state. Earlier state transition from kinship to citizen-based societies established a gender hierarchy inextricable from the metaphysics of identity over difference, mind over body, culture over nature, and order over chaos. Gendered divisions of identity and labour in public and private spheres were formative of and constituted by these other dualisms in the territorial and ideological shift to nation-states. Modern state formation, moreover, has its origins in early Athenian state formation, with the institutionalized separation between the *oikos* (household) and the *polis* (public sphere) and the privileging of Greek elite male citizen-warriors as the source and strength of the democratic polity.

Consistent with this genealogy of gendered state-formation, the boundaries of the state are strengthened by their association with naturalized gender boundaries and masculine agency. Sovereign states require 'others' to establish their very existence: men and states stand against anarchy 'outside', and are distinguished from women and feminised others 'inside'. While it is true that the propriety of moral responsibility distinguishes the private sphere and the domestic state from the international realm in realist thought, the private and international realms are similarly subordinate to the domestic state and its sovereign order of justice and rationality. The ontology of conventional IR thus conceives the private sphere – like the international sphere where order is seen as the primary consideration – as a natural realm of disorder; where women are represented as reproductive beings akin to nature, and who like nature must be controlled. The lower being represented by women, the body, and the anarchical system must be subordinated to the higher being present in the mind, rational man and the order of states. Jean Elshtain insists that the realist narrative of IR in particular pivots on this public–private division and its essentialist construction of femininity and masculinity as the cause of disorder and the bringer of order respectively.[96] She recounts St Augustine's scornful interpretation of the Pax Romana expressed through implicitly gendered representations: he equates sovereign absolutism and the terrible sway of Rome with masculinity and femininity with alien forces, '*aliena*', the unruly She who can disorder. The male, like Machiavelli's virtuous Prince, is the bearer of order who must tame capricious female forces, domestically and externally. Otherness within (women, femininity) and others outside (barbarians, foreigners, other states) threaten the coherent identities of men and states, whose security rests on the establishment of fixed, gendered boundaries.

This symbolic codification of boundaries has real political implications for gender relations and the lives of women. State coercive apparatuses celebrate the agency of soldiers and statesmen and devalue the agency of women who defend homes, families and communities, but are rendered increasingly 'insecure' by war and male violence. The assumption in IR that states are orderly and domesticated masks the masculinist social control that women are subjected to: through direct violence (murder, rape, battering, incest), but also ideological constructs, such as 'women's work' and the cult of motherhood that justify structural violence, inadequate health care, sexual harassment, and sex segregated wages, rights and resources.[97]

Further, Spike Peterson argues that states are directly implicated in violence against women in their non-intervention in domestic violence, their definition of rape from a male standpoint, and indirectly complicit in the masculinist, heterosexist ideology they promote in education, media images, military indoctrination, welfare policies, and patriarchal law.[98] Similarly, dominant IR theories are complicit with masculinist violence against women when they deny or exclude analysis of the gender struggles that go on inside–outside states – that suggest the state itself is a site of struggle. Feminists, however, challenge the constructed boundaries of domestic–international and public–private that distinguish legitimate from illegitimate force, and engender the coercive meanings of order, anarchy and 'security'.

Non-feminist critical IR theories bring historical understandings of the state and state-making, without which a historical understanding of the construction of gender, and the institutionalization of gender hierarchies, is impossible. And yet there is no guarantee that historically-sensitive accounts of modern state-formation will be gender-sensitive: they are, in fact, often blind to gender as one of the most potent ways of constructing and legitimating boundaries of political authority.

Key concepts

Power, rationality, security and sovereignty are the constitutive concepts which underpin the levels of analysis in IR and the hegemonic realist theories which claim to explain 'the reality' of world politics in a more limited sense as 'inter-national relations'. As already argued, these concepts are gender-biased, derived from the above androcentric accounts of men (human nature), the state, and the system of states as ahistorical fixities made self-evident by reference to a gendered state of nature. Feminist scholars of IR have analysed the 'gender-specificity' of each of these key terms and suggested how mystification of their gendered rather than generic foundations limits our ability to explain and understand the multiple realities of world politics.

Because of the dominance of realist accounts, *power* in IR theory is usually and exclusively conceived of as 'power-over': the power to force or influence someone to do something that they otherwise would not. An individual's power rests on one's autonomy from the power of others.[99] In this view, power cannot be shared nor can power be readily increased by relationships with others in the context of interdependent or common interests. The accumulation of power capabilities and resources, according to Hans Morgenthau, is both an end and a means to security. In the context of an anarchical state system which is interpreted as necessarily hostile and self-helping, states that act 'rationally' instinctively deduce their national interests as their maximization of power over other states. The Waltzian notion of power is only marginally different. Kenneth Waltz conceptualises power as a means for the survival of a state but not as an end-goal in itself, to the extent that a stable bipolar balance of power configuration exists between states. Consequently, in the Waltzian world view the only power that really matters is the power-capabilities of 'Great Powers', whose bipolar or multipolar arrangement brings limited order to an anarchic international realm.

How is this concept of power gendered? In her critique of Morganthau's six principles of power politics, Ann Tickner argues that this understanding of power is androcentric.[100] It is particular to male self-development and objectivist knowing in patriarchal societies where men's citizenship and personal authority rests on their head-of-household power over women's sexuality and labour. This concept of power also rests on a particularly gender-specific notion of autonomous agency – man and the state – that makes human relationships and affective connections invisible. If the human world is exhaustively defined by such gendered constructions of 'power-over', how then do children get reared, collective movements mobilized and everyday life get reproduced? It is incoherent to posit self-help as the essential feature of world politics, Christine Sylvester argues, when many international relations go on within households and other institutions, such as diplomatic negotiations, trade regimes and the socialisation of future citizens, that are not based on self-help alone but which take interdependent relations between self and other as the norm.[101] The realist and liberal assumption that men and states are mutually-exclusive and self-sufficient atoms presents power politics as a self-fulfilling prophecy. Power politics, however, is a gendered and therefore partially contingent account of world politics because its conceptualisation of power depends upon the rational agency of political man and the exclusion of characteristics associated with the feminine.

When Cynthia Enloe writes that paying attention to women can expose how much power it takes to maintain the international political system in its present form she is not referring to the sheer coercive power of men and states.[102] Rather, she is intimating that power is a complex phenomenon of social forces that interpolates and reproduces our personal and sexual identities as men, women and national citizens. In order to understand the nature of power at the international level, feminist and other critical theorists urge that we study the domestic and transnational social forces and power relations that not only support the foreign policies of states, but actually constitute the state as the dominant social form.

Rationality in the realist paradigm is the instrumental reason which determines the world-view of states and statesmen. It conditions their perception of the international sphere as an anarchical and hostile space where states are rendered mutually insecure in their attempts to achieve security by offensive-defensive military means. Exclusive national interests and the unitary action of states are deduced from the rationality postulate. To the extent that states share common interests, the theory of rational action tells us that these cannot be realised outside of a juridico-legal order with coercive power and where there is no world government to regulate and enforce agreements.

Feminists argue that this realist form of rationality is gendered. It cannot see relationships, other than self-help relationships, between people and states. State identities and interests are interpreted as exogenous not endogenous to state interaction. This is because rationality is a particularly disembodied and detached masculine way of seeing the world out of historical context and process. This model of knowledge takes the world as 'given' and as inherently conflictual because it portends to know from a position 'outside', removed from the reality of social relations embedded in interdependencies. Further, this rational knowledge is made possible by the gendered division of labour which holds women responsible for human relationships and the reproduction of everyday life, making co-operation for them a daily reality, and relieving men of these necessities. Rational thinkers such as men and states do not figure in their cost-benefit analyses the social costs of foreign policies (military buildup, war mobilisation, economic liberalisation or protection) that are borne by 'private' family-households and communities. This is because the context for neo-realist and liberal conceptions of rationality is the gender-specific, male-dominated preserve of public institutions, the market economy included. The dominance of this objective 'rational' knowledge-interest in IR theory and practice, leaves women and feminist theorists to make visible relationships between the local and the global, the personal and the political.

Security, as theorised by realists and neo-realists, is not what it sounds like from feminist points of view. Rather, security is conventionally defined in IR as the stability provided by militaristic states whose nuclear proliferation is seen to prevent total war, if not many limited wars fought on proxy territory. Typically, security is examined only in the context of the presence and absence of war, because the threat of war is considered endemic to the sovereign state-system where security is zero-sum and by definition 'national'. This conception of security presupposes what Spike Peterson terms a 'sovereignty contract' established between states.[103] According to this imaginary contract the use of military force is a necessary evil to prevent the outside (difference, irrationality, anarchy and potential conflict) from conquering the inside of homogeneous, rational and orderly states. States, according to this view, are a kind of 'protection racket' that by their very existence as bully 'protectors' create threats 'outside' and then charge for the insecurity that these bring to their 'protected' populations 'inside'. In the name of 'protection', states demand the sacrifice of gendered citizens: soldiers through military conscription and mothers who devote their lives to socializing these dutiful citizens for the sovereign state as masculine deity.[104] Like the state which has a monopoly on legitimate force, the institution of marriage has a monopoly on legitimate reproduction and property inheritance and acts as a 'protection racket', specifically for women. Women seek security in marriage and the protection of a husband from the violence of other men or males in general, and from the economic insecurity of a international division of labour which devalues work associated with women. As such, men and states, domestic and international violence, are inextricably related. The limited security provided by 'protection rackets' allows men and states to consolidate their centralised authority over other men and states, but more importantly over women and nature on whom they are dependent as a source of exploitable resources, for the socio-cultural and biological reproduction of power relations.

But how has the national state come to be the ultimate arbiter of power, security and freedom? How is it that we have come to believe in the state's protection from threats of death or conquest? Or rather, from feminist perspectives, '[t]hrough what [gendered] identities do we seek [this conception of] "security"?'[105] Jean Elshtain genealogically traces gendered identities of just warriors and beautiful souls, as the constitutive leading roles in narratives of war and peace, from Hegel's philosophical state to the contemporary state of realist IR.[106] Internalising an identity, a name, is one of the most potent expressions of a power relationship. Indeed,'the status [identity] of the "protector"', Spike Peterson argues 'depends upon structural demands for protection and their embodiment in the "protected" [identity]'.[107]

In sum, as a result of taking women's experiences of protection rackets seriously, feminists urge that 'security' must be redefined. In particular, what is called 'national security' is profoundly endangering to human survival and sustainable communities. State security apparatuses create their own security dilemmas by purporting androcentric control and 'power-over' to be the name of the game; a game we are persuaded to stay in, in order to achieve the absolute and relative gains of state security. Ann Tickner argues that ideas and key concepts such as 'rationality', 'security', and 'power' might also be building blocks of explanation for a feminist theory of international politics.[108] There is nothing inherent in the terms themselves which suggests that they must be wholly discarded, rather it is their narrow and exclusionary meanings in IR theory and practice which is problematic for feminist perspectives. However, Spike Peterson and Anne Sisson Runyan claim that dichotomous thinking (inside–outside, sovereignty–anarchy, domestic–international) prevents IR theory from being able to 'conceptualise, explain, or deliver the very things it says it is all about –

security, power and sovereignty'.[109] Indeed, from their critical feminist perspective it can only re-present the same dualisms, and reproduce the self-fulfilling security dilemma and the perpetuity of masculine power politics.

Gender as Transformative

In the first two sections of this chapter the ontological contributions of feminism to IR were surveyed. However, as Scott Burchill clarifies in his introduction, ontological questions about 'what is a knowable reality' depend upon an epistemological stance. Feminist post-positivists argue that epistemological stances depend upon ontological positions 'from which to know': the positive pursuit of objectivity, for instance, is dependent upon particular masculine subject positions. In contrast, positivist methods in IR subordinate questions of ontology – the specificity of the knowing-subject and subjects of knowledge – to questions of epistemology – universalizing levels of abstraction and the quest for universal knowledge. Feminist perspectives subvert this patriarchal ordering by exposing the male-masculine ontologies behind positivist epistemologies.

In this third section the epistemological significance of feminist IR is discussed in relation to the ontological claims of the category of 'woman', women as an identity group, and gender as a unit of analysis, presented above. By arguing that gender-difference is constitutive of world politics, feminists have deconstructed the defining abstractions of sovereign man and the state and opened spaces for theorising women's experience in world politics. But this is only a starting point for feminist goals of transforming social hierarchies because feminist projects of reconstruction entail the concurrent deconstruction of 'sovereign woman'.[110] In other words, gender is a *transformative* macro-political category, because there is no gender-neutral subject or institution, only in so far as the social-construction of binary gender is itself *transformed*.

Feminist postmodern IR theorists challenge the hierarchical dichotomies of order–anarchy, dependency–sovereignty, domestic–international, subject–object which have traditionally defined the theory and methods of IR. Jean Elshtain in her book *Women and War* (1987) and Christine Sylvester in her article 'Some Dangers in Merging Feminist and Peace Projects' (1990b), refuse to include women in IR on the basis of their dichotomous conflation with peace, co-operation, concrete subjectivity, and domesticated politics, that mirrors men's conflation with war, competition, abstract objectivity and anarchical politics. Instead, they have problematized the defining dichotomies of the field that are reinforced through their association with the masculine–feminine gender dichotomy. They question how gender hierarchies are constructed, legitimated, resisted and reproduced and how they serve to naturalize other forms of superordination in world politics. From this perspective, gender or sexual difference is not just about the relations between male-masculine and female-feminine but about the politics of knowledge, how and from what position we can know, and signifying human relationships of power more generally.

The stance of 'objectivity' is exposed as androcentric for claiming universal validity, when it is actually only congruent with elite male perspectives and masculine attributes.[111] In the same way, the abstractions, sovereign man and woman, are criticised for masking their white, Western identity and rendering differences among women and men according to race, class, ethnicity, nationality, and so on, invisible. But what do the global differences and similarities among women, in addition to those between men and women, say about the politics of knowing and doing IR?[112]

If asking questions about women's location in world politics, addressed in the first section of this chapter, is dependent upon the second section, 'bringing gender in' as a theoretical construct in order to account for women's marginalization in IR, feminist postmodernists rethink binary gender 'not as the essence from which social organization can be explained but as a variable . . . *which must be explained*'.[113] While modern feminist theories created the category of gender to explain the social construction of women's oppression, postmodern feminist theories historicise gender as an analytical device, complicit with patriarchal orderings and harbouring its own exclusions. These must also be deconstructed. It is a tragic irony that, as Ann Snitow eloquently states, 'women become a[n homogeneous] identity . . . to fight the way that women have been relegated to the [homogeneous] category woman'.[114] As an essentially contested political-theoretical movement, feminism expresses the paradoxical tension between 'needing to speak and act as women *qua* woman', and 'needing an identity not overdetermined by our gender'.[115] This makes feminist identity and solidarity problematic in so far as achieving its goal of deconstructing the bonds of binary gender depends on organising 'as women'. Contrary to the tenets of 1970s radical feminisms, there is no easily realized and readily mobilized, global sisterhood. Rather, 'feminist internationality', as Christina Gabriel and Laura Macdonald establish in their analysis of North American women's transnational organising in the context of the North American free trade agreement (NAFTA), must be created by acknowledging and confronting and not ignoring the differences among women.[116] The very tension between modern and postmodern epistemologies which has divided malestream social and political theorists, including IR theorists, is the source of contemporary feminism's theoretical dynamism and political relevancy. Postmodern feminism acknowledges the lack of a foundational collective subject 'woman', and a relatively bounded realm of the political, as well as the need to make a difference to women's daily lives, with the realisation that it is the superordinate category 'woman/women' that has historically served to marginalise females.

In his discussion of Marxism in this volume, Andrew Linklater argues that the status of universalism is the key to the current debate between different modes of critical theory. This debate surrounding the nature of the universal and particular-universal relations of power takes on special and heightened meaning in the context of feminist IR theorising which seeks to conceptualize global-local relations and feminist politics on an international scale. The threefold feminist epistemologies most commonly identified in IR writings as *feminist empiricism, feminist standpoint*, and *feminist postmodernism* are not autonomous or necessarily contradictory approaches to gender-sensitive and gender-transformative knowledge in IR.[117] On the contrary, these epistemologies are distinctive and interrelated feminist challenges to the authority and masculine dominance of science itself.[118] They share a normative struggle to sustain connections to practical feminist politics and the concrete workings of gendered power. The act of feminist theorizing is itself a conscious political practice inescapably implicated with power. Symbolically, 'woman' has been constructed as antithetical to the grand project of abstract theory, and this has had profound implications for women's practice of theorizing, be it feminist or not. Academic feminism is about cultivating connections between theory and practice, knowledge and politics, deconstruction and reconstruction, and nurturing ties between university teaching and a broader women's 'community'. Feminists argue that 'we can't separate our lives from the accounts given of them', that the articulation of our experience is part of our experience.[119] In the field of IR, it is especially apparent that feminist theory-is-practice, given that women are the absences on which the identity of the field itself has been established.

Feminist IR Epistemologies

Cynthia Enloe's work has greatly inspired feminist international relations, perhaps because her research radically subverts conventional ways of knowing and doing IR. To make sense of international politics, Enloe analyses the extraordinary lives of women from below, which the history of the discipline would tell us is the least likely place for 'high politics'. But it is in these 'trivialised' places where 'gender makes the world go round', that the personal is the political and the international.[120] Enloe reveals constructions of masculinity and femininity at the heart of state legitimation, social processes of militarization, nationalist struggles, successful capitalist accumulation and post-Cold War reconstruction. For example, in 'The Morning After: Sexual Politics at the End of the Cold War' (1994), she considers the withdrawal of Russian mothers' support for the Soviet army, due to the gross and unaccountable sacrifice of their sons in the USSR–Afghanistan war, as one of many personal expressions of gendered power that led to the delegitimization of the Soviet regime and the end of the Cold War. Further, analysing the Gulf war from a feminist perspective, Enloe challenges the 'us versus them' construction of the conflict between Iraq and the Rest (symbolised by the veiled Arab woman and the liberated US woman soldier) by focusing on women's war stories and experiences, not featured in the multinational media coverage: the sexual abuse and harassment of US soldiers, the rape of Filipino servants by their Kuwaiti employers, Iraqi soldiers' rape of Kuwaiti women, and Kuwaiti women's struggle to be included in the suffrage of their so-called 'democratic' country.[121] Enloe's method encourages us to broaden conventional ways of knowing 'the truth' of international politics, and to question from whose perspective state 'legitimate' force is the most significant expression of violence and potent explanation for war.

In her book *Feminist and International Relations Theory for a Postmodern Era* (1994), Christine Sylvester suggests an alternative postmodern feminist epistemology, variously referred to as 'homesteading', 'empathetic co-operation', or postmodern feminism.[122] Women as actors and gender as an analytic variable, she argues, are homeless in IR, where the exclusionary homesteads of nation-states dominate without reference to or recognition of the historical centrality of (gendered) households and multiple, shifting political identities. IR theory is also attached to the fixed homesteads of 'man' and 'the state'. However, Sylvester contends that the epistemological practice of 'homesteading' 'reconfigures "known" subject statuses [such as binary gender] in ways that open up rather than fence in terrains of meaning, identity and place in IR'.[123] From Sylvester's postmodern feminist perspective 'all places to speak and act as women are problematic', because they are socially and historically constructed and exclude other contestatory identities.[124] But she argues that women can be agents through creative and mobile acts of homesteading that admit a sense of homelessness in fixed positions and thus refuse our inherited statuses and places in IR. Effectively, Sylvester relinquishes the pure feminist standpoint position that women's experience can constitute the grounds for a more critical and universal theory of IR, in favour of multiple feminist standpoints that question the discipline's exclusionary constitution.

Cross-cultural understanding and feminist strategies in the context of these multiple standpoints and differences among women, however, demand 'empathetic co-operation'.[125] This method advocates intersubjective conversations between selves and others (for example, realists and neoliberals, postmodern feminists and non-feminists in IR) that are not fixed to any one identity but can 'root and shift' from narrowly construed positions and engage in learning processes of mutual transformation. Feminist theory for a postmodern era has the potential, Sylvester claims, to heighten the modern–postmodern epistemological crisis that the field of IR would like to ignore: postmodern feminism demonstrates that it is possible to do research and make knowledge claims, despite there being no given ontological starting points for theories of international relations.[126]

In her article 'The Women/'Women' Question in International Relations', Marysia Zalewski favourably compares the ostensibly opposed feminist standpoint and postmodern epistemologies of Enloe and Sylvester.[127] By making women in world politics visible, she says, Cynthia Enloe adds new voices from new places not traditionally discussed in terms of IR, that contribute alternative ways of conceptualising relations internationally. Enloe's ontological approach actually challenges given ways of thinking about IR, including the dominant objectivist approach: for instance, asking why we have typically only seen statesmen and soldiers in IR leads us to question the identity of the knowers and the particular ways of knowing institutionalised in IR. Moreover, by introducing vastly different world-views of women who are differently situated in the present world order, Enloe exemplifies the postmodern feminist perspective that there are multiple standpoints from which to view IR, and that each reveals diverse realities and relationships.

Sharing Christine Sylvester's feminism for a postmodern era, Spike Peterson suggests that the combination of global contextualisation, comparison and critical reflection are pragmatic but provisional methods for mapping local–global and other relationships across boundaries.[128] She argues strongly that the modern–postmodern debate over the objective *or* relative status of knowledge claims is itself framed by positivism and specifically gendered dichotomies that assume a clear separation between theory and practice, masculine and feminine, subjects and objects. From a feminist relational perspective, Peterson asserts that bringing objects of study into relation allows us to make meaningful comparisons but not absolute claims about the nature of IR. Comparisons enable us to engage in critical reflection and evaluate choices in relation to their anticipated trade-offs. For example, whether we advocate or oppose women's integration into military combat roles depends on the societal contexts, on the relatedness of sexism and militarism, and on our assessment of the political consequences of different strategies. When compared to other public policies and contexts, will women's inclusion in combat roles reinforce the military as an ideology and an institution, and its correlation with masculinity and citizenship?[129] When compared with other feminist strategies will 'women in combat' break down negative gender ascriptions and demonstrate new norms of women as strong, competent, and equal? What are the political consequences of 'adding women to militaries and stirring' for women's practical interests in economic and civil well-being and for their strategic interests in transforming gender-biased institutions and constraining gender identities? As Rebecca Grant argues, homogeneous woman/women, in contrast to sovereign man in malestream conventional IR theories, cannot be a foundational epistemic category for alternative feminist IR theories.[130]

In sum, feminist IR epistemologies emphasise the falsity of knowing international relations from fixed ontological positions and objective epistemological perspectives. Rather, they suggest the importance of contextualising theoretical claims, theorising relationships, situating political struggles and homesteading subjectivities on personal, local, national, transnational, regional, and global levels, in so far as these are interconnected.

Postmodernist IR and Postmodern Feminism: The Third Debate

The importance of contextualizing gender in postmodern feminist theory so that it does not become yet another exclusionary site of universal truth is similar to the importance of specifying the meaning and location of 'the international' in IR theory. Like the exclusive and essentialist use of gender in some radical feminist theory, the international system has been colonised by statesmen and neo-realist IR theorists as the ultimate explanation for war and as a legitimation for state-security.[131] Richard Ashley argues that 'to speak of international politics as a source of causes would be to presuppose the accomplishment of the very effect – the representation of a multiplicity of well-bounded states and domestic societies – *that is in question*'.[132] In the context of the third meta theoretical debate in IR, postmodernists argue that conventional international relations theories are less interesting as substantive explanations of world politics, than they are as expressions of disciplinary and state boundaries *which need to be explained*.[133]

Non-feminist and feminist postmodernisms share their deconstruction of falsely universalizing abstractions endemic to the disciplinary state of IR and their awareness of the inextricable relation between the production of IR knowledge and the reproduction of hierarchical power-over. However, as Rebecca Grant writes 'the newest IR theory is radical but comes without the guarantee of being feminist'.[134] Poststructuralist IR theories crib the insights of feminist theories for mostly deconstructive purposes while remaining blind to the fundamental reconstructive purposes of feminism. Unlike many feminisms, most postmodernisms have remarkably little to say about the concrete practices and knowledges which could replace the current ones. Feminist IR scholars have exposed the (gender) exclusion present in postmodernist, non-totalist theory itself.[135] Ironically, by failing to specify their own gender, race, ethnic, class, multiple and contingent identities, non-feminist postmodern IR is complicit with the universalism that it attempts to repudiate. The habitual refusal of postmodernists to situate themselves as gendered theorists and grasp the transformative potential of – as well as their indebtedness to – 'subjugated knowledges' such as feminism, traps them in the same gendered, hierarchical dichotomies that they claim to invert or transform. Postmodern IR is mancraft without statecraft. It is, Christine Sylvester comments, a struggle for recognition in the sense of having one's views recognised without recognising 'the other'.[136] Taking feminism seriously means taking seriously the modern account of the sovereign subject as gendered. But it also means problematising grounds (or lack thereof) for theorizing and moving beyond abstractions toward specifying particular sites of domination, subordination, and resistance. Postmodernists prefer to engage with the political theories of grand philosophers, rather than the situated politics of critical social and liberation movements. However, counter-memory readings of the IR canon are not a replacement for living conversations that feminists in IR seek to initiate. It is sadly ironic, bell hooks writes, that the contemporary discourse which talks most about heterogeneity, the decentred subject and the recognition of otherness, directs its critical voice primarily to a specialized audience that shares a common language rooted in the very master narratives it claims to challenge.[137] Christine Sylvester has suggested that postmodern IR's marginalization of feminism, and conventional IR's silence, is another effort by men to be autonomous of women.[138]

In spite of this lack of conversation between feminist and non-feminist IR, there is something 'subversive' about the intervention of women in world politics and feminism in IR theory. Adding women to IR, to a field of knowledge constituted by their very exclusion, unsettles the binary gender construction of masculine-feminine and its related political meanings. Ontological inclusion results in epistemological challenges, and post-positivist knowledges require post-essential genders.

Conclusion

The three feminist challenges discussed in this chapter, arguing that gender is a variable, a constitutive theoretical, and transformative epistemic category in IR scholarship, suggest that the actual practice of world politics has suffered from its neglect of feminist perspectives. Feminists argue that malestream visions of international relations distort our knowledge of both 'relations' and the changing constitution of the 'international'. Their adoption and embodiment of positivist forms of knowing has produced only very simplistic correlational (single variable) knowledge claims that reproduce the dichotomies which have come to demarcate IR. These dichotomies, as argued consistently by Spike Peterson, are gendered: they define power as power over 'others', autonomy as reactive and not relational, international politics as the absence of women and the negation of domestic politics, and objectivity as the lack of (feminised) subjectivity. Non-feminist accounts of IR tend to reify the state of gender and gendered states. They render women and gender invisible because they fail to see the political significance of fundamentally gendered divisions of public and private institutionalized within and by the state and state-system. They also ignore the political activities and transformative agency of women: whether they are mobilizing for war, protesting state abrogation of human rights or organizing for the international recognition of women's rights.

Feminist perspectives, however, bring renewed theoretical and political insight to the field of IR by revealing the gendered nature of its foundational assumptions – the masculine identity of the core actors, structures, defining concepts, modes and purposes of social enquiry – that are premised on the exclusion of women, femininity and feminism and on the pervasive presence of global gender hierarchies. Feminist IR research exposes the male-dominance of international political-economic institutions and policy-making, the militaristic construction of masculinity in sovereign states and the dependency of men-masculinity on women and feminized others, who 'run', even if they do not 'rule' the world.[139] Most importantly, by revealing socially-constructed masculinity and femininity as constitutive of (sovereign) identities, (state) structures and ideologies (of nationalism, militarism, capitalist accumulation and science), feminists suggest that there are real possibilities for changing the unequal international order. Developing alternatives to this current order, however, requires challenging the normalcy of gender hierarchy, which Spike Peterson argues 'is fundamental to domination in its many guises', in part because it renders masculine domination over women, nature and feminized groups, acceptable.[140]

The future for feminist international relations looks especially bright as gender analysis is extended to new and existing areas of international studies. What is now the 'sub-field' of feminist IR is growing in interest and research at a rapid rate. The persistent challenge, however, is to develop 'empathetic co-operation' between non-feminist and feminist international relations. Conventional IR empiricists who failed to anticipate, predict or even theorize the possibility of the East–West systemic collapse, for instance, would do well to reflect on the gender bias of their positivist methods and theoretical exclusion of political realities which emanate from alternative theoretical perspectives such as feminism. Analysts who monitored Cold War continuity and change at domestic and international levels tended to focus solely on the public apparatuses of the state, and not on the political role of families in withdrawing support for communist regimes or the associations between domesticity and political dissidence, private morality, the velvet revolutions and civil society in the private spaces of former Eastern bloc countries. Conventional IR has demonstrated only limited understanding of such 'relationships' and was thus unable to explain its own central focus in the post-war period – the bipolar international system. Thus, it would be beneficial for mainstream IR scholars to engage with feminist IR approaches that have analysed the reproduction of the state's and international system's material and symbolic power through authority relations within the family-household and community, where gendered identities get produced and where gendered divisions of power and labour are naturalized.

Currently, there is much empirical and theoretical analysis to be done on the gender-specific dimensions of democratization, nationalism, and global economic restructuring in our radically interdependent post-Cold War world. IR scholars need to consider whose freedom and security these globalised movements are promoting. And why processes of integration and disintegration seem to be occurring on the terrain of gendered social arrangements, and how people are responding to and resisting this new world ordering, as it affects them in different localities below, above, and in the spaces inbetween states. With the knowledge that theory-is-practice, the ongoing challenge for feminist international relations is to engage in meaningful research that brings people's lives and struggles back into the field of IR, and through this work, to forge a different relation to global universalism through the particularities of identity and place.

The challenges that confront us in this 'new' post-Cold War era insist that we learn from the errors of Cold War gender-blindness by constructing gender-sensitive, relational accounts of world politics. Exposing the dependency of the Cold-War standoff and bipolar realist IR on myths and norms of the nuclear family and its gendered division of labour, suggests that there are relationships to be theorized between the 'unbundling of territoriality'[141] and the 'ungendering of world politics'[142], between multipolar feminisms and multiple sovereignties in the late twentieth century. Feminists consistently pay attention to the insecurities that accompany processes of rapid change and deconstructing world orders, including patriarchal orders. As theorists of international relations, we should consider the gender, but also race and class-differentiated causes and consequences of contemporary global shifts, from the sovereignty of states to the sovereignty of global movements in a late-capitalist time without a corresponding political place.[143]

Notes

1. K. *Waltz, Man, the State, and War: A Theoretical Analysis* (New York, 1959), pp. 122–3, 230.
2. R. B. J. Walker, *Inside/Outside: International Relations Theory as Political Theory* (Cambridge, 1993), p. 7.
3. C. Sylvester, *Feminist Theory and International Relations in a Postmodern Era* (Cambridge, 1994a), p. 102.
4. J. W. Scott, *Gender and the Politics of History* (New York, 1988), p. 48.
5. J. B. Elshtain, J. B. *Women and War* (New York, 1987), p. 41.
6. C. Enloe, 'Women and Children: Making Feminist Sense of the Persian Gulf Crisis', *Village Voice* (25 September 1990).
7. R. Grant, 'The Quagmire of Gender and International Security', in V. S. Peterson, (ed.), *Gendered States* (Boulder, 1992), p. 86.
8. G. Spivak, 'French Feminism Revisited: Ethics and Politics', in J. Scott and J. Butler (eds), *Feminists Theorize the Political* (New York, 1992), p. 57.
9. V. S. Peterson, 'Transgressing Boundaries: Theories of Gender, Knowledge and International Relations', *Millennium*, 21, 2 (1992c), pp. 183–206.
10. L. Alexandre, 'Genderizing International Studies: Revisioning Concepts and Curriculum', *International Studies Notes*, 14, 1 (1989), pp. 5–8.
11. W. Brown, *Manhood and Politics* (New Jersey, 1988).
12. V. S. Peterson, (ed.), *Gendered States: Feminist (Re)Visions of International Relations Theory* (Boulder, 1992a), pp. 14–15.
13. Scott (1988), p. 49.
14. B. Roberts, 'The Death of Machothink: Feminist Research and the Transformation of Peace Studies', *Women's Studies International Forum*, 7 (1984), p. 197.
15. C. Enloe, *The Morning After: Sexual Politics at the End of the Cold War* (Berkeley, 1994), p. 55.
16. K. Jones, 'The Trouble With Authority', *differences*, 3, 1 (1991), p. 116.
17. R. Grant and K. Newland (eds), *Gender and International Relations* (London, 1991), p. 4.
18. S. Ruddick, 'Pacifying the Forces: Drafting Women in the Interests of Peace', *Signs*, 8, 3 (1983); S. Ruddick, *Maternal Thinking: Towards a Politics of Peace* (Boston, 1989); S. Ruddick, 'The Rationality of Care', in J. B. Elshtain and S. Tobias (eds), *Women, Militarism, and War* (New York, 1990).
19. B. Brock-Utne, *Educating for Peace* (Oxford, 1985); B. Brock-Utne, *Feminist Perspectives on Peace and Peace Education* (New York, 1989).
20. Sylvester (1994), p. 13; R. O. Keohane, 'International Relations Theory: Contributions of a Feminist Standpoint', *Millennium*, 18, 2 (1989), p. 245.
21. S. Harding, 'Strong Objectivity', *Social Research* (1992).
22. Enloe (1994), p. 21.
23. V. S. Peterson and A. S. Runyan, *Global Gender Issues* (Boulder, 1993); Peterson (1992c).

24. M. Gatens, *Feminism and Philosophy* (Bloomington, 1991); J. Butler, *Gender Trouble: Feminism and the Subversion of Identity* (New York, 1990), p. 7.
25. See M. Zalewski, 'The Women/"Women" Question in International Relations', *Millennium*, 23, 2 (1994), pp. 407–23.
26. Grant and Newland (1991), p. 5.
27. G. A. Steurnagel, 'Men do not do Housework! The Image of Women in Political Science', in M. Paludi and G. A. Steuernagel (eds), *Foundations for a Feminist Restructuring of the Academic Disciplines* (New York, 1990), pp. 79–80.
28. Alexandre (1989), p. 6.
29. Peterson and Runyan (1993).
30. G. Sen and C. Grown, *Development Crises and Alternative Visions: Third World Women's Perspectives* (New York, 1986); N. Kabeer, *Reversed Realities: Gender Hierarchies in Development Thought* (London, 1994); R. L. Blumberg, *Women, Development, and the Wealth of Nations: Making the Case for the Gender Variable* (Boulder, 1992).
31. L. Beneria (ed.), *Women and Development: The Sexual Division of Labour in Rural Societies* (New York, 1982); S. E. Charlton, J. Everett and K. Staudt (eds), *Women, the State, and Development* (Albany, 1989); K. B. Ward, *Women in the World System: Its Impact on Status and Fertility* (New York, 1984).
32. Brock-Utne (1985), p. 7.
33. K. Newland, 'From Transnational Relationships to International Relations: Women in Development and the International Decade for Women', *Millennium*, 17, 3 (1988), p. 507.
34. K. Staudt and J. Jaquette, *Women in Developing Countries: A Policy Focus* (New York, 1983); K. Staudt, *Women, International Development, and Politics: The Bureaucratic Quagmire* (Philidelphia, 1990); N. Kardam, *Bringing Women in: Women's Issues in International Development Programs* (Boulder, 1991).
35. S. P. Joekes, *Women in the World Economy* (New York, 1987); M. Mies, *Patriarchy and Accummulation on a World Scale* (London, 1986); M. Mies, V. Bennholdt-Thomsen and C. von Werlhof (eds), *Women: The Last Colony* (London, 1988); J. Smith, J. Collins, T. Hopkins and A. Mohammed, *Racism, Sexism, and the World System* (New York, 1988).
36. H. Afshar and C. Dennis, *Women and Adjustment in the Third World* (London, 1992); J. Vickers, *Women and the World Economic Crisis* (London, 1991); R. Kamel, *The Global Factory: Analysis and Action for a New Economic Era* (Philidelphia, 1990); V. Moghadam, *Democratic Reform and the Position of Women in Transitional Economies* (Oxford, 1993).
37. I. Bakker (ed.), *The Strategic Silence: Gender and Economic Policy* (London, 1994); J. Brodie, 'Shifting the Boundaries: Gender and the Politics of Restructuring', in I. Bakker (ed.), *The Strategic Silence: Gender and Economic Policy* (London, 1994); V. S. Peterson, 'The Politics of Identification in the Context of Globalization', *Women Studies International Forum*, 19, 1–2 (1996), pp. 5–15.
38. J. Nash and M. Fernandez-Kelly (eds), *Women, Men, and the International Division of Labour* (Albany, 1983); S. Mitter, *Common Fate, Common Bond: Women*

in the Global Economy (London, 1986); J. Pettman, *Worlding Women: A Feminist International Politics* (Sydney, 1996).

39. G. Standing, 'Global Feminization Through Flexible Labour', in C. K. Wilber and K. P. Jameson (eds), *The Political Economy of Development and Under-development* (5th edn, New York, 1992), pp. 346–75.

40. S. Whitworth, 'Planned Parenthood and the New Right: Onsluaght and Opportunity?', *Studies in Political Economy*, 35 (1991), pp. 73–101; C. Hoskyns, 'Women's Equality and the European Community', *Feminist Review*, 20 (1985); E. Vallance and I. Davies, *Women of Europe: Women MEPS and Equality Policy* (Cambridge, 1986); K. Ferguson, *The Feminist Case Against Bureaucracy* (Philidelphia, 1984); H. Pietila and J. Vickers, *Making Women Matter: The Role of the United Nations* (London, 1990).

41. S. Whitworth, 'Gender, International Relations and the Case of the ILO', *Review of International Studies*, 20 (1994), pp. 388–405; C. Hoskyns, 'Gender Issues in IR: the Case of the European Community', *Review of International Studies*, 20 (1994), pp. 225–39.

42. M. Waring, *If Women Counted: A New Feminist Economics* (San Francisco, 1988).

43. A. Rodda, *Women and the Environment* (London, 1991); J. Seager, *Earth Follies: Coming to Feminist Terms with the Global Environmental Crisis* (New York, 1993); S. Dalby, 'Security, Modernity and Ecology: The Dilemmas of Post-Cold War Security Discourse', *Alternatives*, 17 (1992), pp. 95–134.

44. Mies (1986, 1988).

45. C. Merchant, *The Death of Nature: Women, Ecology, and the Scientific Revolution* (New York, 1980); B. Easlea, *Science and Sexual Oppression: Patriarchy's Confrontation with Woman and Nature* (London, 1981).

46. Peterson and Runyan (1993).

47. V. Shiva, *Staying Alive: Women, Ecology, and Development* (Delhi, 1988); M. Mies and V. Shiva, *Ecofeminism* (London, 1993).

48. N. E. McGlen and M. R. Sarkees (eds), *Women in Foreign Policy: The Insiders* (New York, 1993).

49. C. Enloe, *Bananas, Beaches, and Bases: Making Feminist Sense of International Politics* (London, 1989); A. Rao (ed.), *Women's Studies International: Nairobi and Beyond* (New York, 1991).

50. Elshtain (1987); J. Jaquette, 'Power as Ideology: A Feminist Analysis', in J. H. Stiehm (ed.), *Women's Views of the Political World of Men* (New York, 1984); J. Stiehm, 'The Protected, the Protector, the Defender', in J. Stiehm (ed.), *Women and Men's Wars* (Oxford, 1983); B. Reardon, *Sexism and the War System* (New York, 1985).

51. J. Cocks, 'Women in the Military', *Gender and Society*, vol. 8 (June 1994).

52. Stiehm (1989); C. Becraft, *Women in the Military, 1980–1990* (Washington, 1991).

53. J. Bhabha, 'Women Refugees', *Women: A Cultural Review* (London, 1994).

54. Peterson (1992a).

55. F. D'Amico, 'Military Gay Exclusion and Gender: A Comparative Analysis', paper presented at the 35th Annual Conference of the International Studies

Association, Washington DC, 1994; S. Jeffords, *The Remasculinization of America: Gender and the Vietnam War* (Bloomington, 1989).

56. J. Kerr (ed.), *Women's rights as Human rights* (London, 1993); N. La Violette and S. Whitworth, 'No Safe Haven: Sexuality as a Universal Human Right and Gay and Lesbian Activism in International Politics', *Millennium*, 23, 3 (1994), pp. 563–88.
57. Bhabha (1994).
58. V. S. Peterson, 'Whose Rights? A Critique of the "Givens" in Human Rights Discourse', *Alternatives*, XV (1990), pp. 303–34.
59. F. Anthias and N. Yuval-Davis, *Woman-Nation-State* (London, 1989); F. Anthias and N. Yuval-Davis, *Racialised Boundaries* (London, 1994); Vickers (1991); V. Moghadam, *Identity Politics and Women: Cross-National Perspectives* (Oxford, 1993); J. Pettman, *Living on the Margins: Racism, Sexism and Feminism in Australia* (North Sydney, 1992); B. F. Williams (ed), *Women Out of Place: The Gender of Agency and the Race of Nationality* (New York, 1996).
60. S. L. Mayhall, 'Gendered Nationalism and the New' Nation-States: Democratic Progress in Eastern Europe', *The Fletcher Forum of World Affairs*, 17, 2 (1993), pp. 91–99; B. Einhorn, *Cinderella Goes to Market: Women's Movements in East-Central Europe* (London, 1993); N. Funk and M. Mueller (eds), *Gender Politics and Postcommunism* (New York, 1993); G. Waylen, 'Women and Democratisation: Conceptualising Gender Relations in Transition Politics', *World Politics*, 46 (1994), pp. 327–54; J. True, 'Successions/Secessions: Identity, Gender Politics and Post-Communism', *Political Expression*, 1, 1 (1995).
61. M. Molyneux, 'Women's Rights and the International Context: Some Reflections on the Post-Communist States', *Millennium*, 23, 2 (1994), pp. 287–313.
62. D. Stienstra, *Women's Movements and International Organizations* (Toronto, 1994), p. xii.
63. Sen and Grown (1986). See also S. Sharoni, 'Middle-East Politics Through Feminist Lenses: Toward Theorizing International Relations from Women's Struggles', *Alternatives*, 18 (1993), pp. 5–28.
64. C. Pateman, 'Introduction', in C. Pateman and E. Gross (eds), *Feminist Challenges: Social and Political Thought* (Sydney, 1986), p. 5.
65. R. Grant, 'The Sources of Gender Bias in International Relations Theory', in R. Grant and K. Newland (eds), *Gender and International Relations* (London, 1991), p. 21.
66. Peterson and Runyan (1993), p. 3.
67. Peterson (1992c).
68. Walker (1992), p. 191.
69. Peterson and Runyan (1993).
70. C. Sylvester, 'Empathetic Co-operation: A Feminist Method for IR', *Millennium*, 23, 2 (1994b); Walker (1992).
71. Sylvester (1994a), p. 104.

72. Spivak (1992).

73. Enloe (1989), p. 131.

74. L. McEnaney, 'He-Men and Christian Mothers: The America First Movement and the Gendered Meanings of Patriotism and Isolationism', *Diplomatic History*, 18, 1 (1994), pp. 47–57.

75. E. S. Rosenberg, ' "Foreign Affairs" after World War II: Connecting Sexual and International Politics', *Diplomatic History*, 18, 1 (1994), pp. 59–70.

76. R. B. J. Walker, 'Realism, Change and International Political Theory', *International Studies Quarterly*, 31, 1 (1987), pp. 65-86, p. 17.

77. J. A. Tickner, *Gender in International Relations: Feminist Perspectives on Achieving Global Security* (New York, 1992); V. S. Peterson and J. True, 'New Times and New Conversations', in M. Zalewski and J. Parpart, *Feminism, Masculinity and Power in International Relations* (Boulder, forthcoming).

78. Sylvester, in V. S. Peterson (ed.), *Clarification and Contestation: A Conference Report* on 'Woman, the State and War': What Difference Does Gender Make? (Los Angeles, 1989).

79. R. Ashley, 'Untying the Sovereign State: A Double Reading of the Anarchy Problematique', *Millennium*, 17, 2 (1988), p. 230.

80. Tickner (1992); C. Sylvester, 'The Emperors' Theories and Transformations: Looking at the Field through Feminist Lens', in D. Pirages and C. Sylvester (eds), *Transformations in the Global Political Economy* (London, 1990).

81. R. Grant and K. Newland (eds), *Gender and International Relations* (London, 1991), p. 1.

82. A. Wendt, 'Anarchy is What States Make of It: the Social Construction of Power Politics', *International Organization*, 46, 2 (1992), pp. 391–425.

83. C. Gilligan, *In a Different Voice: Psychological Theory and Women's Development* (Cambridge, 1982).

84. See Tronto, in Peterson (1989).

85. J. A. Tickner, 'On the Fringes of the World Economy: A Feminist Perspective', in C. Murphy and R. Tooze (eds), *The New International Political Economy* (Boulder, 1991), pp. 204–6.

86. Tickner (1991).

87. Waltz (1959), p. 188.

88. Waltz (1959), p. 238.

89. Sylvester (1990).

90. J. Ruggie, 'Territoriality and Beyond: Problematizing Modernity in International Relations', *International Organization*, 47, 1 (1993), pp. 149–74.

91. J. Ruggie, 'Continuity and Transformation in the World Polity: Towards a Neo-Realist Synthesis', in R. O. Keohane (ed.), *Neorealism and its Critics* (New York, 1986).

92. A. Linklater, *Men and Citizens in the Theory of International Relations* (London, 1990).

93. Peterson (1992a).

94. Harding (1992), p. 86.
95. Peterson (1992a); V. S. Peterson, 'Security and Sovereign States: What is at Stake in Taking Feminism Seriously?', in V. S. Peterson (ed.), *Gendered States* (Boulder, 1992b).
96. J. B. Elshtain, 'Sovereignty, Identity, Sacrifice', in V. S. Peterson (ed.), *Gendered States* (Boulder, 1992).
97. Peterson (1992b), p. 46.
98. Peterson (1992b), pp. 46–7.
99. Peterson and Runyan (1993).
100. A. Tickner, 'Hans Morganthau's Political Principles of Political Realism: A Feminist Reformulation', *Millennium*, 17, 3 (1988).
101. C. Sylvester, 'Feminist Theory and Gender Studies in International Relations', *International Studies Notes*, 16, 3/17, 1 (1992), pp. 32–38.
102. Enloe (1994).
103. Peterson (1992b), pp. 47–8.
104. Elshtain (19921).
105. Peterson (1992b), p. 53.
106. Elshtain (1987).
107. Peterson (1992b), p. 53.
108. Tickner (1991).
109. Peterson and Runyan (1993), p. 70.
110. Sylvester (1994); Peterson (1995a, 1995b); N. Pershram, 'Politicizing the *Feminine*, Globalizing the Feminist', *Alternatives*, 19 (1994), pp. 275–313; S. J. Ship, 'And What About Gender? Feminism and International Relations Theory's Third Debate', in W. S. Cox and C. T. Sjolander (eds), *Beyond Positivism: Critical International Relations Theory* (Boulder, Colo. 1994); C. T. Mohanty, A. Russo and L. Torres (eds), *Third World Women and the Politics of Feminism* (Bloomington, 1991).
111. E. A. Grosz, 'The Intervention of Feminist Knowledges', in B. Cane, E. A. Grosz and de M. Lepervanche (eds), *Crossing Boundaries: Feminisms and the Critique of Knowledges* (Sydney, 1988).
112. Alexandre (1989).
113. Scott, (1988), p. 2.
114. Ann Snitow, 'A Gender Diary', in A. Harris and Y. King (eds), *Rocking the Ship of the State: Towards a Feminist Peace Politics* (Boulder, 1989), p. 38.
115. Snitow (1989), p. 38.
116. C. Gabriel and L. Macdonald, 'Women's Transnational Organizing in the Context of NAFTA: Forging Feminist Internationality', *Millennium*, 23, 3 (1994), p. 535.
117. C. Weber, 'Good Girls, Little Girls, and Bad Girls: Male Paranoia in Robert Keohane's Critique of Feminist International Relations', *Millennium*, 23, 2 (1994), pp. 337–49.

118. K. McClure, 'The Issue of Foundations: Scientized Politics, Politicized Science and Feminist Critical Practice', in J.W. Scott and J. Butler (eds), *Feminists Theorize the Political* (New York, 1992).

119. M. Lugones and E. Spelman, 'Have We Got a Theory for You! Feminist Theory, Cultural Imperialism, and the Demand for "The Woman's Voice"', *Women's Studies International Forum*, 6 (1983), p. 573.

120. Enloe (1989).

121. Enloe (1994).

122. Sylvester (1994a).

123. Ibid., p. 2.

124. Ibid., p. 12.

125. Ibid., 1995b.

126. Sylvester (1994b), p. 317.

127. Zalewski (1994).

128. V.S. Peterson, 'Shifting Ground(s): Remapping in the Context of Globalisation(s)', in E. Kofman and G. Youngs (eds) *Globalisation: Theory and Practice* (London, 1996).

129. Cocks (1994); Elshtain (1987), p. 239.

130. Grant (1992).

131. K. Waltz, *Theory of International Politics* (New York, 1979).

132. Ashley (1988), p. 258.

133. Walker (1993), p. 5.

134. Grant (1991), p. 21.

135. Sylvester (1994); Peterson and True (1995).

136. Sylvester (1994b), p. 218.

137. b. hooks, *Yearning: Race, Gender, and Cultural Politics* (Boston, 1990), p. 25.

138. Sylvester (1992, 1994).

139. Enloe (1989), p. 17.

140. Peterson (1992a), p. 14.

141. Ruggie (1993).

142. Peterson and Runyan (1993).

143. W. Connolly, *Identity/Difference: Democratic Negotiations of Political Paradox* (Ithaca, 1991).

CHAPTER 9

Green Politics

Matthew Paterson

Green Politics currently has, at best, an underdeveloped position in the discipline of International Relations (IR).[1] However, Green Politics has emerged as a significant political force in many countries from the mid-1970s onwards, and its position is often explicitly global in character. Many writings of Green thinkers, and practices of Green movements, therefore relate to IR. This chapter aims to outline strands of Green Political thought which could be used to develop a Green theoretical position on IR. This position has several features in common with others presented in this volume. The chapter will aim to highlight these in its conclusion. It will focus, however, on what is distinctive about the Green position.

This chapter is organized through a discussion of two main sets of literature which can be used to develop a Green position on IR/global politics. These are the literature on 'Green Political Theory'[2] and that on 'Global Ecology'.[3] It will then draw out the themes from both which help us construct a Green position. Together, these two literatures provide an *explanation* of the destruction of the rest of nature by human societies, and a *normative* foundation for resisting this destruction and creating sustainable societies.

First it is necessary to make an important distinction between Green Politics and environmentalism.[4] This will become clearer later in the chapter, but here it is important to note that, broadly speaking, environmentalists accept the framework of the existing political, social, economic and normative structures of world politics, and seek to ameliorate environmental problems within those structures, while Greens regard those structures as the main origin of the environmental crisis and therefore contend that they are structures which need to be challenged and transcended. Although obviously a crude simplification of the variety of positions adopted by those in the Green and broader environmental movement, it serves a useful function here as a representation of ideal types. This is the case because it becomes obvious that there is no clearly identifiable environmentalist position on IR. From even the most cursory literature survey of the mainstream

IR literature on environmental problems, the environmentalist position is seen as easily compatible with the liberal institutionalist position outlined most clearly by Keohane.[5] In fact most writers within IR who write on environmental problems, and who are clearly motivated by the normative concerns adopted by environmentalists, adopt liberal institutionalist positions.[6] The analytic concern is with the response of the states-system to environmental problems, focusing on the emergence of 'international environmental regimes', while the underlying assumption is that the states-system *can* respond effectively to those problems. By contrast, Green Politics rejects the idea that the states-system, and other structures of world politics, can provide such a response. This is why this chapter will not discuss the mainstream IR literature on environmental problems, as they correspond primarily to a different theoretical tradition in IR.

Green Political Theory

There is now a well-developed literature on Green Political Theory (GPT) which provides a useful base for Green ideas about IR. Three major works suggest slightly different ideas about the defining characteristics of Green Politics. Eckersley suggests that the defining characteristic is ecocentrism – the rejection of an anthropocentric world-view which places moral value only on humans in favour of one which places independent value also on ecosystems and all living beings.[7] Goodin also places ethics at the centre of the Green position, suggesting that a 'Green theory of value' is at the core of Green political theory. His formulation is that for a Green theory of value, the source of value in things is the fact that they have a history of having been created by natural process rather than by artificial human ones.[8]

Dobson has two defining characteristics of Green Politics.[9] One is the rejection of anthropocentrism, as outlined by Eckersley. The other, however, is the 'limits to growth' argument about the nature of the environmental crisis. Greens suggest that it is the exponential economic growth experienced during the last two centuries which is at the root cause of the current environmental crisis. Thus it is not the belief in an environmental crisis which is defining, but the particular (and unique) understanding which Greens have of the nature of that crisis which makes them distinctive.

Dobson's position is arguably the most convincing. A reduction of the Green position to an ethical stance towards non-human nature, without a set of arguments about why the environment is being destroyed by human-beings, seems to lose much of what is central to Green beliefs. In addition, Goodin's formulation is highly problematic, as he posits a notoriously dubious distinction between things which are 'natural' and those which are 'artificial' which cannot be even loosely sustained.

Ecocentrism[10]

For Eckersley ecocentrism has a number of central features. First, it involves some empirical claims. These involve a view of the world as ontologically composed of interrelations rather than individual entities.[11] All beings are fundamentally 'embedded in ecological relationships'.[12] Consequently, there are no convincing criteria which can be used to make a hard and fast distinction between humans and non-humans.[13]

Secondly, ecocentrism has an ethical base. Eckersley rejects anthropocentrism on consequentialist grounds, suggesting that it leads to environmentally devastating results, but also argues for ecocentrism on deontological grounds. Since there is no convincing reason to make rigid distinctions between humans and the rest of nature, a broad emancipatory project, to which she allies herself, ought to be extended to non-human nature. Ecocentrism is about 'emancipation writ large'.[14] All entities are endowed with a relative autonomy within the ecological relationships in which they are embedded, and therefore humans are not free to dominate the rest of nature.

Ecocentrism therefore has four central ethical features which collectively distinguish it from other ethical positions towards the environment.[15] First, it recognizes the full range of human interests in the non-human world. Secondly, it recognises the interests of the non-human community. Thirdly, it recognises the interests of future generations of humans and non-humans. Finally it adopts a holistic rather than an atomistic perspective – that is, it values populations, species, ecosystems and the ecosphere as a whole as well as individual organisms.[16]

Eckersley develops a political argument from this which is statist in orientation. Although she does not adopt the position of the 'eco-authoritarians' such as Ophuls, Hardin or Heilbroner, she suggests, in direct contradiction to ecoanarchism which is prevalent in Green political thought, that the modern state is a necessary political institution from a Green point of view.[17] She suggests that ecocentrism requires that we both decentralize power down within the state, but also centralize power up to the regional and global levels.

For Eckersley, then, new forms of global political structures are required from an ecocentric point of view. This is necessary in order to protect nature. Arguing against the anarchist interpretation of Green politics she says that a 'multitiered' political system, with dispersal of power both down to local communities and up to the regional and global levels is the approach which is most consistent with ecocentrism.[18] If all power is decentralized, she suggests there will be no mechanisms to co-ordinate responses to regional or global environmental problems, or to redistribute resources form rich to poor regions of the world. Her argument is premissed on ecocentric ethics and the priority to protect the rest of nature, the social justice consequences of ecocentrism, and the urgency of the ecological crisis. Arguing against ecoanarchists, she suggests that

> in view of the urgency and ubiquity of the ecological crisis, ultimately only a supraregional perspective and multilateral action by nation States can bring about the kind of dramatic changes necessary to save the 'global commons'. . .[19]

Her arguments are also premissed on the urgency of the ecological crisis. 'Indeed, the urgency of the ecological crisis is such that we cannot afford *not* to "march through" and reform the institutions of liberal parliamentary democracy . . . and employ the resources . . . of the State to promote national and international action'.[20]

This position could be developed within a conventional perspective on IR (such as liberal institutionalism) to look at the character of a wide variety of interstate treaties and practices. The most obvious would be those regarding biodiversity, acid rain or climate change. But it could also be developed for global economic institutions such as the World Bank, or the military practices of states. A broad critique of the major global institutions from an ecocentric position could be fairly easily established, especially considering the very different ethical basis underlying this position in contrast to that which informs international treaties and other international practices. This critique would show how the main international practices are based on an anthropocentric ethic which puts human material interests first, and disregards that of ecosystems or other species. This is even the case for environmental treaties. For example, while ostensibly about protecting biodiversity, the substance of the Biodiversity Convention signed in 1992 is primarily couched in terms of protecting the gene pool for the biotechnology industry.[21] And the objective of the Climate Change Convention, also signed in 1992, while stating that the aim is to 'prevent dangerous anthropogenic interference with the climate system' which could have an ecocentric interpretation, quickly goes on to say that this is 'to ensure that food production is not threatened and to enable economic development to proceed in a sustainable manner'.[22] As a consequence the implications of ecocentric ethics are limited to a critique of the content of international practices, rather than the structure of international relations.

But this interpretation of ecocentrism advanced by Eckersley is challengeable. Ecocentrism is in itself politically indeterminate. It can have many variants, ranging from anarchist to authoritarian, with Eckersley's social democratic version somewhere in the middle of the continuum.

The predominant alternative interpretation within Green thought suggests that it is the emergence of modern modes of thought which is the problem from an ecocentric point of view. The rationality inherent in modern Western science is an instrumental one, where the domination of the rest of nature (and of women by men) and its use for human instrumental purposes have historically been integral to the scientific project on which industrial capitalism was built. Carolyn Merchant's *The Death of Nature: Women, Ecology and the Scientific Revolution* (1980) is the classic account of the emergence of this rationality in the Scientific Revolution of the sixteenth and seventeenth centuries. In other words, environmental ethics are given a historical specificity and material base – the emergence of modern forms of anthropocentrism are located in the emergence of modernity in all its aspects.

This interpretation therefore argues that since modern science is inextricably bound up with other modern institutions such as capitalism, the nation-state and modern forms of patriarchy, it is inappropriate to respond by developing those institutions further, centralizing power through the development of global and regional institutions. Such a response will further entrench instrumental rationality which will undermine the possibility for developing an ecocentric ethic. An ecocentric position therefore leads to arguments for scaling down human communities, and in particular for challenging trends towards globalization and homogenization, since it is only by celebrating diversity that it will be possible to create spaces for ecocentric ethics to emerge. This argument is developed by the 'global ecology' writers outlined below.

Limits to growth

Although the idea clearly has a long lineage, the immediate impetus for arguments concerning limits to growth came from an influential, controversial and very well-known book published in 1972, *The Limits to Growth*.[23] The argument there was that exponential economic and population growth of human societies was producing an interrelated series of crises. This exponential growth was producing a situation where the world was rapidly running out of resources to feed people or to provide raw material for continued industrial growth (exceeding *carrying capacity* and *productive capacity*), and simultaneously exceeding the *absorptive capacity* of the environment to assimilate the waste products of industrial production.[24] The team of researchers led by Donella Meadows produced their arguments based on computer simulations of the trajectory of industrial societies. They predicted that at current rates of growth, many raw materials would rapidly run out, pollution would quickly exceed the absorptive capacity of the environment, and human societies would experience 'overshoot and collapse' some time before 2100.

The details of their predictions have been substantially refuted. However, Greens have taken their central conclusion – that exponential growth is impossible in a finite system – to be a central plank of their position.[25] Dobson suggests there are three arguments which are important here.[26] First, technological solutions will not work – they may postpone the crisis but cannot prevent it occurring at some point. Secondly, the exponential nature of growth means that 'dangers stored up over a relatively long period of time can very suddenly have a catastrophic effect'.[27] Finally, the problems associated with growth are all interrelated. Simply dealing with them issue by issue will mean that there are important knock-on effects from issue to issue – solving one pollution problem alone may simply change the medium through which pollution is carried, not reduce pollution. From this Greens get their notions of sustainability. Whereas environmentalism concentrates on 'sustainable development',[28] which presumes the compatibility of growth with responding to environmental problems, Greens reject this. Sustainability explicitly requires stabilising and in the industrialised countries almost certainly reducing throughputs of materials and energy.[29] This requires a wholesale reorganisation of economic systems.

The implications of this for global politics are clearly considerable. O'Riordan presents a useful typology of positions which emerge from the limits to growth version of sustainability which Greens adopt.[30] The first is very similar to that outlined by Eckersley above – that the nation-state is both too big and too small to deal effectively with sustainability, and new regional and global structures (alongside decentralization within the state) are needed to co-ordinate effective responses.

A second interpretation, prevalent in the 1970s but virtually absent from discussions in the 1980s, is what O'Riordan calls 'centralized authoritarianism'. This generally follows the logic of Garrett Hardin's 'tragedy of the commons' which suggested that resources held in common would be overused.[31] This metaphor led to the argument that centralized global political structures would be needed to force changes in behaviour to reach sustainability.[32] In some versions, this involved the adoption of what were called 'lifeboat ethics'.[33] The idea was that the scarcity outlined by Meadows et alia meant that rich countries would have to practise triage on a global scale – to 'pull up the ladder behind it'. This argument has been rejected by Greens, with a few exceptions.

The third position is similar to the above in that it suggests authoritarianism may be required, but rejects the idea that this can be on a global scale. The vision here is for small scale, tightly-knit communities run on hierarchical, conservative lines with self-sufficiency in their use of resources.[34] It shares with the above position the idea that it is freedom and egoism which has caused the environmental crisis, and these tendencies need to be curbed to produce sustainable societies. In some versions, these communes would be inward-looking and explicitly xenophobic.

The final position which O'Riordan outlines is termed by him the 'anarchist solution'. This has become the position adopted by Greens as the best interpretation of the implications of limits to growth. The term 'anarchist' is used loosely in this typology. It means that Greens envisage global networks of self-reliant communities. This position would, for example, be associated with people such as E. F. Schumacher,[35] as well as bioregionalists such as Kirkpatrick Sale.[36] It shares the focus on small-scale communities with the previous position, but has two crucial differences. First, relations within communities would be libertarian, egalitarian, and participatory. This reflects a very different set of assumptions about the origins of the environmental crisis; rather than being about the 'tragedy of the commons' (which naturalizes human greed), it is seen to be about the emergence of hierarchical social relations and the channelling of human energies into productivism and consumerism.[37] Participatory societies should provide means for human fulfilment which do not depend on high levels of material consumption. Secondly, these communities, while self-reliant, are seen to be internationalist in orientation. They are not cut off from other communities, but in many ways conceived of as embedded in networks of relations of obligations, cultural exchanges, and so on.[38]

Greens also often object to the state on anarchist grounds. For example, Spretnak and Capra suggest that it is the features identified by Weber as central to statehood which are often the problem from a Green point of view.[39] Bookchin gives similar arguments, suggesting that the state is the ultimate hierarchical institution which consolidates all other hierarchical institutions.[40] Carter suggests that the state is part of the dynamic of modern society which has caused the present environmental crisis.[41] He outlines an 'environmentally hazardous dynamic', where 'a centralized, pseudo-representative, quasi-democratic state stabilizes competitive, inegalitarian economic relations that develop "non-convivial", environmentally damaging "hard" technologies whose productivity supports the (nationalistic and militaristic) coercive forces that empower the state'.[42] Thus the state is not only unnecessary from a Green point of view, it is positively undesirable.

The question of scale

This is perhaps the most important theme coming out of Green Politics for IR. One of the best-known Green Political slogans is 'think globally, act locally'. While obviously also fulfilling rhetorical purposes, it is often seen to follow from the two principles outlined above. It stems from a sense that while global environmental and social/economic problems operate on a global scale, they can only be successfully responded to by breaking down the global power structures which generate them through local action and the construction of smaller-scale political communities and self-reliant economies.

One of the best-developed arguments for decentralization is given in John Dryzek's *Rational Ecology* (1987). Dryzek summarises the advantages of decentralization thus; small-scale communities are more reliant on the environmental support services in their immediate locality and therefore more responsive to disruptions in that environment.[43] Self-reliance and smallness shortens feedback channels, so it is easier to respond quickly before disruptions become severe. He also suggests that they are more likely to develop a social ontology which undermines pure instrumental ways of dealing with the rest of nature, commonly identified by Greens (and others) as a cause of environmental problems.[44]

Greens' advocacy of decentralization involves an explicit rejection of the contemporary sovereign states-system. A particular argument is often put that this undermines Greens' claims to global relevance. Decentralized small scale communities, it is claimed, will have little chance of developing effective mechanisms for resolving global environmental problems. The most developed argument of this position is put by Bob Goodin.[45]

Goodin's argument is that since many environmental problems are transnational or even global in scope, global co-operation to respond to these problems is necessary. This is a reasonable enough argument. But he then goes on to argue that the state, with sovereign rights intact, is a necessary political form to procure this co-operation. This turn in the argument is arguably less convincing. Goodin's focus is on the logic of collective action, using game-theoretic arguments.[46] He reviews a number of models of cross-community co-operation on transboundary issues under a Green scenario of decentralization towards small-scale, self-reliant communities, and concludes that even under the most favourable scenario, solutions to this problem 'must necessarily involve revesting at least some of those powers in centralized co-ordinating agencies at the global level'.[47]

Goodin outlines four well-known games which could be said to model co-operation between small scale anarchistic communities: Prisoner's Dilemma, Chicken, Assurance, and Altruism.[48] His concern is to try to show that for each of these, substantial powers may have to be transferred to institutions well beyond the local level, right up to the global level. The problem becomes less acute as we move through his four models towards Altruism (which he reasonably suggests approximates the Green utopia), though he argues it also applies there. This model assumes that all the communities have a fully 'green' culture, in that they follow Green ethical norms as he outlines them, and base their decisions on norms which are global in orientation – they are not purely interested in the quality of their own environment.

As he notes, this does not produce an Altruist's Dilemma mirroring a Prisoner's Dilemma, since each community would be concerned with the total payoffs for all communities rather that simply the payoffs of the other players (which would produce such a Dilemma).[49] However, he suggests that there will still be significant need for co-ordinating mechanisms. In particular, even if Green communities abided by Green norms, they will still need information about what other communities are doing on a particular problem in order to find out what precisely they need to do about that problem. Thus 'there will still be a need for a central co-ordinating mechanism to collate everyone's action plans'.[50]

Goodin then argues that 'the role [of centralized agencies] will be greater, the need for sanctioning powers more urgent, the more the situation resembles the Polluter's-cum-Prisoner's Dilemma'.[51] There seem to be two major flaws in his argument here. First, there is a great difference between 'organized information-pooling' and 'sanctioning powers' which, although Goodin is obviously aware of it, glosses over its importance for Green conceptions of where political authority would lie.[52] If the state is the focus of the discussion, then only where sanctioning powers are concerned would we be talking about something resembling a state. It does not seem to me that Greens who reject the idea of global political authorities should have any problem with institutions concerned with information-pooling across communities.

Secondly, Goodin makes much too much of the need for *sanctioning* powers in the Prisoner's Dilemma situation. Much contemporary theorising about international co-operation has highlighted how extensive co-operation can be produced despite the lack of enforcement powers in international agencies, relying on the sort of information-pooling which Goodin highlights would be necessary even in the altruist case.[53] This undermines his case that institutions with effective authority beyond the local level would be required.

This problem of co-ordination is not one to which Green positions are uniquely vulnerable. All social arrangements, including the present one, require some form of co-ordination of action between social units to respond to transboundary environmental problems. Of course, Greens are arguing for a system where power is decentralized as much as possible, so they may be seen to be especially vulnerable to this problem. However, if Goodin has failed to show that Greens need envisage anything more than information-pooling institutions, then Green proposals are left with the advantage that radical decentralization makes environmental management on the ground more practicable, using many of the arguments given by Dryzek earlier.

Two further arguments could be mentioned from a game-theoretic point of view which Goodin and other critics of the decentralist version of Green politics do not discuss. First, collective action is commonly argued to be easier to achieve in situations where the number of players in a game is small.[54] This is primarily because it is easier for members of a system to monitor the actions of others, so 'defection' (in the game theoretic language) is less likely, and easier to punish.[55] If Green proposals for decentralization were to take place the number of players in a global game would increase, and therefore co-operation would be more difficult to achieve. Dryzek considers this question. However, as he points out, this works in two ways:

> co-ordination among social actors . . . is clearly facilitated by smallness of size in the social unit. This small scale leads, *ceteris paribus*, to the existence of large numbers of such units. And the larger the number of social units, the more problematical is co-ordination above the local level.[56]

In other words this is an inevitable dilemma. We either make co-ordination between units more difficult by decentralizing, or make co-ordination within units more difficult by maintaining centralized forms of social organization.

Secondly, co-operation is usually held to be only possible in situations where player A knows that player B will in fact implement a signed agreement. The confidence needed to make an Assurance game produce co-operation (or make strategies of reciprocity work in a Prisoners' Dilemma) would not be forthcoming, and players would 'defect' to avoid the costs of co-operation without the public good being provided. State sovereignty could be interpreted, and seems to be implicitly by Goodin *et al.*, as fulfilling this condition. If sovereign practices were abandoned, and we were in a situation of loose collections of anarchistic communities confederating at various levels up to the global in forms such as Bookchin's 'community of communities', then at the global level, no player would be able to guarantee that agreements they sign would in fact be implemented.[57]

However, in practice it is currently the case that despite the institution of state sovereignty, there remains a significant implementation deficit on many environmental problems by nation states. It is highly plausible to argue that most agreements signed are done so when negotiators know that implementation will only be patchy. Yet co-operation persists between sovereign states on environmental (and other) issues. There seems no reason to believe that removing sovereignty would make co-operation between communities significantly more difficult to achieve. While the degree of coercion which a Green 'community of communities' would have over communities in matters of meeting basic ecological responsibilities and guaranteeing human rights would be significantly less than those which presently existing sovereign states, the arguments that this would make co-operation between such 'communities of communities' is unconvincing.

A final argument made is that the anarchistic communities would be too parochial and potentially self-interested to provide atmospheres conducive to cross-community co-operation. 'One of the major fears of observers outside the Green movement is that its picture of localized politics smacks of a petty parochialism, which would be both undesirable and unpleasant to live with', writes Dobson.[58] Part of this argument is therefore that it would be stultifying or oppressive for those within the community, but also it suggests that they would be unconcerned with effects across their borders.

This argument is generally empirical in character. In human societies (historical and present) organized on such a small scale, such a parochial character is pervasive, and a universalistic ethics which Greens also espouse only emerged in modernity with its nation-states, cities, and so on. However, it is also heightened by the writings of some Greens. One Green anarchist argues that 'if there is much social mixing between the groups, if people work outside the group, it will weaken the community bond . . . xenophobia is the key to the community's success'.[59] Many other Greens are aware of this argument. Goldsmith *et al.* wrote as early as 1972 that 'we would stress that we are not proposing that they (small-scale communities) be inward-looking, self-obsessed or in any way closed to the rest of the world'.[60]

Whether or not Greens have an adequate answer to this problem, this objection to the anti-statist position is a very odd argument. The objection that small-scale communities may be too parochial could just as easily be a charge levelled against sovereign states. It is the practice of sovereignty which enables states to be primarily self-regarding, and avoid any sense that they have fundamental obligations to the rest of the world.[61] And the sorts of communities Greens envisage are precisely post-sovereign communities. Confederations of small-scale communities could be organised in such a way that effects on other communities would have to be taken into account in decisions. But even if this is rejected as naïve, the point that is missed in this objection is that no particular political form (arguably excepting world government, but that has its own problems) could *guarantee* that communities would be concerned with effects on other communities. Solving that problem is a question of political culture, not political structure.

There are therefore good reasons to be sceptical of critics of Green politics who focus on the inadequacies of Greens' proposed restructuring of global politics. This is strengthened by some of the arguments made below by the 'global ecology' writers, who focus on how the 'commons' are a form of political and social space which are the most conducive to sustainable practices (contrary to the suggestions of Garrett Hardin and others), an argument which strengthens arguments for decentralization.

Global Ecology

In the early 1990s a literature has emerged which builds on the basic Green principles outlined above and provides an analysis of the present situation which is consistent with them. In other words, while GPT provides a normative foundation for a Green view of global politics, 'global ecology' provides an explanatory foundation.[62] This literature can be associated most centrally with the writings of Wolfgang Sachs, Matthias Finger, *The Ecologist* magazine, *Third World Resurgence*, and Vandana Shiva. This literature has two central themes: development as the root cause of environmental problems; and the protection and reclamation of 'commons' as central to the Green vision. After some background discussion, this section will turn to those themes.

A background concern for Sachs and others is that the practices of the environmental movement worldwide have been diluted and coopted in the 1980s. He writes that:

> once, environmentalists called for new public virtues, now they call for better managerial strategies. Once, they advocated more democracy and local self-reliance, now they tend to support the global empowerment of governments, corporations and science. Once, they strove for cultural diversity, now they see little choice but to push for a worldwide rationalization of life-styles.[63]

Reflecting the historical specificity of these works, but also helping illustrate their ideas, a prevalent theme is a critique of UNCED, or the 'Earth Summit'.[64] While mainstream environmentalist accounts of UNCED usually regard the conference as having been a tremendous success for environmentalists and for the environment, marking the culmination of years of effort in getting politicians to take environmental problems seriously, Chatterjee and Finger see it rather differently.[65]

They suggest that UNCED was a failure for the environmental movement, since it marked the final cooptation of environmentalism by ruling elites. 'In fact, the UN Conference in Rio inaugurated environmentalism as the highest state of developmentalism'.[66] Governments managed to shore up their own power by using environmental groups to legitimise them. Mainstream environmental groups made UNCED look like a genuine attempt by governments and other actors to deal with global environmental problems. Also, multinational corporations, organised in such groups as the Business Council for Sustainable Development, were able to use the Conference to present themselves as legitimate actors on the world stage, and as the people with the expertise to deal with environmental problems. They highlight the irony of this by noting that one PR company which offered to promote UNCED free of charge, Burton-Marstellar, had previously worked for Exxon during the Valdez oil spill, Union Carbide during the Bhopal trajedy, and the US nuclear industry after the Three Mile Island accident.[67] Multinationals were given privileged access by the UNCED Secretariat to the proceedings relative to environmental groups. Those groups were used by the Conference's organisers mainly as legitimising tools. Thus the environmental movement, partly because of the tactics of many of its members of co-operation with the governments and multinationals, but also because of the inherent set-up of the Conference which favoured well-organised, large groups over the diverse variety of groups which make up the environmental movement, left the UNCED process more divided than before. Mainstream groups such as WWF (and even Greenpeace) had been co-opted by governments, while those who maintained an oppositional posture were even further marginalised.

The concern of these writers is to reclaim a set of beliefs about the ecological crisis which emphasise that radical social and political changes are necessary in order to respond to those problems. Again the analysis is that it is not possible to simply adapt existing social institutions to deal with environmental problems – entirely new ones will have to be developed. There is a lineage back to Green writers of the early 1970s, such as Schumacher, which is clearly intended.

Against development[68]

Writers such as Sachs do not believe the term development can be retrieved. They are highly critical of the term 'sustainable development', in widespread use in environmentalist circles, suggesting that this merely serves to make it easier for ruling elites to coopt environmentalism. Sachs writes, illustrating this argument well:

> The walls of the Tokyo subway used to be plastered with advertising posters. The authorities, aware of Japan's shortage of wood pulp, searched for ways to reduce this wastage of paper. They quickly found an 'environmental solution'; they mounted video screens on the walls and these now continuously bombard passengers with commercials – paper problem solved.[69]

In other words, elites manage to deal with environmental problems discretely, while in practice ongoing development undermines any ameliorative effect which a particular response, such as changing the medium of advertising on the underground, may have.

One of the reasons why the 'global ecology' writers object to development is the limits to growth arguments, abandoned by much of the environmental movement during the 1980s largely for tactical reasons, in favour of 'sustainable development' or 'ecological modernisation'. Implicit throughout their work is a need to accept the limits imposed by a finite planet, an acceptance which is ignored by the planet's managers and mainstream environmentalists. 'In the eyes of the developmentalists, the "limits to growth" did not call for abandoning the race, but for changing the running technique', writes Sachs.[70] They are also sceptical of the idea that it is possible to decouple the concept of development from that of growth. While many environmentalists try to distinguish the two by stating, in Daly's words, that 'growth is quantitative increase in physical scale while development is qualitative improvement or unfolding of potentialities', others would suggest that in practice it is impossible to make such neat distinctions.[71] For the practitioners of sustainable development, 'sustainable development' and 'sustainable growth' have usually been conflated, and certainly the Brundtland Commission regarded a new era of economic growth as essential or sustainable development.[72]

However, there are a number of more nuanced arguments which they make. While accepting limits in principle, they would be critical of the scientistic fashion in which Meadows *et al.* demonstrated limits – that a computer modelling approach would itself lead easily to a 'global environmental management' form of response which entrenched the power of elites. This was of course one critique of the *Limits to Growth* in the 1970s, that it was too technocratic. They would also agree with another significant criticism of the *Limits to Growth*, for example by Cole *et al.*, that their models had no social content.[73] The social effects of growth, and the social context of developing sustainable societies, is crucial for these writers.

The *Ecologist* (1993) suggests that one of the central features of development is enclosure, or the turning of common spaces into private property. This was central to modernising agriculture in England before the industrial revolution, and they suggest it is a central part of development practice throughout the world at present. It is important to development because it is an act of appropriation which makes commodity production possible. Commons were organised largely (but not exclusively) outside the market, making efficient accumulation difficult. Enclosure makes this possible. However, the effects of enclosure are to take decision-making away from those who depend on local resources, which in turn makes environmental degradation more likely, as well as being socially divisive. This argument is closely tied to the argument in favour of the commons, explored below.

As a consequence of enclosure, access to resources is denied, which concentrates resources and power in the hands of fewer people. Development is thus necessarily inegalitarian, since it depends on continuous appropriation. Inequality has been one of the central ideological arguments governments have often made for economic growth; that within inequality, growth enables the worst off to get better off. An anti-ecological dynamic is therefore built into development. This also illustrates how the global ecology writers make close links between the damaging human effects of development and the damaging ecological effects of development.

Development entrenches the power of the already powerful. This can be seen on the global level – in the global economy in which the North dominates, and can insulate itself from (many) socio-ecological effects of development, such as through exporting dirty industries to developing countries. It can also be seen at the micro-level, for example in the 'Green revolution' of the 1970s, which concentrated power and land in the hands of the rich farmers, at the expense of the poor who could not afford the fertilisers and pesticides to support the new strains of crops.[74]

A central part of this concentration of power is to do with knowledge. The appropriation of spaces previously held in common empowers 'experts' and denies indigenous knowledges as it transforms those spaces into objects for commodity production. This means that the techniques involved in attempts to manage those spaces are turned over to scientists, and other development experts.[75] This involves privileging western technology and knowledge over non-Western knowledges. Thus 'technology transfer' becomes central to solving environmental problems – the idea that 'advanced' Western technology is needed to help developing countries develop in an 'environmentally friendly' way. McCully provides a compelling critique of technology transfer regarding climate change, showing how past attempts at technology transfer, through development aid, have reproduced the problems associated with development outlined above.[76]

As mentioned above, development necessarily is about creating commodity production where previously it had not prevailed. This is of course closely linked to the emergence of instrumental rationality and individualism, which has turned 'nature' into 'natural resources', to be plundered by humans. Development is therefore about an ideological shift of world-view, a major part of which is towards seeing the environment purely in human-instrumental terms. Closely allied to this is the idea that development progressively 'rationalises' the natural world. It turns it into a set of countable species, some of which are useful (to be preserved) some of which are not (to be destroyed if in the way of progress). This way of seeing nature has historically reduced biological diversity, and arguably necessarily so.

The global ecology writers therefore present a powerful set of arguments as to how development is inherently anti-ecological. This is not only because of abstract limits to growth type arguments, but because they show in a more subtle fashion how development in practice undermines sustainable practices. It takes control over resources away from those living sustainably in order to organize commodity production, it empowers experts with knowledges based on instrumental reason, and it increases inequality which produces social conflicts.

Reclaiming the commons

Writers such as Sachs and others resist the 'global' in global ecology, suggesting that the metaphor which implies that 'global environmental management' is necessary is dependent on the further entrenchment of a necessarily destructive system based on growth. Their positive argument is that the most plausibly Green form of political economy is the 'commons'. This argument is most fully developed by the editors of the Ecologist magazine in their book *Whose Common Future? Reclaiming the Commons* (1993). The argument is essentially that common spaces are sites of the most sustainable practices currently operating. They are under threat from development which continuously tries to enclose them in order to turn them into commodities. A central part of Green Politics is resistance to this enclosure. But it is also a (re)constructive project – creating commons where they do not currently exist.

Commons regimes are difficult to define, as the Ecologist suggests. In fact it suggests that precise definitions are impossible, as the variety of commons around the world defy precise description. The first point of definition is a negative one however. The commons is not the commons as referred to by Garrett Hardin. His 'tragedy of the commons', where the archetypical English medieval common gets overgrazed as each herder tries to maximize the number of sheep they graze on it, is in practice not a commons but an 'open access' resource.[77]

Commons, therefore, are not anarchic in the sense of having no rules governing them. They are spaces the use of which is closely governed, often with informally defined rules, by the communities which depend on them. They rely for their successful operation on a rough equality between the members of the community, as imbalances in power would make some able to ignore the rules of the community. They also depend on particular social and cultural norms prevailing, for example the priority of common safety over accumulation, or distinctions between members and non-members. Commons are therefore clearly different from private property systems. However, commons are also not 'public' spaces in the modern sense. Public connotes open access under control by the state, while commons are often not open to all, and the rules governing them do not depend on the hierarchy and formality of state institutions. A further difference from 'modern' institutions is that they are typically organized for the production of use values rather than exchange values, i.e. they are not geared to commodity production. This makes them not susceptible to the pressures for accumulation or growth inherent in capitalist market systems.

Commons are therefore held to produce sustainable practices for a number of reasons. First, the rough equality in income and power means that none can usurp or dominate the system. 'Woods and streams feeding local communities remained intact because anyone degrading them had to brave the wrath of neighbours deprived of their livelihood, and no one was powerful enough to do so'.[78] Secondly, the local scale at which they work means that the patterns of mutual dependence make co-operation easier to achieve.[79] Thirdly, this also means that the culture of recognizing one's dependence on others and therefore having obligations, is easily entrenched. Finally, commons make practices based on accumulation difficult to adopt.

One of the great strengths of the Ecologist's work is the way in which the argument is richly illustrated. I will give just a few examples here. At a general level, they highlight how many people throughout the world are dependent on commons, despite the globalisation of capitalism. For example, 90 per cent of the world's fishers depend on small inshore marine commons, catching over half of all the fish eaten.[80] In the Philippines, Java and Laos, irrigation systems are run by villages communally, with water rights decided at the village level. Even in the North communities still exist which manage resources communally – for example lobster harvesters in Maine.[81] In parts of India, villages based on Gandhian principles known as *gramdam* villages enable sustainable practices to flourish. In these villages, all land within the village boundary is controlled by the *gram sabha*, composed of all the adults in the village.[82] They quote Agarwal and Narain on how one such village, Seed near Udaipur, operates:

> the common land has been divided into two categories – one category consists of lands on which both grazing and leaf collection is banned and the second category consists of lands on which grazing is permitted but leaf collection or harming trees is banned. The first category of land is lush green and full of grass which villagers can cut only once a year . . . Even during the unprecedented drought of 1987, Seed was able to harvest 80 bullock cartloads of grass from this parch. The grass was distributed equitably amongst all households.[83]

The idea of the commons is clearly very consistent with the arguments from Green Political Theory (GPT) about the necessity of the decentralization of power and grassroots democracy. It shows how small scale democratic communities are the most likely to produce sustainable practices within the limits set by a finite planet.

Conclusion

These two literatures mutually support each other. GPT outlines basic principles of ecocentrism and limits to growth. For other IR traditions the central point here is the particular way in which Greens reject the states-system, arguing primarily for decentralizing political communities below the nation-state, rather than for new forms of global political authority. This involves the decentralization not only of political organisation, but of economic and social organization as well. They also argue for abandoning traditional sovereign systems and practices in favour of more mixed locations of authority. Global ecology complements this by suggesting in rich detail how contemporary political-economic practices undermine the sustainability of human societies, and how those power structures need to be challenged to create sustainable societies. Their focus on 'reclaiming the commons' supports the decentralization argument in GPT.

Regarding other IR traditions, Green politics has a number of features in common with many of them. First, it shares the rejection of a hard and fast fact/value distinction with feminism, critical theory, and poststructuralism, by having clearly integrated normative and explanatory elements. Its conception of theory is clearly incompatible with positivist conceptions which have such a clear distinction. Secondly, it shares an interest in resisting the concentration of power, the homogenising forces in contemporary world politics, and the preservation of difference and diversity with poststructuralism and feminism. Thirdly, it shares a critique of the states-system with critical theory and others, although it adopts a position which rejects the idea of global power structures which emerge in correspondence with some idea of a 'global community' in favour of decentralizing power away from nation-states to more local levels. Whereas for critical theorists such as Linklater, the idea of community at the global level is about balancing unity and diversity rather than one which wishes to create a homogeneous global identity, there is a much stronger sense in Green politics that community only makes sense at the very local level – the idea of a 'global community' is for Greens nonsensical. Allied to this normative rejection of the states-system is a rejection of a clear empirical split between domestic and international politics shared in particular with pluralists such as John Burton, but also with Marxists, critical theorists, and feminists. Greens would not think it useful to think, for example, in terms of 'levels of analysis', a form of thinking still prevalent in realism, as it arbitrarily divides up arenas of political action which should be seen as fundamentally interconnected. Finally, there is a clear focus on political economy, and the structural inequality inherent in modern capitalist economies also focused on by Marxists and dependency theorists.

However, it shares to an extent an element of modernist theorizing, in the sense that Greens are clearly trying to understand the world in order to make it possible to improve it. This makes it perhaps more compatible with Frankfurt school type critical theory and feminism than with poststructuralism, as these both have a clear emancipatory normative goal, and in particular a clearer sense that their explanations or interpretations of the world are connected to a clear political project. This is linked to poststructuralism's rejection of foundationalism, which marks a clear difference from Green politics, which relies on fairly strong foundational claims of both the epistemological and ethical variety. However, there are also tensions with the way in which critical theory tries to reconstruct Enlightenment rationality. Eckersley, for example, makes much of attempts by Habermas in particular (she contrasts Habermas to Marcuse) to reclaim science for radical political purposes, suggesting that it necessarily ends up justifying human domination of nature.[84]

Green theory clearly has its own distinctive perspective. The focus on humanity–nature relations and the adoption of an ecocentric ethic with regard to those relations, the focus on limits to growth, the particular perspective on the destructive side of development, and the focus on decentralization away from the nation-state are all unique to Green politics. This chapter has illustrated how the purpose of Green theory within IR is to provide an explanation of the ecological crises facing humanity, to focus on that crisis as possibly the most important issue for human societies to deal with, and to provide a normative basis for dealing with it.

Notes

1. I am grateful to John Barry, Scott Burchill, Richard Devetak, Andrew Linklater, Peter Newell, Ben Seel, and Richard Shapcott for helpful comments on an earlier version of this chapter.
2. For example, A. Dobson, *Green Political Thought* (London, 1990); R. Eckersley, *Environmentalism and political theory: Towards an ecocentric approach* (London, 1992); R. E. Goodin, *Green Political Theory* (Cambridge, 1992).
3. For example, W. Sachs, (ed.), *The Development Dictionary: a guide to knowledge as power* (London, 1992); W. Sachs, (ed.), *Global Ecology: A New Arena of Political Conflict* (London, 1993); P. Chatterjee and M. Finger, *The Earth Brokers: power, politics and world development* (London, 1994); The Ecologist, *Whose Common Future? Reclaiming the Commons* (London, 1993).
4. Dobson (1990), p. 13.
5. R. O. Keohane, *International Institutions and State Power: Essays in International Relations Theory* (Boulder, 1989).
6. This can be seen in major works such as P. M. Haas, R. O. Keohane, and M. A. Levy, *Institutions for the Earth: Sources of Effective Environmental Protection* (Cambridge, 1993); P. M. Haas, *Saving the Mediterranean: The Politics of International Environmental Cooperation* (New York, 1990); O. R. Young, *International Cooperation: Building Regimes for Natural Resources and the Environment* (New York, 1989); O. R. Young, *International Governance: Protecting the Environment in a Stateless Society* (New York, 1994); A. Hurrell and B. Kingsbury,

The International Politics of the Environment (Oxford, 1992), and G. Porter and J. W. Brown, *Global Environmental Politics* (Boulder, 1991).

7. Eckersley (1992).
8. Goodin (1992), p. 27.
9. Dobson (1990).
10. This section will follow Eckersley (1992), largely for reasons of simplicity, but also because her book still represents the most developed application of ecocentric ideas to politics. For other ecocentric works, see for example C. Birch and J. B. Cobb, *The Liberation of Life: From the Cell to the Community* (Cambridge, 1981) and W. Fox, *Toward a Transpersonal Ecology: Developing New Foundations for Environmentalism* (Boston, 1990).
11. Eckersley (1992), p. 49.
12. Ibid., p. 53.
13. Ibid., pp. 49–51.
14. Ibid., p. 53.
15. The other positions which Eckersley identifies are resource conservation, human welfare ecology, preservationism and animal liberation (1992, ch. 2).
16. Eckersley (1992), p. 46.
17. W. Ophuls, *Ecology and the Politics of Scarcity* (San Francisco, 1977); G. Hardin, 'The ethics of a lifeboat', *BioScience*, 24 (1974); R. Heilbroner, *An Inquiry into the Human Prospect* (New York, 1974).
18. Eckersley (1992), pp. 144, 175 and 178.
19. Ibid., p. 174.
20. Ibid., p. 154.
21. Chatterjee and Finger (1994), pp. 41–43; A. Kothari, 'The Politics of the Biodiversity Convention', *Economic and Political Weekly*, 27 (1992).
22. United Nations, *Framework Convention on Climate Change* (New York, 1992), Article 2.
23. D. Meadows *et al.*, *The Limits To Growth* (London, 1972).
24. Dobson (1990), p. 15; Meadows *et al.* (1972).
25. To see this at work in Green writings, see for example P. Bunyard and F. Morgan-Grenville (eds), *The Green Alternative* (London, 1987); J. Porritt, *Seeing Green* (Oxford, 1986); C. Spretnak and F. Capra, *Green Politics: The Global Promise* (London, 1984); F. E. Trainer, *Abandon Affluence!* (London, 1985).
26. Dobson (1990), pp. 74–80.
27. Dobson (1990), p. 74.
28. This concept was originally used in the *World Conservation Strategy* developed by the International Union for the Conservation of Nature (IUCN, *World Conservation Strategy* (Switzerland, 1980)), and popularised by the Brundtland Commission, or World Commission on Environment and Development (WCED, *Our Common Future – Report of the World Commission on Environment and Development* (Oxford, 1987)).
29. K. Lee, 'To De-Industrialize – is it so irrational?', in A. Dobson, and P. Lucardie (eds), *The Politics of Nature: explorations in green political theory* (London, 1993).

30. T. O'Riordan, *Environmentalism* (2nd edn, London, 1981), pp. 303–7; also Dobson (1990), pp. 82–3.
31. G. Hardin, 'The Tragedy of the Commons', *Science*, 162 (1968).
32. Examples of this would be Ophuls (1977) and Hardin (1974).
33. Hardin (1974).
34. Heilbroner (1974); The Ecologist, *Blueprint for Survival* (Harmondsworth, 1972).
35. E. Schumacher, *Small is Beautiful* (London, 1976).
36. K. Sale, *Human Scale* (San Francisco, 1980).
37. M. Bookchin, *The Ecology of Freedom: The Emergence and Dissolution of Hierarchy* (Palo Alto, 1982).
38. The notion of subsidiarity is often used in Green discourse. It is not used in the way that many governments use it – to protect their rights against those of supranational organisations (the classic case being the UK government in relation to the EU). In the Green version, it has radical implications for decentralization of power to the local level, with power only transferred up to higher levels if deemed necessary – local levels deciding what constitutes necessary.
39. Spretnak and Capra (1984), p. 177.
40. M. Bookchin, *Toward an Ecological Society* (Montreal, 1980); (1982).
41. A. Carter, 'Towards a Green Political Theory', in A. Dobson and P. Lucardie (eds), *The Politics of Nature: Explorations in green political theory* (London, 1993).
42. Carter (1993), p. 45. See also D. Wall, 'Towards a Green Political Theory – In Defence of the Commons?', in P. Dunleavy and J. Stanyer (eds), *Contemporary Political Studies: Proceedings of the Annual Conference* (Belfast, 1994).
43. J. Dryzek, *Rational Ecology: Environment and Political Economy* (Oxford, 1987), ch.16.
44. Dryzek (1987), p. 219. See also H. Ward, 'Green Arguments for Local Democracy', Paper for the ESRC Local Governance Programme Conference, 20–21 May 1993, University of Strathclyde, Glasgow (1993) and Ecologist (1993) for extended discussions of similar arguments.
45. Goodin (1992).
46. Ibid., pp. 156–68.
47. Ibid., p. 168.
48. For an introduction to the basics of game-theoretic models and analysis, see for example J. Elster (ed.), *Rational Choice* (Oxford, 1986). For applications to IR, see K. A. Oye (ed.), *Cooperation under Anarchy* (Princeton, 1986).
49. Goodin (1992), p. 165.
50. Ibid., p. 166.
51. Ibid., p. 167.
52. Ibid., p. 167.
53. See for example A. Chayes and A. H. Chayes, 'On compliance', *International Organization*, 47, 2 (1993).
54. R. Axelrod, *The Evolution of Cooperation* (New York, 1984); R. Axelrod and R. O. Keohane, 'Achieving Cooperation under Anarchy: Strategies and Institutions', in K. A. Oye (ed.), *Cooperation under Anarchy* (Princeton, 1986).

55. Axelrod and Keohane (1986), pp. 234–8.

56. Dryzek (1987), p. 231.

57. M. Bookchin, 'Libertarian Municipalism: An Overview', *Society and Nature*, 1, 1 (1992); J. Barry, 'Towards a Theory of the Green State', in S. Elworthy, *et al.* (eds), *Perspectives on the Environment 2* (Aldershot, 1995), p. 194.

58. Dobson (1990), p. 101.

59. Hunt quoted in Wall (1994), p. 19.

60. Ecologist (1972), p. 53; Goodin (1992), p. 153; see also Ward (1993), p. 6.

61. States may have emerged as part of the phenomenon of modernity, and therefore may be affected by the rise of universalistic ethics, but they remain accountable only to those within the territory they control (if to anyone at all), and are therefore unlikely to be particularly concerned about the effects of their actions on those living outside their borders.

62. I use the term in inverted commas here because at times the writers mentioned use it ironically, at other times descriptively. For example, M. Finger, 'Politics of the UNCED Process', in W. Sachs, (ed.), *Global Ecology: A New Arena of Political Conflict* (London, 1993), uses it to denote the environmentalist discourse which emerged in the 1980s which globalised environmental problems for the first time (closely tied to the discourse of sustainable development). On the other hand, W. Sachs, 'Global Ecology and the Shadow of 'Development'', in W. Sachs, (ed.), *Global Ecology: A New Arena of Political Conflict* (London, 1993a), refers to it simply to describe the conflicts occurring over the set of issues often organised around the global themes of environment and development. I am also using a convenient heading to tie together a range of writers, not all of whom would use this tag to define themselves. My point is that there has been a resurgence of radical environmentalist writing in the early 1990s centred around these writers, whose work adds to GPT and some loose heading is required to tie them together.

63. Sachs (1993), p. xv.

64. This was held in Rio de Janeiro in June 1992. It was the UN's response to the wave of interest in environmental issues in the late 1980s and early 1990s. It was the biggest diplomatic gathering on any topic ever held. Among other things, treaties on Climate Change and Biodiversity were signed, and an 800 page document called Agenda 21 was agreed, which is a wishlist of possible actions governments could take to achieve sustainable development. For a straightforward overview see M. Grubb, M. Koch, A. Munson, F. Sullivan and K. Thomson, *The Earth Summit Agreements: A Guide and Assessment* (London, 1993).

65. As do others in this school. See for example N. Hildyard, 'Foxes in Charge of the Chickens', in W. Sachs, (ed.), *Global Ecology: A New Arena of Political Conflict* (London, 1993); Ecologist (1993), pp. 1–2, P. Doran, 'The Earth Summit (UNCED): Ecology as Spectacle', *Paradigms*, 7 (1993), and many contributors to the journal *Third World Resurgence*.

66. Sachs (1993a), p. 3.

67. Chatterjee and Finger (1994), p. 119.

68. I present here what seems to me the strongest version of the argument. Some Greens believe it is more fruitful to try to reconstruct the term development, rather than to reject it. However, they would be equally critical of the forms of development criticised by writers mentioned in this section. A debate about whether to reject or reconstruct notions such as development can easily collapse into a simple terminological dispute which is not particularly helpful. The important point here is that if development is understood as necessarily involving quantitative growth of the system, greater complexity of technological systems, and increasing economic interconnections across the globe, then Greens are clearly opposed to it.
69. Sachs (1993a), p. 3.
70. Ibid., p. 10.
71. H. Daly, 'Toward Some Operational Principles of Sustainable Development', *Ecological Economics*, 2, 1 (1990), p. 94.
72. WCED (1987).
73. H. S. D. Cole, C. Freeman, M. Jahoda and K. L. R. Pavitt, *Thinking About the Future: A Critique of the Limits to Growth* (London, 1973).
74. Trainer (1985), pp. 139–41; S. George, *How the Other Half Dies* (Harmondsworth, 1977).
75. Ecologist (1993), pp. 67–70; see also A. Gorz, 'Political Ecology: Expertocracy versus Self-Limitation', *New Left Review*, 202 (1994).
76. P. McCully, 'The case against climate aid', *Ecologist*, 21, 6 (1991).
77. Ecologist (1993), p. 13.
78. Ibid., p. 5.
79. This has a lot in common with the game-theoretic argument mentioned above which often emphasize how in small scale systems it is easier to generate Co-operation than in large scale systems. E. Ostrom, *Governing the Commons: the evolution of institutions for collective action* (Cambridge, 1990) develops this argument explicitly with respect to commons regimes.
80. Ecologist (1993), p. 7; Ostrom (1990), p. 27.
81. Ecologist (1993), p. 7.
82. Ibid., p. 190.
83. Ibid., pp. 190–1; A. Agarwal and S. Narain, *Towards Green Villages: A Strategy for Environmentally-sound and Participatory Rural Development* (New Delhi, 1989), p. 23.
84. Eckersley (1992), ch. 5.

Index

275